RELIGION, CIVIL SOCIETY, IN NORTHERN IRELAND

Religion was thought to be part of the problem in Ireland and incapable of turning itself into part of the solution. Many commentators deny the churches a role in Northern Ireland's peace process or belittle it, focusing on the few well-known events of church involvement and the small number of high profile religious peacebuilders. This new study seeks to correct various misapprehensions about the role of the churches by pointing to their major achievements in both the social and political dimensions of the peace process, by small-scale, lesser-known religious peacebuilders as well as major players. The churches are not treated lightly or sentimentally and major weaknesses in their contribution are highlighted. The study challenges the view that ecumenism was the main religious driver of the peace process, focusing instead on the role of evangelicals, it warns against romanticising civil society, pointing to its regressive aspects and counter-productive activities, and queries the relevance of the idea of 'spiritual capital' to understanding the role of the churches in post-conflict reconstruction, which the churches largely ignore.

This book is written by three 'insiders' to church peacebuilding in Northern Ireland, who bring their insight and expertise as sociologists to bear in their analysis of four years' in-depth interviewing with a wide cross section of people involved in the peace process, including church leaders and rank-and-file, members of political parties, prime ministers, paramilitary organisations, community development and civil society groups, as well as government politicians and advisors. Many of these are speaking for the first time about the role of religious peacebuilding in Northern Ireland, and doing so with remarkable candour. The volume allows the Northern Irish case study to speak to other conflicts where religion is thought to be problematic by developing a conceptual framework to understand religious peacebuilding.

John D. Brewer is Professor of Post Conflict Studies in the Institute for the Study of Conflict Transformation and Social Justice, Queen's University Belfast. He is Honorary Vice-President of the British Sociological Association and a member of the UN Roster of Global Experts, specialising in the sociological aspects of peace processes.

Gareth I. Higgins is the Executive Director of the Wild Goose Festival, a justice, spirituality and arts gathering in the United States. He has worked as a lecturer and research scholar at Queens University Belfast and Trinity College Dublin, and was the co-founder of the zero28 Project, a post-sectarian peacebuilding initiative in Northern Ireland from 1998–2007.

Francis Teeney is a Research Fellow and honorary lecturer at Queen's University Belfast. He is an active peace campaigner frequently commenting on radio, television and other media outlets. He is a consultative director of Mickel Health Initiatives and a founding member of the Emotions Research Consortium.

Religion, Civil Society, and Peace in Northern Ireland

JOHN D. BREWER, GARETH I. HIGGINS,
AND FRANCIS TEENEY

OXFORD

UNIVERSITY PRESS

Great Clarendon Street, Oxford OX2 6DP

Oxford University Press is a department of the University of Oxford.
It furthers the University's objective of excellence in research, scholarship,
and education by publishing worldwide. Oxford is a registered trade mark of
Oxford University Press in the UK and in certain other countries

First published 2011
First published in paperback 2013

Published in the United States of America by Oxford University Press
198 Madison Avenue, New York, NY 10016, United States of America

British Library Cataloguing in Publication Data

Data available

Library of Congress Cataloging in Publication Data

Data available

ISBN 978-0-19-969402-0 (Hbk)
ISBN 978-0-19-870207-8 (Pbk)

Front piece

Oh yes, oh yes, it needed people to come out of that Protestant woodwork to show that there was another side to Protestantism. You know leadership is a funny thing, there are so many ways of leading, you can stand on your soapbox and you can try to rouse a crowd and it is not the way that many of us are either skilled or comfortable with. What you're doing there is, you're exploiting the fears and the feelings and frustrations of people and that is not a difficult task. Paisleyism was there long before Paisley was born and so, what somebody like Paisley is able to do [is] to gather, you know, and build on those fears and frustrations of people, that's not a difficult thing to do. He didn't invent it, he didn't invent it, all that anxiety was there. If I go into a river people are frightened, whatever it may be, a fire or something, you know, you don't have to start persuading them of danger, you're able to do this, you're actually able to intensify that fear if you want to. But to try and help people to move from a place of fear and suspicion to a place of trust, that's a very different story.

The Revd Harold Good, Methodist minister, former President of the Methodist Church in Ireland, and one of two independent observers of IRA decommissioning, interviewed 24 January 2007.

Situations emerged where one had to take a stand, where you had to say that something was wrong, that murders were wrong, that bombing was wrong, that all these things were wrong, I also had the baggage of Bloody Sunday, around my neck, which was difficult. It gave me very powerful credibility in the Bogside but made me perceived as a Republican in the Unionist, Protestant community, even in some sections of my own community, say the more middle-class folk of my own community would perceive me as having leanings on the Republican side or anti-British side. Whereas, in fact, I wouldn't have been. The thing that Bloody Sunday did to me, it clarified in my mind, it was the only time I actually saw somebody shooting somebody else, the actual man firing the weapon and the fellow being hit by the round. That is a dramatic thing to see, something you would see on films but you never see it in real life. You just see the obscenity of it. I attended many people on the street but it was the first time I was caught in the middle of the thing where I actually saw the shooters and the shot and so it clarified a lot of things in my mind for me, and it settled for me in my mind the incompatibility of the use of violence in our situation, that there were other means of doing it. Afterwards some people would have thought that I should have taken a more anti-British stand, but I just said, I'm not on either side of the conflict. I don't agree with the means that either side is using to achieve its objectives. I cannot accept that violence can be acceptable for any Christian in our circumstances. There may be situations where there is a justification for conflict but I don't think that.

Bishop Edward Daly, former Catholic bishop
in Derry, interviewed 24 January 2006.

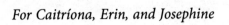

For Caitríona, Erin, and Josephine

Contents

List of Figures   x
About the Authors   xi
Preface   xiii
Acknowledgements   xvii
List of Abbreviations   xviii

Introduction: Civil Society, Religion, and Democratic Transitions   1

1. Contributions to the Social Peace Process   29

2. Contributions to the Political Peace Process   90

3. Opportunities and Constraints in Religious Peace Work   125

4. Weaknesses in the Churches' Peacemaking   172

Conclusion: Religion and the Northern Ireland Peace Process   204

Bibliography   231
Index   243

List of Figures

Figure 1. Forms of active peacemaking   30

Figure 2. Active peacemaking in practice   37

Figure 3. Forms of active peacemaking by the churches   41

Figure 4. Civil society's strategic social spaces   128

Figure 5. The sedimentary layers of the church–civil society–state
           matrix   169

About the Authors

John D. Brewer is Sixth-Century Professor of Sociology (2004–) and former Head of Department (2004–7) at Aberdeen University. He has held visiting appointments at Yale University (1989), St John's College Oxford (1992), Corpus Christi College Cambridge (2002), and the Research School of Social Sciences at the Australian National University (2003). He is a Fellow of the Royal Society of Arts (1998), an Academician in the Academy of Social Sciences (2003), a Member of the Royal Irish Academy (2004), and a Fellow of the Royal Society of Edinburgh (2008). He is a former Leverhulme Research Fellow (2007–8). He is currently President of the British Sociological Association (2009–12), a member of the Governing Council of the Irish Research Council for Humanities and Social Sciences (2008–) and a member of the United Nations' Roster of Global Experts (2010–). He is the author of fifteen books, his most recent being *Peace Processes: A Sociological Approach* (2010). He is Principal Investigator on a £1.26 million project on compromise amongst victims of communal conflict, funded by the Leverhulme Trust (2009–14). With Francis Teeney, he was facilitator for the Northern Irish Faith in a Brighter Future Group of leading ecumenical churchmen and women in their engagement with the peace process (1996–2002).

Gareth I. Higgins is Director of the Wild Goose Festival in the USA (2010–), and formerly Visiting Scholar in Cultural Anthropology at Duke University, Durham, North Carolina (2008–9). His Ph.D. (Queen's University Belfast, 2000) was on notions of the antichrist in Northern Irish Protestantism, supervised by John Brewer. He has written and spoken widely on religion and conflict, art and spirituality, postmodern theology and practice, and film, with his work appearing in *The Independent*, the *Irish Times*, *Sojourners*, and *Third Way Magazine*, amongst others. He appears regularly on BBC Radio. He is co-author with John Brewer of *Anti-Catholicism in Northern Ireland* (1998). He is also author of *How Movies Helped Save My Soul: Finding Spiritual Fingerprints in Culturally Significant Films* (2003) and is currently writing an autobiographical account of growing up during 'the Troubles'. He was founder (in 1998) and director of Zero28, a youth-based peace group, and has worked closely with the Presbyterian Church of Ireland and the Church of Ireland in various peace initiatives, as well as several local projects.

Francis Teeney is Research Fellow in the Department of Sociology University of Aberdeen and Honorary Lecturer in Psychology at Queen's University of Belfast. His Ph.D. (Queen's University Belfast, 2004) was on aspects of the Northern Irish peace process, supervised by John Brewer. He has also been project manager on the EU-funded HUMAINE project on human emotions, which involves thirty-four universities. He has been active in the Northern Irish peace process for several years, most recently in conjunction with John Brewer, coordinating the activities of the Faith in a Brighter Future Group. He is also involved with two cross-border groups, the Meath Peace Group and the Guild of Uriel. He is working with John Brewer on the Leverhulme Trust-funded project on compromise after conflict.

Preface

This is the last in a trilogy of books by John Brewer applying the sociological imagination to the study of peace processes—a topic not normally approached in this way—in the belief that the discipline has much to add. This statement serves as a way of introducing the authorship of this volume: while it has been wholly written by John Brewer, the important roles of Francis Teeney and Gareth Higgins in data collection and commentary on drafts warrant them joining him as co-author. However, it is more a statement about change and continuity in ideas. The previous books in the trilogy were programmatic,[1] making the case generally for sociology's contribution, and it might appear that this volume, focusing on religious peacebuilding in Northern Ireland, has a narrower, parochial interest. On the contrary, it represents the most complete account of the analytical framework John Brewer has been working towards over the last decade. One reviewer of *Peace Processes: A Sociological Approach* was kind enough to remark that it represented the summit of Brewer's life's work. We hope this volume climbs to greater heights; it is the most comprehensive of the trilogy and its attention to Northern Ireland is simply as a case study of an intellectual framework for comparative research that finds its fullest statement here.

A biographer of A. E. Housman once remarked that in many a thick book there is a thin one struggling to get out.[2] The minutiae of Northern Ireland's peace process would make for a very thick book indeed. We have resisted writing it. We are mindful of the advice of Aelfric, the Wessex tutor at Cerne Abbas and later Abbot of Eynsham, at the turn of the first millennium: 'we dare not lengthen this book, lest it be out of moderation and should stir up men's antipathy because of its size.' Our preference for the reader is like that of the Venerable Bede, *lege feliciter*—read happily.

Happy reads are what academic writing should aim to achieve, but seldom do. The novel *Peeler*, by Kevin McCarthy,[3] captures in fictional form the experiences of the pre-independence Royal Irish Constabulary, a police force that John Brewer once studied using oral histories collected from the last surviving members. Years later, Kevin kindly wrote to John on the novel's launch: 'I realise it's a long way to travel from Scotland for an evening of cheap wine followed by Guinness, but I wanted to invite you nonetheless. Your

---

[1] *C. Wright Mills and the Ending of Violence* (Palgrave Macmillan, 2003) and *Peace Processes: A Sociological Approach* (Polity Press, 2010).

[2] Norman Page, *A. E. Housman: A Critical Biography* (Macmillan, 1983).

[3] Mercier Press, 2010.

books on the RIC/RUC were crucial to my research of the novel. Oral histories, I feel, allow for the nuances of human interaction to shine through in a way conventional, secondary historical sources can't. The words of the men you interviewed allowed me to capture some of the subtlety and complexity of the times. Thanks for the books. I couldn't have written mine (for better or worse) without yours.' We sincerely hope to please readers of this book in the same way.

We offer an analysis of the role of the churches in the peace process using analytical categorizations and typologies to help readers make sense of what was going on within the churches, rather than entrap them in the morass of fine detail. We deliberately deploy in-depth interview material at length in order to enliven the intellectual framework with the vivid ethnographic experience of the people involved—using their own words. We, of course, are part of this subject matter: each one of us has been involved in church-based peacebuilding in Northern Ireland. This enables us to give an insider's account, while retaining analytical detachment.

Our arguments are based on a four-year research programme (2005–9), entitled 'The Role of the Churches in Northern Ireland's Peace Process' funded by the Economic and Social Research Council (ESRC), although some interviews were conducted afterwards as respondents became available. We also draw heavily on earlier interviews (1999–2002) by John Brewer, Gareth Higgins, and Ken Bishop, undertaken as part of a project on grass-roots Christian peacemaking organized by the Maryknoll Center for Mission Research and Study in the USA and funded by the Henry Luce Foundation. This supplies us with a further body of interview data that permits reflections spanning twelve years. The ESRC dataset consists of sixty-one audio cassettes and sixty-five data files of transcribed interviews in word format. Some people were interviewed several times. We have nearly a hundred hours of interview data. Interviewees are: rank-and-file members of churches and para-church organizations (26); leaders within church hierarchies (7); leaders of former paramilitary organizations (6); local politicians (6); members of other civil society groups (10); political advisors to governments (1); government politicians (2); miscellaneous (7).

Mindful of Max Weber's exasperation at the reviews of his book on the Protestant ethic thesis, declaring that he had not expected to be so completely misunderstood, there is need for clarification about our focus. Analysts of Northern Ireland's remarkable transition bear a common ailment—the lionization of politicians to the neglect of ordinary people in the background and thus the exaggerated emphasis on the Good Friday Agreement (GFA) rather than the spadework done ahead of it. Given that much of the churches' work was through secret back channels, from which even close colleagues were barred, this ailment is commonplace because outwardly the churches appeared aloof. Roy Garland, in the mix himself as a go-between, repeated this view to us on 4 February 2011: 'sure, the churches had nothing to do with it'. Politicians take precedence, as befits both their personal preference and their ignorance of what the churches were up to.

Sufferers of this malady might note that this book is about the contribution of the churches to the peace process; it is not directly about politicians, political parties, or other civil society groups. We have no doubt that politicians such as David Trimble, Gerry Adams, Seamus Mallon, and the rest, were important to the outcome of the peace process, and that there were sections of other civil society groups who supported them, such as progressive elements of the Orange Order and Gaelic Athletics Association (GAA), the women's movement, the media, trade unions, and businesses. However, our aim to counteract the ignorance about the churches' role in the peace process set our more limited goals. Interest in religious peacebuilding required us to focus on certain people to the neglect of others, and determined the literature we engaged with. Bias against specific politicians whom we neglect should not be read into these choices.

Amongst the politicians we interviewed were two prime ministers (Albert Reynolds and John Major, the latter of whom responded by letter) because of their engagement with the churches in the Downing Street Declaration (DSD), as well as paramilitary political representatives (on both sides), politicians involved in the famous Hume–Adams talks (which were orchestrated by the churches), and politicians at a local level collaborating with the churches in dialogue with paramilitary bodies or in instances of local conflict resolution and the like. We did not interview party leaders *per se* because the parties were not our interest—John Hume and Mark Durkan being the exceptions because of the Hume-Adams talks; hence we also omit scholarship *on* these same politicians in the text. Republicans have never accorded Trimble the respect he deserves in manoeuvring the Unionist leviathan, nor Unionists Adams's deconstruction of the physical force tradition of Republicanism; Trimble and Adams are not irrelevant to the peace process therefore, but Trimble in particular is to religious peacebuilding.[4]

It is worth noting that Trimble was not leader of the Unionist Party for most of the period we look at. While he was leader during the GFA and its aftermath, we make it plain that the churches were excluded from these negotiations. Ten or so years later, when the GFA transformed into the St Andrew's Agreement, when Sinn Féin (SF) and the Democratic Unionist Party (DUP) cut a deal, Trimble had gone and the Ulster Unionists were

---

[4] It is not supporters of Trimble who should complain at our neglect of his contribution to the peace process but supporters of Adams, since Adams was part of the Clonard Monastery-led Hume–Adams talks and thus involved in religious peacebuilding. However, the Sinn Féin (SF) view on this initiative is supplied by Jim Gibney, one of Adams's closest supporters, with a special portfolio to liaise with the churches.

irrelevant. We focus more on the DSD and the 1994 ceasefires (when Trimble was not leader and from which Unionists were excluded), because not only was it pioneering, our research shows the churches to have been heavily involved behind the scenes. The politicians who get a look-in here are the paramilitary political representatives, dealing with the churches and governments, trying to cut deals—such as Gusty Spence, David Ervine, Dawn Purvis, Roy Garland, and Billy Hutchinson, on the one side, and Tom Hartley, Denis Donaldson, and Jim Gibney on the other (note that Hartley and Gibney were designated as SF's representatives to the Protestant churches). Admittedly, these are not mainstream politicians, especially within Unionism, but this highlights the failure for a long time of mainstream politicians to take the same risks as the churches.

Individuals in the churches did many good things, as we shall highlight, but we are also extremely critical of the institutional church, even of some churchmen and women we consider friends. The institutional church was by no means full of saints, but as Nelson Mandela wrote in a letter from his prison cell,[5] we should remember that a saint is a sinner who keeps on trying; and, like him, a number of individual churchmen and women in Northern Ireland tried very hard indeed. It is their story that deserves honour. We feel privileged to tell it.

---

[5] To Winnie Mandela, dated 1 February 1975, cited in Nelson Mandela, *Conversations with Myself* (Macmillan, 2010), page vii.

Acknowledgements

We are grateful for the ESRC's financial support under grant number RES-000–23–1258, and to a series of staff at the University of Aberdeen for managing the grant, including June Middleton, Glenys Milton, and Fiona Elder. John Brewer was Principal Investigator and Gareth Higgins and Francis Teeney were Research Fellows responsible for data collection. We have deposited the tapes and an anonymized verbatim transcription of the data in the ESRC Qualidata Archive and are grateful for the advice and support of Julie Missen in facilitating this. Qualitative research projects are wholly dependent on respondents and we are grateful to the many people who consented to be interviewed. We are pleased to acknowledge our debt to all our respondents, although they and the ESRC are not responsible for the arguments we advance. The interview with the SF activist Denis Donaldson was the last before he was exposed as an informant for the British and later assassinated. Other respondents have died since being interviewed, such as Cahal Daly, David Stevens, Denis Faul, and John Morrow, or become very frail, withdrawing from public life and granting interviews, such as John Hume and Alec Reid. We are very fortunate to count them amongst our respondents.

Many others helped along the way. The School of Psychology at Queen's University kindly gave Francis Teeney a base during fieldwork and we particularly thank Peter Hepper and Roddie Cowie, and acknowledge the significant technical support of Paul Coulter. Rosemary McGarry, Rosemary Nelson, Jennette Neill, and Alison McDonald skilfully transcribed the interviews. We are especially grateful for the comments of the following peace campaigners who have read the manuscript in draft form, none of whom can be held responsible for the final version: Councillor John Kyle, the Reverends Ruth Patterson, Charles Kenny, Norman Taggart, and Earl Storey, and Fr Myles O'Reilly SJ. Some of the arguments have appeared in 'Religion and Peacemaking: A Conceptualisation', *Sociology*, vol. 44, 2010, pp. 1019–37, and we thank the publishers, the British Sociological Association and Sage, for permission to use the material. Lastly, we dedicate this book to our respective families: they know how grateful we are for their love in return.

List of Abbreviations

AIA	Anglo-Irish Agreement
ANC	African National Congress
CFC	Christian Fellowship Church
COI	Church of Ireland
CRC	Community Relations Council
DRC	Dutch Reformed Church
DSD	Downing Street Declaration
DUP	Democratic Unionist Party
ECONI	Evangelical Contribution on Northern Ireland
ESRC	Economic and Social Research Council
FAIR	Families Acting for Innocent Relatives
FAIT	Families Against Intimidation and Terror
FPC	Free Presbyterian Church
FPG	Faith and Politics Group
GAA	Gaelic Athletics Association
GFA	Good Friday Agreement
IICM	Irish Inter-Church Meeting
INGOs	International Non-Governmental Organizations
INLA	Irish National Liberation Army
IR	International Relations
IRA	Provisional Irish Republican Army
ISE	Irish School of Ecumenics
OSCE	Organization for Security and Co-operation in Europe
PACE	Protestant and Catholic Encounter
PCI	Presbyterian Church in Ireland
PCRO	Peace and conflict resolution organizations
PUP	Progressive Unionist Party
SDLP	Social Democratic and Labour Party

SF   Sinn Féin
UDA   Ulster Defence Association
UNIFEM   United Nations Development Fund for Women
USIP   United States Institute for Peace
UVF   Ulster Volunteer Force

Introduction

Civil Society, Religion, and Democratic Transitions

'SAY WHAT YOU MEAN AND MEAN WHAT YOU SAY'

This advice about clarity, taken from the conversation at the Mad Hatter's Tea Party in *Alice in Wonderland*, has several million references in Google. It is clearly saying something that people think is important. The stricture is commonly repeated. 'In the beginning was the word', starts John's Gospel, a phrase made familiar by repetition in every rendition of the Festival of Nine Lessons and Carols at Christmas. And, indeed, we must begin with words. The subject matter of this book is the role of the churches in Northern Ireland's peace process; and already in this simple phrase the potential for confusion and ambiguity—that so bedevils Irish peace agreements—requires clarification of our terms.

We emphasize, first, that we are dealing with the activities of the churches in Northern Ireland. All mainstream churches are Ireland-wide, yet while some Southern-based congregations and dioceses were active in the peace process,[1] Catholic, Anglican, and Presbyterian seats of ecclesiastical power reside in the North. The Northern churches, whose immediate problem the violence and its amelioration was, tended to treat it as a local process, resisting an all-Irish dimension. Northerners felt that their Southern counterparts did not take an active interest in them, something near the truth for a long time. By 'churches' we mean Christian religious groups of all kinds, including the formal institutions that compromise churches, but also 'para-church organizations', which we define as bodies that are not tied to any particular denomination but which have a religious basis, either within a restricted denominational range, such as the Evangelical Contribution on Northern Ireland (ECONI),[2] or ecumenical

---

[1] Border counties in particular had active church-based peace groups, such as the Guild of Uriel (see www.meathpeacegroup.org/activities/).

[2] In April 2005 ECONI changed its name to the Centre for Contemporary Christianity in Ireland but we will use the more familiar nomenclature and the designation by which it was

in character, such as the Irish School of Ecumenics (ISE) or the Faith and Politics Group (FPG). We include work done under the auspices of the churches but carried out by salaried non-ordained staff, such as youth workers, community outreach officers, and others.

The restriction to Christian groups is an obvious consequence of the division between Catholics and Protestants that defines Northern Ireland's conflict, and while we are fully aware that the conflict is not about religion but is over the legitimacy of the state, the conflict is *experienced* as religious and takes on religious forms—religion marks the social boundaries of the groups involved and shapes some of the meaning behind people's identity construction (Mitchell, 2005a, 2005b, 2006 makes the clearest argument for a religious dimension to Northern Irish ethnic boundaries; also see Barnes, 2005). This is only slightly softened by the tendency to refer to Protestants and Catholics as 'communities' or 'traditions'; and such is the elision between politics, religion, and identity that the labels Unionist/Loyalist and Nationalist/Republican more or less neatly overlap with religious-cultural naming. The focus on Christian religious groups, however, also reflects the quiescence of people from the other world religions in Northern Ireland (on the array of Christian groups in Northern Ireland, see Richardson, 1998).[3] The overwhelming response of the non-Christian faith communities in Northern Ireland has been to retain the anonymity that their small numbers provide, by keeping a low profile and avoiding engagement with the conflict (for Muslims in Northern Ireland, see Donnan and O'Brien, 1998; for Jews, see Warm, 1998; Raven, 1999).

As much care needs to be taken over what we mean by 'peace process'. This has both temporal and conceptual dimensions, which give rise to ambiguity. With respect to time, we focus attention on the last phase of the conflict known colloquially as 'the Troubles', from 1968 onwards. Conceptually, we do not limit ourselves to what the churches in this period understood by peace. Peace is one of the key principles of the Christian faith and doctrinally it is central to the belief system of every Christian denomination. In practice, however, some religious groups at times contributed to the conflict. This was sometimes directly, by supplying motivation for combatants—recall the notorious Pastor Peebles who reputedly blessed the pipe bombs timed to kill Catholics and who was later imprisoned when ordnance was found in the boot

---

known during much of its peace work. For excellent studies of evangelicalism in Northern Ireland and ECONI's place within it, see Mitchell (2003) and Ganiel (2008a). It did not survive the departure of its Director, David Porter, to take up a position at Coventry Cathedral, and is now called Contemporary Christianity. It is a much reduced body.

[3] The 2001 Census in Northern Ireland revealed there were 5,028 people from non-Christian 'religions and philosophies', 0.33% of the population. This might be a slight under-enumeration because of the tendency for some people not to disclose their religion or to state 'none', which amounted to 11% in the 1991 Census (the figures are not available for the 2001 Census).

of his car; or Fr Chesney, the Catholic priest who was quartermaster in the South Derry Brigade of the Provisional Irish Republican Army (IRA) and one of those responsible for the 1972 Claudy bombing that killed nine, including three children, and injured thirty.

However, the impact of religious groups on the violence was mostly indirect, by adding to the culture of enmity that sustained the conflict, such as by the perpetuation of negative stereotypes of 'the other'; resistance to strategies that might have alleviated the conflict, such as integrated education or ecumenism; and by fostering sharp identity divisions that garnered zero-sum notions of group interests (Garrigan, 2010, points to the effect of religious ritual and worship practices in stoking sectarianism). Sometimes, religious groups shamelessly fanned the flames while simultaneously denouncing the violence. Hypocrisy is an easy charge to level. Thus, for example, the Catholic Church remained immoveable in its support for segregated education yet bemoaned the sectarian attitudes that their education policies helped to encourage; Archbishop Eames spoke out sincerely, with tears in his voice, after every atrocity but the General Synod always fell back on Anglican notions of governance to excuse imposing a solution on, for instance, the minister of Drumcree Church to bring an end to the Orange Order protest there—one of the longest running series of battles between police, army, and protestors. The churches were not homogenous or united in their commitment to peace, and peace meant different things; they offer no standard against which to clarify the meaning of the term.[4]

Scott Appleby (2000) comments on the ambivalence towards peace even amongst Northern Irish ecumenists, which is part of what Philpott (2007a) refers to as the general political ambivalence of religion. Some churches and para-church organizations showed more ambivalence than others, although in most cases the ambivalence lessened over time as the effects of the continued violence—which went on for longer than anyone in 1968 expected—made them resolve to work more actively for peace. Those religious groups that are regularly criticized for their perpetuation of sectarian divisions, such as the Free Presbyterian Church (FPC) or the Caleb Foundation, which represents conservative evangelicalism—'promoting the fundamentals of the historical Evangelical Protestant faith', as Caleb's website puts it[5]—eventually adopted less hard line and intractable positions. They protested at the nature of the compromise deals rather than peace itself, although the FPC lagged well

---

[4] We are not referring here to any dearth of definitions of peace—the Presbyterian Church's Peace Vocation, statements by the COI's General Synod, the work of the ISE, and publications by ECONI all offered definitions of peace; it is that they disagreed and spoke without unity on their vision for social change. Nor is this meant as a criticism of the many individuals within the churches who fought in vain for years to persuade the churches to adapt to practical peacemaking and develop a unified approach.

[5] www.calebfoundation.org/ consulted 9 December 2010.

behind their former moderator the Revd Ian Paisley, in support for power-sharing with Sinn Féin (SF). Paisley's amazing transformation into dealmaker shows how far some ambivalent people moved over the course of the peace process; Paisley has even criticized his successor as First Minister, Peter Robinson, erstwhile colleague in the Democratic Unionist Party (DUP), for the coldness of his personal relationship with Martin McGuinness, SF Deputy First Minister.

Thus, despite their differences at the starting point of 'the Troubles', and the entrenchment of fixed doctrinal positions at the beginning when the level of violence initially served only to polarize them,[6] it is necessary to admit that towards the end of the peace process most churches and para-church groups came off the fence. But the choice on which side to fall—deal or no deal, peace at any price or only on their terms—differentiates churches and para-church organizations, and it is only possible to make sense of these differences by recognizing the vagueness over the meaning of peace.

In order to unpack the term, we make three critical distinctions, which we elaborate in later chapters. The first is between active and passive peacemaking. The former lives out commitments to peace as a social practice, so that peacemaking is enacted rather than just talked about; the latter is full of idealistic commitment but lacking in application. As we shall emphasize later, some churches and para-church bodies talked the talk but were passive when it came to practice. However, to flesh-out the forms that active peacemaking can take, we utilize Galtung's (1996) famous contrast between negative and positive peace. Negative peace involves working to end violence; positive peace means working towards establishing (or reintroducing) wider principles of justice, equality, fairness, and social redistribution. Some within the Northern Irish churches were active peacemakers when it came to resolving particular incidents of violence, in demanding the paramilitary organizations desist from killing—and entering into dialogue with them to this end. Biblical emphases on justice and fairness notwithstanding, however, few religious groups and individuals saw positive peace as a universal claim relevant to everyone. 'Positive peace for whom?' is a question that must be asked of the churches.

The final distinction is between the social and political peace processes (see Brewer, 2010: 200–2). All too often, peace processes are understood to describe the negotiation process that results in a settlement and the monitoring of conformity to the accord afterwards. Negotiated compromise peace deals, in which parties opt for (or are forced by third parties to accept) second-best

---

[6] Norman Taggart's (2004) analysis of the Irish Council of Churches in the period 1968–72 shows the degree of practical cooperation between the Catholic Church and most Protestant denominations. The polarization occurred after 1972, as the violence worsened, although the gulf was always wider for believers in the pews than for the established church leadership.

preferences in order to resolve conflict, are the foundation of peace processes. We refer to this as the political peace process. However, the negotiated settlement is never the end of peacemaking, for accords mostly leave unresolved the processes of social healing, which we describe as the social peace process. By this we mean reconciliation between erstwhile protagonists, social relationship-building and repair across the communal divide, and replacement of brokenness by the development (or restoration) of people's feelings of wholeness. These concerns are either ignored by negotiators in the political peace process or assumed to follow naturally from the signing of the agreement itself.

The social peace process deals directly with societal healing. It constitutes an important dimension to peacemaking, continuing well after the new political institutions resulting from the accord are bedded in. Progress in societal healing is much slower than political developments. For instance, there are twice as many peace walls now in Belfast than there were at the height of the conflict. For all the increase in shared space arising from the peace process—in bars, recreation and leisure sites, shopping centres, and the like—Belfast people seek more than ever the comfort of return to own-group space, in some cases marked off and separated by peace walls.[7] The churches' expertise lies in the social peace process, which is where their efforts were mostly concentrated prior to the signing of the Good Friday Agreement (GFA) in 1998, but the politicization of religion in Northern Ireland gave the mainstream churches a role also in the political peace process. What the churches have done to deal with the ongoing issues within the social peace process since 1998, however, is another serious question worth examination.

By delineating the various parameters of peacemaking in these ways, we are able to distinguish the different contributions of the churches to different types of peace work. Thus, our typology of kinds of active peacemaking, developed in Chapter 1, is vitally important to help readers understand the differences between various churches and para-church organizations during the social and political peace processes and to locate the assorted behaviours that compromised their peacebuilding. But readers may pose us a question: why the attention on peacemaking within the churches and not, for example, on political change within the parties or transformations within the paramilitary organizations (on which, see Teeney, 2004)? There are good reasons.

---

[7] On 28 July 2009, the BBC reported 'over 40' walls remaining in Belfast (on the religious geography of violence and peace walls see Shirlow and Murtagh, 2006). Their continuance has little to do with the threat of political violence, which has reduced in scale very dramatically, or the travails over decommissioning, which has gone ahead successfully, but conflict over Orange Order parades, most of the contentious ones being in Belfast. What is different today is that there is now a roaring trade in voyeuristic tourism to visit peace walls.

WHY THE CHURCHES?

It can be alleged that there has been too much focus on religion in Ireland. Jonathan Swift thought in the eighteenth century that the country had suffered from enough religion to make its people hate (see Griffin's 2002 review of Irish religion and politics); by the twenty-first century, Kennedy (2004) was still wondering whether religion had bought 'nothing but trouble' to Ireland. When religion is the form through which the conflict is experienced, it is inevitable that it will be perceived as part of the problem. Its capacity to turn itself into being part of the solution, therefore, has some intellectual curiosity.

Our inquisitiveness is lent further value as a result of scholars' neglect of the contribution of the churches. The conventional approach to Northern Ireland's peace process is narrowly political (the best all-round analysis of the peace process, which is exempt from this criticism, is Cox, Guelke, and Stephen, 2006). For example, in an otherwise masterly study of 'talking to terrorists', as they put it, Bew, Frampton, and Gurruchaga (2009) reduce churchmen and women to bit-part players on a stage otherwise commanded by the British state and the paramilitary groups themselves, which overlooks completely the churches' use of back channels to both initiate and facilitate dialogue, and their profound impact on the outcome (the exception is their treatment of the Feakle talks (Bew, Frampton, and Gurruchaga, 2009: 53–4)). The politics behind the GFA has been extensively covered (for an early sociological approach to the peace processes in Northern Ireland and South Africa, see Brewer, 2003c), perhaps to the point of boredom or routine (for a highly selective sample, see: Ruane and Todd, 1999; McGarry, 2001a; Farrington, 2006; Kerr, 2006; Fitzduff and Williams, 2007; Taylor, 2009a). The interviews with twenty-nine political activists undertaken by Fitzduff and Williams (2007) on what respondents saw as the motivating factors behind the peace process overwhelmingly prioritized politics but eschewed mention of the churches.

Narrowing the focus in this way means that those key individuals and parties involved in the final negotiation of the GFA receive the attention and the accolades. Very often they were not connected to the process that brought the appropriate conditions in which the talks could take place. For instance, George Mitchell, Tony Blair, Mo Mowlam, Peter Mandelson, Jonathan Powell, Alastair Campbell, and Bertie Ahern were all post-1994 ceasefire brokers—politicians and their mandarins who rushed in after the 1997 Blair election victory, playing little or no part in ending the violence. Before these people could enter the stage a different set of actors had been instrumental, many of them churchmen, such as Alec Reid, Robin Eames, Roy Magee, Edward Daly, Ken Newell, Des Wilson, Gerry Reynolds, Harold Good, and An Sagairt Maith (*non de plume* for 'the good priest', whose identity he wishes to remain anonymous).[8] This second group worked behind the scenes to secure the ceasefires and it is here that we see the churches acting politically by providing secure space for back channel talks. Contrast this with the GFA talks themselves. The churches were excluded and vanish from the scene. The post-ceasefire brokers at the negotiating table are joined by very few of those who actually contributed to stopping the violence. It is ironic, therefore, that when the agreed political deal got stuck on decommissioning—and stayed so for many years—it was resolved only with the reintroduction of the churches, when the authority and legitimacy of Alec Reid and Harold Good was exploited as appointed witnesses to the destruction of arms.

While this religious dimension is treated lightly or ignored (for exceptions, see Grant, 2004; Power, 2007; Ganiel, 2008a, 2008b), autobiographies by some of the leading politicians and negotiators comment impressionistically on the part played by a few people from the churches (for example, Adams, 2007: 122; Campbell, 2007: 204; Powell, 2008: 273). Journalists who covered the unfolding story repeat these hints (for example, de Breadun, 2008). There is an unfortunate tendency in these casual asides to isolate the charismatic few who are already accorded public recognition and ignore the unsung many.

Sometimes, however, there is no mention of the churches at all, even by people at the centre of events (for example, Mitchell, 2000). Mo Mowlam (2002: xv–xviii), the former Secretary of State for Northern Ireland in Blair's first Cabinet, thanks a catalogue of people for their help in the Northern Irish peace process, even Nelson Mandela, but mentions no one in the churches, although there are two places where the churches are mentioned as a force for good (2002: 211, 307–8). Alastair Campbell (2007: 204), Tony Blair's chief press officer, refers dismissively in his diaries to the churches as 'the holies' and mentions once that they met with Mowlam. David Trimble's biographer, the journalist Dean Godson (2004: 286–7) reproduces Trimble's distrust of the churches and makes only one mention of him meeting with them.[9] The series of interviews with Trimble conducted by the *Irish Times* journalist Frank

[8] 'The Troubles' spurred inventive pseudonyms. Another priest was known as Archangel and a Derry businessman as 'Mountain Climber'. Mountain Climber organized meetings between the Social Democratic and Labour Party (SDLP), SF and the IRA with a senior MI5 agent in Bishop Edward Daly's house in Derry.

[9] Trimble, like Blair, declined our invitation for an interview. John Brewer and Francis Teeney had firsthand experience of Trimble's distrust of the churches, despite his strong personal faith (on which, see Miller, 2008: 23–6). We facilitated two meetings with Trimble for the ecumenical group Faith in a Brighter Future. At the first meeting Trimble was suspicious and seemed to speak only what his advisor, Stephen King, whispered into his ear; at the second he spoke to a group of priests outside Stormont only through an eight-foot wire fence. Trimble was under such attack from all quarters that he suspected the same from ecumenists; he seemed not to be able to tell who his friends were; and he failed to utilize the progressive elements in the churches as an ally, for fear of intensifying criticism from regressive elements in the churches.

Miller indicate that while he has strong personal belief, he wished to separate religion from politics (2008: 23). In order to avoid bringing 'the Lord' into politics—and he would have had his ardent critic Ian Paisley in mind—he kept the churches out too (Miller, 2008: 24). Like Blair and Campbell, Trimble did not 'do God'.[10] Accordingly, there is no mention in the interviews of the contribution of the churches.

This might be expected with a focus on the GFA, from which civil society generally was excluded, but it holds true also for the Downing Street Declaration (DSD), in which the churches were heavily involved. John Major, Blair's predecessor as prime minister and heavily engaged with the Irish government in negotiating the DSD as a precursor to the 1994 ceasefires, makes one-line references in his autobiography to meetings with Anglicans (1999: 457, 467) and to government ministers having met SF in church premises in Derry (1999: 477).[11] It seems strange, therefore, but highly significant for our argument about the neglect of the churches, that in a letter to us reflecting on their contribution, Major should write:

> During the peace process—in which there was so much mutual suspicion on all sides—I often needed a distinctive and dispassionate viewpoint. For this I often turned *in complete privacy* to the church leaders and Robin Eames was on every occasion both helpful and wise. The churches were undoubtedly a strength in keeping the process beyond partisan politics and encouraging the population to accept that a genuine attempt was underway to bring together the political disputants in both Northern Ireland and Eire. The churches were trusted and were invaluable. They seem to me to be a resource often overlooked in modern politics and one that I believe can bring a positive aspect to the search for a solution in very intractable situations. I shall remain forever grateful to Archbishop Eames and other church leaders for their advice in relation to the Northern Ireland peace process. (Dated 4 April 2006; emphasis in the original)

To be able to specify this role comprehensively, bringing it to the centre of interest, and to represent the contribution of the meagre as well as the mighty, therefore helps us meet laypeople's curiosity for more systematic and detailed information.

---

[10] For example, we know Trimble declined invitations to speak at Clonard Monastery.

[11] The one exception to this is Martin Mansergh, the principal advisor on Northern Ireland to the Irish governments of both Albert Reynolds and Bertie Ahern, whose autobiography (Mansergh, 2003) makes voluminous mention. This may reflect his greater respect for the churches, coming as he does from the Irish Republic, his own personal religious observance (as an Irish Protestant), which may influence him to have less dismissive views of religion generally, or the closeness of the Irish government to one of the principal religious actors in the peace process, the Catholic Church. Whichever is the case, the attention he accords the churches only reinforces that there has been deliberate neglect of their contribution amongst other participants to the GFA negotiations.

But our subject matter here is more far reaching than small curiosities. There are important policy dimensions to our focus on the role of the Northern Irish churches in peacemaking. Many conflicts in late modern society are experienced as religious (as discussed in Durward and Marsden, 2009), in large part because of the way globalization has sharpened religious identity as a response to its homogenizing tendencies and simultaneously intensified regional conflicts (see Banchoff, 2008; Smock, 2008), some of which take on a religious hue (even though the substance of the struggle is mostly not religious). Religious differences mark the boundaries of groups in conflict within Sri Lanka, the Philippines, Southern Sudan, Nigeria, Sierra Leone, Kashmir, Israel–Palestine, and the Lebanon, amongst others, where it stands as a surrogate for deep ethnic divisions, differences over the legitimacy of the state or opposing cultural-national allegiances. Northern Ireland offers an example to them all and helps identify the policy strategies that churches and religious groups elsewhere might adopt, as well as avoid, when becoming religious peacemakers.

There is also a corpus of knowledge accumulating on religious peacebuilding to which our study contributes. Instances where religious activists have been largely responsible for bringing warring parties together to negotiate settlements, such as the short-lived peace agreement in Sudan in 1972 or the stable deal in Mozambique in 1992 (see Smock, 2006: 1), are matched with others where the churches worked hand in glove with political groups to realize change, such as apartheid South Africa and communist Poland (discussed at length in Brewer, Higgins, and Teeney, 2010).[12] This spurred the United States Institute for Peace (USIP) in 1999 to establish a research programme on religious peacemaking (as examples of outputs, see Smock, 2001, 2002, 2006, 2008; Landau, 2003; Little, 2007), although their focus is overwhelmingly on interfaith dialogue between the Abrahamic religions. The growing body of literature that is emerging on religious peacemaking (for example, Cejka and Bamat, 2003; Coward and Smith, 2004; Philpott, 2006, 2007a, 2007b; Schlack, 2009; Shore, 2009) acts as useful counterweight to the usual attention given to the link between religion and conflict (for example, Juergensmeyer, 2000; Bruce, 2003; Larsson, 2004; Norris and Inglehart, 2004; Durward and Marsden, 2009).

However, while the literature on religion and conflict is quite theoretically astute, that on religious peacemaking adopts the case-study approach, including the extensive work of the USIP.[13] On one level, our book appears to supply

---

[12] In reviewing the many cases of religious peacemaking Appleby (1998) draws a distinction between those where the churches were brought within the political process and those where they remained external. We will come back to this distinction in Chapter 3.

[13] The case studies of religious peacemaking collected by Smock (2006) exclude Northern Ireland. This is because he focuses on conflicts between two or more of the Abrahamic faiths (mostly Christian–Muslim and Muslim–Jewish conflicts) and ignores intra-Christian conflicts,

yet another case study of religious peacemaking; and an instance much discussed already (Brewer, Bishop, and Higgins, 2001; Brewer, 2003a), particularly the contribution of ecumenism (Appleby, 2000; Grant, 2004; McCreary, 2007; Power, 2007), although Ganiel (2008a, 2008b; also see Ganiel and Dixon, 2008) has broadened the focus by addressing the consequences for the peace process of religious and political change within evangelicalism. Individual peacemakers in Northern Ireland from a religious background who have written autobiographies (Morrow, 2003; Patterson, 2003) or who are the subjects of biographies reinforce the impression of particularism inherent in the case-study approach (on Robin Eames, see McCreary, 2004; on Ken Newell and Gerry Reynolds, see Wells, 2005; on Eric Gallagher, see Cooke, 2005). There is value in adding to a corpus of knowledge, of course, but we see our study operating on another plane by theorizing the relationship between religion and peacemaking; making it the first of its kind. We use the Northern Irish case as a way into developing a conceptual framework for the comparative analysis of religion and peacemaking in conflict societies where religion is part of the problem.[14]

The Introduction to this book is not the place for detail, but we can sketch the outlines of our conceptualization before its elaboration in later chapters. The key to it is civil society and the four socially strategic spaces that religious groups can occupy within civil society (which we call intellectual, institutional, market, and political spaces) and by means of which they can play a role in peace processes as 'bridging' social capital across groups, rather than just forms of 'bonding' social capital within groups. However, religious peacemaking is mediated by the wider civil society–state nexus. This shows itself in two sets of variables that simultaneously constrain and facilitate the relationship between religion and peacebuilding: the majority–minority status of churches and religious organizations; and the official–unofficial nature of their intervention. Civil society and the state are dominating elements within religious peacework and we argue that the connection between religion and peacemaking has to be understood within the bounds of church–civil society–state relations. Religion matters greatly in peace processes but its role is dependent on this wider relationship. We use the Northern Irish case to substantiate and illustrate this conceptualization.

which is consistent with his emphasis on interfaith dialogue as the primary form of religious peacemaking (an approach established in Smock, 2002). It is for this reason also that none of the (inter)faith-based NGOs active in peacemaking mentioned by Smock (2001) have any presence in Northern Ireland.

[14] Beck (2010) has theorized the relationship between religion and peace and portrays the link as lying in the nature of late modernity, which he calls 'reflexive modernity', that propels people 'to make gods of their own', which has the potential to make religion a source of inclusivity rather than division precisely because 'truth' is irrelevant now to most believers. Self-righteous religion can give way to religions that seek peace not 'truth'.

There is a final reason for the focus on churches. In the case of Northern Ireland, they represent the largest single set of voluntary groups within civil society and supply the greatest number of voluntary members (Morrow *et al.*, 1991). Marie Fitzduff (2010: 4–5) notes that this centrality is cemented also by the church hall being a community site used by several different civil society groups. In 2001, Taylor (2001: 43) reported that there were 'about 5000 voluntary and community groups' in Northern Ireland, with an annual turnover of £400 million and about 5 per cent of the workforce. Compare this with the near million people noted in the 1995–6 *Irish Christian Handbook* as belonging to one of Northern Ireland's Christian denominations, upwards of two-thirds of the total population (worked from figures in Richardson, 1998: 6).[15] Churches also have a wide geographical spread and a centralized coordinating structure, giving them a visible presence throughout the North and a coherent voice. In contrast, other groups, such as many women's groups, community development projects and the like are by nature small, localized, and uncoordinated, with limited capacity to direct debate or demand media attention outside their immediate locality. The churches, in contrast, move between central and local spaces at the same time, they are literally everywhere—Belfast is a landscape of spires (on which see Brewer, Keane, and Livingstone, 2006)—and they have not completely lost their authority.

While there is evidence of liberalization in what Christians believe in Northern Ireland and some fall-off in the regularity of observance (see Brewer, 2003b), there is no evidence of decline in belief. So-called 'religious independents' (people who in surveys do not identify with any religious group) are a stable proportion of the sample at around one in ten people (Hayes, Fahey, and Sinnott, 2005: 30–57). Put differently, nine out of ten people identify themselves as belonging to a religion, even if the meaning of this identification has changed and is held with less intensity (see Mitchell, 2005b; for an analysis of elements of change and continuity within Protestantism, see Brewer, 2004; for Catholicism, see Mitchell, 2005c). In the absence of much secularization in Northern Ireland, therefore, civil society is populated by a very large number of religious groups to an extent that is unusual in Western Europe. Northern Ireland has never experienced the privatization of religion, its retreat into the domestic sphere of family and the home; for good or ill, the churches and para-church organizations continue to dominate civil society.[16]

As a way of reinforcing the centrality of the churches within the voluntary sector, Morrow and colleagues concluded their 1991 survey by pointing out

---

[15] The actual number was 942,911. Lest it be thought that the *Handbook* might deliberately overcount, Richardson also supplies figures from the 1991 Census, which show 1,339,527 people belonging to a Christian denomination (1998: 6).

[16] Casanova (1994) argues that there is a process of deprivatization affecting modern society generally and there has been trenchant debate in the USA over the political dangers of the entry of religion into the public square (see Audi and Wolterstorff, 1996).

that churches were 'communities of people whose whole lives are lived in the light of their church experience and knowing', and when 'in the workplace, in pubs, bringing up children or whatever, they remain partly in church' (quoted in Fitzduff, 2010: 6). It is hard to support this claim any longer. The churches may speak, but whether people listen as much is debatable. The churches' capture of civil society sits uneasily with many people's sense of frustration towards the churches, arising from their being seen as partly responsible for 'the Troubles' in the first place, leading to a weariness at their pronouncements (rather than outright hostility). A growing anticlericalism, nourished by sex scandals and child-abuse atrocities, combined with antipathy to churches as large and anonymous institutions, and feelings of cultural outdatedness, especially amongst the young, complete this sense of frustration. But, regardless, the residue of legitimacy the churches retain supports our view that they are—exceptionally in late modernity—a major component of Northern Irish civil society.

Demonstrating this is important for the next stage of our argument. We use the churches as an exemplar of civil society activism in conflict societies, from which vantage point we seek to critically engage with the extensive literature that promotes civil society as an antidote to war (Kaldor, 2003) and as essential to the stability of democratic transitions after communal violence. However, before we locate our research within this debate, it is necessary to outline the form it takes.

CIVIL SOCIETY AND DEMOCRATIC TRANSITIONS

The connection between civil society and democratization has both empirical and theoretical sides and we first wish to map the extent of their relationship in practice. In a recent analysis of the role of civil society in peace processes, Bell and O'Rourke (2007: 297) noted that of the 389 peace agreements between 1990 and 2007, 139 made explicit reference to civil society involvement. This included civil society allocation of resources and humanitarian aid, the monitoring of parties' obligations under peace accords, the provision of participative forums and direct involvement in constitution building. Van Leeuwen (2009), in a practitioner approach to civil society peacemaking, identified on the basis of several case studies their roles as diplomacy and peace negotiations, security enhancement and the provision of safe environments, assistance with economic reconstruction and development, reforming governance structures, justice and human rights protection, and societal healing (2009: 32–3). This heavy involvement in peacemaking is in part the consequence of the sizeable funds available to civil society groups to facilitate it. Three things are important here: the number of International Non-Governmental

Organizations (INGOs) and other associations with a remit that bears upon peace and post-conflict reconstruction; the level of influence they have on peacemaking beyond the numbers of people who are formal members; and the funds available from charities and philanthropic foundations to support them.

Evidence is difficult to find on the first two issues, but it is nonetheless there. Mary Kaldor has described the last two decades of the twentieth century as experiencing a 'global association revolution'. In a survey of the non-profit sector in twenty-two countries, she has revealed that the sector contributed 5.1 per cent of total employment and could call on an additional 10.4 million volunteers (Kaldor, 2003: 88–9). Whilst these figures cover only a small number of countries, they refer to only one form of voluntary association, the non-profit sector. More broadly, during the 1990s registered INGOs rose by one-third to 13,206 and their membership to 263,000, with an increasing proportion of official aid being channelled through them, ranging from 85 per cent in the Swedish case, to 10 per cent for the UK (Kaldor, 2003: 89). While membership of INGOs per million of population in 2003 shows this form of civic engagement to be dominated by the West and OECD countries (see Kaldor, Anheier, and Glasius, 2005: 19), their activities are focused on the poorer countries. Thus, countries with communal conflicts or a history of communal conflict have very few citizens as members of INGOs per million of population (Eritrea had 42.3, Sri Lanka 69.2, and Nicaragua 160.2, as compared to Iceland's 6,353.3, Norway's 987.3, and Denmark's 932.1), but statistics capture the growth in the presence of INGOs in 'low income economies' over the ten-year period to 2003. Economically poor countries have seen a substantial growth in INGO involvement (the following figures taken from Record 15: Country Participation in INGOs in Anheier, Glasius, and Kaldor, 2005: 304–9). Countries with a history of violence witnessed some of the largest percentage increase in INGO presence, such as East Timor at 767 per cent, Bosnia and Herzegovina 891 per cent, and Eritrea 2,933 per cent. Equally revealing is that some countries with fragile peace processes often had a low presence by INGOs, such as Sri Lanka, with only an absolute growth between 1993 and 2003 of 24 per cent, Sudan 11 per cent, Nepal 65 per cent, Haiti 19 per cent, and the Philippines 37 per cent; Liberia suffered 7 per cent decline, when INGOs withdrew as the violence deteriorated. These figures suggest an obvious connection between civil society and peace processes, but it is mediated by philanthropy and the funds available to encourage peacemaking.

Charity and aid are increasingly becoming mechanisms of democratization (for elaboration of this point see Brewer, 2010: 37–42; Vogel, 2006), something perhaps difficult to associate with the army of kindly, elderly volunteers with their small charity boxes standing outside supermarkets on chilly weekends. Traditional charities, however, need to be distinguished from what Karl and Katz (1987) call 'modern philanthropy'. New large-scale philanthropic organizations have emerged, such as Rockefeller, Carnegie, Ford, and MacArthur, which focus on finding long-term solutions to the major public problems of the day. This does not just involve the alleviation of harm and illness but challenges the root causes of problems; aid is directed to facilitate social and political change. This is done in several ways (see Anheier and Daly, 2005: 162). Some endowed foundations award grants for specified purposes, some develop their own projects and programmes consistent with their aims and remit, while others are linked to multi-national companies and businesses. They function within the developed market economies and established democracies of the West but direct attention to the social problems in the Global South or on transitional societies that have geostrategic value to the West. Foundations in the United States are more active internationally than European ones (Anheier and Daly, 2005: 163), and the amount of their aid is mesmerizing; the top fifteen US foundations gave more than $US19 billion in 2001 (worked from figures provided in Anheier and Daly, 2005: 164).

Much of this philanthropy specifically targets peace initiatives. The Ford Foundation funds a Governance and Civil Society Programme,[17] and the Woodrow Wilson Center's programme on leadership and state-building held a major event in October 2009 on civil society inclusion in peace processes. The Carnegie Endowment for International Peace, for example, describes itself as an international donor that has embraced civil society aid as a key tool for democracy promotion and supports thousands of groups around the world in the name of civil society development, investing precisely in those organizations that say they promote democratic participation and free market principles (see www.carnegieendowment.org). It funded a 'democracy and rule of law' research programme in Washington, the results of which were collated by two permanent researchers from Carnegie under the revealing title *Funding Virtue: Civil Society Aid and Democracy Promotion* (Carothers and Ottaway, 2000), addressing South Africa, the Philippines, Peru, Egypt, and Romania. Anheier and Daly (2005: 164) outline that amongst the top fifteen charitable foundations in the United States, for example, the Ford Foundation (which awarded grants of $US6 billion in 2001) 'seeks to strengthen democratic values . . . and promote international co-operation'; the MacArthur Foundation ($US94 million in grants in 2001) 'seeks to promote international peace and security . . . and human rights'; the Hewlett Foundation ($US66 million in 2001), 'supports conflict resolution and US–Latin American relations'; the Starr Foundation ($US53 million in 2001), 'supports international relations'; the Carnegie Foundation ($US44 million in 2001), 'supports international peace and security'; the Mott Foundation ($US31 million in 2001), 'supports the strengthening of civil society globally'; and the Open Society Institute ($US24 million in 2001) 'promotes open societies through support for civil

---

[17] Its director, Michael Edwards, is author of a book on civil society (Edwards, 2004).

society...and human rights'. This is not just a feature of US foundations, although they tend to dominate modern philanthropy. The Hallows Foundation in Australia and the Nippon Foundation in Japan also give generously to 'overseas co-operative assistance'; 353 public benefit corporations in Japan list 'international relations' as the field of their charitable activity (Anheier and Daly, 2005: 165). In their analysis of five trends in global giving, Anheier and Simmons (2004) refer to two that bear upon our point: the tendency for aid to be directed to post-conflict societies and to compensate for 'deficiencies in government or market failures'. These private foundations work alongside, but sometimes in conjunction with, governments, the United Nations, the European Union (EU), and INGOs as part of a global network of organizations involved in post-conflict scenarios. The global network of women's organizations, for example, is heavily involved in empowering women as peacemakers, with several umbrella bodies involved in funding local groups, lending international advice and acting as encouragement, such as Hunt Alternatives, the United Nations Development Fund for Women (UNIFEM), and the Initiative for Inclusive Security (see Brewer, 2010: 95–7).

Some philanthropic foundations have focused on civil society in Northern Ireland. The Joseph Rowntree Charitable Trust always apportions part of its money annually to Northern Ireland. The Barrow Cadbury Trust in the United Kingdom has a justice and peace programme that has seen monies go to the promotion of civil society in Northern Ireland (and the Middle East), and the US-based Atlantic Philanthropies has been a significant funder of peace and reconciliation initiatives in Northern Ireland through civil society capacity-building. This is complemented by the British and Irish governments and the EU devoting huge resources to peacemaking; the latter's Special Peace and Reconciliation Programme in Northern Ireland was in excess of £1.5 billion by 2001 (see Brewer, 2003c: 133). The third stage of the EU's Peace Programme is funded to the scale of €267 million. According to an economic audit by the *Regional Monitor*, the EU has allocated a further £575 million to Northern Ireland and the six bordering counties in the Irish Republic under the 2009 Transitional Objectives I programme. The size and vitality of Northern Ireland's voluntary sector is in part a reflection of the survival of tight-knit communities that 'the Troubles' helped to reinforce,[18] but also of the

---

[18] One of the interesting consequences of the communal violence was the unintentional encouragement it gave to the survival of close-knit communities, which was a by-product of reduced population relocation, the persistence of extended family networks in local areas, low amounts of inward migration, and strong senses of in-group solidarity fostered on resistance to out-groups, all of which were rooted in 'the Troubles' and which had the effect of suppressing levels of ordinary crime rate and enhancing mechanisms for the local management of crime. Despite high levels of political crime, therefore, ordinary crime during the height of 'the Troubles' remained lower in Belfast than in Dublin and comparable cities in Great Britain (see Brewer, Lockhart, and Rodgers, 1997).

impressively large amount of funding available to sustain the activities of local civil society groups. For example, there were 26,000 applications for funding under the second phase of the EU's peace-funding programme for Northern Ireland, half of which received some level of aid (Fitzduff and Williams, 2007: 14)—a staggering number given the travails in introducing peace beforehand. To strike home this point, in the five-year period following the 1994 ceasefires, nearly as many inter-church ecumenical projects were formed as in the preceding fourteen years (Power, 2007: 73). They flourished in part because space had been opened up for them to function more safely as a result of the ending of violence, but more money was also now available to support them.

It bears asking, therefore, what value philanthropists and governments see in civil society peacemaking. The way the concept of civil society has been theorized gives the clue (for contrast, see Kaldor, 2003; Keane, 2003; Edwards, 2004). The political and sociological treatments of the concept are mutually reinforcing. Sociologists associate the term with participation in the voluntary sector, from which follows enhanced sociability, a heightening of the social bond and increased trust, reciprocity and tolerance between members of voluntary groups. These social virtues are seen to spread beyond voluntary group members to society generally. Political science treatments associate it with political participation in the public sphere, the provision of, and involvement in, deliberative forums for debate and articulation. This encourages people's interest in politics not apathy, political engagement not boredom, and feelings of efficacy not indifference. Democratic societies are thought to be strongest where apathy is weakest. In political and sociological treatments, indifference by people (to each other as much as towards politics) is dangerous. The way to avoid this risk is the same for both approaches: civil society is the locus for civic virtues such as trust, respect and tolerance, altruism, and senses of belonging, which imprint themselves on the quality of social *and* political bonds.

There is an unfortunate tendency to narrow down these virtues to the single idea of social capital. This is a concept developed independently by many social scientists (on its various definitions, see Portes, 1998), although the framework of Robert Putnam (1993, 2000, 2007) dominates, where it describes people's social connectedness via the social networks in which they participate.[19] It was Putnam's penetrating analyses of social capital that motivated renewed interest in civil society in US sociology and the global discipline, but the terms are not interchangeable. However, as a result of the

---

[19] Rival formulations of the idea of social capital, such as by Pierre Bourdieu, never penetrated US sociology because of American insularity. French influences have been stronger in British sociology, where Bourdieu is more popular. However, the Americanization of global sociology gives Putnam's formulation the edge. Bourdeiu's death in 2002 also leaves the terrain open for Putnam's work to flourish.

influence of Putnam's study of lonely, isolated, retreatist modern America in his book *Bowling Alone* (2000), in which social capital becomes the mechanism both for making democracy work and for enhancing sociability, social capital has come to represent civil society. While it has been claimed enthusiastically that social capital is the raw material of civil society (Onyx and Bullen, 2000), the equation of civil society with protection against individualism and authoritarianism goes back to earlier concepts in US sociology in the 1950s, such as David Riesman's notion of 'the lonely crowd' or the concern of people such as C. Wright Mills and William Kornhauser with the critique of mass society. Discussions of trust, tolerance, compassion, humanitarianism, and the like—as modern virtues—should be separated from the narrower debate about social capital (for example, Delanty, 2009 subsumes discussion of these virtues under the broader notion of the 'cosmopolitan imagination'; for an application of this idea to the sociology of peace processes, see Brewer, 2010: 2–7).

It was no coincidence that Putnam's analysis, introduced in 1993 with *Making Democracy Work*, became so quickly popular (and that the idea of social capital has defined the debate since), for it occurred simultaneously with two seemingly contradictory processes. On the one hand, organized violence escalated in this period and transformed into what Kaldor called 'new wars' (1999), dominated by intra-state conflict, without a set battle zone and involving large numbers of non-combatants; violence of a kind that no longer involved professional armies but engaged the whole of society and the resolution of which equally prompted a broad response from civil society (a point emphasized by van Leeuwen, 2009: 38). At the same time, we witnessed the downfall of several different kinds of authoritarian regimes— the collapse of apartheid, the ending of Soviet communism, and the overturning of dictatorial regimes in Eastern Europe and Central and South America. This seemed to reinforce the impression that future conflicts could be prevented through democratization via civil society transformation (van Leeuwen, 2009: 37).[20] This was also the time when neoconservatives in the USA were forecasting the end of history, and Fukuyama (1992) predicted the universalization of Western liberal democracy as the final form of government. This helps explain why US perspectives on social capital assumed authority. Putnam's ideas got wrapped up in post-Cold War triumphalism in the USA, since he explicitly outlined the incipient threats to the dominance of the West coming from within, as democracy rotted inside through lack of the social capital to sustain it, and supplied an implicit endorsement of the means

---

[20] It is in this time period that some International Relations (IR) specialists broadened their focus beyond the narrowly political dimensions of peace processes and began to recognize the value of civil society in bringing wars to an end, notably Paris (2004).

by which Western hegemony could be extended to all the newly democratiz-ing societies.[21]

A critical shift in nomenclature occurred in the use of the term civil society towards the end of the 1990s in the face of the obdurate persistence of ethnic and political rivalries in transitional societies (notably the Balkans and Sri Lanka); the continued threat of 'spoiler violence' seeking to undermine peace settlements (Stedman, 1997; Darby, 2001); the unbending commitment of a small minority of protagonists to a war-based economy of corruption, patron-age and warlord gangsterism (Keen, 1998); and the difficulties in embedding political and institutional reform. Distinctions were made between in-group and out-group social capital—the development of trust, tolerance, reciprocity, and enhanced social and political bonds inside or outside the group—giving us intra-group bonding social capital (socially exclusive) compared to inter-group bridging social capital (socially inclusive). Leonard (2004: 927) notes that while Putnam later tried to deal with the negative effects of social capital by means of this distinction in *Bowling Alone* (2000), his analysis is flawed because bonding capital rarely progresses into bridging capital, so that social capital can become solidified into prejudicial practices and beliefs and thus becomes a constraint on peacemaking (a point made earlier by Portes and Landolt, 1996).

With this came the realization that social capital could be used for anti-democratic purposes, when it fostered solidarity and political activism within racist, xenophobic, and authoritarian groups, leading to Putzel's (1997) depic-tion of the 'darker side' of social capital and to Chambers and Kopstein's (2001) identification of 'bad' civil society.[22] Civil society cannot be restricted only to groups who are 'civil'. Contrary to Farrington's suggestion (2008b: 115), the prefix 'civil' has never been used as an adjective in social science discussions of civil society (Berger, 2005, is the exception), for there is suffi-cient evidence of civil society groups who operate outside the boundaries of 'civility' and 'civilization'.[23]

---

[21] Tying philanthropic aid to democratization by funding civil society was, therefore, the inevitable conclusion drawn by US governments, think tanks and philanthropic foundations. The flip side to this is that the threat of withdrawal of aid gave them control over civil society activities. Leschenko undertook a case study of two private foundations, the Mott Foundation and the Soros Foundations Network (reported in Anheier and Daly, 2005: 170–1), and showed that they tended to fund local NGOs that were involved in promoting good governance, assisted in the training of officials and politicians and policymakers to improve governance and worked to promote the idea of open, civil society, which was conditional upon the Foundations being satisfied that they continued to serve these ends.

[22] Critics of the idea of civil society when applied to Northern Ireland point out that the Orange Order and the Gaelic Athletics Association (GAA) are the two largest civil society groups (see McGarry, 2001b: 117), but this comment reflects the failure to distinguish progressive and regressive factions within civil society.

[23] 'Civil' has its roots in the Latin *civilis*, meaning citizen, rather than referring to politeness.

A further shift in nomenclature occurred with Jeffrey Alexander's (2006) exploration of the 'civil sphere'. Written from within cultural sociology as a challenge to the valorization of social capital, which he describes as naïve (2006: 97–8), Alexander's approach to the stabilization of democracy is to emphasize social solidarity and the importance of the social bond, qualities that are not the by-product of social connectedness (and hence social capital) but the result of an effective 'civil sphere'. The civil sphere is not populated by third-sector voluntary groups and associations, as traditional civil society and social capital theorists conceive it, but consists of a set of values towards 'the democratic life' that are communicated by discursive and cultural practices and disseminated by the mass media as well as cultural, legal, and other institutions (2006: 4). This might be thought of as tautological: democracy is viable and stable in societies where democratic values thrive. Alexander's contribution, however, is to show how democratic values can establish themselves and survive against the 'uncivil forces' that threaten the civil sphere through a range of communicative practices and movements that disseminate notions of justice, fairness, and equality, and engage in 'social repair' whenever uncivil tendencies (such as, for instance, slavery and the Holocaust) weaken it. The civil rights movement, feminists and peace movements, for example, not only mobilize the interests of racial, gender, and national minority groups, they are 'about the reconstruction of social solidarity, about its expansion and repair' (Alexander, 2006: 5). Self-referential, inwardly directed, voluntary associations play no effective role in the civil sphere (2006: 103); they must have normative commitments to the wider civil sphere and integrate with its communicative, cultural, and institutional frameworks and codes.

The notion of the civil sphere introduces key advances because it places emphasis on the 'dark side of civil society' (Alexander, 2006: 6), the contradictions in civil society around 'race', religion, gender, and its other structural social divisions that 'bonding social capital' does not seem adequately to capture. At the same time, the term is associated with commitment to a cosmopolitan humanitarianism of disinterested love, as Alexander put it (2006: 5), in which the civil sphere can triumph over incivility when structures, institutions, and discursive practices assist people to see they have common feelings for others who they do not know personally but whom they respect out of principle. Solidarity, in other words, is premised on a sense of community that is culturally defined and discursively and institutionally reinforced. It means more than civility, although this is implied by it; it is mutual respect, garnered not by social connectedness, since it extends in principle to people well beyond our personal social networks, but nurtured by public opinion, people's ways of talking about and thinking about others, as well as society's cultural codes, institutional arrangements, and values. The civil sphere not only includes the practices by which mutual respect is disseminated, it contains the strategies for social repair when mutual respect is absent or diminishes. As a form of morality that is sociologically structured by various social practices that reproduce solidarity, the civil sphere is at one and the same time the object of its own reproduction; it is a goal that pro-democratic peace groups can aspire to as subaltern civic communities within an uncivil society, as well as the strategy by which they will realize this goal. The civil sphere is the key that opens up itself.

In many ways, Alexander's work is an attempt to marry commitment to the idea of civil society with the evidence of very uncivil tendencies in modern life, where some forms of identity politics close down the civil sphere. In response to situations of intractable conflict and persistent ethnic, religious, national, and racial segregation, Putnam's further elaboration has been to develop the notion of 'constrict capital' (2007). People who prefer to live in mixed communities against the trend to segregation are said to 'hunker down' and withdraw even from their own group, reducing inter- and intra-group solidarity and social capital still further, with commensurate loss of trust, community cooperation, and altruism. Weak ties between liberal-minded people get even weaker in the face of continued diversity, as they turn inwards and away from all forms of social capital. It is not diversity that is the problem here, however (as many observers have pessimistically concluded as a commentary on race relations in the USA (Oliver and Ha, 2008) and elsewhere[24]), but incorrigible, incurable inequality. Putnam makes clear that the reduction in social capital in diverse societies is short-term while new pluralist identities develop. Yet this supplies even more evidence, in the short term at least, of the limits of civil society in dealing with intractable social structural divisions—and is another warning against romanticizing the contribution it can make in divided societies undergoing democratization.

Another shift in nomenclature occurred with the emphasis placed on 'global civil society' as the primary type associated with peacemaking (see Kaldor, 2003). Here the connection made with peaceful transitions occurs because global civil society allows small civil society groups in localized wars to move in their peacemaking between local, national, and global arenas, drawing international attention to their work and allowing them to benefit from wider and richer networks in order to aid their efforts. Global activists are— in the famous phrase—urged to think globally and act locally by addressing the local manifestations of global problems. But they also move in the other direction by taking local concerns on to a global stage by marshalling global civic networks. The capacity of civil society groups to negotiate their way between the local and the global allows them to be simultaneously national

---

[24] Quite a lot of work has been done by British and European social scientists because of high levels of migration within Europe and the implications of marked diversity of the EU for the development of European identity (see, for example, Gesthuizen, van der Meer, and Scheepers, 2008; Letki, 2008; Stolle, Soroka, and Johnston, 2008; Hooghe *et al.*, 2009).

and international, within and outside a nation state's borders. This makes civil society groups an effective go-between on two levels, mediating between the grass roots and the state within a national context and also between national and transnational peacemakers. This gives local grass-roots people the opportunity for their private troubles to be transformed by civil society into public issues on national and global stages.

The idea of global civil society is not universally accepted (for criticisms see Keane, 2003). There are, however, several factors that are beginning to make civil society global. For example, forms of geostrategic governance have emerged associated with the United Nations, particularly since the then General Secretary Boutros Boutros-Ghali in conjunction with the EU, NATO, and the Organization for Security and Co-operation in Europe (OSCE), developed the notion of international trusteeship for the comprehensive reconstruction of war-torn societies and for the regulation of the conduct of war. Forms of cosmopolitan and humanitarian law have also emerged to impose international accountability for the conduct of war that transcends national legal systems (see Hirsh, 2003). The emergence of global politics has ensured that civil society political engagements take place now on a broader space than the nation state, and civil society groups are required to be international in their political focus and activities (Kaldor, 2003: 79 *passim*). There are now also networks of exchange and collaboration that are transnational. These global networks place the activities of national groups in a broader framework, moving them literally on to a global stage. Civic networks in the past have linked together national civil society groups across different fields of interest (which thus amplified their range of involvement) or within their field of interest (which thus added weight to their campaigning), but these networks are now global, which raises exponentially the scale of their activities. While there is no global state, as it were, to provide a legislative framework for civil society activities—as there is with national NGOs—there are geostrategic governance structures and rules of law that global civil society groups both work within and help to reinforce. Global civil society is thus both cause and effect of the growth of international organizations and treaties and the emergence of regional blocs of cooperation over security, health, economics, and the like (Huddock, 1999).

However, the global civil society rhetoric tends to conveniently sidestep the problems around regressive elements in civil society by portraying global civil society as a progressive movement of activists, committed in values to cosmopolitan humanitarianism and in behaviour to social democracy (a point emphasized by Keane, 2003: 151). A healthy dose of Alexander's realism is needed here. The problem, as Brewer (2010: 205–6) has shown, is that there is no single global civil society. It is best to conceive of it in the plural, with factions occupying different spaces and on occasions working in opposition. Human rights groups in Rwanda, for example, took a critical position on the infamous *gacaca* courts, because they trampled the rule of law, which was contrary to the stance of women's groups, who saw them as a form of gender mainstreaming and empowerment (discussed in Brewer, 2010: 2006). It is important therefore, even with the focus put on progressive activism, not to overlook forms of peacemaking where civil society groups work in counter-productive ways.

Religion has recently been made an element in the debate about social capital through introduction of the notion of 'spiritual capital'. Putnam has endorsed a research programme by the Metanexus Institute on Religion and Science (www.metanexus.net/spiritual_capital), based in Bryn Mawr in Penn-sylvania and funded by the John Templeton Foundation, which has been exploring evidence for spiritual capital. Several working papers and a literature review on spiritual capital (www/spiritualcapitalresearchprogram.com/ research_articles.asp) have been generated. The Metanexus Institute's website describes religion as 'by far the largest generator of social capital in the United States, contributing to more than half of the social capital in the country', justifying the isolation of this subset of social capital. The website goes on to define spiritual capital as 'the effects of spiritual and religious practices, beliefs, networks and institutions that have a measurable impact on individuals, communities and societies'.[25]

The idea builds on earlier work within the sociology of religion by Iannac-cone, who developed the term 'religious capital' (1990) to explain patterns of religious beliefs and behaviour over the life cycle between generations and among family and friends. Stark and Finke (2000), two further doyens of the sociology of religion and collaborators of Iannaccone, later described the social and cultural dimensions of religious capital, having in mind the extent to which religion and religious observance were culturally disseminated. This yields a definition of religious capital as 'the degree of mastery of, and attachment to, a particular religious culture' (Stark and Finke, 2000: 120).

Spiritual capital proffers potentially a major conceptual stride forward by addressing the social *impact* of religion on believers and society generally, specifically linking with Putnam's familiar arguments that church attendance enhances social connectedness, and garners and culturally disseminates trust, reciprocity, and a sense of community (2000: 67). This is the motive behind the formulation of spiritual capital; it is not about people's feelings towards religion but the social *consequences* of these feelings for inculcating the virtues associated with social capital. Religious and spiritual forms of capital are thus not equivalent, as suggested by advocates of the earlier term (such as Finke, 2003: 5), for spiritual capital does not touch on the quality and strength of a person's religious beliefs but their social connectedness to others inside and

---

[25] www/spiritualcapitalresearchprogram.com/what_is.asp consulted 24 February 2010.

outside sacred spaces, by means of which virtues such as trust and reciprocity are socially disseminated. As Woodbury (2003: 2) puts it, spiritual capital 'helps us see religion as a resource; one that people draw on to meet various challenges—sickness, political oppression, ethical choices, or social problems'.

To this list one can add, for our purposes, also churched people's social engagements with reconciliation and societal healing during and after conflict. The Northern Irish churches' roles in the peace process are thus a measure of the level and quality of spiritual capital in Northern Ireland. It is clear that secularization impacts negatively on the capacity for spiritual capital, since social connectedness based on church attendance weakens with the decline in observance (as it does also for participation in very large 'mega-churches' and small independent 'house churches'). While Putnam expressed anxieties about trust relations in the USA as a consequence of its decline in religiosity (2000: 67), the relatively high levels of observance in Northern Ireland potentially make spiritual capital a useful resource that the churches could exploit.

This brief excursion into the literature on civil society, democratization, and forms of social and spiritual capital sets up a pertinent case study. The churches' contribution to Northern Ireland's peace process acts as a test of the efficacy of civil society in situations of conflict where civil society is itself part of the problem. The attention on church-based peacemaking allows the further possibility of establishing whether spiritual capital is a notion relevant only to socially cohesive societies or can be applied to settings where religion is implicated in the conflict. Before we proceed to this, however, it is necessary for one final digression in order to outline existing knowledge on the role of civil society in Northern Ireland's peace process.

CIVIL SOCIETY AND THE NORTHERN IRISH PEACE PROCESS

Civil society has wide currency in the debate over Northern Ireland's democratization. A few studies of the peace process have noted the important role of Northern Ireland's non-sectarian sectors of civil society (for example McCartney, 1999), placing it as one dimension alongside others in a holistic explanation (for example, Farrington, 2008a) or in contrast with other peace processes (Maney, Higgins, and Herzog, 2006), particularly the role of integrated education NGOs (see Stephen, 2006) and women's groups (Morgan, 2003; Fearon, 2006). Rupert Taylor (2001, 2009b), sees civil society as part of a model of social transformation in Northern Ireland that is an alternative to consociational models of political change (on which, see Taylor, 2009a). Guelke (2003) focuses on two civil society initiatives for their political effects, the 1992 Opsahl Commission and the non-party 'Yes Campaign' in the

1998 GFA referendum. He concludes that they were politically significant but that civil society influence was evident only during these high points. Cochrane (2001: 152), in his review of the voluntary sector, thought they had achieved indirect influence by encouraging political education and debate but he noted, sardonically, that the major turning points that moved the political process were violent events not peaceful ones (2001: 151).

Three points are worth making about this putative literature: its conceptual simplicity in understanding civil society; the rather indifferent evaluation made of its contribution because of the prioritization placed on its political effects; and the neglect to mention the role of the churches. Conceptual confusion arises because the literature treats Northern Irish civil society as a homogenous sector, so that authors get puzzled when some of the largest groups are clearly regressive or when systemic sectarianism in some groups co-exists with commitments to social transformation in others, as if this was not an inherent part of its fragmentary nature. Civil society is a notoriously uneven landscape, with groups occupying different spaces; some groups reproduce the sectarian divide, while others surmount great difficulties in transcending the divisions but nonetheless succeed in working across the lines of cleavage. For instance, in Sri Lanka, civil society is structured along ethno-religious lines, with parallel Tamil and Sinhalese groups (Orjuela, 2008): van Leeuwen (2009: 41) reports on many cases where civil society groups aligned themselves politically, were co-opted by political factions (by state-led and revolutionary groups), or became part of clientelist systems of patronage. As this example shows, we need a more sophisticated conceptual apparatus that allows us to focus on varying capacities to move from bonding to bridging social capital, from exclusivity to inclusivity. In Alexander's phrasing (2006), our analytical apparatus must enable us to distinguish the civil and uncivil tendencies in the civil sphere and identify processes of social repair for dealing with the latter. We should not get carried away and romanticize the contribution of civil society but we need the proper lens through which to scan the various roles played by its different groups.

Assessments made of the contribution of civil society to the Irish peace process in part reflect the narrowness of the conceptual field within Northern Irish scholarship. Interviews with civil society activists undertaken by Fitzduff and Williams (2007: 13) reveal that some failed to understand that politicians kept them at bay because specific civil society groups reproduced the divisiveness of sectarian society. Being rejected by politicians yet working on political terrain meant civil society groups had an unhappy lot. Cochrane (2001) queries whether or not they are unsung heroes, later describing them as deserving two cheers rather than three (2006; also see Cochrane, 2005). This is a cautious endorsement because the terrain on which they are judged is solely political; namely their contribution to the political peace process. Farrington (2008b: 113–14), in perhaps the best attempt to chart the contribution of civil society in Northern Ireland across the several meanings given to the term, says that civil society had no causal or deterministic effect in bringing about the GFA and that civil society had a diminished role subservient to politics. Cochrane and Dunn (1997), reflecting arguments before the GFA, described civil society in the North of Ireland as osmosis-like, with almost imperceptible political effects. These harsh judgements are right only if we overlook contributions to the social peace process and focus on formal, front-stage politics, rather than back-channel political engagements.

This emphasis has implications for the churches. The failure of the literature on Northern Irish civil society to mention the churches (with the exception of Ganiel, 2008a, 2008b) reflects the narrow focus on the politics of the peace process, and within that on 'high' politics rather than 'low', the politics of the final negotiation process rather than smaller-scale political engagements leading up to the peace accord. As we shall stress, the churches played a considerable role in the social peace process and engaged in significant 'low politics' initiatives, something hinted at in personal accounts of the peace process but not fully acknowledged. This omission in the literature leaves a significant gap in our understanding of Northern Ireland's peace process, which we intend to fill. The foregoing review, however, suggests we should do this critically, with an eye to the different spaces that particular churches and para-church organizations occupied in diverse sorts of peacemaking at various times, occasionally in opposition to one another and in ways that were sometimes regressive and counterproductive.

LOCATING THIS BOOK

Our ambition is to assess the contribution of the churches in Northern Ireland's peace process as a case study of the strengths and weaknesses of civil society peacemaking in situations of conflict. This choice is strategic in that some churches and religious groups opposed the peace process or engaged with it in limited ways, while the positive contribution of others has been neglected on the popular view that religion is part of the problem.[26] Our book therefore has three objectives: to compensate for the relative neglect of the churches in accounts of Northern Ireland's peace process by critically analysing their contribution; to use our data to reflect on the wider role of civil society in peace processes; and to assess the usefulness of the idea of spiritual capital in settings where religion is itself wrapped up in the conflict.

---

[26] Since we began our research in 2005, Power's (2007) analysis of the ecumenist churches and Ganiel's research on evangelicalism (2008a) have been published, but it is still the case that the contribution of churches more generally has been neglected.

We outline the churches' contributions to the peace process through a series of conceptual advances rather than by detailed chronological description. In Chapter 1 we focus on the social peace process, terrain on which the churches should have expertise, and develop a typology of kinds of peacemaking engaged in by the Christian churches in Northern Ireland between 1968 and 2011. In Chapter 2 we focus on the political peace process, terrain on which the churches have received criticism in the literature, by adding two further forms of peacemaking activity to our typology, which have been formerly unacknowledged. In Chapter 3 we try to make sense of these forms of peacemaking through two broader conceptual distinctions. First, we identify four strategic social spaces in which churches and para-church organizations acted within civil society and which gave the churches weight beyond the numbers in the pews (which we call intellectual, institutional, market, and political spaces). Second, we incorporate these distinctions into a conceptualization of the link between religion, civil society, and the state, pointing to the ways in which church–state relations can both constrain and facilitate engagement with peace. The conceptual apparatus allows us to plot the uneven landscape within Northern Irish civil society, the different locations some church groups occupied, including positions that allow us to suggest that some represented regressive, 'bad' civil society. In Chapter 4 we concretize these discussions by identifying other limitations and challenges in church engagements with the peace process.

We make three conclusions, which mark the distinctive contribution of this book. First, is the failure of Northern Irish ecumenism.[27] Ecumenism in Northern Ireland can be judged against two standards. The first is in improvements in the quality of relations between Catholics and Protestants, something that can be measured with respect to the relationships between church leaders and, quite separately, ordinary adherents in the respective pews. On the first of these measures it has done very well (most recently celebrated by Power, 2007); personal and ecclesiastical relations between bishops and the like are truly excellent. The second standard is in transforming Northern Irish society by means of these improved relations, as measured against the erosion of sectarianism. This is a high bar when set against four centuries of injustice built into the social structure, but it is realistic to have expected ecumenism to foster positive cross-community relations on a wider plane than in sacred spaces and amongst a broader constituency than committed ecumenists. It failed at this. Despite the valorization of the ecumenical movement in the academic

---

[27] Terminology is important at this point. Ecumenicalism describes the formal coming together of the denominations and world faiths, in effect the collapsing of religious boundaries, while ecumenism is at one and the same time something narrower and broader, describing the improvement in relations between members of denominations and world religions rather than institutional merger.

literature, much of which is US-based, Northern Irish ecumenism was conservative with an exclusionary mindset, restrained in the level of challenge it offered to the mainline churches. Ecumenism made considerable institutional advance in the early stages of the last phase of 'the Troubles', such as the Irish Inter-Church Meeting (IICM), the FPG, and the establishment of ecumenical communities, but failed to break out from their laager of ecumenically minded Christians and could not/did not engage with conservative evangelicals or move much beyond religious-cross-community forms of peace work. They remained locked in sacred—and in even narrower inter-church—spaces and did not form part of a general pro-peace coalition with secular groups.

Ecumenism did, however, universalize the discourse of peace and reconciliation. The most significant religious transition that presaged the peace process was the conversion of mainstream evangelicalism to the language of peace; it is shifts within evangelicalism rather than ecumenism that mark the major religious contribution to the peace process. This was achieved, mostly, by ECONI, which has played the single most significant role above that of Methodism, progressive Presbyterianism, and the Redemptorists in Clonard, significant as these were, since ECONI was the conduit by which the peace vision of ecumenical groups such as the Corrymeela Community and ISE, for example, and the activism of some within the mainline churches, came to influence evangelicals to embrace peace.

Our second conclusion points to the failure of civil society. Despite the valorization of civil society in democratic transitions, pushed by US philanthropic foundations, research centres, and Peace Studies researchers, and notwithstanding all the positive peacemaking undertaken by the churches, we should not exaggerate the role of civil society. It can be regressive as well as progressive; it is a contested landscape in divided societies and can reproduce the main lines of social cleavage. It can seem an alien idea associated with colonial memories, such as its reduction by some Republican intellectuals to imported British notions of multiculturalism. The churches rarely transcended the sectarian divide in Northern Ireland and ended up reproducing sectarian identities. Civil society, therefore, is not necessarily an antidote to war, or a necessary bulwark against conflict; it has a 'darker side' that can either resist peace or define it in negative ways, being passive rather than active in its commitments. Civil society groups that are parochial and place themselves outside global civil society cannot benefit from global processes, because they either lack the international networks necessary to make global connections with others or only link themselves with groups that are marginal to the progressive forces in global civil society. Religious peacemaking is more effective when made part of a national and international coalition of progressive peace groups. Self-referential and inward-looking churches, disengaged from the rest of civil society, fail to exploit the advantages of their position in the civil sphere.

Third, we point to the failure of spiritual capital in Northern Ireland. Spiritual capital in societies where religion is problematic requires two qualities: churches need to be active in the public sphere disseminating spiritual capital as if in a form of moral economy; and the capital needs to garner societal trust, hope, reconciliation, togetherness, healing, and the like. These virtues should circulate within the moral economy to build bridging social capital. During 'the Troubles', however, the Northern Irish churches were weak at bridging social capital and very strong in bonding social capital; and in the post-conflict phase they have largely evacuated the public square, ignoring their expertise in the social peace process by treating as pastoral concerns within their congregations all those questions important to societal healing that they should be translating into public issues. The churches in Northern Ireland feel uncomfortable in the public sphere in the post-conflict period, being stuck in a model of pastoral care to their own flock, and strengthening exclusive bonds within traditions at the expense of bridging community divisions. This suite of problems arises because churches either fail to admit they were part of the problem (feeling they have no special responsibility for the future), or they are not sure how to be part of the ongoing solution (and thus turn inwards).

CONCLUSION

'Meaning what you say and saying what you mean' can appear to be a poor start to 'a happy read'. However, we have set out the subject matter of our book as unambiguously as we can, in order to eliminate potential confusion deriving from the enigmatic meaning of our terms. We have alluded to a series of conceptual advances, which we explore in the following chapters, in order to bring sense to the varying types of engagement and disengagement that church people had with the peace process. We have documented what we see as the weaknesses in the current literature on the Northern Irish peace process and civil society's part in it, deriving from the near total neglect of religion, which explains why our attention to the churches is pioneering. In filling the gaps in our knowledge of conflict resolution in Northern Ireland, however, we have also highlighted the broader literatures for which the Northern Irish case is relevant, setting up subsequent chapters as an opportunity to reflect upon the contemporary enthusiasm for notions such as civil society and spiritual capital. In broad strokes, we have pointed to the churches' strengths and weaknesses and their progressive and regressive elements, and it is to the detailed analysis of all these matters that we now turn.

1

Contributions to the Social Peace Process

INTRODUCTION

Two stereotypes of Christian peace activists dominate the public imagination in Northern Ireland and, like all 'social imaginaries' that act as cultural tropes in late modernity (on which see Taylor, 2004), their public reproduction—through culture, in the media, and in lay people's speech—gives them a more solid grounding than they actually deserve. The first is of the soft-spoken bishop, Anglican or Catholic, hand-wringing in impotent despair at yet another senseless act of violence, speaking from the pulpit or graveside of one atrocity after another, their previous heartfelt words ignored, once again. The second is the firebrand fundamentalist Reformed pastor, vilifying violence from only one side and accusing Rome of being behind everything that is 'wrong' with Northern Ireland (and elsewhere), spitting hellfire and damnation in every cursed mention of Vatican-sponsored 'terrorism'. In a society where a disproportionately high number of people claim personal Christian faith, there are many and varied types of Christian peace activism but these caricatures represent popular perceptions of Christian peacemaking that must be challenged.

In this chapter we begin to outline the first stages of the conceptual framework by which we analyse the Christian churches' contribution to Northern Ireland's peace process between 1968 and 2011. This involves elaborating on three sets of conceptual distinctions: between active and passive peacemaking, negative and positive peace, and the political versus social peace process. Once passive peacemaking is eliminated from serious consideration, because it is vacuous, we are left with the social scientist's proverbial fourfold box to describe types of active peacemaking, as in Figure 1.

In order to fill in the cells and represent the various kinds of active peacemaking, we develop a typology to comprehensively describe the churches' activities, which we illustrate with copious examples. The typology is weighted towards activities that we conceptualize under the rubric of social peace process; this is as it should be, since this is where the expertise of the

	Positive	Negative
Social		
Political		

Figure 1. Forms of active peacemaking

churches ought to lie. However, the elision of religion and politics that characterizes Northern Ireland's conflict means that the churches deliberately sought and appropriated a political role. In return, they were courted assiduously by one or other set of protagonists and encouraged to get politically involved in order to afford moral legitimacy to various constitutional positions. In this chapter, the attention is on that part of the typology that covers the social peace process, leaving consideration of the political peace process to Chapter 2. The typology, along with the examples used to illustrate it, represent some of the positive achievements of the churches in the peace process, strengths which demand acknowledgement.

CONCEPTUALIZING PEACEMAKING

Northern Ireland's conflict was deeply paradoxical. One enigma in particular concerns us here. Despite the tragic loss of nearly 4,000 lives and direct injuries to upwards of 40,000 people (Fey *et al.*, 1999) over three decades, exceeding in proportional terms the number of Americans killed and injured in the Vietnam War and representing the equivalent of 100,000 deaths in the United Kingdom, the violence was never intense. Grass roots and civil society groups were not decimated under the body count; rather, they flourished. However, thirty years elapsed before a credible political settlement was negotiated and a further ten before it was finally implemented. This suggests that peacemaking was neither a priority nor seriously undertaken. This is the wrong impression to draw. However, identifying the strength of religious peacemaking in Northern Ireland, as we intend here, discloses another irony. Because the conflict had a religious appearance and the groups contesting it were defined in part by religious boundaries, the churches perforce *had* to become one of the principal arenas for peacemaking. They had no option but to engage with peace, making religion both a site of conflict and reconciliation, at the same time part of the problem and the solution. It is *how* the churches engaged that differentiates them. This is both an analytical and empirical question. The empirical dimensions of this question are mapped through our typology of kinds of religious peacemaking, to which we will come shortly, but a prior set of analytic issues first needs to be charted.

We begin by making a distinction between what we term active and passive peacemaking. This conceptual contrast was first mooted in earlier work (Brewer, Bishop, and Higgins, 2001; Brewer, 2003a) but bears repetition because it is the cornerstone of our new intellectual apparatus, allowing us to distinguish a form of peacemaking that does not deserve its name. Passive peacemaking involves commitment to or affirmation of peace as an ideal without actively practising it. Peace is, after all, socially desirable to the point that it equals apple pie as a virtue unchallenged. For churches especially, the backcloth of Jesus' peace vocation ensures that no Christian denomination can hold steadfast for violence; they just wriggle with Scripture uncomfortably. One way to manage the tensions between a pragmatic position taken on violence and the teachings of Jesus on peace is to adopt passive peacemaking. This involves ritualized expressions of the social desirability of peace, trenchant denunciations of violence and atrocity, sometimes against all sides, occasionally one-sidedly, and criticism of perpetrators, again, sometimes partisan. It forms a reliance on the power of 'the statement', on 'the word', and the 'good news' explicit in Christian teaching, as if oratory is all-important. Preachers might be excused belief in the efficacy of oratory but the witness of the scriptures gives rise also to a social gospel, with Jesus' promise expected to be fulfilled in 'good works'. Set against the demands of *living* Jesus' word in social practice, passive peacemaking ends up merely as speechifying. From bitter personal experience, Dr Cecelia Clegg expressed this well: 'one of the things that frustrated me most was that we never seemed to be able to get people to agree a programme of activity, of actual actions. We had prayer meetings, we had conversations, we would have discussions; we might have seminars and conferences. But the bit that was always missing was getting to the action bit at the end of it' (interview 29 November 2007).

Active peacemaking, by contrast, lives out the commitment to peace as a social practice. This reference to social practice is not meant loosely. The notion of social practice is a meeting point for philosophy and the social sciences and has a technical meaning. Tuomela (2002) describes social practices as the specific mental states of agents that are orientated towards collective attitudes and social interests ('we' attitudes), and as such are the building blocks of intersubjectivity and eventually of habit, custom, and tradition in society. In sociology, the term social practice is treated almost as an equivalent to social action, describing forms of relations, activities, and discursive strategies that are normative. Normative is meant in both its sociological senses: something that is based on norms (that is, grounded in actual values, beliefs, and behaviours) and is also socially desirable (that is, it has virtue attached to it as an ideal). Sociologically, therefore, social practices constitute the norms, values, habits, and behaviours that describe the regular patterns of social life (the way of living together and talking to one another as practised in society) and the aspirational ideals on which social life ought to be lived (the virtuous way to practise living together and talking to one another in society). Social practices are not rendered in sociology as forms of mental state where 'we' attitudes dominate but as forms of social relationships that reproduce society, either as it is mundanely practised (made into the norm) or idealized into something better (made normative). Active peacemaking, therefore, involves commitment to behaviours, values, beliefs, and discursive formations that put peace into practice, in which peacemaking is a habit, custom, and tradition, as well as an ideal, in which peace affects the kinds of social relationships practitioners have and the social actions they perform in order to make a peaceful society in the future normative. This will include speechifying. Primarily, however, it means trying to implement peace by action.

Understood in this way, active peacemaking is still a very broad process. With respect to active peacemaking by the churches, it conceals as much as it reveals. One way to unpack different forms of active peacemaking is through the famous distinction between positive and negative peace. This conceptual contrast was first introduced by Johan Galtung, the founder of the discipline of Peace Studies in the 1950s, and it has since become hegemonic (for one of Galtung's clearest statements see 1996). Kemp (1985), in an international survey of leading researchers in Peace Studies, noted the supremacy of this distinction (which resides in part in the intellectual respect Galtung commands). It has remained in wide currency as definitive of the conceptual field in Peace Studies.[1] Negative peace involves the cessation of violence. It best describes conflict resolution rather than peacemaking. Working to stop the killings by negotiating a ceasefire or to intercede between warring factions to resolve an instance of violent conflict is active peacemaking in its negative sense. Positive peace, conversely, is what is done *after* the violence has been resolved and the ceasefire won. It refers to the (re)introduction of justice, fairness and equality, the repair in social relationships, and the return to wholeness in place of brokenness. Positive peace is built on negative peace— these things first require the killings to stop—but goes well beyond it in what it seeks to achieve. It is about realizing a different kind of society once the conflict has come to an end.

'Negative' may seem an unfortunate adjective for examples such as this, where something plainly undesirable—violence—is prevented from happening again (or until the next time), since the word carries pejorative connotations. As a noun, it is associated with refusal and denial, while as an adjective it usually means unenthusiastic or harmful. In its technical sense, however,

---

[1] For example, Clark (2009) has recently wondered whether international war crimes tribunals are useful practices for assisting the transition from negative to positive peace in Bosnia and Herzegovina.

negative peace refers to an absence; and even though it might be preferable that it is absent—the elimination of violence—it describes a situation where nothing has replaced it. 'Negative' is used almost to mean 'void' and 'emptiness'; what fills the space is positive peace. This helps us understand Martin Luther King's deployment of similar terminology in his famous letter from Birmingham Jail, dated 16 April 1963, when, in a remarkable piece of anticipation, he referred to 'obnoxious negative peace' and 'substantive positive peace' (www.hartford-hwp.com/archives/45a/060.html). Denis Donaldson, a former IRA member and not yet exposed as a British informant, summarized the distinction very well, clearly wishing to retain his 'cover' in the interview:

> [name deleted]'s motivation in all this, this is what I firmly believe, was nothing more complicated than to get the war stopped, which is fair enough, that's totally honourable and justified from his point of view. But that doesn't remove the causes, 'cos the IRA weren't the cause of the violence, the IRA were a product of it. It sort of sounds like clichés now but the IRA came out of certain political and social conditions, the causes of violence, the injustice at the heart of it. The only way you can deal with violence is to deal with the causes of the injustices, the discriminations, the inequality, the nature of the state itself. (Interview, 14 November 2005)

A simple way to represent the differences between negative and positive peace is that the former is oriented towards *conflict* transformation, the latter *social* transformation. People often differ on what is preferred to fill in the void left by negative peace. By definition, peace accords are second-best compromises in which people give up their first preferences for a common agreement (Brewer, 2010: 27). But the peace settlement may not stipulate the content that is to be given to positive peace or may leave it open for subsequent negotiation (much like the 1998 GFA which was constructed as ambiguous). In these circumstances, notions such as equity, justice, and fairness remain contested (although differences between the factions are now pursued in non-violent ways). What constitutes positive peace, therefore, can remain a source of disagreement despite the preference for social transformation in one form or another. It is obvious that conflicts involving marked distributive injustice and political exclusion—and which are terminated without a clear winner owning the moral high ground—will leave significant problems for peace settlements that have to implement degrees of social redistribution. The level of agreement symbolized by the signing of the peace accord is unlikely to extend to consensus amongst people over what is good and bad for themselves and society as a whole. This lack of consensus increases the threat of renewed violence.

Two consequences follow for how we should conceptualize peacemaking. First, what peacemakers do *after* the signing of the peace accord to develop consensus over the necessary positive peace reforms continues to be important as a form of peacework against which they can be measured. Second, peacemaking is not solely about garnering political agreement. Human rights legislation, political and institutional reform, and fairer forms of voting systems and political representation are celebrated achievements in creating positive peace but they leave untouched the messy problem of societal healing, reconciliation, and restoration. For this reason, we need another conceptual distinction, namely between social and political peace processes.

This distinction only entered the lexicon of peace research with Brewer's explication of a sociological approach to peace processes (Brewer, 2010). The political peace process describes political developments that succeed in the negotiation of a peace settlement and which introduce the regulatory procedures within the new political environment that monitor conformity to its terms afterwards. It persuades a political explanation of the transformation, with emphasis placed on factors such as political change within the electorate, internal shifts from formerly fixed political positions, the role of international intervention and third-party brokering by external political actors, and political developments inside the parties leading to movement change. Peacemaking here assists in bringing parties and factions to the negotiating table and keeping them there. As a corollary it also includes dialogue in the midst of the violence with groups considered beyond the pale, when political talks cannot be seen to be taking place and thus deployment of secret backchannels of communication. It involves assisting combatant groups to make the transition from a military to a political strategy, mobilizing connections with constituencies important in making this decision, such as with the military leaders whose hands are stained with blood, prisoners with lengthy terms for perpetrating past atrocities, and political leaders noteworthy for their public intransigence. Peacemaking in the political peace process may also involve taking part in the negotiations themselves as a representative at the table or participating in the subsequent debate about the new constitution.

The political peace process not only delivers a negotiated peace agreement it assists in subsequent 'statebuilding' as a mechanism to consolidate the accord. The attention to 'statebuilding' rather than 'peacemaking' in some recent literature (for example, Chesterman, 2004; Chesterman, Ignatieff, and Thakur, 2005; Call, 2008a)[2] arises because peace evidently depends in part on strong state structures; weak states lack the authority, resources, and intent to resist

---

[2] Statebuilding is different from peacebuilding. Galtung (1976: 297–8) sees the latter as building sustainable peace by examining the root causes of the violent conflict, and peacemaking to be mediation and conflict resolution. Statebuilding is about bolstering the structure of the new state as a bulwark against renewed violence. It is one strategy for what Galtung would refer to as peacebuilding.

the travails in peace processes and to face down detractors. Weak states cannot eliminate what Braithwaite and colleagues call 'revenge conflict' (2010: 9), motivated by grievances over earlier phases of the fighting. Statebuilding after the signing of an agreement, however, is invariably portrayed as a political process, in which building institutional capacity to improve the organizational arrangement of state structures is valorized as the way to build peace, an approach best represented by Call (2008a). While Call (2008b: 366 *passim*) makes the valuable observation that statebuilding does not necessarily guarantee peace, statebuilding is perceived as a 'deeply political process', and the core activities by which peace is realized through statebuilding are themselves political, save for the acknowledged contribution of justice and balanced public finances. And as Call (2008b: 374–9) portrays it, the guarantee of peace after statebuilding is dishonoured solely because the state is imperfect politically—it has gained too many powers too quickly, or with powers undermined by international peacebuilding agencies, there are insufficient power balances and checks, too narrow a political base and too much short-termism. The connection between statebuilding and peacebuilding may not be easy, as Call is right to point out, but peacemaking is still rendered by him as a political process.

Political peace processes, however, either neglect the matter of societal healing or assume it follows naturally once problematic politics are resolved and the violence stops. There are two grounds on which to dismiss this as naïve. The first has to do with negative peace. The violence never stops completely, or reduces in scale only gradually (Darby, 2001), leaving the constant threat in the medium turn of renewed outbreaks of violence, ensuring that the political peace process has to deliver the negotiations while violence or its threat is ever-present. Indeed, ongoing violence can be a tactic to add leverage in the negotiations.[3] Societal healing needs negative peace; it is impossible to heal injuries that are yet to occur, through violence yet to happen. The second has to do with positive peace. Constitution building, institutional reform, democratization, human rights law, and new forms of voting systems are procedures on the way towards equality, justice, and fairness, but genuine social transformation is premised also on societal healing, reconciliation, and restoration of broken relationships. Something more than a political peace process is needed to realize these ends. The social peace process has these goals as its purpose.

---

[3] There were more politically motivated deaths during South Africa's constitutional talks than in the whole apartheid period, most of it called Black-on-Black violence as opposition parties and factions vied for influence in the negotiations (see du Toit, 2001), particularly between Inkatha and the African National Congress (ANC). For comparisons between the nature and levels of violence in Northern Ireland and South Africa see Brewer (2003c: 79–86).

The social peace process describes forms of peacemaking designed to bridge the social cleavages around which violence coheres—in order to restore broken relationships, effect reconciliation, and achieve something akin to forgiveness and compromise. This involves building relationships that cross the community divides, establishing citizenship education programmes that, amongst other things, help to deconstruct violent masculinities in ex-combatants and assist with gender mainstreaming, introduce restorative justice policies, assist with new forms of memory work, as well as implement truth-telling and truth recovery projects, and manage the problems of victims (for a fuller depiction see Brewer, 2010). It pays attention to emotions, identity, well-being and other nebulous touchy-feely matters normally outside the realm of 'rational' politics.

In his account of social transformation after political violence, Hamber (2009), one of the foremost analysts of Northern Ireland's peace process, sees the job as revolving around managing trauma and mental health problems in individuals but also instituting procedures and public policies at the societal level for reparations (symbolic and financial) and truth recovery, and attending to justice issues. The impressive body of work on transitional justice done by researchers in Northern Ireland—particularly at the University of Ulster's Transitional Justice Institute[4]—lends weight to this emphasis on truth recovery and justice as vital augmentations to the political approach to the peace process (for example, Lundy and McGovern, 2005, 2006, 2008; Simpson, 2009), although truth recovery has disabling weaknesses that are often overlooked by enthusiasts (see Brewer, 2010: 156–63) and the idea of 'non-truth' has also been shown to be important to reconciliation (Braithwaite *et al.*, 2010).

Hamber's account proffers a very limited set of goals for social transformation but his attempt, in work with Grainne Kelly, to flesh out the meaning of reconciliation gives a more fulsome vision of societal healing (see Hamber, 2009: 159–60). Reconciliation involves five strands: the development of a shared vision; acknowledgement and management of the past; building positive relationships; cultural and attitudinal change; and equity and equality. It is easy to quibble with this specification. It might be added to by including notions such as compromise and forgiveness—and some of the items are naïve, as if suggesting attitude change has first to occur before relationships can be restored, or that a shared vision is more important than people agreeing to disagree by developing a pluralist vision that incorporates diversity (which is the lesson of South Africa, see Brewer, 2010: 150, despite Hamber's close concentration on this case). It is also likely that local circumstances embedded in history and the nature and course of the conflict make reconciliation so contextual that its meaning cannot be generalized into whatever number of strands. But notwithstanding these caveats, something like Hamber and

---

[4] See www.transitionaljustice.ulster.ac.uk/publications

Kelly's five-strand model of reconciliation is implied by the social peace process. In this respect, it is clear that the social peace process is not exclusively the responsibility of the new state or regime, but also civil society groups with remits in these sorts of areas.

In his analysis of the intersection of the social and political peace processes, Brewer (2010: 203) noted that their relationship is recursive, each facilitating and enabling the other; one should not be prioritized at the other's expense. While the social peace process only fully blossoms in the post-agreement phase, after the political peace process opens up space for it to develop, the political agreement implants itself and becomes secure only if the social peace process is addressed simultaneously. Political deals without commensurate social healing often unravel. The social peace process can also facilitate the negotiations, opening up opportunities for the political peace process to flourish. Peacemaking in the social peace process can be a violence-reduction strategy as much as a mechanism for societal healing and thus a precursor of negative peace. It assists developments in the political peace process that open up dialogue with militarists, seeking to end the violence (either in the lead up to, during, or after the negotiated settlement), and it continues the brief of societal healing once the political peace process has delivered institutional reform.

These conceptual clarifications enable us to map the diverse forms of 'active peacemaking' as we defined it above. It can be differentiated into whether the active peacemaking is oriented towards negative or positive peace and is part of the social or political peace processes. This is diagrammatically presented in Figure 2.

	Positive	**Negative**
Social	Involves civil society and grass-roots groups working in areas of expertise to focus on social transformation and societal healing, whether in pre- and/or post-agreement phases.	Involves civil society and grass-roots groups working in areas of expertise to focus on conflict transformation by intervening as mediators in specific instances of violence and/or campaigning to end the violence generally.
Political	Involves political parties, negotiators and politicians incorporating social transformation and societal healing into the terms of the accord and/or using the new political structures to address social transformation and societal healing.	Involves political parties, negotiators and politicians negotiating ceasefires and campaigning for all factions to desist from killing.

Figure 2. Active peacemaking in practice

This gives visual form to some of the preceding arguments. Political peace processes rarely concern themselves with the bottom-left cell (positive/political), for peace agreements rarely address social transformation, or, at least, the success of the institutional reforms in embedding new political values and democratic practices is dependent on the extent to which the new state, in conjunction with civil society and grass-roots groups, also works in the top-left cell (positive/social). Similar sorts of cooperation are required to negotiate ceasefires, where active peacemaking in both of the right-hand cells involves civil society and political groups working to stop the killings, although rarely together or in coordination.

Finally, it is worth emphasizing that the cells are not hermetically sealed. As noted above, the relationship between the variables is recursive. Positive peace is only feasible once negative peace has been won; with the violence over, the real job of positive peacemaking can take top priority (although always being mindful to manage the threat of renewed violence). The social and political peace processes enable each other; the social peace process can be used as a conflict-reduction strategy (top-right-hand cell) preparing the space for political negotiations (bottom two cells), and a successfully negotiated peace accord gives civil society and grass-roots groups the opportunity to address the range of issues involved in social transformation and societal healing (top-left-hand cell), safe within a secure context established by the accord, where political freedoms, the rule of law, and human rights pertain. There should be constant movement, therefore, between the cells—up, down, and across—and collaboration between the new state, civil society, and the grass roots in making these transitions.

As informative as Figure 2 is for fleshing out the content of active peacemaking, there is a final building block to be inserted before the basic foundations of our conceptualization are laid. The broad sweeps by which we painted the cells need finer detail in order to complete the picture. To this end we have developed a typology of kinds of active peacemaking that fill in the cells. While we focus on the churches' activities, the typology is not unique to them and could apply to other progressive civil society groups. We first present the typology in schematic form, after which we illustrate it with examples from our data. Note that the final two activities in the typology refer to the political peace process and will be addressed in Chapter 2. The focus in the rest of this chapter is on the social peace process.

TYPOLOGY OF ACTIVE PEACEMAKING

Our typology begins conventionally enough at the starting place for all previous discussions of the peacemaking roles of the Northern Irish churches, namely ecumenism, but we see their contribution ranging much wider. In the following sections, we first sketch a few examples of the sorts of activities we see as representative under each heading, which we then go on to discuss in more detail.

a) Ecumenical activity (breaking down barriers, stereotypes, and developing contact in a religious context)

Church-to-church activities in the form of joint worship, shared Bible study, prayer, and clergy-to-clergy groups; major ecumenical organizations (Corrymeela, Cornerstone, etc.); ecumenical public events; joint declarations of doctrine, belief, and commitment; Irish bishops and Irish Council of Churches establishing the Irish Inter-Church Meeting; 'informal' or 'non-structured' ecumenism in the form of open invitations to preach in other pulpits, everyday ongoing interactions between people of different churches.

b) Mediation (conflict resolution and prevention)

Formal mediation organizations with Christian input (such as Mediation Northern Ireland); informal involvement in mediation by local Christians (such as Holy Cross); Christian dialogue with protagonists to the conflict, such as clergy meetings with paramilitary organizations; the development in some clergy of what might be called 'mediatorial behaviour', that is, adopting a posture of mediation that motivates specific formal mediations; transitional justice work with prisoners and ex-prisoners.

c) Cross-community activities (entry into secular spaces to try to break down barriers)

Large-scale Christian involvement in integrated education, integrated holiday schemes, home-building schemes, etc.; local Christian involvement in neighbourhood initiatives, such as issue-based mobilization on drugs, crime, women's issues, etc.

d) Peace initiatives (espousing peace and monitoring the conflict)

Church involvement with formal peace organizations and initiatives; clergy engagement with populist peace activity—peace train, rallies, peace marches, etc.; public interventions by church leaders and others, including sermons at funerals; peace advocacy by churches, such as Church of Ireland's (COI) Hard Gospel and the Presbyterian Church's Peace Vocation.

e) Anti-sectarianism (challenging the conflict and redefining it)

Engagement by churches and para-church organizations with the nature of sectarianism and its negative features, such as ISE's project on transcending sectarianism, IICM's project on non-sectarianism or ECONI's deprivatizing of religion by creating public spaces to meet to discuss sectarianism; church involvement with the trade union-led peace rallies against sectarianism.

f) Dealing with the problems of post-violence (assisting with post-conflict adjustment)

Work with victims and victim support groups; dealing with memory and narratives of atrocity; dealing with the issue of hope, forgiveness, and reconciliation; reintegration of protagonists, such as church-facilitated ex-prisoner and family support groups, job creation schemes; citizenship education workshops that try to inculcate the skills for living together in tolerance.

g) The churches as backchannels of communication (provision of 'safe' private political spaces)

Mobilizing secret meetings between British and Irish governments, local politicians, and leaders of the main paramilitary groups; the use of sacred spaces for informal, exploratory political talks; churchmen and women as 'go-betweens'.

h) Churches' participation in negotiations over the GFA and its iterations and contributions to selling the deals (the churches' public political role)

The politicians' exclusion of the churches from the negotiation process was to eliminate their discordant voices on wider justice and equality issues (this included minor political parties as well as religious figures), but there were attempts by parties to the agreement to try to get the churches to sell it afterwards; the churches and decommissioning; the churches and historical memory.

	Positive	Negative
Social	a), c), d), e), f)	b)
Political	h)	g)

Figure 3. Forms of active peacemaking by the churches

It is useful to plot this typology on to our fourfold chart in order to synchronize the elements of our conceptualization, as in Figure 3.

As this makes clear—and we have repeated many times thus far—the churches' expertise lies in the social peace process and this is where the bulk of their peacemaking has taken place. Figure 3 puts into particularly stark relief another point raised earlier that now warrants repetition before we validate the typology with examples. Religious peacemaking ought to circulate around the cells—up, down, and across—incorporating negative and positive peacework and moving between social and political peace processes. Locating the activities represented within the typology in one or other cell should not be taken to mean that this is their only domain; Figure 3 is a heuristic device for presenting the primary and initial purpose of the activity. In the real world, these activities blend into one another at the edges, having consequences (often unintended) for other forms of active peacemaking, so that an activity in one cell can often lead into other types of peacemaking in different areas.

ACTIVE PEACEMAKING IN PRACTICE

a) Ecumenical activity (breaking down barriers, stereotypes, and developing contact in a religious context)

As one of its chief architects in Northern Ireland, the late John Morrow crystallized the point of ecumenism when he said in one of the last interviews before his untimely death, 'until we have proper relationships we can't build peace' (7 December 2005). The Revd John Dunlop stressed in the interview, however, how difficult it can be to build right relationships: 'you move from isolation into empathy but never total identification. That is not just an intellectual journey that is an emotional journey at the same time' (23 March 2006). Ecumenism, in other words, cuts deep into people's emotional ties and presents them with a serious challenge, rewarding as it might be in helping with 'proper relationships'.

Most people begin with ecumenism when thinking of religious peacework in Northern Ireland and, as part of our typology, we need to supply some detailed background. Ecumenicalism describes the formal coming together of the denominations and world faiths, while ecumenism is at one and the same time something narrower and broader, describing the improvement in relations between members of denominations and world religions rather than institutional merger. Religious peacemaking as interfaith dialogue, in the mode of the USIP, represents ecumenicalism; Northern Ireland had ecumenism. The Catholic Church's resistance to ecumenism in the 1960s was initially overcome only by seeing it as ecumenicalism in disguise, a way of returning the separated Protestant brethren to the one true church, which, ironically, fitted the view of some extreme Protestant fundamentalist groups that likened ecumenism to three other dangerous 'isms'—Romanism, liberalism, and communism. As ecumenism became more widespread as a response to the violence, even the Irish Catholic hierarchy appropriated the label, reinforcing the suspicion of Protestant extremists. Power (2007: 19) discusses how Cahal Daly, later to become cardinal, worked with Eric Gallagher, a Methodist minister later to become its president, on the Working Party on Violence in the early 1970s that helped institutionalize Catholic support for ecumenism, although some priests still refuse forty years later to minister to Catholic pupils in integrated or mixed schools, demonstrating that ecumenism for them is about improving Catholic-Protestant relations in a specific political context, and for limited purposes, rather than an enduring theological preference.

At the time, however, the Catholic Church took risks in their support for ecumenism that, as William Crawley observed, people in the FPC thought they were incapable of (interview 23 September 2007). This initial resistance by the Catholic Church leads to problems over dating the origins of ecumenism in Northern Ireland, for in the sense of Catholic–Protestant relationship-building it begins only with the outbreak of violence in the late 1960s (Fitzduff, 2010: 10), but ecumenism within Protestant denominations goes back to the beginning of the twentieth century (on its history, see Power, 2007: 10–26).

The specialist and mainstream expressions of ecumenism need distinguishing, however. There was considerable institutional growth in specialist ecumenist bodies and organizations in the first years of 'the Troubles', as some churchmen and women saw in it the way to improve relations between Catholics and Protestants, such as the IICM, the FPG, and the establishment of various ecumenist communities, although the most well known of these, Corrymeela, began a few years prior to the outbreak of the violence. As John Morrow said in an interview 'Corrymeela Community was founded in 1965 before "the Troubles" even began because we could see that we were living in a cold war, which as we later saw became a hot war, and we were trying to build those relationships at a time where we thought there was a hope of a different way, before things broke down. Luckily we at least established enough trust to be able to carry on and at least make some contribution, but the situation had gone so far it wasn't going to be easy for anybody to bring an end to the conflict overnight' (7 December 2005).

Ecumenism also spread into the mainstream churches for the same reason, with small ecumenical groups springing up in some congregations pursuing local initiatives, such as the Fitzroy–Clonard group and its programme of dialogue between Presbyterians and Catholics premised on the personal relationship between the Revd Ken Newell and Fr Gerry Reynolds (see Wells, 2005). Its growth was naturally slower in mainstream settings because of the broader positions represented within diverse congregations. The Revd John Dunlop summed up the problems for clergy with diverse congregations: 'in Ireland you come into a very restricted kind of thing where things are cautious, very rigid, a lot of suspicion going on and into a society which is deeply divided, deeply suspicious' (interview 23 March 2006). One of the Clonard priests, Fr Adrian Egan, repeated similar fears from the perspective of the Catholic Church: 'Gerry Reynolds, Al Reid, would cross the peace line to go into the Shankill to visit the homes of Protestants killed by the IRA. Back then [this] was quite a step, a risk to take. Just the physical act of doing that, of making physical contact with people who were grieving because of the troubles was itself a witness and a breaking down of barriers, a reaching across' (interview 22 November 2007). One Protestant clergyman, who wishes to remain anonymous, described how 'Taig lover' was daubed on his church door because of his openness to ecumenism. Another brought out a postcard he had received years earlier but had kept, on which was drawn a coffin with his name on it, signed by a Loyalist organization.

The smaller Protestant churches within the evangelical and Reformed tradition oppose ecumenism on theological grounds, not seeing interdenominational contact as an opportunity to proselytize but rather feeling themselves under the Old Testament injunction to 'separate out and be different' from the heathen.[5] Some people from the evangelical wings of the mainstream Protestant churches feel this also, at least with respect to relations with Catholics: one well-known Presbyterian minister, active in the Orange Order and with

---

[5] Evangelicalism in Northern Ireland is represented as the dominant position in some Protestant denominations, such as Baptists, Brethren, and various independent churches, such as the Free Presbyterians, but also exists within sections of the mainstream Protestant churches, especially Presbyterianism. It comes in conservative and more liberal versions. Protestant congregations in the large mainline churches contain both liberal and conservative members. According to a survey of churchgoers in Belfast undertaken by Boal *et al.* (1997), liberal evangelicalism was the popular position amongst respondents, which highlights the difficulties ecumenism has in setting root in mainstream churches (for other studies of evangelicalism in Northern Ireland, see Jordan, 2001; Mitchell, 2003; Ganiel, 2008a).

Loyalist political groups, said in interview that he had no issue with ecumenism so long as it was restricted to Protestants (interview for the Maryknoll research, 13 July 2001). The Presbyterian Church in Ireland (PCI), for example, has a strong anti-ecumenist group known as the Movement for Presbyterian Reform (see Power, 2007: 63–8) and the PCI's liberal and conservative wings rotate the moderatorship every year. The Revd Mervyn Gibson, a Presbyterian member of the Loyalist Commission, announced himself in interviews as 'not an ecumenist', explaining that in his view many evangelicals initially opted out of engagement with the peace process precisely because 'there was an ecumenical tag attached to it' (27 January 2006). The uneasy relations between evangelicals and liberals cause problems when liberals are in office as moderator, constraining their expressions of ecumenism while their gestures to Catholics result in fierce complaint. The Revd Ken Newell, for example, was described by his opponents as causing them offence when, as Moderator Elect in 2004, ten years on from the signing of the DSD, he invited Archbishop Brady to the General Assembly; a group from Paisley's FPC protested outside the meeting. Only the very small Methodist Church in Ireland, with its long and proud history of engagement with global peace, was without doctrinal conflicts as a mainstream church in its commitment to ecumenism (see Vignette 1).

William Crawley, a perceptive analyst of current affairs in his role as broadcaster and journalist, observed that 'the Methodist church in Ireland has over the years been one of the most ecumenical minded churches in Northern Ireland and that facilitated openness to peace questions and openness to even the word reconciliation. The Presbyterian Church in Ireland has struggled tragically and drastically at times with the notion of ecumenism and that has closed off access to the concept of reconciliation' (interview 23 September 2007). From the Catholic position, Fr Egan from Clonard Monastery confessed in interview, 'you did not find many Protestant churches coming to visit us or too many of them inviting you' (22 November 2007). Ironically, therefore, the Catholic Church gave amongst the strongest commitment to ecumenism despite its poor start and the residue of ideas about Christian reunification that lay behind it. Several Catholic priests reported how their tentative contacts with Protestant clergy, at least until the 1994 ceasefires, had to be secret—for fear of the Loyalist paramilitaries as much as a hesitant, conservative, Protestant church hierarchy.

The opposition to ecumenism within large sections of Protestantism explains the proliferation of specialist ecumenical institutions and communities as a way of providing ecumenists with spaces where they could mix with like-minded people. Besides the noteworthy exception of Methodism, individuals from mainstream Protestant churches prominent as leading ecumenists, such as the Revd Ken Newell within Presbyterianism and Bishop Harold Miller and the Revd Charles Kenny within the COI, received a harder time and less

---

Vignette 1: *Methodism and the Peace Process*. Extracts from the Revd Harold Good's interview, 24 January 2006

[At first] a couple of ministers [were involved] and then we had another grouping of people within the council of social responsibility, and some of us from within the council of social responsibility felt that, I remember saying, 'look, we've got to move beyond sitting in our formal Church council, talking about the situation, analysing it and being academic about our Christian response', and writing very good papers. I would have to say, I think [these were] very good papers, we had some very good people, very able people who wrote very good papers on behalf of the Church, on which the Church then based its conference pronouncements on the situation in Northern Ireland. We had a little ginger group which was made up, not exclusively of Methodists, this was another ginger group, a thing called a consensus group, the consensus group, which was five or six people, they were people like Des Rea, Bob Stout, and a couple of others, lay people, David Hewitt was in there, too. Des Rea, the policing man, and they were meeting away, way back trying to, as lay people, to draw up a five-point way-forward document. Really, you could say it was the blueprint for the Good Friday Agreement. Take a look at it, take a look at it and this was adopted by our Church, our conference, away back. The Connolly House thing, that was happening, that gave me contacts within the Republican movement and then I introduced some of my Methodist friends and we had this little group within the council on social responsibility, which was totally free, didn't have to run back to the Church to say, can we go and meet with somebody or can we do this or can we do the other. It was a very clear understanding, look you're free to talk with whomsoever you wish, whenever you wish. If there's anything that you have to feed back that you think will be helpful to us in our understanding of where we are going or any of the statements we are going to make, that's all right, but you don't have to. That was very important because it gave us a freedom to go, when and to whom and whatever, we weren't accountable and there was a trust, a trust and that was very important, that trusting thing was. Whereas, most of the other churches have to work through very tight structures and have to report to each other and have to get permission.

---

institutional support than might be imagined from the speechifying of senior church leaders who proved to be very mindful of doctrinal differences over ecumenism within their traditions. Miller, of course, has authority in his own patch as a bishop and said in interview, 'I have a kind of policy that unless I know that somebody else is in the situation or involved in the situation I want to see these situations for myself, right, and I want to understand the situation for myself. I mean, the fact that there was no real relationship there [example deleted by request], really worried me, now there is' (25 January 2006). Kenny was critical of his church leadership: 'One of the things that I hold against [name deleted] is that he kept it all to himself, absolutely and completely' (interview 14 September 2005). He was also frustrated at the slow pace with which the COI moved: 'we did not have combined services straight away: we exchanged choirs. But all this took a couple of years. For at least ten years before this you did have the annual combined services for Christian Unity. That happened in January every year and that had been going from the early 1980s, but it was very much a one off, once a year type thing' (14 September 2005). The Catholic priest involved in this initiative admitted that from his view the 'partnership was more a flagship than an actual coming together of minds' (interview 15 March 2006).

One of the enduring features of religious peacemaking in Northern Ireland can be directly related to this resistance, for at a national level, ecumenism was forced to work its influence through the specialist ecumenical organizations, institutions, and communities, hence the symbolic significance and practical efficacy of Corrymeela, ISE, and the like, and the attention they have received in the literature. As Sean Farren, from the SDLP, said in interview when assessing the contribution of the churches, 'my experience would be of organizations outside the authority of the Protestant churches, such as Corrymeela [which] was doing an awful lot more than I ever became aware of. The official churches were tied in a way because they interpreted their immediate role as providing pastoral care to their own congregation' (27 May 2008). This is not strictly true as an assessment of mainstream churches, but the impression is valid enough because ecumenism in mainline Protestant churches had to be restricted in scale to small local initiatives, where common platforms and programmes could be more easily negotiated depending upon the demographic profile of the neighbourhood, personal motivation, and the history and nature of the conflict locally. Working-class Christians in areas at interface, such as at peace walls and at sites of contentious parades, were, not surprisingly, more actively involved in these local responses than middle-class suburban Christians, who tended to dominate the ecumenist communities. This is epitomized by the location of Corrymeela and the Rostrevor Centre in sleepy coastal regions, deliberately far away from the violence for purposes of calm reflection, although it is worth noting that the Cornerstone Community is based at an interface in West Belfast in a deliberate attempt to break down mental walls. But the paradox remains. The interface areas, where ecumenist activity might have been thought to be most needed, showed the greatest resistance to it, leaving flashpoint areas open to violent protest and intimidation of those involved in ecumenical programmes. The leafy suburbs offered ecumenists the greatest protection.

The opposition towards ecumenism from within mainstream Protestantism was widely perceived. Roy Garland, a Loyalist politician and community activist, said in interview when assessing Corrymeela, 'it was sidelined from the churches. If you ask me I think the churches were not all that keen on Corrymeela' (13 September 2005). This resistance to ecumenism, however, gave it another permanent stamp, forever bestowing on it a conservative mentality with a preference for relating to other ecumenists across the sectarian divide rather than dialoguing with opponents. As Bishop Harold Miller said: 'it [was] much easier to relate to Roman Catholics than to Free Presbyterians' (interview 25 January 2006). Given the opposition to ecumenism in some quarters of the COI, the BBC producer Bert Tosh quipped that it was easier for Harold to talk to Catholics than some Anglicans (interview 7 May 2010). This view is endorsed by Grant (2004: 270) and is alleged to be common among ecumenical clergy.

The strength of the diatribe against ecumenists, however, especially from very vociferous conservative evangelicals, made restricting dialogue to like-minded ecumenists a reasonable option. Conservative evangelicals were always more energetic in the public square, in defending their own position and attacking others, in large part because they were led by fiery political preachers, of which Paisley is the most well known, leaving ecumenists both ambivalent about their public presence and diffident when too far away from their comfortable silo of like-minded 'reasonable people'. Liberal evangelicals in ECONI offered more fruitful engagement for ecumenists, as we shall emphasize in later chapters, but ECONI, too, operated in spaces where it felt most comfortable, mostly behind the scenes, working by stealth rather than bombast, and appealing to the intellect not the passions. The rhetorical style of the firebrand conservative evangelical preachers in politics captivated the moment and the media,[6] and while ecumenism contained some of the leading religious intellectual figures of the generation, such as David Stevens, Cecelia Clegg, Geraldine Smyth and Johnston McMaster, as did ECONI with David Porter and Alwyn Thomson, they were cerebral not orators, and their intelligent, complex writing was not matched by a charisma on the stumping ground. Withdrawal from confrontation with conservative evangelicals did not necessarily mean retreat from the public sphere but a presence there that was less dramatic and 'public'. The large number of clergymen who were also Unionist Party MPs, MLAs, and councillors always came from the evangelical wing of Protestantism; no ecumenist went into formal politics. As Cecelia Clegg noted, 'there was the failure to act publicly and support the prophets, support the ones out there on the margins doing the difficult stuff that nobody else wanted to do or was afraid to do. Too many of the churches left them to hang in the window' (interview 29 November 2007). The key to ecumenical growth over the course of 'the Troubles', therefore, is the expansion in the numbers

---

[6] The evangelical preaching tradition in Ulster, with its characteristic flourishing and hectoring rhetorical style, easily blended in with the needs of Unionist political speeches, whipping up frenzy against a collection of apostates, pagans, Catholics, the Irish, and the duplicitous British, as the need demanded, as noted from the very beginning with respect to Paisley by Abbott (1973) and Scott (1976), such that Wallis, Bruce, and Taylor (1987) correctly noted the elision of ethnicity, evangelism, and electioneering. What this ignores, however, is the pragmatism Paisley displayed, which is not normally a feature of evangelicalism.

committed to ecumenism as a strategic response to violence rather than ecumenists breaking out from their constituency to convert evangelicals to inter-church dialogue.

The broad distinction between specialist and mainstream ecumenism helps us better understand the types of ecumenism that Appleby (2000: 181) distinguishes in Northern Ireland: churches and their leaders, reconciliation communities, and high-profile ecumenically motivated individuals, although Maria Power, another of Irish ecumenism's chief chroniclers, defines it as inter-church relationships manifested in national level dialogue between church leaders, local relationship-building, and peace and reconciliation education initiatives (2007: 4–5). National dialogue between the leaders of the four main churches (Catholic, PCI, Methodist, and COI) has been the most constant feature of ecumenism, she argues (although clearly in its most minimal meaning), but its more active forms are found in local relationship-building between Catholics and Protestants, whether by the specialist institutions or the local initiatives undertaken within mainstream churches. Among the examples of the former are the reconciliation workshops, interdenominational retreats, and education courses by ecumenical communities such as Corrymeela, Cornerstone, and ISE, and of the latter various clergy-led discussion groups, inter-clergy meetings, and neighbourhood church fora. This illustrates that the kinds of activities to be included as ecumenist are widely different in sort, ranging from small prayer fellowships and avowedly spiritual activities to social action programmes in inner cities (also see Brewer, Bishop and Higgins, 2001: 18–49; Power, 2007). However, relationship-building was always at its heart, giving participants a form of 'cat flap' into another person's world.

i) Church-to-church activity

This category relates to ecumenical groups that seek to promote Christian understanding through relationship-building between the Christian denominations in Northern Ireland. This dialogue is promoted through shared teaching, research, and outreach activities, and is marked by efforts towards reconciliation. Within this general category one can sub-divide this type into two categories: ecumenical communities; and inter-church groups that include both clergy and laypersons. Among the most obvious ecumenical communities involved in church-to-church dialogue in Northern Ireland were the Christian Renewal Centre (see Vignette 2), and the Corrymeela Community. Other notable ecumenical communities included the Columba Community, Columbanus Community of Reconciliation, Conerstone Community, Currach Community, and the Lamb of God Community. Central to the aims and objectives of these ecumenical communities were reconciliation and challenging religious ignorance, suspicion, and fear. Reconciliation was promoted through contemplative prayer and retreat as well as training courses. Prayer

---

Vignette 2: Christian Renewal Centre

The Revd Cecil Kerr and his wife Myrtle established the organization in Rostrevor in 1974. They left the COI chaplaincy at Queen's University Belfast to create a place where people could come together in the uniting love of Jesus Christ. It is an established ecumenical community of Christians across both traditions in Ireland. Members of the charity remained members of their own churches and sought to share with each other in faith and prayer the work of the centre. The Centre's aims and objectives were:

- Reconciliation: 'We encourage and facilitate the coming together of people, in an atmosphere of prayer and worship, allowing the Spirit to melt our hearts, lead us into repentance, and forgiveness of one another, enable us to accept one another in Christ, thus restoring fellowship.'

- Prayer: 'Recognising the transforming power of God through prayer, we, as a community, are committed to growing in our understanding and practice of prayer and intercession.'

- Renewal: 'Being committed to Jesus Christ as Saviour and Lord, who baptises us in the Holy Spirit and renews His Church, we work with Him to encourage personal renewal, renewal in the local Church and restoration of the gifts of the Holy Spirit, so that His Church may be an effective witness to His power and healing love for the world.'

- Community: 'Finding our primary identity in Christ, we are called as a community to be a sign and an instrument of reconciliation, to identify with and serve the whole body of Christ, as the Lord directs us. We are not called to become another self-sufficient entity breaking away from an already broken body.'

The Centre's activities included youth camps, school outreach, clergy fellowship, clergy inter-church work, prayer events, and Faith Alive weeks. Held each July, the Faith Alive weeks focused on praise, prayer, and biblical teaching with national and international guest speakers. The children's programme played an important part in the week. The total residential membership of the Centre varied between 10–16 with a number of international volunteers and supporters. In 2008 the Centre folded and the premises were handed over to Youth With a Mission. Cecil Kerr died in August 2010.

---

was an important activity for the ecumenical communities. However, social awareness and responsibility were not neglected; in some it was the primary focus. For example, Bishop Edward Daly, a prominent member of the Catholic hierarchy in Derry, worked with other church leaders and the mayor to establish the Waterside Churches Trust in 1987 (now the Churches Trust) as an inner-city youth project for the unemployed, designed as a social action project with 'a very powerful ecumenical witness'; 'it was a contribution for young people to see that *building* was the way, not destroy-ing' (interview 24 January 2006). There are many similar examples in our data of ecumenism garnered through social activism, with relationship-building working alongside practical action (these examples will be picked up again in Chapter 3).

The promotion of a pastoral support presence to local families, individuals, and community groups was encouraged, so ecumenical clergy put themselves alongside the hurting people in their own and other denominations. Fr Alec Reid, from Clonard Monastery in Catholic West Belfast, said in interview, 'we were in a situation where you couldn't but try to do something, you know, not much choice and we did what we could, which I hope did some good' (8 February 2011). On radio he told the following story from his personal experience:

> I knocked at this door and a middle-aged women opened and she kind of drew back when she saw the collar and all that and then I said I've come around about the recent trouble just to assure you that the people over there don't want to cause you any harm and she said come in and I sat down in the arm chair. I was feeling a wee bit uneasy and I looked around and on the stairs was a plaque which said 'God answers prayers' and then on the wall beside me was another big one which said 'The Lord is my Shepherd'. I said to myself well you know I feel at home here. Now her name was [deleted], she was a Presbyterian a very saintly woman she became very friendly with us here and I remember one night phoning her and saying now don't forget to pray for me and she said you know every night I pray for you and I blow two kisses over the peace line, a kiss of love and a kiss of peace. I could go around there eventually because I got to know them; I got to know the people along there.[7]

Putting themselves alongside hurting people was a strategy established by ecumenists at the very beginning. The Revd Harold Good recalled the first Loyalist attacks in Catholic Bombay Street at the start of the last phase of 'the Troubles': 'The next Sunday, after Bombay Street had been burned out, my car was laden with stuff that people brought for the children of West Belfast. As I stood at [my church] door and shook hands with the congregation that morning [of the attacks], the people were putting money into my hands and saying "you'll know somebody who could use that"' (interview 24 January 2006). Importance was placed on sharing common life-experiences, struggles, and needs. The Columba Community in Derry, for example, has a visitation programme for prisoners, ex-prisoners, and their families. Organizations such as the Cornerstone Community on Springfield Road in Belfast offer senior citizens' luncheon clubs, and support for women's groups, after-school clubs, and youth clubs. Another key activity for the ecumenical communities in

---

[7] Taken from the BBC Radio 4 programme 'The Clonard Priest', 29 November 2006.

Northern Ireland was offering hospitality and accommodation to specific individuals and groups away from their own communities. Open residential events were common for people from all traditions on social, cultural, political, and religious topics.

Inter-church groups, including both clergy and laypersons, were another kind of ecumenical peacemaking. They were locally organized and focused on formal community relations work, shared prayer, and fellowship, as well as Bible study. Their work was primarily focused in ways that allowed the churches to cooperate by addressing commonly shared social and community needs, reconciliation issues, and community life in the local area. The difference between ecumenical communities and inter-church groups is that inter-church groups are local grass-roots initiatives between individual churches and have a much lower public profile. Some groups, such as Churches in Cooperation from Derry, sought to provide joint denominational structures or forums in order to develop and implement community peace initiatives. Others focused on more informal community initiatives such as joint services and seminars. Good examples were Belmont and District Council of Churches, Community Relations and Christians, and Magherafelt Interdenominational Group. The main aims of these groups were to build relationships of confidence and trust and to create an 'open space' to respond to local community issues.

Some Protestant and Catholic churches developed a structured twinning relationship with other churches in the same neighbourhood or further afield. Groups where two churches had an ongoing partnership included the Clonard/Fitzroy Fellowship, St Comgall's Roman Catholic Church Derriaghy/ St Columba's Lisburn Church, and St Matthew's/St Oliver Plunkett Group. A member of the Clonard/Fitzroy Fellowship said of the initiative in an interview conducted as part of the Maryknoll research: 'we want to know about each other's denominations, we want to deal with each other to show that we are not all angry stereotypes. We want to show that we can live with our next door neighbour whoever they are. We want to make a difference' (cited in Brewer, Bishop, and Higgins, 2001: 21–2).

ii) Clergy-to-clergy groups

A large number of clergy groups existed in Northern Ireland involving Catholic and Protestant clergy coming together in acts of reconciliation and for practical benefit. Many were under severe constraint prior to the ceasefires and mostly conducted their activities in secret. For instance, Fr Toner said of his engagement with clergy in nearby Protestant Sandy Row, 'they didn't want it known because of the paramilitary elements in Sandy Row, they had to keep quiet, really secret in a sense. I would have been welcome in [his] church but he couldn't invite me. He would have been welcome here but it [would have] to be kept secret' (interview, 15 March 2006).[8] As Anglican Archdeacon Gregor McCamley said, there was a 'general fear of getting involved, of talking to the other side or moving away from the Protestant line. Two examples. David Armstrong, moved by his parishioners from Limavady just because he wished the parish priest a happy Christmas, and Earl Storey petrol bombed because he wrote a book on the Orange Order' (interview 14 September 2005).[9] For these reasons, the activities of these groups depended on the strength of the personal relationship between the clergy, and mostly included less public activities such as prayer and fellowship, as well as sharing resources on pastoral skills and congregational issues. For example, Castlederg Clergy Group stated its main aim was 'to promote mutual understanding, respect and tolerance; to help the community to live in peace and harmony'. Clergy groups also offered an opportunity for the different denominations to meet informally to directly engage in discussion and dialogue about social issues that affected their respective communities. The Ballynafeigh Clergy Group often attempted to mediate in the parades issue on Ormeau Road in Belfast. These groups are less formal than inter-church clergy and lay groups; meetings are hosted in each other's homes or church halls in order to facilitate privacy.

iii) Ecumenical organizations

There were a number of formal ecumenical organizations in Northern Ireland that had a peacemaking agenda of their own, as well as supporting the peacemaking activities of the churches, local clergy, and laygroups by providing resources for training, advice, information, and support in community relations and peacebuilding.

Two examples are ISE (see Vignette 3) and the Irish Commission for Justice and Peace, both established in 1970 by the Catholic Church in response to Vatican II, and strongly ecumenical in policy and practice. Perhaps one of the most well known is the IICM established in 1973. It had departments dealing with theological issues from an inter-church perspective, social issues, and faith and politics; and had an extensive peace-education programme. Also, the FPG was particularly active in challenging the nature of the conflict in the North. Through education programmes, lectures, and the sponsoring of research, these organizations addressed issues such as forgiveness, sectarianism, identity, and grass-roots peacebuilding. Their education programmes

---

[8] Sandy Row is a working-class Protestant area, where Loyalist paramilitaries and firebrand preachers thrive.

[9] See Storey (2002) for the book concerned. While it is widely believed that Storey's house was bombed, this is not in fact the case (email from Storey, dated 11 February 2011). And to prove Kaufmann's (2007) point about political splits within the Orange Order, some Orangemen visited the house when it was attacked to offer Storey condolence and support and were outraged.

Vignette 3: The Irish School of Ecumenics

Its founder, Michael Hurley, from the Society of Jesus, had a vision to bring people of all cultures and faiths together in dialogue and study within an ecumenical framework. ISE is a centre for teaching and research with a commitment to reconciliation and peace. Masters/Diploma courses in Peace Studies, Reconciliation Studies, and Ecumenical Studies are taught in association with Trinity College, Dublin. Adult education takes place in Belfast, Derry, Armagh, Newry, Enniskillen, and Dublin. ISE completed a major five-year research project based in Belfast called 'Moving Beyond Sectarianism'. This project was initiated to examine the causes, expressions, and consequences of sectarianism in Ireland, as well as to develop insights and models for moving beyond it. The focus was on the role of the Christian churches in both maintaining and challenging sectarianism. ISE is also involved in organizing public seminars and workshops on various ecumenical themes. ISE is based in Dublin and Belfast.

---

sought to empower local peacemakers to intervene effectively. For example, the Irish Commission for Justice and Peace stated that their emphasis on educational programmes was to 'encourage mutual understanding and dialogue; to break down prejudice, sectarianism and divisiveness and to help create a society of peace and justice'.

iv) Ecumenical public events

Ecumenical work was dominated by the work described above, occasionally, however, public events took ecumenical policies and practice on to the streets. Ecumenical marches focused around Christian worship and celebration, as well as conferences and events. The most notable example was the United Prayer Breakfast, which was both ecumenical denominationally and organized across the North and South of Ireland. Key leaders and opinion-formers were invited to regular breakfasts held across the island, at which they were enjoined to pray for peace and reconciliation. The organizing team was composed of churchmen and women from all denominations, as well as public figures with strong personal faith drawn from both sides of the border. The Revd Martin Smyth, a leading Unionist politician who is also a Presbyterian minister, was criticized publicly by some conservative evangelicals for participating in the event alongside Catholic priests; Free Presbyterians always protested outside the venue.

v) Joint declarations of doctrine, belief, and commitment

This form of ecumenical activity was not well developed in Northern Ireland. The sorts of joint declarations common in the United States, between, for example, Lutherans and Catholics or amongst evangelicals and Catholics, were a step too far for Christian peacemakers in Northern Ireland. There were two exceptions. The Evangelical Catholic Initiative, run by Paddy Monaghan, produced several pamphlets and books attempting to define common ground between Catholicism and evangelicalism, such as *What is an Evangelical Catholic?* Other tracts introduced Catholics to reading the Bible, as well as collated testimonies of evangelical Catholics. A similar theme lay behind the second initiative. A sixteen-page document entitled *Evangelicals and Catholics Together in Ireland* was prepared by a group of fourteen people and endorsed by 130 clergy and leaders from different traditions from the North and South of Ireland. It proposed an agreed basis of faith between evangelical Protestants and Catholicism as well as calls for Christians to explore their common faith and to build friendships in order to bear joint witness in a divided society. It was launched in 1998 by the internationally known evangelical theologian Jim Packer, and asked all Christians in Northern Ireland to subscribe to a new confession: 'We repent of attitudes, words and actions that have fostered hatred and divisions within and among our traditions... We humbly ask the forgiveness of God and one another, and pray for the grace to amend our own lives and to actively seek in every way possible to help change divisive attitudes.'

Some of these activities, to use Alastair Campbell's dismissive phrase (2007: 204), appear particularly 'holy' for a setting where holiness is tainted; and to the thoroughly anti-religious they seem slight, even pointless. Ecumenism is about building relationships in sacred settings, with the intention of them spreading outwards to others parts of the churches and secular spaces. These spiritual forms of relationship, though easy to parody, were very important, in that they represented new forms of ritual and symbolic behaviour designed to introduce 'social repair' and bring about enhanced social connectedness. Religion is the epitome of ritualized behaviour, and anthropologists and sociologists of religion tell us that rituals affirm shared views of the world; for someone like Roy Rappaport (1999) ritual is the heart of religion. In this respect, rituals and myths work together (for a discussion of their relationship see Segal, 1998, 2005). The most common view, going back to James Frazer's *The Golden Bough* (1922), is that myths speak what rituals enact. Rituals instil behaviour—and myths communicatively spread what is instilled. Changes to familiar religious myths and rituals can be problematic for believers. Vatican II, by eliminating Latin prayers, offended traditional Catholics, and in Judaism the status of *kashrut* is divisive. Indeed, Reform Judaism broke with Orthodoxy by introducing the vernacular in services and by allowing musical instruments in the service.

But rituals can effect, not merely reflect, beliefs. The hard part is getting people to accept new or even revised rituals, but this resistance likewise attests to the power of change. Rituals tied to changed performances and new beliefs can help people confront taken-for-granted world views and thereafter assist in transforming them. As part of the commitment to improving Catholic-Protestant relations in sacred spaces, various symbolic rituals were developed within ecumenism, such as shared liturgy for forms of joint worship, shared Bible study, common prayer meetings, and, in the absence of the possibility of shared communion, other rituals of reconciliation such as foot-washing ceremonies and sharing the carrying of the cross at Good Friday worship. (Ecumenical sorties often coincided with key Christian festivals, such as Easter and Christmas, as well as key local dates, such as Christian Unity Week and ECONI Sunday.) The occasional Presbyterian service conducted in Irish (such as in Fitzroy Church in South Belfast, where at one time they were held monthly) represented a symbolic ritual of equal import, as did clergy and priests sharing pulpits. The peacebuilding workshops, educational courses, and initiatives conducted by ecumenists almost always supplemented the discussions, conference statements, and declarations with symbolic rituals of this sort in order to cement the reconciliation through performed behaviours not just words (see Landau, 2003: 47 for similar rituals used to try to consolidate Arab-Jewish peace initiatives). Church-led peace walks or prayer breakfasts in large hotels and conference centres (which for a time became very popular on both sides of the Irish border) took these symbolic rituals of reconciliation into secular spaces. Such rituals symbolically instilled participants' sense of the social transformation within themselves and in their social relationships with others, irrespective of whether this is understood as representing new forms of social connectedness, in Putnam's terms (2000), or the emergence of civil sphere social solidarity, using Alexander's words (2006). The problem, however, is that participation in news forms of ritualized behaviour impacted primarily on those ecumenists performing them and did not expand too far outwards into a generalized repair. Ecumenism, on the other hand, was not the sole type of religious peacemaking.

b) Mediation (conflict resolution and prevention)

The second category of religious peacemaking in our typology is mediation. This involves intervention to resolve specific instances of violence (such as de-escalating tensions over particular Orange marches, intervening in the Holy Cross affair and the hunger strike, for example, and moderating the internecine killings within the paramilitaries). It also involves dialogue with the perpetrators and combatants as a form of conflict prevention (building up a rapport and establishing contact to be able to encourage a non-violent form of politics). While the latter used backchannels, with meetings at 'special sacred spaces', such as at church premises or the homes of church people, this is different from the typology of political peace-process activities that will be discussed in Chapter 2, activities in which backchannels were used to promote political engagement (such as between the paramilitaries themselves, between the paramilitaries and certain politicians or perpetrators and governments, and so on). In the mediation sense discussed here, the backchannels were exploited for meetings between church people and paramilitaries to desist from violence; in the broader political sense, as used in the next chapter, backchannels were used by the churches to bring together politicians and the paramilitaries. This is a clear—if fine—distinction; clearly the long-term intention of mediation was political, what distinguishes it is that the churches were not conduits to bring paramilitaries and politicians together in political talks but were themselves the purpose of the mediation so as to be enlightened about the paramilitaries, establishing rapport with them over time so that they could eventually urge upon them the need to desist from violence.

The mediation undertaken by the churches involved two processes. The first was assisting individuals or communities to develop their own resources for handling conflicts; the second was direct conflict resolution, either by intervening to stop incidents of violence or relationship-building with combatants and perpetrators for purposes of long-term conflict prevention. Mediation in both senses was particularly feasible in Northern Ireland. There were occasional flashes of high-intensity violence in 'the Troubles', which required direct intervention, but normally the low-key character of the conflict provided some space for local people to be taught mediation skills. We distinguish three sorts of mediatory peacemaking: that done by formal and professional mediation organizations; informal mediation done at a local level by local parties; and dialogue with the paramilitaries and protagonists. Christians by no means did all the conflict resolution in Northern Ireland, but there was a pronounced Christian input into all three kinds of mediation.

i) Formal mediation organizations

The main peacemaking activities common to this type were mediation in specific instances of conflict, counselling amongst protagonists, the facilitation of discussions and local consultations, and training local community figures in conflict transformation. Ecumenical communities such as Corrymeela, Cornerstone, and ISE did this kind of work. For example, Columba House of Prayer and Reconciliation based in Derry was formed by Fr Neal Carlin in 1980 as a response to the need for reconciliation and counselling, 'not just about healing the world of divisions within the body of Christ, but about the integration and wholeness of individuals as well'. There were, however, few formal professional organizations in Northern Ireland for which mediation was the sole purpose. The most well-known was Mediation Northern Ireland (see Vignette 4), originally formed as the Northern Ireland Conflict and

---

Vignette 4: Mediation Northern Ireland

The group was formed in 1986 by a number of individuals wishing to develop alternative, non-violent approaches to conflict and disputes. In Mediation Northern Ireland's own words, it 'seeks to make a contribution to Community Relations in Northern Ireland by promoting the use of third party intervention in situations of conflict... We believe that mediation is a useful way to manage enmity, assist communication, improve understanding and support creative thinking in situations of conflict. Mediation is also a method of building long term peace by assisting in the growth of mutual respect and right relationships in our society.' At one time the Presbyterian minister Doug Baker was the development officer responsible for 'The Churches Programme', which sought to work with and alongside local churches in building better community relations. Its director at one time, Brendan McAllister, went on to be one of four Victims Commissioners set up by the devolved administration.

Mediation Association in 1986 and then Mediation Network, to promote alternative non-violent approaches to community conflict and disputes (for further details see Power, 2007: 187–92). As the organization's vision statement stated: 'The Mediation Network for Northern Ireland promotes the use of third party interventions in disputes, and supports creative responses to conflict in the community.' Its principal objectives are the provision of training and support services to enhance the skills of mediators, but the organization offers its own mediation services in instances of conflict. Mediation Northern Ireland was involved, for example, in a number of high-profile disputes, notably the controversy surrounding Orange parades. Mediation Northern Ireland also works with individual parishes and congregations, as well as with local inter-church groups and denominational committees, in an attempt to empower local Christians in conflict resolution. It assisted in bringing international conflict mediators to Northern Ireland, including the well-known Mennonite peace campaigner John-Paul Lederach. The majority of the organization's staff are volunteers, some are Christian, although the organization is not formally Christian. As significant as Mediation Northern Ireland was, however, it must be admitted that the churches' most valuable contribution to mediation was done informally.

ii) Informal involvement

A high number of non-specialist clergy groups and individuals were involved in mediation at an informal level as emergency-style intervention in disputes in the local neighbourhood. Because of the sensitive nature of the mediation process and the need to maintain confidence between parties, it is sometimes difficult to identify those involved in any given dispute. As the Revd John

Dunlop said in interview, 'what am I going to do about this, I can either talk about this man at a distance or engage in some kind of discussion, so I discovered there were discussions which were private in Clonard and behind closed doors and the condition of getting involved is that you were not to talk about it' (23 March 2006). Local clergy did not function separate from community residents and leaders, community development workers, politicians, and the police, and behind the scenes there was better cooperation across a wide front than there was in public. The secrecy was not only used to protect the negotiations, it guarded the negotiators. Prior to the ceasefires, one Presbyterian minister involved in mediation commented that he always felt threatened by Loyalist paramilitaries and feared the burning of his church. Local Catholics were not the source of threat, said another Protestant minister, but the Loyalist paramilitaries who objected to his contacts with Catholic clergy.

In a strange way, however, the public-private dichotomy collapsed for some clergy whose public profile gave its own protection to their work behind the scenes, blurring the distinction between public and private witness. One response to fear was for senior church figures to do the mediation—in the view that they were too famous in the public sphere to be touched by the paramilitaries. For example, Archbishop Robin Eames, Anglican Primate during much of this period, along with Presbyterian minister Roy Magee, was able to broker the Loyalist paramilitary ceasefire in 1994 because they were untouchable. As Eames said in interview after he had retired as primate, 'we were having cross-community discussions through some of the darkest days of the 1970s and 1980s. I think that even if it allowed "x" to feel they knew "y" a bit more, that was worth doing' (29 January 2008). Reflecting on Eames's role, Roy Garland's insider knowledge of Loyalism allowed him to say that Eames was important because 'he stood up and gave legitimacy'. But he went on to comment, 'Alec Reid was in there trying to bring about a better society. Eames never came across in the way that Reid came across, getting his hands dirty. Eames was seen as somewhat aloof' (interview 13 September 2005). This view is perhaps influenced by Eames's tendency to mix with the high players (see Vignette 5).

But social class considerations also seem important, at least when looking back. Of the Protestant working class, Garland said years later, 'some of them would have more in common with Reid than Eames' (interview 13 September 2005). Reid reciprocated Loyalists' trust and friendship: 'I had many contacts with Loyalist politicians, and would have been friendly with them. They were helpful because they saw [we] were trying to do something to get the IRA to stop. They then became very friendly, supportive. I got on very, very well with Gusty Spence—we were personal friends' (interview 8 February 2011). This confirms that Gerry Reynolds and Alec Reid, the Clonard Redemptorists, had much the same iconic 'public' status that afforded them protection in their 'private' peace work.

Vignette 5: *Eames/Magee and the Loyalist Ceasefire.* **Extract of an interview with Brian Rowan, former security correspondent of BBC Northern Ireland, 4 April 2006**

I mean just to go back to Eames and Roy Magee, for example. You had in 1993 the Loyalists producing their six principles, they make their way into the Downing Street Declaration on the basis of contacts going on between Eames and Albert Reynolds. Then in March 1994 [you] have a meeting between Robin Eames facilitated by Roy Magee and there are two representatives of the Combined Loyalist Military Command there and they at that stage present their terms for a ceasefire which they want Eames to take to the two governments. You then have that ceasefire being pushed away because of the killings that are going on. It then gets to the point of writing the Combined Loyalist Military Command ceasefire statement and Eames is behind the line of [them admitting] 'abject and true remorse' in the statement and [having] to say sorry. Eames continues to be involved in the background, you have that stalemate over decommissioning and Eames then persuades the Loyalists towards this statement of 'no first strike'. This is about giving greater confidence to the nationalist community. So they are talking to Eames about needing to get prisoners out, Eames is saying to them well you're not going to get prisoners out or you're not going to get greater remission on the basis of a ceasefire, you need to offer something more. So out of that the Loyalists offered this 'no first strike' statement. [Patrick] Mayhew [Secretary of State for Northern Ireland] restores 50 per cent remission and they begin to talk about the issue of the early release of prisoners, which takes you through to the Good Friday Agreement. So Eames is in there not just simply taking messages from the Loyalist to the two governments but in there saying to them these are the things you need to do to build confidence.

Another response to the insecurity of church people when involved in mediation was to localize it, planting mediation firmly in solid relations built up in small areas between people who were personally known to each other. Fr Adrian Egan put this well: 'the main stuff happens at the grass-roots level. You can have [all] sorts of wonderful inter-church documents giving out and pontificating and so on, but the vast majority of ordinary people won't pay attention to it and it doesn't make a difference. It is the physical things that [make things] happen' (interview 22 November 2007). This local mediation is often built upon the ecumenical relations established by clergy groups, neighbourhood church fora, and church-to-church groups, pulling in favours to help intervene in local conflicts. This sort of activity, however, very much represented private witness, and is little known. Reflecting on mediation in the many small, nameless incidents, Bishop Edward Daly said, 'in conflict situations everyone uses you, everyone uses you, everyone. I mean if you don't want to be used, don't get involved' (interview 24 January 2006).

The hunger strikes in 1980–1 offer an example of this in practice. Protesting against the British government's withdrawal of political status for prisoners, Republican prisoners began a dirty protest and, when this proved ineffective, they initiated two hunger strikes. With hindsight, the strikes became moments of transition when SF realized the potential of a political strategy (Brewer, 2003c: 98). Commenting on his work with Cardinal O'Fiaich during the first hunger strike, Bishop Edward Daly noted how his priestly role quickly became political and involved him having to liaise with a range of interested parties who were more politically skilled. 'Well', said Bishop Edward Daly, 'it blew hot and cold, there were times when we were miles apart. Cardinal O'Fiaich and myself worked together very closely with those on the hunger strike, with the families of the hunger strikers, with the Northern Ireland Office, with the Westminster government, Thatcher, and ultimately we thought we had a solution but it didn't work out. The British certainly deceived Cardinal O'Fiaich and myself. I think Thatcher, there was an agreement reached and there was a Cabinet meeting on the Thursday in which it was to be announced, and I think it must have been Thatcher's intervention that changed things, which I think ultimately caused the second hunger strike' (interview 24 January 2006). Of course, we know from the secondary literature that the Catholic Church was heavily involved at an institutional level in trying to negotiate with the British government to bring the second hunger strike to a close, and that local priests worked tirelessly to try to persuade prisoners to come off the protest and thence to pressure their families to the same end.

The most influential clerical figure was Monsignor Denis Faul, who was interviewed at length for this research. After long bedside discussions with Bobby Sands, Fr Faul was convinced that the prisoners were prepared to starve to death. The Catholic hierarchy hoped that their injunctions would influence the men to take food. The Pope sent his special envoy to speak directly to the prisoners; Cardinal Hume in England even made an intervention. Local priests such as Faul had more influence, however, recognizing that a new strategy was needed. Fr Faul ran a parallel set of negotiations with the prisoners' families, hoping to convince families to take their fathers, sons, and brothers off the fast. He succeeded but only after ten men had already died (this is discussed in Taylor, 1998). Rank and file clerics (who had more or less avoided politics up to this point) found themselves offering prayers and Masses for the hunger strikers. Indeed the Catholic Church in Ireland could do little else, as the vast majority of Irish Catholics at home and abroad supported the prisoners' five demands. Furthermore, Cardinal O'Fiaich told the world media that he had visited the jail where the hunger strikers were being held and that one would not allow animals to live in such conditions never mind human beings. He then compared it to the slums in Calcutta and by doing so allowed Catholics to support the prisoners' demands without actually supporting IRA violence.

This distinction became the principle for all future engagement between clergy, Catholic and Protestant, and paramilitaries.

The hunger strikes came about in protest at the government withdrawing special category status for paramilitary prisoners. The prisoners wanted rights restored to wear their own clothes, have extra visits, and have access to bibles in Irish. The question of the religious issue of bibles was, paradoxically, difficult for many Protestants to accept, subverted as it was by the question of national language. DUP MP Sammy Wilson famously said that every word spoken in Irish was like a bullet fired from a Republican gun. But ordinary Irish Catholics and the Catholic hierarchy did not see it that way. Therefore, the hunger strikes brought Catholic church leaders into the conflict on opposite sides to their Protestant counterparts. Catholic clergy had to bury the dead and look on as hundreds of thousands attended each of the funerals. As a negative social force, the hunger strikes polarized communities and as a consequence forced the Catholic Church in Ireland to publicly take sides (Beresford, 1987). The Catholic Church in Ireland found itself the conduit of outrage in its flock, not least because of papal involvement, Irish government participation, and lay Catholic beliefs in the reasonableness of the prisoners' demands. Catholic leaders found this to be an uncomfortable position, and ambivalence towards this political role largely explains why O'Fiaich's successor as cardinal, Cahal Daly, preferred to keep the Catholic Church out of politics. The fact that Mrs Thatcher overturned a deal brokered by Cardinal O'Fiaich and Bishop Edward Daly compounded their anxiety at the situation, as Catholic leaders saw it, being concerned at finding themselves in opposition to the state. But it also finished Fr Faul as a go-between, as the Republicans sidelined him—from that time on he was known by them as 'Denis the Menace'—and by the Catholic hierarchy under Cahal Daly, for whom he was a dangerous maverick.

The Holy Cross protests in 2001–2 is another example of a localized incident in which clergy mediated, and which quickly nourished international interest and became hugely public, blurring the private–public witness by transporting local clergy into high politics. Loyalists protested at Catholic children and parents walking through their area each day on their way to a girl's primary school. This was motivated by a sense in which growth in the Catholic population meant encroachment on areas in North Belfast traditionally understood as Protestant, thus touching at the emotional core of territory and identity in a way that overruled prudent constraints around gender and children (the gendered nature of the conflict has been addressed by Ashe, 2006, 2007). The protests became very vociferous and violent, and pictures travelled the world of hectoring Protestant mothers spitting hate at cowering, frightened Catholic schoolchildren. Bottles of urine were thrown at the children and the Ulster Defence Association (UDA) even lobbed a pipe bomb into the middle of a group of schoolchildren, which exploded but luckily injured no one; this earned the UDA universal contempt and other Loyalists said in the media that they were ashamed to be Loyalists. Again, the contribution of local clergy as mediators, such as the Revd Norman Hamilton (Presbyterian) and Fr Aidan Troy (Catholic), is well known without us needing to repeat it.

One dimension that is worth explaining is the deep chasm the Holy Cross incident caused amongst Protestant clergy. It confirmed to outsiders what seemed to them as the irrationality of Protestant positions on the impasse around the GFA; and nuanced distinctions locally between Unionism, Loyalism, and Protestantism were eschewed. Some well-known liberal Protestants called for greater understanding and less pillorying. In an article in the *Guardian*, even the moderate Presbyterian the Revd John Dunlop expressed concern at the outside world's interpretation of what happened (www.guardian.co.uk/politics/2003/dec/01/northernireland.faithschools). Visits by Archbishop Desmond Tutu to the area only served to make matters more frustrating for Protestants, some of whom believed that only white South Africans and Israelis sympathized with them (Teeney, 2004). In reality, most Protestants did not support their co-religionists in Holy Cross and objected to the stereotypes of Protestants that were publicly circulating. Other Protestant clergy worked tirelessly to mediate the conflict; and complaints alleged against the aggravating role of the Catholic Church overlook the contribution of Fr Aidan Troy to its reconciliation. The image of Fr Troy leading schoolgirls through a daily torrent of abuse was flashed around the world and became as iconic as that of Edward Daly and his white handkerchief on Bloody Sunday. In truth, he could have pressed home a propaganda advantage, yet he chose to make friends with the Revd Norman Hamilton, the local Presbyterian minister, in the hope that together they could try to bring resolution to the conflict.

It is worth noting in passing that in interview, the Revd Norman Hamilton reflected on some of the dilemmas he faced in deciding to get involved, and how he managed the overtly political role foisted on him: 'Well, I mean, I obviously had to work my way through this very carefully and I remember one particular TV piece with a close [up] of me standing on my own with my arms folded, wearing my dog collar, standing on my own in my usual spot and then panned back to the wider riot or protest that was going on. What I was trying to do there, and I was actually quite grateful for that shot because I was very deliberate about my body language in public. I was very deliberate about my dress in public. I famously wore the same coat every day, now this was very deliberate, to say I am here, I am OK with being here but can you please try and understand that I am desperately trying not to be part of the problem. So that even the public imaging of dress was part of my positioning. When the protest would be over in the morning you would then be talking to all sorts of people and the dog collar would come off' (interview 26 January 2006).

One of the lasting benefits of the churches' involvement in mediating the protest, as Hamilton sees it, is its positive impact on subsequent relationships that assisted in mediating later conflicts, especially over contentious parades. For example, the relationships built up in mediating Holy Cross facilitated the development of the North and West Belfast Parades Forum, a grouping that includes the paramilitaries, political representatives, community people, and the churches. Hamilton said, 'within that grouping you have a number of relationships. You sometimes have some very uneasy discussions, so you talk politics and you talk parading and you talk community stuff, but at the same time you are building real relationships with the paramilitary guys there, as for example, personally I was able to build during and out of the Holy Cross dispute. For me the [principle of] building of relationships has been, I must go and get to know the paramilitaries and do whatever I am going to do with them. It has come out of saying, these folks, like the churches, are part of the fabric of this society, for good or for ill, and in the normal course of what you might call social dialogue and social intercourse, we will be engaging with each other' (interview 26 January 2006). Some of these meetings were with the Orange Order and the Ulster Volunteer Force (UVF). This brings us seamlessly to the final type of mediation.

iii) Dialogue with conflict groups

A significant part of conflict resolution is the development of dialogue with protagonists as a form of relationship-building, with this social connectedness intended to develop rapport and trust sufficient to try to dissuade them from violence, now and in the future. Opening up constructive dialogue with conflict groups reaped benefits later when the churches acted as backchannels in the political peace process, as one form of peacemaking merged into another. SF activist Jim Gibney, who himself played a significant role in developing dialogue with the churches for nearly twenty years, is worth quoting at length on this:

There are individuals inside those institutions, ministers of the various churches, Protestant and Catholic, who I believe did serve the people very well, made a valuable contribution to the political changes that we have on this island today. They had to battle against apathy and indifference, prejudice inside their respective churches. So all praise to those individuals and there were a handful of them, compared to the size of the respective Christian churches on this island. And I think that in the writing up of the history of this, it has to be accurate. It has to be clear, crystal clear, to ensure that the churches as institutions do not get the credit for what we have today. In actual fact the individuals who led from the front, they [should be] given the recognition. And I am thinking particularly of people like Fr Alec Reid, Fr Gerry Reynolds—these are the two names that strike me. The

Monastery itself, the way in which it put itself at the disposal of the peace process, and the roles that they played in that, and particularly I have to say the freedom that the Redemptorist Order gave to Fr Alec Reid to continue his work with Gerry Adams and John Hume in the first instance. And I am also mindful of people like Harold Good and the Methodists; John Dunlop who I believe for a very long period of time was very influential in his engagements with Sinn Féin. And I also think David Porter should be given recognition for the work that he did in ECONI. Myself and Tom Hartley and indeed our party generally found David Porter's advice indispensable in terms [of] understanding what was going on inside Unionism. And the regular meetings that we had with that group of people over a long period of time—some fifteen years I would say, of intense dialogue with them. Another person who isn't remembered for this type of background work was Jack Weir. Jack Weir was also involved and I met Jack several times. And there were other people around Jack Weir who because I don't know them I can't remember their names and they need to be recognized. John Morrow, for example, was part of that small group. Ken Newell would have been involved in it as well. And the Corrymeela Centre had some connections to it. And I think it is important to identify those individuals and those small organizations because [of what] they pioneered in terms of cross-community work. Certainly John Dunlop took great risks in his engagements with Sinn Féin, as did David Porter. But that is the business of conflict resolution. Risks are taken, people step over the line in all sorts of ways. (Interview 3 September 2008)

This idea that institutional and individual contributions need to be distinguished was also the theme of Roy Garland's assessment from the Loyalist perspective. 'Reflecting on my own experience', he said, 'the church was not a major player, with the exception of one or two people. The church leaders coming out together has not got much impact on the ground. Some of the churchy people would not even have met with the UDA, would not even talk to them. I remember saying to some of them, you need to talk to these people and they were unwilling' (interview 13 September 2005).

Garland is referring to a strange paradox that fashions Loyalist views of the churches. Based on years of personal experience in dialogue, the Revd John Dunlop opined that church mediators should walk tentatively to avoid heading straight into the other's camp: 'there is no point in getting two feet into the other community otherwise you are useless or two feet back in your own community and not doing any of this [dialogue]' (interview 23 March 2006). Identification and detachment, empathy and distance, are needed at the same time: a foot in each camp, as it were. However, Protestant ministers were often more willing to talk to Republicans than Loyalists, and Catholic priests were more frequent interlocutors with Loyalists than Protestant clergy. Protestant ministers could see dialogue with Republicans as part of the gospel of reconciliation, morally acceptable as a form of conflict prevention; Loyalists, on the other hand, were often seen through class lenses as disreputable, meetings with whom had greater moral challenge. As Garland said, 'within churches and the

Unionist Party to this day, with some exceptions, paramilitaries are just criminals. In prison Gusty [Spence] mentions that a bishop and one or two clergy did things for them, especially Methodists, but he found more sympathy from the Catholic clergy' (interview 13 September 2005).

Catholic dialogue with Loyalists was rooted in the way priests perceived Republican combatants. This is not meant in the cheap sense that they were hand in glove, as many Unionists alleged. Alec Reid, when confronted once with the accusation that he was naïve in meeting with groups labelled terrorist, replied 'I'm trying to take the conflict off the streets. I'm trying to prevent people being killed, there's no point in me talking to the peaceful party. If I'm going to stop it on the streets I'm going to have to talk to the people who have it on the streets. You're working with them trying to persuade them to stop using armed force.'[10] In interview Reid recognized that the key to wider political progress was persuading the IRA to desist from killing, as this would unlock everything: 'We got involved mainly to stop people being killed. That in practice meant trying to stop the IRA. We felt if the IRA stopped, the Loyalist paramilitary people would stop also. We did succeed in persuading the IRA to stop, with a lot of help from Sinn Féin politicians, with the advice that they gave us. When that happened, it opened the way for negotiations between all the groups because the Unionists would not engage in negotiations with Republicans or Nationalists while the IRA was active. So we could not get the dialogue going to settle the conflict until the IRA stopped' (8 February 2011).

This sort of view was common among our Catholic respondents and enabled Catholic clergy to dialogue with greater moral abandon than their Protestant equivalents. That having been said, some Protestant ministers overcame resistance. In a way, the deepening atrocities forced it upon them. As the attitudes of laypersons polarized in response to the violence, some Protestant clergy were forced to relax their moral constraints in speaking to conflict groups, which only increased the feelings of pressure they felt under— and thus their courage in breaking through it. Some Protestant clergy matched their Catholic counterparts to meet with the paramilitaries; some restricted contact to particular paramilitaries, others dialogued with all conflict groups, and some focused on prisoners. Speaking of Presbyterians in particular, the Revd Lesley Carroll described them as natural politicians and for Presbyterians to 'think they weren't political would mean they hadn't read their own history' (interview 10 January 2008). In the view of another churchman, from the 1980s onwards the churches took seriously engagement with paramilitaries (Walter Lewis, interview 8 October 2007), not un-coincidentally in the post-hunger strike growth of SF. However, contrary to this view, there is a long

---

[10] BBC Radio 4 interview, 29 November 2006.

history of such dialogue for a minority of ministers. Some Protestant church-men first began dialogue with the IRA in 1974 at the Feakle talks,[11] leading to the Christmas ceasefire of that year, from which developed much later a regular channel of communication between some Protestant ministers and SF; these ministers also facilitated Catholic priests to meet Loyalist paramilitaries.

This early contact had several knock-on effects for later conflict prevention, as well as assisting change in the paramilitaries, and the opening up of other forms of dialogue. Alongside church-led dialogue, successive British govern-ments had been having on-off secret talks with Republicans from the early 1970s, yet they failed to provide the breakthrough. Sociologically it is neces-sary to ask why the churches succeeded when the professional politicians failed, and this is an issue we will return to in Chapter 2. Here, we restrict ourselves to describing the knock-on effect of church-led dialogue. For example, it is no exaggeration to argue that church dialogue helped facilitate change in the paramilitaries. It is doubtful whether Denis Donaldson's views on the meetings he and other Republicans—some of whom were ex-IRA combatants—had in Fitzroy Church under the auspices of the Revd Ken Newell are affected by his later exposure as an informant for the British. Reflecting first on the importance of Clonard as a special sacred space for secret dialogue, he said, 'it allowed church people from the Protestant, Methodist, and Presbyterian background to engage with Republicans and to try and get an understanding of just what Republicans were about'. Fitzroy was clearly another key secret and sacred space. His meetings there were good 'because it was very challenging, 'cos it forced us to think some of our notions about them. And it forced us, it challenged some of our own misconceptions, so I thought it was useful' (interview 14 November 2005). Jim Gibney's views quoted above, which endorse Donaldson's, confirm the claim that Donald-son's peculiar biographical position does not impugn his judgement that dialogue between the churches and paramilitaries was critical to social trans-formation and repair.

The dialogue that church people entered into with prisoners can perhaps best demonstrate this. Prisoners were critical to the move from a military to a political strategy, on both sides, and when consulted on the inside by their political representatives they overwhelmingly supported their respective cea-sefires. The bridge-building done by prison chaplains and other church visitors was also important to this choice. Roy Garland revealed that Gusty Spence, the nearest to a putative leader of the very schismatic Loyalists, met often with Fr Alec Reid, saying 'Gusty has a great respect for clergy. His prison experience taught him that this society had to change. He was on board with

---

[11] These talks have become iconic, both for their success and failure, and we discuss them in Chapter 4.

regard to the peace process' (interview 13 September 2005). It is for Reid's work with Spence in persuading Loyalists to agree to a ceasefire that Garland praises Reid above Eames for 'getting his hands dirty', although this overlooks the separate talks Eames and Magee were having about a Loyalist ceasefire, highlighting the factionalism of Loyalism and contradicting the positive assessment Brian Rowan makes of Eames's contribution (see Vignette 5 above; also see Chapter 2).[12]

Protestant clergy sometimes found it easier to visit prisoners than to dialogue with paramilitaries, since prison visiting is a more normal part of pastoral work. Prison visiting was also popular as a practical form of ecumenism. Bishop Samuel Poyntz recalled going to visit prisoners with Cardinal Cahal Daly, 'and we used to meet both sets of prisoners together' (interview 23 September 2005). The Revd David Armstrong, now a COI minister in Cork, during his travails as a Presbyterian minister in Limavady was also a prison chaplain in Magilligan, and said that distinctions of Catholic and Protestant did not matter inside and that prison chaplains befriended all prisoners regardless (interview 2 December 2005). Through prison contacts, Armstrong established dialogue with David Ervine and the UVF as well as with the Irish National Liberation Army (INLA). Even more beyond the pale than the IRA, Armstrong's talks with INLA were described as 'long, very, very long [and] apart from speaking to you about it, there's very few people know'. Not all Protestant clergy were as open, especially after prisoners were released, for fear of giving legitimacy to Loyalist paramilitaries and worries about being exploited as support for armed struggle. Bishop Edward Daly recalled an incident when he and Cardinal O'Fiaich organized sessions for released prisoners that were attended regularly by Loyalists, who were there on the instruction of their wives because 'their own church was not interested in them at all, they disowned them virtually' (interview 24 January 2006). He also wrote letters for Loyalist prisoners.

c) Cross-community activities (entry into secular spaces to try to break down barriers)

In an authoritative analysis Maria Power (2007) argues that the ecumenical churches and para-church organizations transformed over the course of 'the Troubles' into community relations agencies as their only way to succeed. There is some point to this. If ecumenism (as distinct from ecumenicalism) is designed to improve relations between Catholics and Protestants, they are more effective in doing so when this is conducted in secular as well as sacred

---

[12] Garland discusses the role of Spence (see Garland, 2002); and Rowan's assessment of Eames in his fuller account of the ceasefires (see Rowan, 1995).

spaces and taken from church settings into the community. And this is precisely what they intended by their cross-community activities. A caveat needs to be made, however. It is a moot point whether ecumenists succeeded in improving wider Catholic-Protestant relations amongst non-ecumenists in secular settings, and if they did, they certainly did not do this separately from the impressive range of secular initiatives that formed part of the community relations agenda in Northern Ireland, which had been well funded by various British, US, and EU initiatives, nor did they do so alone from a range of other church activities done outside the ecumenist framework.

We have already seen how some forms of social action and outreach into the community were perceived as practical forms of ecumenism, but to give some sense of the balance between sacred and secular community work, Frazer and Fitzduff (1986) estimated in 1984 that of the forty-five groups classified as undertaking community relations work, only nine were allied to the churches. It was only in 1996 that the Community Relations Council (CRC) appointed its first project officer for the churches, who said, 'when I started there was very little going on' (cited in Power, 2007: 193).[13] While the CRC was only set up in 1990, Fitzduff (2010: 13) notes that by 2008 its website listed 129 organizations as pursuing community work, of which only 20 had a church affiliation or foundation. Church people, however, give the impression that their contribution was greater. The late David Stevens, writing for the CRC (2005: 10), felt that 'much of the voluntary effort in this society is focused around churches and they contribute enormously to social capital'. Time matters here: Stevens is reflecting on the expansion of church activity post-1998 when the signing of the GFA facilitated the social peace process as they moved into spaces opened up by the political peace process—the increase in community relations work as a whole after 1998 is a measure of that, too. Definitions matter also: some of this disagreement resolves around what is meant by community relations work.

Cross-community work involves bringing Protestant and Catholic communities together in secular spaces in an attempt to break down barriers and forge peaceful social relations. The Revd Mervyn Gibson, from the PCI and Chair of the Shankill Community Forum, noted that one of the advantages of community work such as this was that it fostered all sorts of useful relationships in other forms of peacemaking, including relations with the Loyalist para-militaries in the Shankill, whose 'brothers, wives, and sisters sit on these committees, so that you come to know them and they know you are helping the community' (interview 27 January 2006). Gibson, as a committed non-ecumenist, would not like the idea, but cross-community work is the secular equivalent of the ecumenism done in religious settings. By definition, however,

---

[13] The CRC's Churches Advisory Group was disbanded in 2001.

in secular settings the churches work alongside those with other faiths or none, and in settings where a Christian ethos is missing or incidental.

Another paradox of this type of religious peacemaking is that relationship-building across communities is mostly low profile, yet to succeed has to be done by organizations and individuals with a sufficiently high profile to have the legitimacy to make contact and build trust, possessing the skills to foster good social relations across the sectarian divide. 'Local' work was often done by national and international agencies and by people well known in the neighbourhood but with much wider credibility. And there lies the rub for the churches. It was very difficult for them to be identified in the public mind with this kind of peacemaking, working as they did as second fiddle to secular organizations. The churches' speechifying made regular reference to the necessity for 'good' community relations but the low-profile nature of this kind of relationship-building and its concentration around specific bodies and persons with skill and credibility meant the churches as institutions found it difficult to make an impression. The Revd Ruth Patterson, from Restoration Ministries, drew no doubt on her own experiences in encapsulating this: 'I believe that there was an awful lot of work going on pre-peace process with individuals and groups that wasn't publicized otherwise the process would not have been possible, there would have been no foundation on which to build it. I mean, groups like Corrymeela, groups like Cornerstone, like the Christian Renewal Centre at Rostrevor, like the Columba Community in Derry and lots of other groups, all with a different way of going about it [and] one mightn't always have felt particularly comfortable with it, but all were contributing their little bit towards the creation of something, including all the secular bodies towards the creation of something which made the peace process possible' (interview 29 November 2005). There are two kinds of Christian involvement in cross-community work, however, that which is large scale, often done on a countrywide basis involving specialist organizations and initiatives, and the local work done in neighbourhoods in informal ways.

i) Large scale

Central to cross-community peacemaking is the reconciliation of religious, political, and social difference between Catholics and Protestants. The involvement of large-scale actors such as the US government and its Northern Ireland Peace Envoy, the EU, the International Fund for Ireland, Northern Ireland's CRC, and the Equality Unit of the Office of Northern Ireland's First and Deputy First Minister has been extensive. These actors, along with other government departments North and South, have had a dramatic positive effect on peacemaking in Northern Ireland. The problem is disentangling the specifically religious dimensions. Some anti-peace Protestant groups resented outside interference in their 'wee province' irrespective of the coffers they brought with them, but for pro-peace churches, in one sense these wider initiatives are relevant because they funded grass-roots Christian groups. Large-scale groups involved in supporting cross-community activities included Co-operation North, Protestant and Catholic Encounter (PACE), the YMCA, the Northern Ireland Council for Integrated Education, the Northern Ireland Mixed Marriage Association, and the Sports Council for Northern Ireland. Some of these have had a strong Christian input, most notably the Northern Ireland Mixed Marriage Association and PACE. The development of integrated education also began in the commitment of individual Christians who wanted to move away from divided education in the belief that children grow together when adults if educated together while young. Integrated education is now well established.

This represents a good example of what sociologists call institutionalization, for the personal faith of some committed Christians became bureaucratized into large-scale organizations, which pursue their vision on a grander scale but lose the Christian ethos of the original visionaries. An exception is perhaps Habitat for Humanity, a large-scale cross-community initiative that is still avowedly Christian, concentrating on bringing ordinary Catholics and Protestants together in low-cost home-building schemes that sees them building homes with and for each other. Many Christians assist beside them in the manual labour. It is also the case that the main churches and ecumenical communities and organizations have been involved in large-scale cross-community activity distinct from their ecumenical work but as part of their ongoing programme of reconciliation and peacemaking. This includes cross-community holiday schemes, summer clubs, youth clubs, and identity work with local women's groups. As evidence of the way civil society prospers according to the level of funding available to resource it, a lot of the grants made available to these organizations were dependent on them having a cross-community element. While there is strong evidence of groups from different communities joining forces to get the funding, some did not survive the loss of funding.

ii) Local

There exists a wide range of local secular and Christian cross-community activity. The types of groups involved in local cross-community work include community development associations, community interface projects, and children and women's organizations. One of the more unusual was commented upon by the Revd David Armstrong who was for a time Chaplain to Glentoran FC, in the heart of Protestant East Belfast, noting that by the time he left, the normally all-Protestant team had six Catholics as regular first-team players (interview 2 December 2005). All such initiatives seek to promote cooperation and reconciliation through education and understanding in settings in which Protestants and Catholics come together. Groups such as Ballynafeigh Community Development Association are taking 'active steps to realise the community relations development potential of a mixed communi-ty'. It does this by activities designed to attract both communities, such as workshops and seminars; the community centre is a building shared by more than twenty groups from the area, representing both traditions. There is often little Christian input into community development groups—indeed, these bodies are often escapes for people committed to cross-community peacemaking activity but who do not want to work in a Christian environ-ment. Churches, however, have often come together to address the social and community needs of neighbourhoods in ways that bring the two communities together. Such projects often promoted practical social ministries and com-munity volunteering placements in the context of prayer and fellowship. The Churches' Voluntary Bureau, Clogher Care, and the Downpatrick Area Inter-Church Caring Project were examples of projects that provided a range of services to local neighbourhoods on a cross-community basis, such as help with the elderly in both communities, working with people with learning difficulties, playgroups, youth clubs, and community employment schemes. Forthspring Inter-Community Group states this objective well: 'To encourage local people to actively seek for themselves a future free from violence and sectarianism' (see Power, 2007: 84–100 for detailed consideration of Forth-spring). Community Dialogue, set up in 1997, brings together community development workers interested in cross-community work, and churchmen and women with the same ambition. It seeks a 'cross-community solution to political, social and economic problems' and has community activists and church people as members.

The mobilization of people across the two communities in terms of their social needs rather than strictly as members of one religion or another—bringing together categories of people such as the elderly, the young, mums and toddlers, victims of crime, or people concerned about drugs, the environ-ment, or hospital closures—not only unites communities across the sectarian divide but it reduces the saliency of religion as an individual's identity marker. This is perhaps most apparent with respect to the cross-community mobiliza-tion of women. It is not too much of an exaggeration to claim that local women's groups have had the most profound effect on cross-community activities in Northern Ireland (women have played a significant part in the Northern Ireland peace process, see Morgan, 2003; Potter, 2008). Groups such as Women Together for Peace and Women's Information Group actively sought to bring about a cessation of sectarian violence in Northern Ireland by giving women a 'voice in society'. Mainstreaming gender issues is widely accepted as a peacemaking strategy by deconstructing the lines of fissure around which conflict adheres (see Brewer, 2010: 68–102), although women's groups aligned with the combatants always offer an alternative form of engagement for women (women's groups from West Belfast, for example, for a time used to protest outside meetings of Women for Peace Together, referring to them as 'Informers Together' after the organization told women to inform on the IRA). In terms of their local peacemaking, the mission statement of the Women's Information Group put its objectives well: 'To bring women together and provide quality information which can be used to enhance their lives, that of family, project and local community.'

The empowerment of women as peacemakers in their local communities is the aim of an initiative formerly based in Armagh and run from the Queen's University outreach campus in the city and now based in Belfast. As the ecclesiastical capital of Ireland for two of the main denominations, it was fitting that the Women and Peacebuilding Programme began in Armagh. It involved joint training courses for women from both traditions to enhance their personal and peacemaking skills to enable them to take up a proactive role in their local communities. The programme was a cross-community initiative intended to foster positive relations between women as strategic peacemakers, which they then take into their neighbourhoods. There was a Women's Resource Centre on the campus that facilitated the programme as well as providing resource material for local women's groups. Young people were also mobilized as a social category, although significantly less so than women. Special initiatives among the young included Community Cross Links, a Christian young person's drama project, and Zero28, an initiative aiming to provide space for active peacebuilding that used culturally relevant ways of engaging with the conflict.

In order to connect to an argument made in the Conclusion about the post-conflict flight of the churches from the public sphere, it is important to emphasize here that the churches tended to mobilize people as Christians, even more narrowly as denominational Christians, rather than in terms of other identity categories, such as women, youths, the elderly, or conflict victims. Churches had, in particular, their specialist youth organizations and women's groups but these social categories were not mobilized specifically as peace activists, such that in the post-conflict period, there was no legacy of active youth and women's organizations, let alone victim groups, able to be turned into agents assisting in societal healing and by means of which spiritual capital could be disseminated within the moral economy. Women's groups within the churches faced powerful constraints, in that they confronted institutions that were patriarchal; as youth groups faced ageism that taught them that elders knew best. For this reason, some women's groups were only incidentally Christian, while others were hostile to religion. It is also noteworthy that youth organizations such as Zero28, while avowedly Christian, operated outside any church authority structure, finding space to develop a youth response to the conflict outside ageist religious institutions. The flip side of this patriarchal and ageist structure is that women clergy and youth activists often found it difficult to develop the autonomy and freedom to engage fully with the peace process, although there were some notable exceptions, such as Gareth Higgins, Lesley Carroll, and Ruth Patterson.[14] Nuns found it easier than the women clergy, precisely because of their independence from the male-dominated churches, such as Cecelia Clegg and Geraldine Smyth; Clegg has since left her religious order.

Some leading ecumenists felt the need to go softly in their community relations work. The Revd Ruth Patterson expressed the tentativeness of her first steps towards cross-community work: 'we began, very gently behind the scenes, and then also, very, very gently, some cross border activity' (interview 29 November 2005). The mainstream Protestant churches, however, lagged some way behind these specialist cross-community initiatives. The PCI's Peace Programme was pitched at young people, for example, but it did not require them to be involved in encounters across the sectarian divide, and this, as broadcaster and journalist William Crawley emphasized, 'is after "the Troubles"' where it is still 'too controversial a proposal to even consider' (interview 23 September 2007). The parish structure of the Catholic Church institutionalizes its engagement with local communities but cross-community activity that is distinct from social activist ecumenism is equally slight. If we put this reticence in the context of the growing homogenization of neighbourhood communities, as they become increasingly more ethno-religiously exclusive, we have the institutional churches hunkered down in a form of 'constrict capital', as Putnam (2007) termed it, happy enough (but not ecstatic) to break down barriers in sacred spaces through ecumenism but fearful of doing so in secular spaces, thus hunkering down—a term Putnam uses extensively to mean withdrawal—within themselves. The Revd John Dunlop expressed Putnam's point for him rather well:

> One of the most worrying things about Northern Ireland at the present is that we are moving into homogeneous communities, the demographic shifts of the population in Northern Ireland are very serious and very worrying. Now, the only way in which you can start to overcome that, or one of the ways in which it can become addressed, is when local church communities decide that they are going to move across these divisions and try and sustain integrated communities or mixed communities or sustain mixed communities or sustain good neighbourliness. That is a part of the Christian vocation where they have to have a concern not just for their own congregation but have a concern for the community. The danger is that you get a very strong Sinn Féin attitude of ourselves alone, ourselves alone as Republicans, ourselves alone as Unionists, ourselves alone as Presbyterians, ourselves alone as Methodists, ourselves alone as Catholics but ourselves alone won't work because God never meant us to work that

---

[14] Gareth Higgins founded Zero28 as a youth peace group. The Revds Carroll and Patterson were female ministers in the PCI.

way. That is essentially divisive, inward looking, selfish, just ourselves alone. What that does is to reinforce the sense of your own identity without having any concern for the well-being in the wider community. (Interview 23 March 2006)

d) Peace initiatives (espousing peace and monitoring the conflict)

A caveat has to be made at this point. It appears superfluous to have peace groups and initiatives as a separate category since all the types in the analytical framework are examples of peacemaking. It is worth keeping this as a special category, however, because there are groups, organizations, and initiatives that self-consciously constitute themselves in these terms. Peace is not a by-product of other aims or activities but an espoused ideal and the central intention of practical action; and peace groups also often monitor events and incidents for their threat to peace. For these purposes, the mainstream churches all had their peace committees, although under various names, or peace envoys; the PCI even appointed 'Peace Agents' in presbyteries, and the COI established the Hard Gospel project to monitor and address sectarianism and had its 'Think Again' programme in the diocese of Down and Dromore. The progress was slow, however. William Crawley commented on how PCI statements were 'nervously formulated to avoid giving offence to [a] section of the church' (interview 23 September 2007). The Revd Lesley Carroll, herself Presbyterian, noted how difficult it was for liberals like her—even after several atrocities affected their congregations directly—to get motions passed at General Assembly, 'which got an awful rough ride despite many people being glad of it' (interview 10 January 2008). But the Revd Earl Storey, in charge of the COI's Hard Gospel project, said that it was action that was important not motions (interview 21 September 2005), the sort of action that Bishop Harold Miller from the Anglican diocese of Down and Dromore himself encouraged: 'Well, I have been involved in lots of things. Most of what I have been involved in has been across the Catholic, Protestant divide and over five years I have encouraged parishes, churches, individual clergy, through all sort of different programmes and things to try to break down that particular dividing wall' (interview 25 January 2006).[15] We can begin to describe this action by dividing it into two subsections: peace bodies and populist peace activities.

---

[15] Miller had spent time in Cork before moving North and as such had a more open mind to cross-community, ecumenist, and peace work than others for whom the North has been their sole arena of activity.

i) Peace bodies and initiatives

Peace bodies can be described as those formal organizations that seek to promote and support the activities of peacebuilding and are constituted solely on this basis; many organizations lay claim to having supported peace and assisted in the peace process but the focus here is on those bodies and initiatives for whom it was their *raison d'être*. Some of the bodies and initiatives are Christian, others not; some of the secular bodies have Christians working in them. Some of the Christian bodies and initiatives are local and are tied to specific churches or parishes. Good examples are Hillsborough Parish Bridgebuilders Group, which sought to examine issues of peace, conflict, and reconciliation in a Christian setting, and Strandtown Christian Fellowship Church's Bridges Forum, which aimed to contribute to peace by inviting speakers whose words might inform Christians with the knowledge, skill, and commitment to work for peace. Some of the initiatives were large scale. For example, the Anglican diocese of Down and Dromore, which includes the greater Belfast area, had a Diocesan Reconciliation Operational Group. Bishop Harold Miller's personal vision for peace and reconciliation led the diocese to establish in 1999 (within two years of his appointment as bishop) a systematic programme of reconciliation and peace activity known as 'Think Again'.

The initiative asked people to 'think again about investing in people', and focused on reconciliation, outreach, and youth issues. The five-year programme was funded to £725,000, half each from the COI and the EU Peace Fund, and had several full-time staff; it was money well spent according to Miller, 'it transformed attitudes' (interview 23 June 2010). It was intended to spiritually renew the COI around the theme of reconciliation, outreach, and youth. One of its guiding principles was expressed in its brochure as follows: '*Think Again*, in recognition of the deep divisions which exist within society, will place a particular emphasis on developing projects and programmes which help to heal these divisions.' These included the following: the Community Bridge Builders programme, intended to improve relationships with Catholics in local parish areas; the appointment of two Community Bridge Builder coordinators in each parish to take forward this vision; the development of a range of training events and activities focusing on the theme of reconciliation, dealing with issues such as sectarianism, identity, peacemaking, conflict resolution and ministries for peace-building; and provision within the parishes for access to specialist support agencies and organizations involved in peacemaking and reconciliation. The initiative produced a regular newsletter *Think Again News*, and its March 2001 edition stated: 'Not many churches in Northern Ireland embrace the need and Christ's call to reconciliation, and if they do it is with conditions. One large stumbling block is the notion that others must be like us before we can accept them or have any dealings with them. Instead [we] need to behave rather like an engaged couple for whom planning a future together is a delight.'

When asked years later if he considered it a success, Bishop Miller focused his view first on the programme's ambition to stem the haemorrhage of young people from the pews: 'It was a great success. We had an assessment at the end carried out by a stats person from the Church of England and he observed a plateau or slight growth in places. Had we not have had the programme we would have lost numbers. The programme helped people and parishes focus on the task in hand' (interview 23 June 2010). Asked about its contribution to peace, however, Miller was naturally less sanguine: 'Very hard question to answer. It certainly made people see the church as being there for the sake and good of the community. I inherited a diocese with poor community spirit. We changed that and that helped peace.' He added, 'there [were] loads of obstacles. It was hard to create a different mood but we managed it. Reconciliation was difficult as we had obstacles around joint worship and this was mostly from Presbyterians who did not want to joint worship with Catholics. Thankfully at the end of the five-year programme this was less of an issue. Certainly for the COI it became normal behaviour. I take all my priests to a Benedictine Monastery in Rostrevor every year and it is totally accepted. But the objectives were fulfilled and it helped to create a different mood.'

As part of 'mood change' amongst church congregations, the PCI also outlined what it called its 'peace vocation'. To coincide with the ceasefires in 1994, eighty-two years after its moderator signed the Ulster Covenant that enshrined the narrow sectarian interests of Protestants in Ireland, the General Assembly passed the following recommendation: 'We affirm [ourselves] to be Christian peacemakers in our own situation. We must therefore be prepared to meet and talk together with those from other churches whose practices and beliefs differ from our own, with those from whom we are politically divided. We understand peacemaking to be an affirmation and accommodation of diversity. Our own particular history makes it imperative that we reassert the Church's proper calling to seek peace and the things that make for peace in our day.' The IICM had a peace education initiative as did ISE and ECONI (see Vignette 6). The latter was formed in 1987 to reflect the shared peacemaking concerns of evangelical Christian leaders who felt that an evangelical voice on Northern Irish issues was speaking at that time only of enmity and not reconciliation. The liberal evangelicals in ECONI were connected to European and North American theological ideas about reconciliation and transformation and tried to apply them locally, including Catholic liberation theology, which, being opposed by the Catholic Church, did not have a Catholic stamp on it. As Ganiel (2008a) notes, evangelicals with social networks and biographical experiences that took them outside Ireland, giving them expanded horizons, tended to be the least parochial and conservative.

Vignette 6: Evangelical Contribution on Northern Ireland

ECONI emerged in 1987 as a response to the shared concern of a number of evangelical Christian leaders. It worked 'to apply Biblical principles and perspectives to the situation in Northern Ireland'. In particular it sought to 'address evangelical Christians in order to facilitate a continuing process of engagement with God's Word and the hurts facing our divided community'. ECONI's goal was to 'encourage change in values and attitudes which will lead to evangelicals being active as makers of peace and agents of healing'.

The group was involved in a number of programmes including:

- Training courses, residential meetings, conferences and workshops on issues of peace, sectarianism, identity, and forgiveness.
- The production of written materials and resources relevant to the situation intended to empower others to confront the challenge of peace.
- Provision of speakers, trainers, and facilitators.
- Public events, such as ECONI Sunday, Christian Citizenship Forum, and Clergy Days, to publicize ECONI and its work.

These activities were designed to resource Christians to develop a Biblical response, raise awareness of the issues to be considered in a divided society, facilitate research in Biblical and theological perspectives, and to encourage people to engage constructively in the search for peace and healing. ECONI subsequently changed its name to the Centre for Contemporary Christianity in Ireland.

This was something Higgins (2000) picked up on earlier with respect to undermining Protestant beliefs in the antichrist. Many ECONI leaders attended theological colleges overseas, for example, and often invited speakers on reconciliation from Great Britain and North America (thus lacking the 'our wee province' mentality of hardliners).

As we shall emphasize in later chapters, what made ECONI particularly instrumental to the peace process was its roots within the evangelical tradition, enabling it to utilize the symbols, terminology, and arguments of evangelicalism put to the service of peacemaking. It was the bridge between the avowedly pro-peace groups within the ecumenist tradition, some of whom sat on ECONI's board of trustees and wrote in its journal *Lion and Lamb*, and those evangelicals who, though anti-ecumenist, were transformed into being pro-peace. The Revd Mervyn Gibson, for example, on the evangelical wing of the PCI and not a member of ECONI, expressed frustration at the association of peace with ecumenism and went on to acclaim the contribution of evangelical pastors and ministers in moving their hardline constituencies in the direction of peace: 'I spoke at [a] local Ulster Rally at the Shankill. I made an extremely conciliatory speech at a hardline rally and that speech was cleared by everybody present, because I wrote it and then said to everybody, "this is what I'm going to say, anybody with any objections, tell me now, so I'll not get it the neck afterwards." Everybody said, that's great, and that speech accepted IRA decommissioning, that speech said we need to build new relationships with our neighbours and with the South. All those things are in that speech and that was a hardline rally. So you can say things coming from those sectors that [other] people can't, but the idea is that you can bring people with you' (interview 27 January 2006). ECONI helped make it acceptable for evangelicals such as Gibson to use that kind of language.

Bridges, of course, can be approached from both ends and ECONI made it possible—and comfortable—for ecumenists to dialogue with evangelicals as well. Bishop Miller's confession that, 'it [was] much easier to relate to Roman Catholics than to Free Presbyterians' (interview 25 January 2006), highlights the importance of ECONI as the link to pro-peace evangelicals, although a majority among the FPC eventually supported the peace process after their moderator, Ian Paisley, determined it was in the interests of the DUP to join in coalition with SF (on God's supposed instructions to Paisley about dealing with SF see Bruce, 2007). ECONI's then director, David Porter, felt that its work would 'never get acknowledgement from the political world' but that what 'the more liberal, ecumenical side of the church and ECONI did was very significant' (interview 24 September 2007). People never had to look back at the bridges they were burning, as ECONI kept open channels of communication.

A number of small peace organizations have evolved outside the churches in response to specific instances of atrocity—and often not sustained much beyond the memories of it—as well as to espouse a more general and sustained campaign for peace and reconciliation. The former tend to be independent groups organized by local people who want to do something positive in a conflict situation. They face difficulties in sustaining themselves. The Enniskillen Together Peace Group has its origins in the aftermath of the bomb that exploded on Remembrance Day 1987, killing twelve people, but is now not high profile.[16] The Drumcree Faith and Justice Group first came together in response to the violence associated with Orange parades through Catholic areas near Drumcree but is now little known. Families Against Intimidation and Terror (FAIT) was mobilized by a mother after her son's grievous treatment in a punishment beating by the IRA and, for a time, had a very high public profile in monitoring punishment beatings as a form of violence and in leading the public campaign for peace. FAIT was stymied by various allegations against its founders and is now defunct.

---

[16] Eleven died on the day and a twelfth person some thirteen years later, having been in a coma for the intervening period.

There are other peace groups that are not mobilized around a specific atrocity and as a result can sometimes more easily sustain their activities, although not necessarily garner the same popular support. The Peace and Reconciliation Group, Peace Committee, Peace Pledge Ireland Campaign, and Women Together for Peace are good examples. Other examples include Counteract (a trade union-sponsored organization), and the Non-Violent Action Training Project, which seeks to 'explore imaginative, effective and non-violent ways of working in Northern Ireland'. These are, again, little known. Community Dialogue sees its central aim to progress the GFA and has undertaken an initiative to encourage community groups to think through peace issues. It has developed a Community Dialogue Discussion Pack, available to community group leaders in order to assist groups in thinking and talking through Northern Ireland's peace negotiations. These groups face the classic catch-22 problem however, for in lacking the initial spark on which to mobilize arising from an atrocity, they often fail to make a public impression. For our purposes here, however, we will note in passing that the church-based peace groups very rarely linked up with other peace groups in civil society, a theme to which we return in Chapter 4.

ii) Populist peace activities

There have been a number of populist activities that have had a positive effect on the peacebuilding process. For example, many of the peace groups above held public meetings, trying to advance peace by highlighting the plight of all who suffered through sectarian violence, as well as discussing specific contentious issues, such as decommissioning or policing, and holding meetings on the GFA. But populist peace activity was something broader. It was mass public participation in peacemaking events, such as the 'Light A Candle on Christmas Eve' peace campaign, 'Friendship Seats' in parks throughout Northern Ireland, and the 'Stamp Out Sectarianism Roadshows' held in public places such as shopping centres, festivals, and sports arenas. PACE, established in 1968, pursued its peace objectives by means such as drama, carol services, poetry readings, as well as anti-sectarian projects, ecumenical services, and prayer meetings. Media attention focused on Women Together's peace vigils and other symbolic events to challenge sectarian violence. The 'People Moving On' project was the best known of these. Coinciding with a difficult period in the peace negotiations over the GFA, Women Together facilitated the People Moving On initiative, which organized public 'peace witnessing' events to give people everywhere an opportunity to show continuing support for the peace process. This initiative gained substantial media coverage and was recognized widely as crucial in keeping hope alive during a difficult period.

An earlier example of a populist peace initiative that received wide media coverage was the 'Peace Train'. This involved a series of train journeys between Belfast and Dublin in the late 1980s and early 1990s. Church and civil representatives along with members of the public travelled between the two cities in an act of mutual respect for each other's traditions and in a spirit of reconciliation. As the main route to Dublin, the train line was bombed on more than one occasion. Another initiative saw people enjoined to plant a tree in Israel in a unique gesture of peace and reconciliation. It was called the 'Ireland peace and reconciliation forest' and is near Jerusalem. The four main churches in Northern Ireland and the government in the Irish Republic supported it, and its purpose was to reconcile Christians and Jews as well as Christians in the North and South of Ireland. And two daily newspapers, the Catholic-read *Irish News* and the Protestant-read *News Letter* held a joint phone-in petition against violence. There was no dramatic pay-off from populist activities such as this that are traceable to a specific outcome but they kept the idea of peace alive when the violence might otherwise have destroyed hope—they did not offer 'moments of transcendence' (see Brewer, 2010: 138), when fundamental shifts appeared to have occurred (at least when looking back) but they had an incremental effect in popularizing the idea of peace and disseminating its language, allowing others later to buy into peace again.

e) Anti-sectarianism (challenging the conflict and redefining it)

If Christian faith is held strongly enough that believers would die for it, it seems perverse to want to kill for it. However, as the Revd David Armstrong admitted, doctrine has been something a few Northern Irish Christians have been prepared to kill for (interview 2 December 2005). This might be construed as misnaming the nature of the conflict, as one about hermeneutics rather than the legitimacy of the state. However, the religious form that essentially political disputes took in Ireland makes religion matter because it was the modality through which 'the Troubles' were experienced. Thus it is a significant part of religious peacemaking to challenge the *nature* of the conflict by seeking both to name it for what it is—centuries old sectarianism—and to redefine its terms. Sectarianism is the use of denominational boundaries in a political project to enforce social exclusion by one religious group against others (see Brewer, 1992; Brewer and Higgins, 1998). Identifying this as the basis of the conflict is a contribution to peacemaking by disabusing the dominant group of any moral superiority in the conflict and challenging their self-belief that they are uninvolved, despite being beneficiaries of a sectarian social structure. This type of religious peacemaking goes one stage further when it leads on to redefinition of the problem. It becomes a form of peacemaking to subvert the impression that the conflict is absolutist, zero-sum and rooted in identities that are thought of as resistant to social change—and to redefine it, instead, as contingent, dependent upon sociological, historical, and political forces that are fluid and open-ended. In this manner, religious peacemaking involves Protestants and Catholics being encouraged to transcend absolutist sectarian mindsets and identities—and to focus on what unites them.

This is what we mean by anti-sectarianism as a form of religious peacemaking. The churches, in this type, recognize and address the sectarian nature of the conflict, as well as the contribution of religion to sectarian divisions, establish various measures to tackle sectarianism in their own institutions and the wider society, and proffer alternatives to sectarianism as a way of restructuring Protestant Catholic relations. Mainstream Protestant churches were coming to a realization of their shared responsibility for conflict just at the outbreak of 'the Troubles (see Brewer and Higgins, 1998: 116), only for the violence to polarize the communities and put back the process of self-reflection. The Revd Gary Mason recalled years later thinking as a teenager in the early 1990s how slowly the churches came to the realization they needed to address sectarianism, asking 'how has it taken the church twenty plus years into a sectarian conflict to decide to have a working party on sectarianism' (interview 14 February 2006). The persistence of that violence eventually impressed itself upon some progressive churchmen and women to the point where today virtually all the different Christian organizations are involved in anti-sectarian activity of some sort, just as they are in peace. But this can be fairly minimalist. Cecelia Clegg, co-director of ISE's Moving Beyond Sectarianism project, noted the difficulties in getting some Christians to reflect on these issues: 'there were many groups that thought they were achieving things, who had been meeting for years; and I'm sure they did achieve good things. But when we started actually to get them to talk about the issues of sectarianism, it nearly ripped the groups apart' (interview 29 November 2007).

Individual churches and other ecumenical organizations developed a number of specialized Christian anti-sectarian initiatives. For example, Nazarene Compassionate Ministries aimed to address the causes of sectarianism and the problems confronting the poor and powerless. Restoration Ministries does likewise. The Corrymeela Community consistently addressed the issue of sectarianism and amongst other things provided training in anti-sectarianism and produced a booklet for this purpose (Williams and Falconer, 1995). Perhaps the most thorough confrontation with the nature of the conflict was the work done by the FPG. This group represented some of the leading personalities within Irish ecumenism, most being leaders or key figures within peacemaking and reconciliation organizations in Northern Ireland. The group was ahead in its thinking of most Christians in Northern Ireland but always represented a good measure of the ecumenist and peace vision of IICM. It has tackled through position papers all the contentious issues around sectarianism, including in 1993 the roots of sectarianism in Ireland (see FPG, 1993), breaking down enmity, how to handle history, especially contested and divided history, the handling of remembrance and forgiveness (FPG, 1996), and issues such as paramilitary funerals and self-righteous boasting (on which, see FPG, 1989).

In the first of its pamphlets on history (see FPG, 1991), the group tried to place in a new light remembrance of the key events of 1690 (the victory of the Protestant King William over the Catholic King James, dear to Protestants) and 1916 (Dublin Easter Rising by Republicans, dear to Catholics) by helping groups realize what each affair means to others and correcting some of the mythology that surrounds them. Their call for re-remembrance was significantly extended when in 1998 it recognized that the GFA of that year would require a new approach to remembrance and forgetting (FPG, 1998). Showing extraordinary foresight, they argued that building a future for Northern Ireland required that Irish history be reckoned with—rather than having a line drawn underneath it (1998: 3)—by recovering certain memories, and forgetting or re-remembering others. In *Transitions* (FPG, 2001) it addressed itself to the issue of identity in a non-sectarian and peaceful Northern Ireland.

The COI had its Hard Gospel project intended to confront the issue of sectarianism, directed by the Revd Earl Storey. It represented a practical, active form of peacemaking amongst young people. Speechifying was not enough for Storey: 'In a sense if that is all the church can do about sectarianism or dealing with difference—to a drowning person [just] describe the water—well that is not enough. [The] churches' contribution has got to be much more incisive, much more proactive than just condemnation' (interview 21 September 2005). ISE also completed a six-year project called Moving Beyond Sectarianism, which resulted in a book (Liechty and Clegg, 2001; for some of Liechty's earlier work on anti-sectarianism, see Liechty, 1993), as well as two resource packs and materials geared separately towards groups of adults and young people to use as prompts to their own rethinking of the nature of the conflict. This was the central significance of the project, for it fed directly into the practical peacemaking of organizations, churches, community groups, and other civil society bodies who used the resources, material, and training courses in their own setting. This empowered participants to seek alternatives to the narrow mindsets and identities of the past. Workshops on identity or anti-sectarianism, for example, taught people the skills to help them assist others in the local community to move on beyond sectarianism.

Of course, a large number of secular organizations were also involved in anti-sectarian work, such as those working in local government, integrated education, or in anti-racist, mixed marriage, and trade union settings, all of whom developed anti-sectarian policies and practices (on the development of non-sectarian social work, see Brewer, 1991; for the anti-sectarian policies and practices of the child-centred organization Playboard, see Playboard, 1990;

Brewer, Bishop, and Higgins, 2001: 46). Where these organizations had Christian input, and many did not, it was incidental—most of the Executive Board of the integrated education pressure group All Children Together at one time were Christian, but this did not affect its operation—and there were no formal attempts to link what was going on in the churches with these related developments elsewhere in civil society.

Republican politicians, however, were positive in their assessment of the churches' work on anti-sectarianism. And not just because this was consistent with the way SF wanted to present the conflict as the political problem of the British in Ireland; they learned from clergymen and women something of what Britishness meant to Protestants. Jim Gibney, ex-Republican prisoner and now a leading peace activist, recalled the impact of his early discussions with the Presbyterian minister Jack Weir:

> I remember Tom Hartley and myself speaking to Jack Weir and the group around him and we asked them 'What is it, can you define for us your British-ness? What does it mean to be British in Ireland?' Jack Weir, I think probably for me, gave what I consider to be maybe the clearest exposition of it at that time. He said 'look, being British on this island for us is more than just carrying a British passport, in the same way that being Irish for you is more than carrying an Irish passport. We have lived on the island for close on 400, 500 years; we are part of its cultural identity, its history [and] all of that stuff'. He crystallized it in a way for us in terms of understanding. And he said after 1916, there was only one set of heroes on the island and that was those who went out to fight for their own defence. The people who came back from the First World War, Protestant and Catholic and he said in towns right across the southern part of the island, people died in the First World War and the state ignored them. What happened after partition was that, the historical facts of this is another matter, but this was [what] Jack Weir on that particular day [was] saying to us. 'Look the Protestant community in the southern part of the island were ignored by the state. Those who fought in 1916 were elevated into heroes. In the Northern part of the state, those who fought and died in Flanders in 1916 were considered heroes.' So he said there was a mirror image of prejudice, or whatever, but he always said that Protestants on the island wanted to play a part on the island. He was an island man. (Interview 3 September 2008)

The Revd Harold Good, one time President of Irish Methodism, agreed about the priority to facilitate common understanding of the conflict. 'The big gap, the big gap', he said in interview, 'was the Protestant community and the Republican community. That is, the Republican community needed to discover that the Unionist community and the Protestant community weren't necessary always the same thing. That was the big discovery for them. They had to discover that the people they needed to do business with were people from within the Protestant-Unionist community, and those were things that we [the Protestant churches] needed to help them [with]' (24 January 2006).

f) Dealing with the problems of post-violence (assisting with post-conflict adjustment)

Peacemaking does not stop with the signing of the peace agreement. The new structures and institutions established as part of the political peace process need help to be embedded and the social peace process only really starts with the accord as societal healing and social repair start apace, with the opportunities opened up by the ending of violence. Negative peace (conflict transformation) needs to be replaced by positive peace (social transformation). Making the transition from a society racked by violence to post-violence is never easy, as South Africa and Latin American countries show. The legacy of bitterness, hurt, and anger is literally a dead weight; and the memories of atrocity, and the grief and pain just add to its pull. Post-violence societies therefore face acute problems associated with history, memory, remembrance, and victimhood. Ways have to be found in which people's personal plight—the memories of loved ones, the empty chair at the dining table, the constraint of the wheelchair, the experience of intimidation, harassment, and atrocity—are recognized, validated, and commemorated while encouraging society as a whole to move forwards. Past protagonists need to be wedded to the peace of the future, ex-prisoners need to be socially re-integrated, the guns silenced, and the wounds healed. Questions of fairness, justice, equality, and social redistribution have to be raised and ways found to change society so that it meets these policy injunctions. Without citizens developing senses of fairness and justice, and experiencing a real improvement in their well-being, peace will not flourish. The moral landscape of post-conflict societies needs to change, as do their systems for allocating distributive justice and equality of opportunity. Dealing with the problems of post-violence is therefore an important peacemaking category: as we wrote earlier, what people do *after* the signing of a peace accord is as important as what they did to help bring it about.

There are various dimensions against which peacemaking efforts can be measured in the post-conflict phase. Attempts to help reshape the moral landscape, for example, are critical in consolidating the social peace process, as reflected in debates about trust, empathy, hope, forgiveness, justice, compromise, and compassion as virtues appropriate for societal healing. Policies with respect to recognition of victims are another measure of post-conflict peacemaking, as is debate about remembrance and new forms of memory work. Practical help for victims and others in the way they think about and recall the conflict must sit alongside other forms of practical help with the legacy of medical and emotional trauma. Historical re-envisioning of the future—the way the past is understood to speak to the future—has to be encouraged as much as social policies that implement an equality agenda, improve people's life chances, and enhance their well-being. All these things are part of the ongoing social peace process and carry on years after the signing of the political accord. Failure to tackle them leaves the political peace process fragile, since institutional reforms remain unstable unless implanted in new social relationships, societal healing, and social repair.

These things are the responsibility of the state, civil society, and the grass roots, and, clearly, some are more relevant to the churches than others. But if the churches are genuinely to garner and disseminate spiritual capital as a form of moral economy, they have to be active in Northern Ireland's civil sphere in the post-conflict period, mobilizing Christians to make the leap of trust into the future so that they can then bear witness to others in their own healing. The churches thus have to be active as institutions and as individual believers in working alongside victims and others in promulgating the new moral landscape and in providing practical assistance. Spiritual capital also requires the churches to utilize the civil sphere in two ways: first, to address publicly issues within their provenance, on forgiveness, remembrance, justice, hope, compromise, victimhood, and personal and societal healing; and, second, as institutions, church leaders, and ordinary believers to campaign for public policies that institutionalize social transformation, such as those policies dealing with transitional justice (for victims and ex-prisoners), housing, employment, education, and racial and ethnic tolerance—the nuts and bolts by which equality, justice, and fairness are worked out for Christians.

The churches' contribution to this phase of the social peace process is poor. The COI held a series of public lectures on forgiveness and brokenness in 1996 in St Anne's Cathedral, producing an informative booklet (COI, 1996) and ECONI published a series of fifteen reflections on forgiveness. Lecture series by ECONI, ISE, and other ecumenical organizations invariably raised these sorts of issues. ECONI's courses under the rubric 'Journey into Understanding' offer an excellent example. These courses involved cross-community contact designed to promote reflection on the future needs of people living together after 'the Troubles', and deal with issues such as identity, sectarianism, and divided history. This was the strength of the ecumenists, they were not afraid to deal with difficult issues; their weakness was that they attracted audiences only of other ecumenists. The mainstream churches, Protestant and Catholic, have treated them as pastoral concerns to be dealt with inside congregations as part of their healing ministry. As institutions, the churches have evacuated the civil sphere and are not raising openly the sorts of concerns that transform their members' private troubles into public issues.

Individual churchmen and women have been publicly active in some arenas. The Revd Harold Good and Fr Alec Reid were used by the British government to witness acts of decommissioning and to stand over this momentarily very problematic part of the GFA. More than half the members of the Consultative Group on the Past were Christian, the body headed by former Archbishop Eames and former priest Denis Bradley, for ever associating the question of remembrance of the conflict with the churches; and as if to epitomize its marginalization, the government and local politicians rejected its key recommendation on reparations. Victim issues, truth recovery, and transitional justice matters, however, are not dealt with by the churches. Church-led public debates about forgiveness have closed and those on themes such as hope, compromise, and trust, never started. The churches expertise in moral matters remains fixed on time-old questions of sexual morality, making it unequipped to address the needs for a more general reconfiguration of the moral landscape for societies coming out of violence. Northern Ireland might have changed as a result of the political peace process, but it also remains very much the same when it comes to this part of the social peace process.

This is with the exception of transitional justice matters. Daniel Philpott (2006, 2007a, 2007b) has noted the potential contribution of religion to the politics of transitional justice. More than forty transitions from authoritarian rule to democracy have occurred since 1974 and with them the problem of how to deal with the past. Transitional justice has encouraged the re-enchantment of our discourse. The Christian ethos of South Africa's Truth and Reconciliation Commission (on which, see Shore, 2009), the writings of theologians on the concept of political forgiveness (Shriver, 1995), the contribution of Christian social scientists to the idea of healing between nations (Amstutz, 2004), the search for the spiritual roots of restorative justice (Hadley, 2001), the placing of discussions of hope within the messianic Christian tradition (Desroche, 1979), and the overt references to Christian love as the pillar on which to rest the management of emotions after violence (Ure, 2008) all reflect this potential. Philpott's equation of transitional justice with reconciliation (2007b: 100) and the judgement that Christians have offered the majority of arguments for political reconciliation (2007b: 97), assist him in taking this view about the primacy of religion, although transitional justice is a field in civil society dominated by liberal human rights groups that are normally inimical to religion. The number of truth commissions managed by the churches is remarkable, although human rights advocates might point to the fact that the churches did so in societies where civil society was so squeezed by repressive regimes that they were the last part left standing, such as in apartheid South Africa and especially Latin America.

The churches' contribution to transitional justice in Northern Ireland was not through advocacy of truth recovery procedures, nor the development of a practical theology of peace, but restorative justice. Their contribution here was substantial. Philpott (2007b: 105) was puzzled by the churches' failure in Northern Ireland to push for truth commissions; the other instance is El Salvador. He blames the British government's resistance to the idea of a truth commission (2007b: 106). The answer is much simpler: they were busy elsewhere in the transitional justice field. Their work with prisoners has already been noted as part of pastoral ministry and this was easily extended in the post-conflict stage to restorative justice. More important for this focus, however, was the tendency in Northern Ireland for prisoners to undergo a religious conversion in prison and to emerge outside as key religious resources working amongst erstwhile colleagues.[17] The LINC Resource Centre and Restorative Justice Ministries are examples of two Christian-based organizations formed from amongst former combatants that address ex-prisoner issues. When interviewed for the Maryknoll research, the director of LINC said that the personal experiences he had as an ex-prisoner were important in his work but so was his faith: 'I became a peace builder because I am a Christian' (cited in Brewer, Bishop and Higgins, 2001: 49). Jim and Ann-Marie McKinley's Pax Works was another example, premised on Jim's experiences as a former UVF prisoner; and while Pax Works was short-lived, Jim McKinley remained working in restorative justice. Many ex-prisoners in Northern Ireland left with educational qualifications earned inside prison, reducing the impact of economic marginalization once released, and many work in local community development groups and associations active in the social peace process. Jean-Paul Lederach calls ex-prison peace activists 'insider partials' (1997), and this type of person features strongly in peacemaking, in having pasts that make them specially suited to developing rapport with militants that assisted in conflict transformation. Paradoxically, some liberal Protestant churchmen and women had problems in relating to this kind of peace activist because of their prison background, but, ironically, not the evangelicals if their conversion was accompanied by being 'born again'. Transitional justice aside, however, the churches have not developed a post-conflict role and spiritual capital is absent, a theme to which we return in later chapters.

CONCLUSION

Peacemaking is a many-faceted skill. In the social peace process it is done in various ways and consists of many things. Some Christian groups and churches developed clear aims and objectives for peace and earned success in developing local initiatives and activities for societal healing, relationship

---

[17] The cliché that Republican prisoners came out with degrees while Loyalists with pill-induced bodybuilding muscles, has an element of truth to it, as do all clichés. On the basis of his prison visits Bishop Daly commented on this in interview: 'the contrast between the Provo [IRA] and Loyalist wings was quite incredible. The Provos were all studying politics and sociology and the Loyalists were doing weightlifting and helping to tattoo each other. One was looking after body and one was looking after the mind. It was quite a contrast' (24 January 2006). On the other hand, the marked tendency towards religious conversion inside prison was overwhelmingly a Protestant trait. Not all conversions are to evangelicalism, despite the attractiveness to prisoners of being 'born again'; many conversions were to ecumenism.

building, and social repair. It is almost impossible to trace these to specific outcomes, except in the most direct of cases such as the hunger strikes and Holy Cross, but they helped maintain in the midst of violence those 'islands of civility' or 'zones of peace' (Kaldor, 1999: 138) that kept alive the hope of better things, and which proved effective spaces where peacemakers could ply their skills beside the 'zones of war'. It is also clear, however, that peacemaking was not the preserve of the churches and para-church organizations, and although a large number of Christians worked for secular organizations, the ethos of such groups remained non-religious.

Christians dominated some forms of peacemaking within our analytical framework more than others. The churches were very successful in relationship-building in sacred spaces in the form of ecumenism, although more so within specialist settings than mainstream churches. While on the one hand this kind of religious peacework has been unwarrantedly valorized by advocates who overlook its conservatism and exclusivity in restricting itself to its own, conversely, attempts to deride this sort of work as excessively 'holy' and spiritual misunderstand the importance of its new forms of ritual and behaviour as emblematic of wider change. One can put it no stronger than that, for while ecumenists were active in cross-community work, as sacred and secular spaces elided, the 'proper relations' that ecumenism saw as its purposes never spread beyond its constituency of like-minded people in inter-church settings. 'Right' relationships were never accomplished within the wider space of secular society, at least not by the churches. It has been argued that the churches succeeded in the broader community because their ecumenism migrated into community relations, but it is hard to sustain the argument that good community relations were achieved prior to the political process—being the outcome, if at all, of the GFA not its cause—or that the churches were responsible for this, separate from the array of secular bodies with vastly more money and skills working in the community relations field. 'Proper' relations remained 'wrong' in another sense. While the churches were active in promoting anti-sectarianism at the level of church policy, it still remained a challenge to the main churches to address the sectarian attitudes of some in their congregations. The serious challenges to sectarianism were mounted by the para-church organizations and ecumenical groups marginalized within the mainstream. And the churches have neglected the wealth of problems faced in the post-conflict phase, being less active now in the public sphere than during the violence. Their failure to recognize that peace processes do not come to an end with political concordats, and that the social peace process is an ongoing project of societal healing in which they have to continue to play a major part, is unchristian. We need to return later to the question of what this means for the efficacy of spiritual capital in settings where religion is wrapped up in the conflict.

On the other hand, the churches did sterling work in conflict mediation and prevention in the social peace process, developing excellent relations locally that enabled them to intervene in neighbourhood disputes and to dialogue efficaciously with Republican paramilitary groups. These relations were mobilized effectively in the social and political peace processes and can be said without hesitation to have helped change the mindsets of the militants. Loyalists' assessments of the churches are more malign, especially of the Protestant mainstream churches, and, ironically, the Protestant churches were more ambivalent about working with Loyalists than with Republicans. Religion worked its effect on Loyalist prisoners more by religious conversions than pastoral witness by their clergy. Contrary to some suggestions, the Northern Irish churches excelled in transitional justice, nearly as much so as in ecumenism, especially in their work with prisoners, inside jail and on release. It is also clear, however, that as institutions the churches made less advances in peacemaking than did organizations working separately from the mainstream churches or did individuals working locally with ambiguous institutional support.

This raises questions about the role of church leadership, the contrast between official and unofficial interventions by the churches, and the level of constraint the churches felt under as institutions to support the peace process, which we address in Chapters 3 and 4. Before this, however, we should complete consideration of our typology by examining the churches' contribution to the political peace process. Given the valorization of ecumenism in the literature on the Northern Irish peace process, and the universal view of commentators that the churches had little impact on the politics of the peace process, our arguments in the next chapter will be surprising to most, for backchannel political communication was the churches' single most effective achievement.

2

Contributions to the Political Peace Process

INTRODUCTION

The churches' expertise is primarily in the social peace process. But the historic elision of theology and politics in the Irish conflict, going back to the seventeenth-century Plantation and beyond (see Brewer and Higgins, 1998; Brewer, 2003d), always gave the churches a political role. Politics from the pulpit was mostly subtle, but at key tipping points in Irish history the churches made their political preferences abundantly clear and were overt in their political campaigning. Outside these periods of political storm, however, the churches rowed quietly, confidently in the direction of one ethno-national tradition or the other in Northern Ireland's political seascape, resolutely Unionist or Nationalist, eliding Protestantism and Catholicism with opposite political interests in the zero-sum portrayal of people's political loyalties. Religion was a principal cultural resource in the construction of two mutually exclusive identities, reproduced seamlessly in religiously segregated schools, religiously divided neighbourhoods, and separate friendship networks and marriages, amongst other things. The social reproduction of sectarian divisions was so taken-for-granted and such a routine part of broader cultural reproduction that the politicization of religion was disguised and the churches appeared, at least in times of normality, as politically aloof.

It is not paradoxical, therefore, that the churches saw themselves as above the clamour of party politics. In 1981, Cahal Daly, then Bishop of Down and Connor, in evidence to the New Ireland Forum,[1] said: 'the Catholic Church in Ireland totally rejects the concept of a confessional state. We have not sought

---

[1] The Forum was established in Dublin in May 1981on the initiative of John Hume, leader of the SDLP, to give politicians in the Irish Republic an opportunity for a wide debate on the Irish question and Northern Ireland's constitutional position. Its membership was dominated by Southern Irish politicians and the SDLP. It held eleven public meetings, at which various oral submissions were given. It later published a report (see Kenny, 1986). A delegation from the Irish Episcopal Conference appeared before it, headed by Cahal Daly. Needless to say, Unionist politicians berated what they alleged was the disastrous influence of the Catholic Church on Southern Irish politics (Kenny: 1986: 57ff).

and we do not seek a Catholic State for a Catholic people. We believe that the alliance of church and state is harmful'; and when asked by a Forum member why, if divorce could be permitted in a thirty-two county Ireland, as part of the separation of church and state, it could not also in a twenty-six county Ireland, replied 'that is a political question which is not appropriate for us to answer' (cited in Kenny, 1986: 40). Daly's views had not changed years later when we interviewed him on 24 February 2006: 'The church is not involved in politics and it's very dangerous for the church to be seen as if it were in [a] political party or a pressure group or whatever. The church encourages its members to work for peace but the work of peace is a complicated issue, it requires a great deal of skills, which are not necessarily the skills of a pastor of souls. If asked to craft a blueprint for a future without violence—that is not the pastor's role'.[2]

Supposedly existing separate from the political realm, leaving to Caesar that which is his, the mainline churches were shocked at exceptions such as the FPC and its umbilical links to the DUP. Paisley was seen as vulgar in his extremism. The flip side of this desire to distance themselves from Paisley was that the moderate church leaders ostracized him, failing, in Dawn Purvis's words, 'to take Paisley on theologically' (interview 11 September 2007). She described this as 'the biggest mistake' of the churches. As a Methodist and former head of Edgehill Theological College in Belfast, Dennis Cooke's biography (1996) came closest to doing this. It was left to para-church organizations such as ECONI to challenge Paisley directly as evangelicals (as we explore later). Throughout the course of one interview, a leading ecumenist could not even speak Paisley's name, referring to him continually as 'that certain gentleman', and another senior member of the ecumenical wing of the PCI explained that whenever they met, Paisley would always tell him he was going to hell, offering him the opportunity of personal salvation there and then, 'an embarrassingly stupid thing for a public figure to be doing'.

Yet for all this criticism of Paisley, when push came to shove in stormy times, the mainstream churches took equally clear positions on the Union. They saw themselves as party-neutral yet they reinforced sectarian political identities by their constitutional preferences. There was no clamorous political evocation of peace, save from the very small Methodist Church, liberal wings of the mainstream Protestant churches, and the marginalized and largely unpopular ecumenical movement; mainstream churches could minimally agree to condemn terrorism but wider political differences negated any greater agreement on the political solution to Northern Ireland's conflict.

---

[2] Cahal Daly did get very heavily involved with the campaign to free the Birmingham Six. This was because he genuinely thought they were innocent, as British law courts eventually showed them to be. In his interview with us, he often mentioned Billy Power (one of the six) as being a devoutly Christian man. He refused to get involved in anything else, including notorious aspects of the 'dirty war', such as the shoot-to-kill policy, the Stalker Affair, supergrasses, Diplock Courts and the rest.

The worsening violence, climaxing in the early 1990s in some horrendous atrocities, ought to have forced a political response from the churches, but, conscious of their political differences, the aim amongst the leadership of the mainstream churches remained as it was in the early 1970s (on this time period see Taggart, 2004), to get along with each other in good interpersonal relations by avoiding political offence as far as was intentionally possible, leaving undisturbed the constitutional backdrop against which they befriended each other. The point that is most relevant for our purposes, however, is *not* that this interpersonal agreement to desensitize politics disguised widely understood political preferences, but that the largely unspoken consensus amongst mainstream church leaders had implications for religious peacemaking. An avowal of negative peace, the almost universal call for the ending of killings, was comfortable common ground that allowed political differences over the solution to 'the Troubles' to remain, without threatening their good interpersonal relations or undermining their self-perception that they were above the fray of party politics.

Positive peace, however, is a more problematic entity altogether. This required the churches to make political pronouncements and take campaigning positions on issues such as human rights abuses, unemployment and inequality, housing and poverty, and the elimination of sectarianism and abolition of election gerrymandering, thus potentially undermining the consensus amongst the church leaders to avoid overt politics. The churches resisted the temptation to make political issues of these matters, maintaining their consensus to desensitize politics—hence the dissatisfaction of most political and civil society activists at the silence of the churches on these sorts of issues. There was also dissatisfaction from proponents of the social gospel. Despite Methodism's strong social emphasis, the Revd Gary Mason felt obliged to argue:

> I think anybody as a Christian who says they are not involved in politics, then, I would want to say they are rather lopsided in their Christian faith; and I am not talking about political parties, I am talking about engagement with politics because politics is life. Unemployment is a political issue, homelessness is a political issue, what youth do is a political issue. I think of Jesus engaging with society. I would challenge a lot of Christian churches that they are not, they are basically salt depositories; they are not salt dispensers. I would be saying strongly that the church has got to be a salt dispenser. You have got to dispense the salt of Christian faith into the street. I mean the purpose of salt is to purify society, one of the reasons society is the way it is, I would say is because Christians hide behind fortress doors, have their lovely little worship service on the Sunday morning, tuck their Christian faith into their top pocket until next Sunday. There is no meaningful engagement with society. (Interview 14 February 2006)

The Catholic Church's position on the hunger strike, for example, is a good demonstration of how the hierarchy tried to balance twin pressures—from the Catholic community worldwide to respond to the demands of the prisoners and from the internal alliance of religious leaders that they not overturn the consensus and become overtly political; a position they managed by treating the strike as a pastoral issue that required ministering to the prisoners and their families to get them to desist. While this ended up being consistent with the British government's stance, the Catholic Church did not cave in to Margaret Thatcher's hardline stand against the prisoners, for behind the scenes the Catholic Church and its representatives were energetically trying to bring a political solution. The little publicized efforts of Archbishop Eames to promote a Loyalist ceasefire in 1994 as part of the Irish and British governments' negotiations over a political settlement offer the same example within the Anglican tradition.

Cautionary political statements in public, matched by frenetic activity in private, was a strategy that the churches on all sides adopted to deal with the tension between maintaining peace commitments and the interpersonal obligations of the religious consensus to desensitize politics. This means that the distinction between official and unofficial, and public and private, peacemaking becomes critical to understanding the contribution of the churches to Northern Ireland's political peace process, as we shall see in Chapter 3. To allege that religious people do one thing in public and another in private, or permit unofficially activities that cannot be owned up to officially, is mostly meant as a criticism intended to render them powerless by hypocrisy (a strategy that is understandable). This is not our intention.

Societies where politics has become violent require one or both of two things of the churches' peacemaking: overt intervention in politics to implement political change as a way of ending violence; and the desensitization of politics as a way to break the spiral of politically motivated violence. There are occasions where there is little moral ambiguity surrounding political violence, when the moral high ground is clearly claimed and the violence is made easier to justify and one set of perpetrators is lionized, such that overt political interventions by the churches are popular. The political role of the Polish Catholic Church in supporting Solidarity in its action against the communist government (see Herbert, 2003: 197–228) or the support of opposition churches—as well as some elements of the DRC—in the anti-apartheid movement in South Africa (Protzesky, 1990; Shore, 2009) come to mind as examples. In Northern Ireland's case, however, the morality of the armed struggle was always contested. The solution was thus to avoid adding to the intensity of political conflagration by limiting overt political interventions and resisting potentially damaging political statements, thereby permitting certain peacemaking activities to take place unofficially or in private so that they could be denied if public revelation made them problematic for the churches.

Two contributions to the political peace process, therefore, need to be distinguished: a) the churches as backchannels of communication (provision of 'safe' private political spaces); b) churches' participation in negotiations over the GFA and its iterations and contributions to selling the deals (the churches' public political role). These elements form the last part of our typology of active peacemaking and focus the discussion in this chapter. The backdrop to our argument is the common perception in the literature on Northern Ireland's political peace process that the churches were minimally involved and marginal. This view can be sustained only if we neglect their use as backchannels. Those commentators who point to an indirect political role for the churches have this hidden set of activities in mind. By bringing to public attention the role of the churches as backchannels of communication we are able to correct the misapprehension that they were minor actors in the political peace process. We begin, however, by expanding on the issue of church leadership and the consensus amongst mainstream churches to desensitize politics.

POLITICS AND CHURCH LEADERSHIP

The Revd Harold Good, himself a former president of Irish Methodism, reflected on his father's experience as president before him, commenting on the failure of an earlier generation of church leaders to act in concert (see Vignette 7). At the time of the last phase of 'the Troubles' such inaction was impossible to contemplate. However, while a leap forwards was taken by the leaders agreeing to form a group, the stride was not huge. In his positive assessment of the contribution of ecumenism to the peace process, Appleby (2000: 236–7) misses the mark again when he describes the 'highest official' leadership of the mainstream churches—'and other churches'—as encouraging peacemaking efforts, criticizing their belligerent co-religionists and fostering joint social and economic activities to elicit cross-community cooperation and build trust between erstwhile antagonists. Good's comments rue the smallness of the steps taken. It is also worth reminding ourselves of Archbishop Eames's comment in interview that the church leadership talked a lot but were in the end irrelevant because real progress is built on local actors coming together (29 January 2008). The demonstration of togetherness was itself useful, although it marginalized the scores of smaller churches excluded from the consensus, but many political and civil society activists agreed with Eames about leaders' lack of practical impact on the ground, especially, as Roy Garland said, in working-class areas where people tended not to go to church (interview 13 September 2005). Locally active clergy, disappointed at the lack of thrust from their leaders, were in accord. As the Revd Norman Hamilton

---

Vignette 7: Extracts from the Revd Harold Good's interview, 25 September 2007

God forgive us for our lack of leadership. Let me go back in years, my father was the President of the Methodist Church in 1958, 1959 and that was [time of] the IRA border campaign. He was in Enniskillen at that time and I can remember, one of the first policemen to be killed belonged to his congregation and he felt it very deeply, very, very deeply. I have correspondence there which bears that out, but within his papers when he died I found three letters which I found very interesting, one was from the Church of Ireland Primate of the day and one was from the Roman Catholic Cardinal of the day and one was from the Presbyterian Moderator of the day. In those days there were no church leaders' meeting like there is now between the four main churches. His letter to them must have been saying perhaps the time has come when we should meet and see what we should say or do about what is happening in our land as leaders. Each of the three letters I have got are saying in one way or another 'thank you for your letter, it's a nice idea but the time is not right'. Now, I believe it would have made an amazing difference to this period of conflict if back in those days those four church leaders had grasped their responsibility as leaders and had stood together and had refused to deviate from the position of strength that they had, which was much more significant than it would be today.

---

said when referring to the potential role of church leaders in persuading political agreements in these sorts of areas, 'if you want some of this sold to the Loyalist community don't bank on the church leaders being the ones to sell it' (interview 26 January 2006). David Porter, himself heavily involved in the political peace process, but as Director of ECONI at the time excluded from the church leadership consensus, responded irritably to the 'myth', as he put it, 'that the senior church people did nothing, that they reiterated all their regular statements and all the rest of it' (interview 27 February 2006), going on to point to his own involvement and the much earlier behind-the-scenes work of people such as Jack Weir and Eric Gallagher. Much depends here on what is meant by leadership and who are considered leaders inside the consensus. We have in mind the hierarchy within the four mainstream churches, our point being to highlight the disconnection between church leaders and those they led, and the contrast between national and local level religious efforts in the political peace process. Porter is right that the main leaders did more than they are credited with; our argument is that they tended towards particular kinds of things in the political peace process that preserved the public consensus to avoid politics.

It is normally understood that the consensus began in 1969 with the Irish Council of Churches (Power, 2007: 17), when it encouraged leaders of the Protestant churches to write to Cardinal Conway for meetings to develop 'a better understanding of each other's position and where possible joint action' (cited in Power, 2007: 17), from which followed the Ad Hoc Committee (known also as the Heads of Churches' Consultative Committee, amongst others, see Power, 2007: 226 fn 34). Looking back as a young minister at the time, Harold Good thought the leaders had been rather shamed into establishing consultation as a result of Ulster Television hosting a live debate between them, 'much too late, much too late' he said (interview 24 January 2006). The leaders quickly displayed a willingness to avoid controversy. We do not mean withdrawal from engagement with the conflict—the leaders established their Joint Group on Social Questions in 1970 and the Working Party on Violence in Ireland in 1973—but avoidance of politics. Statements on the violence were nervously formulated to avoid giving offence to each other. Indeed, IICM, as one medium for consultation, had the policy of wanting first to resolve theological questions as a way of establishing good relationships between the churches. Even as late as 1985, the IICM was writing that the 'Irish problem' was too complex and that inter-church dialogue could not be expected to solve it or end violence (cited in Power, 2007: 33). They expressed the hope, however, that the coming together of the church leaders to think and pray would remedy the problem. The IICM's two departments—theology and social issues—eschewed politics and it earned the reputation of being 'only a talking shop, talking around in circles about things of no great interest', according to the Revd Norman McAuley (quoted in Power, 2007: 37). Hence the Jesuit priest Fr Brian Lennon criticized the narrowness of leaders' notions of consultation for neglecting 'social and political justice issues' (quoted in Power, 2007: 51).

There was a political lesson intended here, where close personal relations between the leaders would be the model for political compromise and reconciliation, but without the mention of politics. And relations between them were good; and some clergy felt the model actually worked. David Porter again: '[it] set the tone and context whereby liberal Unionism was able to engage with Nationalists and Republicans, so you had a religious movement first, an ecumenical world, followed by a liberal political movement' (interview 24 September 2007). Personal relations underwrote this. To the Clonard priest Fr Egan, the churches' contribution to the political peace process was the result 'very much because of the leadership, the friendship, inspirational men who had the courage of their conviction' (interview 22 November 2007). Porter referred to the 'qualitative difference of something that happened' as a result of the good personal relations developed by leaders, which percolated down to the next generation of torchbearers and improved their dialogue in the political peace process.

> The older clergy, out of the Clonard talks, along with the Republican leadership, they had a relationship, they could phone each other. It seems to me that there

was a younger generation of us, like Lesley Carroll and myself, the relationship that we built up with the Republican movement was more akin to a friendship that was more peer to peer than leader to leader. I think that [this] added value to what had been built by the leaders, something happened underneath that was more organic, more relational. (Interview 27 February 2006)

The older generation of senior church leaders were, however, risk averse. Risk taking, of course, is not a common feature of any form of leadership in divided societies (Gormley-Heenan and Robinson, 2003: 260), except by those who make all the difference, because of fear of weakening their position—fear of finding themselves too far ahead of the people on whose continued support their leadership is built. Conflict situations where leadership is strong on one side but weak on the other are more irresolvable because the weaker leaders can deliver less, precisely because of their weakness (Rothstein, 1999). However, it has also been noted that the transformation of conflict is directly linked to the transformation of the actors involved (Nordlinger, 1972). The close personal relations between the senior leaders in the mainline churches, most of them in strong positions within their respective churches, was a transformation in itself, which, according to people such as David Porter, was inspirational for changing wider relations some time later.

But three caveats need to be stressed here. First, the Moderator of the PCI was always in a weaker position because of the annual switch between conservative and liberal wings. Not only did this disrupt continuity of personal relationships, but the extent to which any particular moderator could break through the consensus was constrained by the broad constituencies they were expected to represent. The change in moderator concealed a bigger problem, however. The constituencies inside the PCI were, to use the words of an 'insider' who wished to remain anonymous, 'always warring'. The PCI Moderator was, in Rothstein's terms, the weaker of the leaders unable to make concessions in fear of causing mayhem in the presbyteries. Hence Ganiel's observation (2008a: 52) that liberal Presbyterians continually faced *religiously* motivated opposition to their peacemaking. This is one of the chief reasons why the PCI was always the most ambivalent of the mainstream churches towards involvement in the peace process—it was the one most racked by internal division, lacking a strong leader with a position of near perpetuity who could either stamp a direction on the church, such as the Catholic Church, or do the high-profile political brokering themselves, the option of the Anglicans. The second caveat to stress is that the other senior leaders, in searching for consensus, were always pulled back to the minimalist position, being unwilling to isolate the intransigent or reluctant leaders amongst them. They never criticized each other in public, nor spoke against each other. If the leaders were to be a model for political compromise, unity was the key. And they had enough foils around them—Paisley, the paramilitaries—to focus their ire in unison. Third, it was critical to their ability to deliver that they remained strong leaders, located squarely in the mainstream of their respective religious and political communities even if they themselves were ahead as a vanguard. This meant they had to give the appearance of being behind their constituency, leading from the back, while searching for ways in which they might stretch their constituency from a position out in front. John Dunlop, a former PCI Moderator, expressed it thus:

> One of the challenges which faces anybody in the church is being able to do the things that you think need to be done, to say the things that need to be said, without losing contact with the people that you are trying to talk to on either side and particularly on your own side. You can't get so far ahead that you lose contact with your own people or you lose credibility with your own people. And yet at the same time, you feel an obligation to move across some of these divisions and to do things constructively. (Interview 23 March 2006)

Gormley-Heenan and Robinson (2003: 268) refer to this style as 'elastic band leadership', and while they had Northern Ireland's political leaders in mind, it applies well to church hierarchies (see Fitzduff, 2010: 22–3), taking followers forwards but not so far that the elastic breaks. Appleby's positive portrayal overlooks leaders' inherent caution and conservatism, eager to move things along but without—to use another metaphor—cutting free the anchors that bound them firmly to their ethno-religious constituencies, so they went only as far as the chain would drag.

However, 'elastic band leadership' offers only one characterization. 'Leash leadership' was just as prevalent. By this we mean the desire amongst leaders to keep on a very tight leash what they saw as the potentially damaging forms of mass populist action loitering just beneath the surface. Desensitizing politics not only required stretching the boundaries in moderation, it required that the potential for political disruption be reined in. This was hard enough for the churches to do even within their own institutions. For example, in the aftermath of Bloody Sunday in 1972 many Catholic clerics were to the fore in expressing vociferous community outrage, while after the signing of the Anglo-Irish Agreement (AIA) in 1985 many Protestant clerics joined in expressing the anger, taking part in rallies, waving gun certificates, and leading prayer services for deliverance. Fr Denis Faul, an ardent critic of the British and often silenced by the Catholic hierarchy, was generous enough to admit that the Catholic Church often did not speak out 'because they were afraid of splitting the parish, that it [speaking out] would make life impossible for us. They wouldn't go to Mass and they'd stand outside the church shouting and roaring' (interview 23 January 2006). 'The instinct of the leaders of the church', he said, was 'the terrible fear of the whole thing becoming sectarian. The church is in a very delicate position and they had to try always to restrain people'. Incapable of realizing that the violence was already sectarian, the

Catholic Church feared inflaming support for the IRA, likewise Protestant leaders for Paisleyism (rather than for Loyalist paramilitaries). With respect to the latter, the COI clergyman Charles Kenny observed that leaders, 'especially Presbyterians' were 'terrified of the Paisleyites' (interview 14 September 2005).

Conscious of the significance of his words and determined to be fair, Albert Reynolds reflected on his experience of church leadership when Irish Taoiseach, 'well, it's a hard one to call because the community was so divided as I saw it in the North of Ireland, that both sides probably were conscious, it's not for me, it's only an outside judgement, but they were conscious of the hatred that was inbuilt in some areas. They didn't want to aggravate an already aggravated situation between the communities up there' (interview 21 March 2006). A good illustration is provided by Cardinal Conway's response to the knowledge that in the early years of 'the Troubles' Republican internees and prisoners were being tortured by the British. Fr Denis Faul picks up the story. 'Cardinal Conway was told about the torture, he could have got into the pulpit and blazed about it and everyone would have joined the IRA and there would have been all-out sectarianism. He didn't. He went to see Mr Heath [British prime minister] and he also notified the Archbishop of New York; he spoke about it. Cardinal Conway wouldn't do it himself, rightly so. The IRA would have grabbed the opportunity to recruit a whole lot of people' (interview 21 March 2006).

'Leash leadership' such as this is the reverse of 'elastic band leadership', but has the same effect in desensitizing politics within the consensus. Both are essentially unambitious leadership styles—going only so far as followers will accept and never as far that they will become uncontrollable. These styles bear no relation to what communities wanted or might accept; some individuals within the churches, let alone in the wider community, thought them moral cowardice. Jesus led from the front to the extent that He died on the cross, as Archdeacon McCamley put it, and leaders' reluctance to see this as a model for their own leadership meant that they lost their moral voice in politics. As David Porter said, they faced a situation 'that increasingly was getting out of their control and they lost [a chance] to bring a political moral voice into the church' (interview 24 September 2007). Desensitizing politics meant that church leaders not only tried to keep disruptive identity politics from their churches, as best they could,[3] they did not articulate in public a prophetic vision for the politics of compromise, leaving their close personal relationship as a silent witness to an alternative form of politics for Northern Ireland.

Years later, after retirement from church leadership, former Methodist President Harold Good could admit with hindsight: 'about the past, we failed

---

[3] The paradox, of course, is that paramilitary funerals and Orange Order ceremonies are only two of many examples that display the inability of church leaders to control the entry of disruptive identity politics into religious space.

to be the prophetic church', leaders needed to 'paint a vision of what the world could be'. Alongside everything else 'we've got to be painting the vision' (interview 24 January 2006). The absence of this prophetic voice was noted by many peace activists within the church. As Gary Mason said, church leaders were 'very good personally, appalling prophetically'. In peacebuilding, he observed, leaders have to be prophetic, but they were 'afraid to say things that irked, upset and annoyed people'. 'We were very pastoral, go and visit wee Brigit there, go and see wee Jimmy there, eat a wee bun with her and see how she is but, critique Jimmy or Brigit's sectarianism and bitterness, oh no. People sometimes are more in love with King Billy than they were with Jesus Christ, they are more in love with Mother Ireland than they were with Jesus Christ, so a real prophetic voice in Catholicism or Protestantism was challenging these false idols...I think a lot of our church stuff, personally, [was] a disaster' (interview 14 February 2006).

These twin styles of leadership nonetheless had a profound effect on the nature of religious peacebuilding. The leaders did not idle while Belfast burned (although critics allege they merely told people it was wrong to play with matches), but these forms of leadership meant in practice that the main leaders adhered to a minimum consensus to speak out against violence but avoid overt politics; that they tolerated *most* of the mavericks who were the real vanguard and doing the important peacemaking at the edge in local settings; that they preferred in their own peacemaking to operate in secret, in case public exposure threatened their leadership and the elastic band snapped or political hysteria was unleashed; that they favoured their clergy and priests working in backchannels rather than through the formal political process; and that some truly transformative religious peacemakers kept their church leaders in the dark for fear of retrenchment—or could flourish only by placing themselves in locations where church authority was weakest, such as in para-church settings like ECONI and the ecumenical organizations, or in religious orders such as the Redemptorists or the Society of Jesus.[4] This meant that more of the religious peace work was 'unofficial' in the political peace process than in the social peace process, a theme we explore further in Chapter 3. It also explains the widely divergent opinions activists expressed about church leaders. They were attacked by some in their own churches and

---

[4] Jesuits were 'allowed' to work in Northern Ireland only in 1987–8 and then cautiously as a result of the controversy surrounding their role in South American liberation theology. Bishops were required to give permission, retaining this autonomy from the cardinal because the latter position was honorific. When Bishop of Down and Connor Cahal Daly refused the Society of Jesus permission to operate in his diocese—which is why they were not active in Belfast for much of the time; and when he became cardinal, Daly lacked the power to prevent other bishops from granting them permission. The Jesuits in Armagh diocese, for example, especially Fr Brian Lennon, were very active in negotiating with the protagonists a resolution to the Drumcree Orange parade stand-off.

outside for not going far enough, for being risk averse, cautious and apolitical, for pushing adventurous and potentially more transformative actions off the agenda; by some for going too far, for being too political and ecumenical, allegedly soft on terrorism and obsessed with reconciliation; while others applauded their model of personal reconciliation with each other and the valued lesson it taught about political compromise. We address some features of this style of religious peacebuilding in the next section.

BACKCHANNELS OF COMMUNICATION

The former Director of ECONI, David Porter, himself actively involved in mobilizing backchannels of communication, summarized their purpose: 'soldiers know that you need to talk to end war. It's politicians that don't want to talk to end war. I have never met a soldier either in a terrorist organization or in the British Army or in the RUC [Royal Ulster Constabulary], of calibre, I'm not talking about just hot heads and grunts who don't know that you need to talk and [be] prepared to sit in the tent and work out the cease fire and the amnesty. That is what soldiers do because soldiers know that fighting is not nice: it's politicians that play games with peace talks' (interview 24 September 2007). It was realized by many men and women in the churches that if they were telling politicians that they ought to talk, the church should be prepared to do so, too. This often came with the self-awareness that politics need not always be grubby. As the Revd Lesley Carroll admitted, Presbyterians were historically political, and churchgoers fooled themselves by thinking they could separate themselves from politics. Her fellow Presbyterian and former moderator John Dunlop reiterated the point: 'The politicians' job is to do the negotiations, we can't do the negotiations but we can create an environment where negotiations have been possible' (interview 23 March 2006).

If this provides the motivation for dialoguing with paramilitaries and their political branches, the procedure through which talking works is relationship-building, from which trust develops. The relationship-building, however, has to include the paramilitaries *and* the politicians. John Dunlop again: 'the church can't do the negotiations but you can encourage politicians to do it. You can try to create the atmosphere and the body politic where people see it is as necessary.' The space where this kind of relationship-building is more likely to realize results is secret backchannels, facilitating opportunities in private for people who otherwise would not meet and talk in public. Conflict situations impose particular restrictions on backchannel spaces. They are often, at first, not deployed for the purposes of peace but more general relationship and trust-building over the 'wee cup o' tea', as experienced church peacemakers routinely described it. 'If you go to a paramilitary with peace as your priority', Bishop Edward Daly said, 'they will immediately turn off' (interview 24 January 2006). A classic example was Gordon Wilson whose daughter was killed in the 1987 Remembrance Day bombing at Enniskillen. That evening he was interviewed on television and said he bore the bombers no ill will. This projected him to unwanted fame. He subsequently asked to see the IRA; they agreed. But he had only one issue and that was to ask them to end violence—the meeting ended with him saying he was disappointed. He did not take time to build the rapport. Initially, a form of *social* engagement is needed that takes place through backchannels. David Porter is quite clear on the sequence: 'first you had a religious movement, an ecumenical world, followed by a liberal political movement' (interview 24 September 2007)— engaging with Nationalists and Republicans, at first about nothing in particular, later encouraged wider political progress. Lord Eames said that, as a young cleric, at first his contacts could not be described as dialogue: 'that is far too grand a word, I had openness, a contact' (interview 29 January 2007).

It is beneficial for later political communication that politics first be avoided in preference for simple relationship and trust-building. Conventional political spaces are not best suited as channels of communication when politics is at first to be avoided. The churches, on the other hand, offered suitable spaces precisely because their main focus was not political. As a cleric heavily involved in backchannel dialogue, Fr Alec Reid said of churches: 'It was a question of trust. People would believe that the churches had no selfish interest in it and they were not following some kind of agenda—private agenda or personal agenda; they were following the principles of the Christian faith, the principles of peace' (interview 8 February 2011). In practice, sacred spaces have five advantages as backchannels, which we explore in turn: neutrality, confidentiality, secrecy, entrée, and redemption.

Ironically, the (mis)perception of the churches as above party politics, made them appear neutral spaces, whereas it is their political identity that really contributes to their effectiveness as backchannels. Harpviken and Roislien (2008) note that religious brokers, whether they function for 'liaison', 'co-ordination' or 'representation', as they put it, work best when they share cultural identity with the conflict parties. Precisely because of cultural and political connectedness, religious brokers from all sides can facilitate wide-spread dialogue across the divide. The lines of communication between the Catholic Church and Republicans, between individual Catholic clergy and vanguard Protestant ministers, and between Protestant clergy and the Loyalists, was something like a holy alliance. This allowed conflict groups to see the others' sacred spaces as being as equally neutral as their own, something that is facilitated, of course, when the conflict is not about religion, as in Northern Ireland.

These connections between people and spaces made it possible for SF, for example, to request a meeting with the then Anglican Primate Robin Eames in

Clonard Monastery, Eames thought 'about mid- to late 1980s'—and for Eames to go to this Catholic heartland without hesitation because of the space in which it occurred: a meeting unknown until now: 'It was awesome. These were the faces of those I had condemned, but when I found them, I didn't think of the baggage they were carrying, I found them open to talk, open to listen. Not dogmatically attacking the position that I held' (interview 29 January 2007). The evangelical Presbyterian minister Mervyn Gibson emphasized the importance of neutrality in his first, tentative backchannel contacts with Loyalists:

> All our early meetings were in church halls, they were difficult meetings, the two sides wouldn't sit in the same room, there was walk outs; there was all the usual stuff you have around getting people together. These people had killed people, and each other, up to the week before. I think there was a significance that church people were involved and it had the backing of the major denominations because there was integrity seen by the paramilitaries within that, and there was neutrality seen there. After we met in church halls we thought it would be better meeting in their territory, so we started to meet in clubs or pubs which were affiliated with one group or the other and the paramilitaries came back and said, no, this isn't right, if we are bringing Archbishop Eames or anybody out we are not going to bring him to a pub, we'd rather meet in a church. For respect they changed the venue back. (Interview 27 January 2006)

Sacred spaces also have the quality of confidentiality. The delicacy involved in the very fact of the meeting, let alone its subject matter, often requires confidentiality. Every party to the backchannel communication manages the delicacy by means of discretion in order to protect themselves as much as the others. Albert Reynolds, Taoiseach at the time of the negotiations over the 1994 ceasefires and, with John Major, the force behind the DSD, very much therefore an insider to key talks, is explicit about this: 'I made it clear from the start that I wouldn't talk to the IRA or Sinn Féin directly, but I would indirectly and that I would talk to them directly as soon as I got a permanent ceasefire.' These indirect routes were through the churches and normally involved his advisor Martin Mansergh, and Reynolds stated: 'I could rely on all the religious leaders I met to keep confidence and confidentiality. I mean, you could rely on the church, they are used to confidentiality, it doesn't matter whether you are talking Catholic Church or Protestant Church, or whatever' (interview 21 March 2006).

Secrecy is another defining feature of sacred spaces. Secrecy can be problematic when, as people in Northern Ireland say, 'even the dogs in the street know' what is happening—that is, when confidentiality breaks down. Much for this reason, Cardinal Daly said that he personally objected to participating in private talks. 'I have always believed that any dialogue must be in the open. There must be transparency; there must be no backstairs and no secret deals because it is wide open to grave misunderstanding. I was quite certain that if I engaged in talks with the paramilitaries this would very quickly become public knowledge, that it would be exploited as an indication of the church's secret sympathies with people of violence' (interview 24 February 2006). How this public stance worked out in private we shall shortly elaborate in two case studies, but, paradoxically, it forced many Catholic priests into acting clandestinely to keep what they were doing from the hierarchy, although Daly also had a remarkably far-sighted blind eye. As a general principle, openness might be desirable, but in conflict situations, privacy is often the foundation on which later public activities are based. The churches operated in different spaces therefore, both public and private. Norman Taggart, a Methodist minister active in ecumenism, expressed this well: 'I think we have got to do what we can and, as far as possible, do it publicly and yet do other things quietly and away from the public eye. You have got to build relationships which enable you at a later stage to take more prophetic action' (interview 30 January 2006).

The secrecy of some of the churches' peace work, as we shall see in Chapter 4, fed critics' notions of conspiracy and promulgated fear, but as far as political relationship-building was concerned at the beginning, secrecy was a must. The churches demanded it, so did the politicians and the paramilitaries. Speaking of his experience of meeting Protestant clergy in Fitzroy Church, the former IRA prisoner Denis Donaldson said the meetings were not publicized 'because the Protestant church people didn't want any, neither did we for that matter because that [secrecy] was their point. For them to go back into their community, it would be "ah", "traitor", you know, Lundys and all that' (interview 14 November 2005). The cost for the churches was the public misapprehension that they were not proactive. Even people in the churches were in the dark. 'I did not know what was going on', Archdeacon Gregor McCamley said, 'I knew things were going on but I did not know what it was' (interview 14 September 2005). Mark Durkan's experience as John Hume's deputy during the Hume–Adams talks, in which the churches were instrumental, made him reflect on the importance of sacred spaces: 'The Catholic bishops facilitated talks between SF and MI5 in a safe house [Bishop Edward Daly in Derry] and the business community could not. The reality is, a pastoral house is a different sort of location and people make assumptions about sanctuary and confidentiality that they wouldn't elsewhere. People have a degree of confidence about a pastoral agenda or pastoral interest [than] if you just had some business people suddenly taking this sort of initiative' (interview 17 February 2006). Thus it was that John Dunlop continued to keep his counsel by saying that he was not prepared to betray any of the details of secret meetings he had participated in (interview 23 March 2006).

Another quality of sacred spaces is their capacity to open access to further backchannels as an entrée or admission to yet more secret and special spaces because of the churches' position as gatekeepers. 'Why did the Loyalists talk to

Robin Eames?' the journalist Brian Rowan asked rhetorically in interview, 'they talked to Eames because they knew Eames could walk through 10 Downing Street and they knew he could walk into the Irish parliament and see Albert Reynolds' (4 April 2006). Backchannels are, in effect, social networks with degrees of connectedness where relationships spread in all directions, giving us backchannels within backchannels that effectively linked the churches, mainstream politicians in Ireland, Britain and the USA, and paramilitary combatants and their political representatives. Thus it was, for example, that Clonard priests mobilized contacts with Albert Reynolds to get President Clinton to grant Gerry Adams a visa to visit the USA as part of the political co-option of SF. But the channels within channels got very complicated, as Albert Reynolds explained:

> Alec Reid came to my house, whatever was required, whether it was two o'clock in the morning or whether it was six o'clock in the morning.
>
> Question: By the way, what was he asking you at two o'clock in the morning that couldn't wait until 7.30 the next morning?
>
> Well one of the times was to get a visa, to get Gerry Adams entry into the States. I set out from the start to change the whole approach, change the policy, change everything in relation to our approach to the North of Ireland. Coming from where I came from, Longford and Roscommon, not very far from the border, thirty odd miles, I understood it better than most people. I knew more people in the North on all sides. In fact to try and get a view on Paisley, I rang a Protestant in Ballymena; a man who had a [deleted] up there, [name deleted], he died about nine months ago. I rang him and I said I wanted him to find out for me privately, quietly, confidentially where Paisley stood [on the peace issue]. [Name deleted], I says, come back to me, please do me a turn that's all and save me time and effort and everything. He came back to me after a week and said that he had sat down with him for about four hours and told me that he had said no all his life, he wasn't changing and that when he asked him why, he eventually got it out of him, he wasn't going to allow anybody the opportunity of putting Lundy on his headstone. So I didn't go after him, I didn't go after the DUP. (Interview 21 March 2006)

The final quality of sacred space that marks them out as special sites for backchannel communication is that they convey the idea of redemption. 'Redemptive scripts', as Shadd Maruna terms them (cited in Braithwaite *et al.*, 2010: 23) are forms of talk and cognitive mapping used by former criminals to denote that their resort to violence in the past was unavoidable, not the 'real them', but explicable due to the circumstances of their past. Braithwaite and colleagues apply the term to combatants in political violence (2010: 23–4), where militants deploy redemptive scripts—explaining away violence as an inevitable option given former conditions—so that they can participate in the subsequent politics of peace and reconciliation. Its extension is limitless however. Every person and party to negotiations needs redemption of some sort. Recalcitrant politicians unbending and uncompromizing, hot-headed orators, preachers stoking up hell fire against enemies of God, extremists of a political or militant hue, all have to be redeemed for their contribution to the conflict in the past. This may or may not be expressed through words such as 'sorry' or in pleas for forgiveness, although these specific redemptive scripts can move political negotiations along; political developments in Northern Ireland after the GFA often got stuck over competing formulations of the words used to convey the intent without actually saying sorry (on the role of apologies in the sociology of peace processes see Brewer, 2010: 110–12). Redemptive scripts, of one form or another, can thus unblock bottlenecks in political dialogue; their absence can obstruct the flow. They make political dialogue possible.

Our point is that sacred spaces exude redemption. It seeps from the walls of the cloisters; it reverberates with the echoes in the church halls and drifts along with the bells and smells. Sacred spaces make redemptive scripts easier to issue, they encourage and facilitate them and enforce the realization on everyone that it is not just combatants who need redemption. They are secret, safe, secure, confidential places where the first words of redemption can be spoken—I understand you, I know where you are coming from, I want to know your position, I see your point of view. And this is precisely how respondents described their experience of meeting their nemesis—Republicans on hearing Protestant ministers explain that they are not to be treated as settlers, Catholic priests or the Irish Taoiseach when they encountered Loyalist hard men for the first time, or Protestant clergy when introduced to the feelings of injustice and discrimination experienced by Catholics or the conditions faced by prisoners. We will let Jim Gibney, SF activist and former prisoner, stand for them all when he articulated in interview the impact of meeting the Revd Jack Weir and hearing his exposition of the Protestant position on Britishness: 'he crystallized it in a way for us in terms of understanding' (3 September 2008). And we will treat Clonard Monastery as emblematic of all the sacred spaces used, when Fr Egan, himself based there, explained, 'it was about trying to provide a space for people to come and just find out about what it meant to be Catholic' (interview 22 November 2007).

Of ripples and rumours

The point about secret sacred spaces is that, some unspecified time later, the dialogue can ripple out to a wider constituency than was involved in the original dialogue and have broader effects. We have already seen how confidentiality is impossible to guarantee and that occasionally leakage of the news is designed for its consequences, either giving wider support to the interlocutors or heaping coals on their head.

We might call some leaks 'improper disclosure' since they potentially harm the outcome of the dialogue; it is normally done by investigative journalists putting together a story or by spoilers deliberately seeking to scupper the dialogue. Given the opposition to backchannel communications from those sections of the churches opposed to the peace process or to peace not on their terms, spoilers responsible for improper disclosure can be other churchmen and women. It was the Revd William McCrea, from the FPC and a DUP MP, for example, who broke the news that John Major's government was having secret talks with SF. Major said it would turn his stomach if true and he denied it. However, within two days McCrea was proved right and Major and Patrick Mayhew, the Northern Ireland Secretary, owned up to them in parliament. The dialogue they were having was between MI5 and Martin McGuinness and Gerry Kelly, facilitated by Denis Bradley and taking place in Bishop Edward Daly's house with the 'Mountain Climber'. Unionists were furious. The excuse used by Major was that they got a message from the IRA to say that the war was over and they needed the government's help to bring it to an end, something the IRA denied. The improper disclosure did not disrupt backchannel dialogue for long because the British and Irish governments were eager interlocutors.

There is also 'imperfect disclosure'. Knowledge that the dogs in the street seem to have about secret meetings, where nothing is deliberately leaked but everyone seems to know that something is going on, can feed rumours, suspicions, and conspiracies based on the imperfect understanding of what it is. Rumours are dangerous to backchannel dialogues and can defeat their purpose. Rumours are thus negative features of secret, sacred spaces. Even if the parties accord sacred spaces authority as spaces of sanctuary, secrecy, and confidentiality, and the tight lips of the churchmen and women involved might *not* be the source of the imperfect disclosure that circulates the rumours, such rumours exist as a natural part of imperfect knowledge. It is noteworthy that church people familiar with sacred spaces tend to have greater access to this imperfect knowledge and thus to be the source of rumours.

Rumours and ripples proliferate outwards, like wash on a pond, in exactly the same way, moving through channels that broaden the range and scale of their reach. Ripples, however, are different to rumours and can have a positive or negative impact. Rumours are spread by imperfect disclosure, with the uncertainty itself prompting speculation; we see conjecture, gossip, and guesswork as always negative because it is ill-informed or misinformed. On the other hand, ripples are spread by what we call 'authoritative disclosure'. This can be helpful or not. Authoritative disclosure normally occurs some time later, once secrecy and confidentiality are no longer prerequisites. It may not involve full disclosure, in that some confidences may be honoured and discretion applied, but it is always authoritative, done by parties with direct and personal involvement in the backchannel dialogue, with, or sometimes without, the permission of other parties. Disclosures without the permission of others may have negative effects, since they are open to denial by those whose confidentiality and privacy is breached. Where the interlocutors agree to authoritative disclosures, however, the ripple effects can extend well beyond the dense social networks represented at the original dialogue to impact generally on others. The ripples might extend to other clergy, not themselves yet involved in peacemaking, and the personal friendship networks and social circles of the interlocutors, including politicians, paramilitary members, ex-prisoners, and others not engaged in the dialogue but heartened to hear of it or inspired in their own peacemaking by it.

It is important not to be naïve, however. Ripples can cause a backwash, where their onward progression is stymied by coming up against an obstruction or hindrance. This is the more serious negative effect of ripples. Authoritative disclosures of backchannel developments need not always encourage others' peacemaking, for the ripples can reach people whose opposition to the peace process is strengthened by hearing about secret meetings and secret deals. Sometimes the obstacles come from other churchmen and women, who either oppose the outcome of backchannel communications or, as occasionally happens, complain because the disclosures are not fulsome enough, of being kept still in the dark. However, the authority of the person making the disclosures is also important to the size of the ripple effect. When the disclosures of secret meetings and backchannels are made by people with legitimacy, with authority owed to them as individuals because of their personal qualities or accruing by respect for their office, the knowledge they reveal of secret meetings in the past is accepted more generously and can help congregations, constituencies, and audiences move on in their political thinking and social relationships, no matter how incrementally. Indeed, some authoritative disclosures are done strategically by parties to the dialogue as a way of testing the reaction of constituencies and congregations, information that is then taken back into the backchannel dialogue to strengthen or change it. For example, we were told of a charade that Fr Alec Reid, Fr Des Wilson, and Gerry Adams used to play when they encountered each other outside of backchannels, asking each other 'what position was the Holy Spirit playing'? Apparently this was code for requesting knowledge about the state of play within the ceasefire negotiations, which was then fed back into their own separate backchannel meetings. However, 'strategic authoritative disclosures', as we might call them, can close debate as well as open it up. The view was often expressed by critics of Eames within the Anglican clergy, claiming that he used strategic disclosures as a way of stopping debate at Synod, not facilitating it, hinting to delegates that the COI was doing something but urging them not to ask for more detail since this might limit his capacity for movement.

Our argument is that churchmen and women, speaking with the authority of their office from the special sacred space of the pulpit or from a position of personal loyalty as a charismatic pastor or priest, can move their congregations in this way to a greater extent than other civil society activists speaking from outside sacred space. Authoritative disclosures in sacred spaces allow congregations to pledge their agreement and use the disclosure as personal or collective motivation. Paul Reid, for example, former leader of the Christian Fellowship Church (CFC), someone with authority as a popular, charismatic speaker and head of a vibrant and growing community of churches within the CFC umbrella, helped the middle-class people in his Protestant East Belfast congregation move forward when he announced unexpectedly that he had been in dialogue with Republicans for some years. The new church movement, best represented in Belfast by CFC, with a background in Brethren pietism, responded slowest to the peace vocation felt by progressive churches,[5] the Revd Charles Kenny referring to these sorts of groups as 'late comers' (interview 14 January 2011), but Reid's CFC congregation developed various 'bridge building' initiatives and supported the peace activism of its individual members. Talks and seminars were held introducing the congregation to members of other denominations, to politicians and paramilitaries from the 'other' tradition, and which called members, particularly its large number of young people, to action in the peace process. This cannot solely be attributed to Reid's authoritative disclosures about his contacts with Republicans, but this was part of a mood change within CFC that assisted its overwhelmingly Protestant middle-class membership in thinking the previously unthinkable—and doing something about it. Advocates of the political process model in social movement theory refer to this as 'cognitive liberation' (McAdam, 1982), where new interpretative frames slowly emerge, the effect of which is to assist movement change.

It would be wrong to give the impression that sacred spaces were the only venues for backchannel communications or that churchmen and women were the only go-betweens—religious peacemakers went to politicians' houses, apparently sometimes late at night, and other venues were mobilized by non-religious peacemakers. John Dunlop recalls meetings of the British-Irish Association in Oxford, which included SF and the Progressive Unionist Party (PUP), the latter aligned with UVF; there were many more, too numerous to

---

[5] This might be thought unusual given they carried no denominational baggage and were free of church history and tradition, but as we shall see in Chapter 3, the origins of the new church movement in the charismatic pursuit of a personal experiential relationship with God initially directed attention inwardly and it was only some years later that outward expressions began with the social gospel and then 'the Troubles'. They were non-sectarian in the sense of transcending denomination, only later in the sense of confronting sectarian divisions.

list. However, it is possible to assess the impact of sacred space through two case studies that allow us to delve beyond the superficial detail that, perhaps, even the dogs in the street knew: the Hume–Adams talks, and the 1994 ceasefires as part of the DSD.

The Hume–Adams Talks

In a lecture at Queen's University on 9 February 2000, organized by John Brewer and Francis Teeney, Gerry Adams announced that since 1971 Republicans had never been *out* of dialogue with the British government. 'There was dialogue in 1974, 1975 and then during the hunger strikes, and so on, right up to the present time' (see Brewer, 2001: 21). He disclosed that SF had a broad raft of contacts within the churches, civil society, business, and the Unionist political parties. What he did not say, but which the dogs in the street knew, was that they had also been meeting MI5. The Hume–Adams talks, however, were orchestrated by the churches in a specific political context that made sacred space perhaps the only possible backchannel at that time. SF had placed itself further beyond the pale than normal by the 1984 Brighton bombing and the IRA's attempt to kill the entire British Cabinet, and yet the British and Irish governments' response to this attack,[6] the 1985 AIA, had made Northern Ireland a more troubled place than usual as the Protestant community, including some churches, protested en masse. Paisley was in his element, collecting groups of embittered men halfway up mountains, wearing berets, and waving gun certificates (on the AIA see as a selection: Kenny, 1986; Cox, 1987; O'Leary, 1987; Cochrane, 1997). What added to their ire was that the Protestant church leaders were not consulted over its terms; nor, incidentally, were local politicians. Kenny (1986: 125) records that two former Stormont prime ministers were approached, the Viscount Brookeborough and James Chichester-Clarke, but no prelates or parties; it was a top-down London–Dublin led initiative that ignored all local groups. Protestant attacks on the police and civil servants, huge public protest rallies, and disruption in the business of direct rule was matched with the electoral growth of SF post-hunger strike to form the backcloth to Fr Alec Reid contacting John Hume in 1987 about possible meetings with Gerry Adams.

There was great delicacy about the proposal. Mark Durkan, appointed as Hume's shadow in the talks (Adams had a shadow, too), said they wanted the

---

[6] It was said by the Cabinet Secretary at the time, John Chilcott (quoted in Mallie and McKittrick, 2001: 13), that Mrs Thatcher had to be dragged, kicking and screaming, into the AIA, but her reluctance was assuaged in large part by memory of the bombing and how lucky she had been in surviving it. As an IRA statement ominously warned, she had to be lucky all the time, they just once.

talks postponed until after the 1987 general election 'in case it got out [and] would be misunderstood, misrepresented, and misinterpreted' (interview 17 February 2006). Even then, Adams, Hume, and Reid all wanted the dialogue conducted in private, 'because', as Hume said 'when it became public I would be crucified'. Sacred space was critical to this: 'we wanted to meet in a private place, we didn't want to be meeting in hotels and Fr Reid provided the place, Clonard' (interview 11 March 2006). Indeed, according to Bishop Edward Daly, confidentiality was breached precisely when they moved venue for one meeting and Adams was spotted by a journalist coming out of Hume's house in Derry. Hume was very upset, he reports, and Daly spoke out publicly at Mass about the importance of supporting the dialogue. If churches are sacred spaces with particular qualities suited to backchannel political dialogue, the pulpit is a special sacred space within them, for even if militarists are unmoved by what is said from pulpits, they know that many in the community—whose support they need—*are* moved. Pulpits provide insulation for preachers, allowing them to say things that in other spaces would be more dangerous and problematic; if only preachers had realized this and used pulpits more bravely.

Knowledge of the talks met with a visceral response from Protestant churchmen and women, as well as the British government, even though they had been having their own secret talks with both militant Loyalists and Republicans. While the British government was not formally involved in the talks, the Irish government's Martin Mansergh was and, according to Bishop Daly, through Mansergh there was a link to the British; a connection provided also by Hume's own dialogue with the British government. Bishop Daly also confirmed that Cardinal O'Fiaich (who died in 1990) acted as an entrée for Reid to the then Irish Taoiseach Charles Haughey. Upon public exposure, however, it was as if they were all ignorant of the talks. What matters in backchannel politics, of course, is that breaches in secrecy force a public response that reproduces for public effect the outrage of their community. Durkan was shocked at the hypocrisy of the Protestant churches that did this, 'people who were more than happy to see their role as trying to work to bring Loyalists forward' (interview 17 February 2006).

It is not only that participants to the talks did not appreciate the particular problems posed by secrecy when confidentiality is broken, they did not realize that Protestants would perceive the talks as a 'pan nationalist front', to use Roy Garland's term (interview 13 September 2005), something Protestants feared most in the face of their own fractures and schisms. The talks were not seen as the political co-option of SF but the radicalization of the SDLP, the latter being at that point the only hope amongst moderate Unionists for any sort of deal. It is for this reason that normally fair-minded and progressive civil Unionists reacted so vehemently. Temporarily, Fr Reid became a hate figure (in the same way that Jesuits always were to most Protestants). David Porter recalls that

Protestant ministers, before agreeing to attend meetings that he was organizing, would ask if Reid would be there (interview 27 February 2006). ECONI
arranged for other Catholic clergy to attend, who it was known would report
back to SF.

However, Reid remained the orchestrator of the Hume–Adams talks, which
continued in private, despite the public knowledge that they were happening.
'Oh, he was the architect', Bishop Edward Daly said, 'he was the instrument,
providing an environment in which they could phone one another, safely and
out of view' (interview 24 January 2006). It was important to Hume and
Durkan, when looking back, that it appeared as if Reid was doing this with
the sanction of the hierarchy. 'The fact that they supported what we were
doing', John Hume said, 'strengthened our approach', feeling that if knowledge of it leaked out the church would be able to moderate it (interview 11
March 2006). Durkan was equally clear: 'the advice we were given at the time
was that Fr Reid was acting in the knowledge of the hierarchy, so while they
weren't implicated they were aware and were giving it some sort of encouragement' (interview 17 February 2006). This support never materialized at an
institutional level when public furore ensued. When the talks were exposed,
Hume was castigated by the usual suspects in Northern Ireland, but he felt the
strain particularly when the Catholic Church failed openly to back him, and
the Southern Irish media turned on him. The latter kept up their attacks for
days but then, interestingly, popular opinion rallied. The South Irish media
was swamped with people who had had enough of the castigation of Hume.
Overwhelmingly popular support forced the media to retract and then belat-
edly back him. The institutional church, however, never did.

The whole attraction of backchannels to 'rubber band' and 'leash' leaders is
that their knowledge of them is tacit and unofficial, allowing damage control
to be managed by disowning knowledge and disclaiming support. Thus,
despite the tacit understandings at the time, public exposure meant participants to the talks were abandoned by the church hierarchy. Durkan said: 'no
I don't think the churches were giving political cover. Whenever John Hume
was getting all the flack, particularly in the Southern media, there was no cover
coming from the church or anybody else. So while church people would have
privately indicated to John they were supportive, we were disgusted about this'
(interview 17 February 2006). According to Bishop Edward Daly, Reid suspected that he would be disowned by the hierarchy and be portrayed as 'doing
this off his own bat' (interview 24 January 2006).

While this might be construed as an illustration of the moral cowardice of
'rubber band' and 'leash' leaders—further evidence of their failure to be a
prophetic moral voice in politics—backchannels are not only favoured by
leaders because they can be renounced, but mavericks adopt them because
they offer autonomy from official leadership. While on the one hand Reid
wanted protection to cover his back, he wanted to be free of hierarchical

control. Reid put it this way: 'It was better to do it one's own way without involving the official church as you would get yourself tied up in knots. You would have to get the permission of the official church—and you wouldn't get it. The official church would never agree to talk to Sinn Féin people or IRA people. You would then have been held up—completely held up' (interview 8 February 2011). Bishop Daly again: 'Alec wanted to be free of any control, acting as an independent agent. But at the same time he wasn't acting unknown to us, at least not Cahal Daly, but Tom O'Fiaich and myself were very much involved. I don't know how much Cahal was involved. Cahal was always rather nervous about any negotiations with Sinn Féin' (interview 24 January 2006). Edward Daly, on the other hand, was keen on backchannel and secret dialogue with militants, ensuring that Derry was more often the site of private dialogue than Belfast—British government ministers travelled secretly to Edward Daly's house in Derry as much as the other way round; and when Catholic sacred spaces were used in Belfast it was in Clonard, since as a Redemptorist monastery Clonard was less under the command of Cardinal Daly.

Derry was also where Denis Bradley lived, as well as the 'Mountain Climber', both active in backchannel dialogue between MI5, Republicans, and the British—and Derry had benefited much longer from a *de facto* ceasefire arranged between Bishop Daly and the IRA. Edward Daly also thought that the Belfast bishops had more academic backgrounds 'and had never been down on the ground or getting their hands dirty with people'; as bishop for Derry, the fourth largest Catholic diocese in Ireland, Edward Daly thought he had 'street cred that was important when the going was tough' (interview 24 January 2006)—legitimacy earned as a young curate on Bloody Sunday in much the same way in South Africa as Archbishop Tutu won respect later arising from his anti-apartheid credentials.

The way Alec Reid balanced the twin pressures inherent in backchannel political activity, between isolation and interference, was to have a tight knit group of church-based advisors around him—a system that ironically replicated the cell structure of the paramilitary groups he was dialoguing with. They read the various iterations of the agreed text between John Hume and Gerry Adams and mobilized their own backchannel networks to pass on versions to the Northern Ireland Secretary of State (Peter Brooke at the time) and the British and Irish governments. Brooke's statements were themselves cleared by the British and Irish governments, thus, Bishop Edward Daly asserted, 'none of those statements were off the cuff, they were all pre-arranged and part of a very carefully programmed choreography' (interview 24 January 2006). Bishop Edward Daly was also the contact person connecting Reid, and thus the Hume–Adams cell, with the separate backchannel communication of Denis Bradley and the Mountain Climber between British civil servants, MI5, and the IRA. According to Edward Daly, Martin McGuinness—himself

Derry-based—had his own contacts with the British government at the same time and fed information back through the networks, showing the web-like spread of this connectedness.

Religious peacemakers were therefore at the centre of an extensive network, with Fr Alec Reid at the hub. Throughout our interviews, Reid was lauded for his contribution from Loyalists, such as Spence and Garland, by Republicans, such as Jim Gibney, SDLP leaders such as Hume and Durkan, and other religious peacemakers. Even those who criticized the churches as institutions, named Reid as one of the key individuals whom they respected.

The DSD and the Paramilitary Ceasefires

If Reid might be construed as a maverick, working under the shadow of the church but very much keeping the hierarchy in the dark,[7] our next case study of backchannel activity by the churches covers the secret activity of some of those at the apex of the hierarchy. The DSD was a joint statement of the British and Irish governments issued in December 1993 by John Major and Albert Reynolds. It included for the first time the assertion that the people of the island of Ireland had the exclusive right to solve the issues between North and South by mutual consent and promised that parties linked with paramilitaries could take part in political talks, so long as they abandoned violence. The statement was designed as part of the orchestration leading the announcement of ceasefires, and both the IRA and the Combined Loyalist Military Command obliged the following year.

A little cameo is revealing. The Loyalist ceasefire was planned to go first, in July 1994, but the IRA murdered Ray Smallwood four weeks beforehand, delaying the announcement by some months and until after the IRA agreed theirs. Smallwood was one of the principal members of the UDA pushing for a political strategy, although he had been imprisoned years before for the attempted murders of Bernadette Devlin and her husband. He was one of the few Loyalist combatants to find politics in prison rather than God or bodybuilding. Smallwood had been in liaison with the Revd Roy Magee, as the main Protestant contact with the Loyalists, as well as Fr Alec Reid and Fr Gerry Reynolds, as the main go-betweens with Republicans. The Combined Loyalist Military Command was keen to steal a march on the IRA by announcing their ceasefire ahead of them. Smallwood's murder changed the sequence. Gerry Reynolds and Alec Reid prayed beside his coffin and attended

---

[7] This sobriquet seemed to stick when later he equated Protestants with the Nazis, an off-the-cuff remark uttered in Fitzroy Presbyterian Church of all places, and in response to comments from a well-known victim of 'the Troubles', although they did result from goading and he apologized almost immediately.

his funeral—a remarkable demonstration of the strength of their reputation as mavericks and the belief in their physical safety as a result. They also paid a visit to the IRA in which they admonished them severely for the outrage. It was never understood why Smallwood was murdered. One speculation is that it was done to permit the IRA to go first in the declaration of a ceasefire. More likely, they were clearing the ground before the cessation of violence prevented them from settling old scores. The vignette is instructive, however, by highlighting the role of church people in orchestrating the ceasefires and the space that religious peacebuilders had opened up for themselves for effective political intervention. We can take this point further by discussing the role of the churches in the development of the DSD.

Some of the networks exploited in the negotiations linked back to Reid and the Hume–Adams dialogue. Backchannels can lie dormant for a very long time and if people remain in place within their respective social networks, they can be resurrected very quickly. While Durkan described Reid as a facilitator, Reid on this occasion asserted his own opinions over substance and strategy. For example, when Major and Reynolds imposed a series of conditions on SF and the IRA before they could be admitted to talks, Durkan admits he was inclined to accept these conditions within a generous time period (perhaps because Reynolds endorsed them as well) and recounts that it was Reid who persisted in persuading him and Hume against engaging in debate about conditions (interview 17 February 2006). Later, when Tony Blair sent Shadow Northern Ireland Minister Paul Murphy secretly to Belfast, ahead of the 1997 election to explore the possibility of talks, by which time the first IRA ceasefire had broken down precisely because of the delay in political dialogue with SF, it was Reid to whom they turned, in Durkan's words, 'to get on the talks and to handle the whole question of SF in terms of entry'. Durkan was still disagreeing with him about tactics, 'so I remember at the time saying to Fr Reid, "you should listen more to other ideas and other opinions", but he obviously has his own way of doing things and he will let you know' (interview 17 February 2006). Backchannels, in other words, were networks that allowed some church people to be overtly political.

But Reid was not the only cleric involved in backchannel networks that gave entrée to politicians. It is worth highlighting the role of Archbishop Robin Eames, someone at the other end of a religious bureaucracy, who needed no gatekeeper for access to prime ministers and had no ambivalence about giving direct political advice to them, even if in secret. Albert Reynolds was asked in interview about his relations with Eames: 'Oh, very good, very good. I called him in, from the first time he came to see we had a long chat about it in the office, and he saw where I was coming from. I called him in at the time when I was putting the Downing Street Declaration together and I showed him what was in it. I gave it to him to read. I mean I know what Major's limitations are, where is he coming from and I know what might run [and] what certainly won't. So as far as I was concerned I was going to produce something that hopefully would bring peace or certainly contribute in a big way to peace' (interview 21 March 2006). Eames was given a veto, according to Reynolds, to 'put down your community's position and what would be acceptable to them'; and Reynolds changed his draft document on one occasion because he was told by Eames that what he was being shown would not work. Eames used Presbyterian minister Roy Magee's backchannel networks that supplied connections to the Loyalist paramilitaries to ensure their input.[8] Reynolds admitted to putting a clause into the DSD that repeated verbatim a Loyalist document prepared by them under Magee's tutelage: 'Paragraph 5 was what Roy Magee had written at meetings on the Shankill Road. I read it and I was happy to run with it.' Reynolds also met Gusty Spence, from the Combined Loyalist Command, and David Ervine, along with three 'big tall fellow[s], about six foot two or six foot four, [who] you wouldn't want to meet on a dark night', and was told that Loyalists would reciprocate with a ceasefire if the IRA's stuck for six weeks. Of Cardinal Cahal Daly's input, however, Reynolds was unsure whether he was in the loop: 'Oh he was, I'm not so sure if he, he came in on a Saturday morning, he may well have read it, I have a feeling he probably did.' Bishop Edward Daly, however, confirmed that up to his death in 1990, Cardinal O'Fiaich was heavily involved. Daly pulled out a yellowing document from the drawer in his home where we interviewed him—'stuff here I've never shown before'—to allow us to glimpse the pencil-corrected draft.

It is worth emphasizing that Eames went down to Dublin while O'Fiaich and Cahal Daly never went to London. It is tempting to see this as conspiracy or as some legacy of Catholic colonial-historical memory, making London forbidden space for Irish Catholic leaders. Much simpler is the suggestion that Eames was Primate of all Ireland, with responsibilities in Dublin, whereas Catholic ecclesiastical authority ended at the Irish Sea. And it would have been harder to keep secret a trip to London by Catholic leaders, thus destroying the purpose of the visit in the first place.

Eames had no qualms about visiting London and was simultaneously negotiating with John Major and Albert Reynolds. Eames was eager to talk directly in case Jim Molyneaux, leader of the Ulster Unionist Party at the time and one of the minority parties assisting Major with his low majority in the House of Commons, might assume greater significance. While Eames and Molyneaux were described as 'very pally, very close' by Reynolds, Eames's

---

[8] Roy Magee died on 5 February 2009 and had been too ill to be interviewed for our research. His obituaries were universal in praise for him as a peacemaker and as someone instrumental in negotiating the Loyalist ceasefire in 1994. He travelled so far in his political journey, however, being a popular speaker in the Irish republic, that Loyalists ostracized him, in much the same way as they criticized Eames, whose own journey was remarkable in its distance from his Unionist roots. Perhaps it is the way of obituaries, however, but Magee is singled out for realizing the ceasefire to the neglect of Eames.

direct connections to Major allowed him to bypass Molyneaux and counteract any potential negative leverage. Molyneaux declared the IRA ceasefire as the most destabilizing event to have occurred in the history of Northern Ireland. This marked the level of fear Unionists had at political transformation, suggesting that religious leadership, rubber band variety or not, was ahead of political leadership in this moment of transition. The whole point of the churches' use of backchannels is that it allowed those who occupied them to be more risk seeking because the secrecy and confidentiality gave them more flexibility than politicians operating openly in the public sphere. This is a point we return to in the conclusion to this chapter.

At the centre of this web of sacred backchannel networks, on this occasion, was Eames. Loyalists had problematic relations with him, portraying him as unwilling to get his hands dirty and comparing him unfavourably to Fr Alec Reid, and thus Loyalists refer to the Revd Roy Magee, one of their gatekeepers controlling entrée, as the 'Reverend ceasefire', as the journalist Brian Rowan described it. 'But really, all Roy was', according to Rowan, 'was a means of the Loyalist organizations getting to Eames and what Eames presented was someone who could get their message into Downing Street and into Albert Reynolds's ear' (interview 4 April 2006). Rowan articulated how far ahead Eames was of the political leaders based on his own interviews with him (see Rowan, 1995): 'Well Eames talked to me about the aloneness of all of this and the struggle in his mind about the rights and wrongs of it. Remember that he was way out ahead of the political posse in terms of the Unionist community at that stage. He was talking to Republicans privately when it wasn't political[ly] acceptable to do so. It was a risk and even to this day he has refused to meet Adams publicly, he has talked to Adams privately on a number of occasions' (interview 4 April 2006). To us, Eames admitted just how far ahead he was, when he said, 'I tried to get more Protestants, Unionists, and Church of Ireland to accept that long before "the Troubles" there was great injustice in the Catholic community' (interview 4 April 2006). 'Without realizing it' at the time, he said, he was 'on a journey of self-realization'.

In this case, his unpopular leadership style was to wider advantage. Eames's tendency to centralize control around himself within the Anglican synod—to use his position as Primate to ensure that Standing Committee would not change the rules to permit devolution of decision-making, his political skill in presidential addresses to rule out of order discussion of controversial issues, and his single-mindedness to ensure that the secret backchannel dialogue was done by him (complaints repeatedly made by several Anglican respondents)—nonetheless placed control in someone ahead of Unionist political leaders. This forms a strikingly sharp contrast with the approach of Cardinal Cahal Daly to the political peace process; and to others, too. John Dunlop, for example, former Moderator of the Presbyterian Church and for a long time co-convenor of the PCI's Church and Government Committee (as it was then called), likewise saw a clear distinction between the political and religious aspects of leadership, and while in his personal witness he engaged in many forms of backchannel dialogue, he drew in his own mind a contrast between what churchmen and women should and should not do:

> It's very important that it be distinguished in the churches' role. The politician's job is to do the negotiations, we can't do the negotiations but we can create an environment where negotiations might have been possible. I never thought it my job to be involved in the talks as such but you were encouraging people to be involved in them. You know what political negotiations are like; you are going through a thousand and one drafts of a sentence so it is not our job to do that; that is what politicians are elected to do. (Interview 23 March 2006)

This view not only impacted on what Dunlop, and those like him, saw as the proper purpose for the churches in utilizing backchannels—that they be used for relationship-building and conflict transformation not political negotiation— it shaped their approach to the second type of church engagement with the political process, participation in top table discussions around which peace accords are settled and then sold to the public.

CHURCHES AND THE FORMAL PEACE NEGOTIATIONS

It must be said that Eames, Magee, and Reid were untypical in the level of their involvement in writing drafts of peace statements, even if in secret. With respect to formal political negotiations, Dunlop's is the common approach. The churches tended to be excluded from the top table anyway. It is not difficult to understand why. Formal peace talks need to be inclusive in the parties to them, with all the key groups sat around the table. Some peace talks have even included sections of civil society to guarantee their inclusivity. Northern Ireland's churches were divided and some sections were ambivalent about peace talks. To invite the ecumenically minded, pro-peace sections only would have itself been divisive, adding to the clamour of voices in some parts against negotiations. They were excluded, in short, because the churches were not expected to be unanimously in favour of compromise: a sad reflection.

Of course, many in the churches in their diverse ways had helped prepare the conditions for talks through the social peace process and backchannel political dialogue. However, once the conditions were in place, most progressive elements in the churches withdrew to let politicians take over: 'We can't turn up and negotiate the Good Friday Agreement', Dunlop said, 'it's not our job' (interview 23 March 2006). This view had the unfortunate consequence, however, of leaving the field open for those critics of the peace negotiations inside the churches to mobilize politically against the process; they had no similar reticence and they already had the advantage of being directly represented at the talks by Paisley. Critics of negotiations within the churches, given their oratorical evangelical style, dominated the public square and the progressive elements, already inclined to withdraw and leave politics to the politicians. If backchannel politics was dominated by the pro-peace parts of the churches, then formal politics allowed the ambivalent sections to dominate.

Rubber-band and leash leadership played its part in constraining some progressives within the churches, for numerically very significant sections of the mainstream churches were nervous about the GFA. In William Crawley's view, progressive elements in the mainstream churches wanted to encourage the peace process but did not know how to (interview 23 September 2007). One way that leading ecumenists tried to make a difference was by forming the Faith in a Brighter Future group, the idea of the Revd Ken Newell, which used backchannels to meet politicians, civil servants, the paramilitaries, and their political representatives, including Trimble's internal party critics such as Jeffrey Donaldson, although this eventually folded once the go-between mechanisms formally established under the GFA bedded in. This took some time and John Brewer and Francis Teeney were facilitating its meetings as late as 2002. Delegations of concerned clergy and priests visited Trimble in Stormont on several occasions, especially before Ulster Unionist Council meetings, encouraging him to stick with the Agreement in the face of fierce criticism, including from within his own party and some of which was from prelates. John Morrow recalls that the PCI produced several reports and documents, circulating around the insiders before being sent on to government (interview 7 December 2005).

But this was backchannel dialogue again, keeping up the pretence of church disavowal of politics. John Morrow continued: 'we didn't expect to be involved in the direct negotiations but reports by various committees of the [Presbyterian] church were sent to governments and meetings took place with government which weren't public. The churches did have some input into the bricks and mortar.' Some of the papers concerned the issue of amnesty. Talking to Trimble in private, however, further silenced the moral voice in public politics that the pro-peace churchmen and women could have provided. It is also questionable whether Trimble needed more pressure from progressive and ecumenical Protestants, since this only fed his critics' conspiracies. They might have served him better if they had dialogued with the anti-Agreement members of their own congregations by using the sacred space of the pulpit as insulation. Church unity, however, was their primary concern. For the same reason they feared publicly challenging anti-Agreement para-church bodies such as the Caleb Foundation, and the FPC. Dawn Purvis, then a member of David Ervine's PUP, noted that to the pro-peace churchmen and women it was 'more important to hold on to your congregation [than] stand up for what you believe in' (interview 11 September 2007). Indeed, she said that Trimble's lack of statesmanship was not the problem: his dithering, uncommitted, unenthusiastic failure to sell the Agreement was less important than the religious peacemakers' failure to support him publicly and to lobby anti-Agreement Unionists.

This is not how anti-Agreement sections of the church saw their religious opponents' actions. Cedric Wilson, for example, felt constantly under pressure from the badgering of religious peacemakers, whose efforts behind the scenes to influence people like himself, as well as Trimble, he resented. When asked if pro-Agreement Christians tried to persuade him, he replied:

> Yes, always. That is a very good example of the type we actually resented, that sort of an approach. When I say resented it, [it] was really that we thought people didn't really understand exactly what was being presented to the people here. There is this thing abroad, and I was aware of this more particularly when I travelled to the United States and Europe and spoke to journalists, the idea of being anti-Agreement just sounds very evil in its essence, terrible. I mean how can you be against an agreement? So we had to start by explaining to people what it was we were opposed to. I would have said those who held a Christian point of view, and who actually believed in the principles of the Bible, actually support our position; saying that people who have murdered or killed and maimed and who have held the community to ransom, that those people should not be brought into a political process. You cannot blur the line between democracy and terror. You have to say OK, here is the line. (Interview 1 September 2008)

It probably confirmed the impressions that people such as Cedric Wilson had of the progressive parts of the churches when, years later, the British government was looking to bolster the fumbling peace process, it called on them to assist with confirmation of decommissioning (Fr Alec Reid and the Revd Harold Good) and packed with them the Consultative Group on the Past when seeking to deal with the problem of memory and remembrance.

CONCLUSION

In their account of the peace process in Indonesia, Braithwaite and colleagues (2010: 432) argue that it was driven less by front-stage peacemaking by national leaders than by backstage aggregation of countless little reconciliatory actions in everyday life. If formal front-stage politics is supposed to be interest led, backstage channels provide fulsome opportunity for acts of emotion-led reconciliation, openness, empathy, forgiveness, hope, and redemption. It is for this reason that the pro-peace elements in the churches focused their attention on backstage work—they could act there like clergy do in their pastoral ministry. They felt they had no gifts suitable for formal politics.

This view is regrettable, for it lost formal politics in Northern Ireland a moral voice when it needed it most. Sacred space, however, always felt more comfortable, pulling them back to settings where they felt their Christian qualities were best suited. It should not be forgotten, though, that these sacred spaces were particularly suitable to involvement in the political peace process, giving neutrality, secrecy, confidentiality, entrée, and redemption. But the pulpit, perhaps the most special part of sacred space, was rarely used to articulate a new political vision for Northern Ireland. And secrecy brought its own problems, making backchannels problematic. It garnered suspicion, nurtured feelings of resentment, fed rumours and, not least of all, disguised the high level of engagement that sections of the church had with the political peace process. The perception of political disengagement, which was practised by the minimalist consensus amongst the religious leadership and seemingly reinforced by the churches' exclusion from front-stage political negotiations, which was both forced on them and self imposed, completes the image of the churches' as having a limited role in the political peace process. It is not as simple as that however. Albert Reynolds, drawing on his vast direct experience and knowledge, said the churches 'were very helpful, there is no question about it in my book' (interview 21 March 2006).

To understand how in particular, we need to return to the conceptual distinctions we introduced in the last chapter. Most churches practised passive peacemaking, proclaiming its desirability and denouncing the violence. Some were active in their peacemaking, getting their hands dirty as so many respondents phrased it. They were better at this in local settings than national ones, in part because the national leadership operated to maintain a false consensus that pulled them to the minimum; and as institutions the pro-peace churches preferred to maintain the delusion that they were apolitical, above the party fray. Leaders offered no moral vision for an alternative form of politics. But a lot was done behind the scenes, including by some of these leaders themselves. Backchannels spread like a web, with social networks overlapping that connected the churches to governments, paramilitary combatants, political parties, and MI5. The networks extended so far that there was potential for misinformation,[9] not deliberately planted for dissimulation but misunderstood like in games of Chinese whispers as it transforms in the many times of its retelling; meetings sometimes had to be called by the churches to clarify what it was that people actually knew. These connections

---

[9] The well-cited example is Martin McGuinness's alleged remark that the IRA's war was over but they needed help in ending it, denied by him but stated as fact by others. In reality, some years later, Denis Bradley admitted that he had said it, not McGuinness. This illustrates our point well. The problem with backchannel conversations is not only their deniability, although this can be important initially in case the dialogue goes wrong, it is also that information is mistakenly misheard in the many retellings that occur across the stretched web-like networks involved in backchannels.

were like tentacles spreading so far and wide that it seems impossible to trace back to an identifiable visible centre. But some had churchmen and women at their core. As we saw, knowledge of church-led backchannel dialogue, mostly disclosed sometime later, could have ripples well outside the social networks involved in them, washing out to congregations and constituencies well beyond the backchannels to encourage others in their own peacemaking. But it was negative peace that they were deployed to serve—the ending of violence, calling of ceasefires, and the political incorporation of former militants to consolidate the conflict transformation. The withdrawal from front-stage politics meant that positive peace—social transformation—had no opportunity for avowal and expression, except in the few local instances where the social gospel was practised aplenty.

The churches did all this while oscillating between the social and political peace processes. In Chapter 1 we emphasized the various kinds of relationship-building and restoration within our typology, which were epitomized by the ecumenists but by no means confined to them. In this chapter we have drawn attention to kinds of political involvement, especially backchannel dialogue and facilitation. In working at these kinds of activities, pro-peace sections in the churches illustrate well the recursive nature of the relationship between the social and political peace processes. As John Dunlop said, churches can help establish the conditions for political talks through involvement in the social peace process by creating 'the atmosphere and the body politic, where people see it as necessary and where people will be supportive of the process' (interview 23 March 2006).

It is essential to note, however, that they conspicuously failed to achieve this for much of the previous twenty years, until the early 1990s when the political parties themselves began to realize they would have to negotiate in earnest (for some of the sociological and political factors lying behind this awareness, see Brewer, 2003c). For example, Eames and Magee only started to make real progress in their engagement with Loyalist paramilitary organizations when political developments in the UDA and UVF resulted in the formation of the Combined Loyalist Military Command. Before that, the churches were talking to small groups and Loyalism was inchoate and divided. This weakened Loyalist leadership and inhibited the capacity of any particular leader to deliver Loyalist participation in a ceasefire—as the collapse of the Combined Loyalist Military Command some years later showed. Relationship-building and restoration through the social peace process is part of the conditioning for political talks, opening up an opportunity for political talks to take place and succeed, something reinforced by the relationship-building achieved in the process of backchannel political dialogue itself. But negotiations succeeded only when the political peace process was opened up by the readiness of most of the parties to the conflict to take dialogue seriously. At that point, the social peace process was given a lift and relationship-building in society was mutually reinforced by political developments.

There is a final conclusion to be drawn. Some Protestant clergy, at least in private, were ahead of Unionist leaders in their political adventurousness (there was no similar gulf on the Catholic-Nationalist side; indeed, critics of Cardinal Daly's leadership would claim it was the reverse). Unionist politicians refused to speak to John Hume for a year or so after the revelation of his talks with Gerry Adams, for example, while some Protestant clergy showed a willingness to dialogue with anyone, no matter how far beyond the pale, including even INLA. Molyneaux thought the ceasefires the most destabilizing event in Northern Irish history, but his co-religionists had been active in bringing it about. David Trimble was fond of saying that leaders should be a step beyond followers, but only one step; religious leaders in some cases were ahead by streets. Those that were involved in the Protestant churches in peacemaking—and it was only a minority—showed more flexibility than the politicians. There are likely to be many personal incentives behind this in each individual's case but the essentially *religious* reasons for it are worth highlighting.

Part of the cause is motivational, a greater commitment to the idea of peace (even if primarily negative peace) deriving from the way they interpreted Christian doctrine. It also has to do with the capacity of church people—and particularly of religious leaders themselves—to act, if they so wished, relatively autonomously. The churches are institutions with their own authority and hide-bound traditions but, in relative terms, there are no elections to be fought, no electors to cajole, no holding to account, and no constraints imposed on flexibility arising from past positions. It is not that clergy refused to impose conditions on the paramilitaries before they would enter into dialogue but these conditions were less stringent. Church leaders could ignore the conservative views of members, if they wished, while ordinary clergy could do likewise with respect to their more conservative leaders. Some members in congregations would have complained had they known what the pews were being used for in backchannel meetings, but their pastors had the autonomy to do it anyway. There is more room for pragmatism in religion than in politics even though it may seem that theology is as much a prison as the party manifesto.

Pro-peace churchmen and women were also encouraged by the spaces in which they operated. Sacred spaces, as we have argued at length, are private, meaning that religious peacemakers risked less than politicians by their adventurousness. Unionist political history is littered with the headless corpses of politicians, lopped off when the rubber band snapped. Maverick church people were also reined in but unconventionality is more permissible in the churches than in political parties. The very nature of religious space, therefore, gave those who were not risk averse (indeed, those who were risk seeking), the opportunity to be brave.

Time is as important here as space. Formal politics operates with time scales that prioritize the immediate. Formal politics does not cope well with long hauls. Politicians want results and they want them now. Clergy, however, inclined as they are to the hereafter, can operate on a slower timescale, taking the time to develop relationships and build rapport. The slow pace of sacred space thus gave pro-peace clergy opportunities denied to politicians.

Unionist political history, however, also reveals that politicians showed a remarkable ability to ignore vanguard clergy who were ahead of them. There are many reasons for this: we wish to mention one religious factor. The Protestant churches are schismatic—a house divided as Steve Bruce put it (Bruce, 1990)—and decentralized. Authority is dispersed and localized. Church governance might identify an apex to the hierarchy—the Anglican Primate, the Presbyterian Moderator or the Methodist President—but these are titular and temporary and individuals occupying these offices had to be artful and skilful to sidestep the democratic structures within the institutions that constrained them (as so many respondents alleged of Eames). Protestant churches did not present a unified position and the smaller and more enlightened sections carried little authority and weight; para-church and ecumenical organizations even less. This diffuseness deflected their criticism of Unionist politicians. Politicians could turn to other sections of the church where there was support and readily ignore anyone they wished.

It would be foolish to allege that we are claiming Unionist politicians were intransigent; the evidence of the GFA attests some were not. We are arguing, however, that some Protestant clergy were a vanguard ahead even of the least intransigent Unionist politician.

3

Opportunities and Constraints in
Religious Peace Work

INTRODUCTION

It might be useful at this point to summarize our argument and survey the
state of religious peacebuilding during 'the Troubles'. So far we have emphasized the churches' contribution to the social and political peace processes by
means of a typology of kinds of peacemaking. The typology enables us to see
that the churches placed their emphasis on the social peace process, concentrating on relationship-building between Catholics and Protestants within and
outside sacred spaces. Outside the group of committed ecumenists, however,
the building of trust, empathy, and understanding through new forms of
Catholic-Protestant relations was not extensive or successful. Paradoxically,
as supposedly apolitical institutions, the churches were more successful in
building relations of trust with the paramilitary organizations, which were
later mobilized for purposes of effective backchannel political communication.
Thus, they contributed with greater effect to the political peace process. This is
the reverse to how their contribution is presented by commentators, who
herald their efforts in the social peace process.

The focus of religious peacemaking, however, remained primarily on the
realization of negative peace, thus on conflict transformation, by facilitating
the ending of violence. Social transformation through advancement of positive
peace was advocated by a small few through the social gospel, people who
were not usually ecumenists, dominated as this was by the intelligentsia and
the middle classes, but activists in hard-hit areas, Loyalist and Republican,
moved by the poverty in their surroundings, or those whose ministry brought
them into the arena of transitional justice, involving pastoral work with
prisoners and their families. The case for positive peace—the (re)introduction
of equality, justice, fairness, and social redistribution—was on the whole
ignored and assumed, beyond the small few, either to be outside the bailiwick
of the churches or to follow naturally from statebuilding in the political peace
process.

Useful as it has been in illuminating these features of religious peacemaking in Northern Ireland, the conceptual framework needs to be extended in order to locate religious peace work in the context of broader civil society peacemaking. This enables us to identify further opportunities and constraints affecting the churches, and to place their kinds of religious peacemaking in the broader relationship between the churches, civil society, and the state. The church-civil society-state nexus is the main prism through which religious peacemaking in Northern Ireland should be approached; shedding light on what otherwise appears as inchoate and haphazard activities. This is the purpose in this chapter.

One of the serious limitations of the literature on civil society is its tendency to treat civil society as a homogenous entity, devoid of division and complexity. While the contrast between 'good' and 'bad' civil society is well known (Chambers and Kopstein, 2001), and the civil sphere is recognized as having 'regressive' elements that require civil repair (Alexander, 2006), including, often, the exclusionary features of bonding social capital (Putnam, 2000), other fissures remain untheorized. In this chapter, we develop our conceptualization further by identifying four strategic social spaces in civil society that the churches occupied in pursuing their peacemaking activities. Various opportunities and constraints are associated with these particular spaces, which help to set religious peacebuilding in context.

To help non-sociologists understand what is meant by this, a distinction needs to be made between space and place. Places are physical spaces, existing as bricks and mortar. The churches occupied many different places during the peace process, encountering all sorts of different people who occupy these places; these can be secular places such as prisons, schools, and hospitals, and sacred places such as church premises. In particular, we have emphasized the importance of prisons as secular places critical to the churches' dialogue with paramilitary organizations in the social peace process and, out of such dialogue, their utilization of sacred places for backchannel political communication in the political peace process.

Space can include place but is conceptually different. For example, sacred spaces are places that exist as physical locations—pulpits, particular church buildings, monasteries and the like—but they also transcend place by having social and cultural qualities beyond any one physical place. We emphasized the particular qualities sacred spaces had that made them eminently suitable as physical places for backchannel political communications. These qualities did not reside in the bricks and mortar of actual places—meeting in a tin shack halfway up a mountain can provide as much secrecy as Clonard Monastery; these qualities were found in the association of these physical places with cultural and social values such as honesty, integrity, confidentiality, and anonymity. Space, in other words, also includes cultural, economic, political, and intellectual environment. The geography of place, from its emphasis on locality and neighbourhood through to national and imperial places, is thus joined with approaches that emphasize space as environments where sets of ideas, values, beliefs, and social practices provide a framework for social and personal life. This is the sense in which we use space in this chapter to demarcate the various environments of ideas, values, beliefs, and practices of which civil society is made up. Civil society has tangible and material venues—it is comprised in part by physical locations and groupings with visible structures— but, conceptually, civil society is also constituted by different sets of ideas, values, practices, and beliefs about itself and the wider social world.

We wish to critique the naïve view that civil society is a unified and homogenous space, with a common set of practices, ideas, values, and beliefs. We emphasize four socially strategic social spaces—intellectual, institutional, market, and political—as important to the peace process that go well beyond the now familiar distinctions between 'good' and 'bad', or progressive and regressive, civil society. These strategic spaces help us understand further the difference in the kinds of engagements that churches and para-church organizations had with the social and political dimensions of the peace process. They are important also for illustrating that the churches retained cultural authority beyond the numbers that practised regularly, for these spaces potentially integrated churches with other key parts of civil society, giving them significance beyond the number of adherents weekly in the pews. However, as we shall emphasize in Chapter 4, the failure of the churches to link up with secular civil society, with whom they shared these spaces, is all the more regrettable.

These strategic spaces are: *intellectual spaces* (as places for discussion of peace, development of visions for peace, ideas for conflict resolution, new ideas for reconciliation work, envisioning the new society, etc.); *institutional spaces* (religious organizations putting peace into practice in their own activities and behaviours); *market spaces* (their employment of social, symbolic, cultural, and material resources to actively support peace and peace work); and *political spaces* (their engagement with the political peace process, engagement with political groups and their armed wings, with governments, etc.). If we combine this typology with those in Chapter 1, we suggest that in intellectual spaces we find the churches doing many forms of ecumenical activity and anti-sectarianism; in institutional spaces we see the churches engaging in cross-community activities and involving themselves in national and local peace initiatives; in market spaces the churches were involved in those post-violence adjustment problems that involved expending material and cultural resources, notably transitional justice work with prisoners and their families, and other forms of faith-based social action; in political spaces we see the churches involved in mediation, especially in dialogue with paramilitaries, acting as backchannels of communication, facilitating engagement between the various factions, including paramilitaries and governments. This is presented diagrammatically in Figure 4.

Intellectual	Institutional
Ecumenism, anti-sectarianism	Cross-community activities, peace initiatives

Market	Political
Transitional justice work with prisoners and families, social gospel	Mediation, backchannel political communication, formal political representation

Figure 4. Civil society's strategic social spaces

As a preface to the discussion of the importance of these four strategic social spaces in civil society to an understanding of the opportunities and constraints on religious peacebuilding in Northern Ireland, we must first unpack the idea of civil society peacemaking.

CIVIL SOCIETY AND ITS CONTRADICTIONS

The notion of civil society is much in vogue in peace research (see Kaldor, 2003; Orjuela, 2008; van Leeuwen, 2009; Brewer, 2010). In part this is an empirical observation reflecting the large number of peace agreements that involve the participation and contribution of civil society groups (see Bell and O'Rourke, 2007). There is also a conceptual argument, deriving from the analytic linkage between civil society and democracy.[1] The conceptual link is portrayed in three different ways, with civil society working to support democratization via discourse, values, and institutions. We will explore each briefly in turn.

The suggestion that the public or civil sphere involves a specific form of dialogue is well enmeshed in social science. The claim owes much to the early intellectual prominence of Habermas ([1981]1983) in the modern theorizing

---

[1] Northern Ireland is different from most transitional societies in having a democratic deficit—inadequate and incomplete democratic representation—rather than authoritarianism, the military campaign against which, of course, temporarily only enlarged the deficit in the form of Direct Rule (for a consideration of how political violence impacted on the democratic deficit in Northern Ireland and South Africa, see Brewer, 2003c: 129–39).

of civil society, who argued that civil society is the only arena where free dialogical exchange is possible, comprising a discursive space in which people can discuss, debate, and shape public opinion free of ideological and other encumbrances. The approach of deliberative democracy theorists to civil society peacemaking is premised on arguments such as this, in that civil society groups help in the introduction of deliberative democracy by comprising forums for discursive deliberation that desensitize and eventually transcend violent politics (for example, Dryzek, 2005). This parallels the emphasis in peace research on eliminating forms of 'hate speech' and intolerant talk as part of post-conflict democratic dialogue (for example, Paris, 2004: 196–9) and as ways of reinforcing reconciliation in restorative case conferences by avoiding insult (Scheff, 1997: 11). Roland Paris, for example, emphasizes the importance of socially responsible public media in peace processes and the importance of excluding from the public sphere forms of talk that are divisive, such as by establishing rigorous but enforceable codes of conduct for journalists or by jamming 'incendiary broadcasts' (2004: 197–8) on radio. It also infuses the attention on the important role of the media in post-conflict restoration (for example, Lynch and McGoldrick, 2005; Servaes, 2008, 2010), which is in part about the peace advocacy role of the media but also the management of 'hate media' (Servaes, 2010: 62) and sensationalist and partisan reporting.[2]

The notion that civil discourse is the characteristic form of dialogue in civil society also enters the recent revival of the term tolerance. Toleration does not mean being uncritical towards others but being polite, giving them recognition, accepting their rights, and according positive value to them, even when there is disagreement (see Jones, 2006); differences are conducted within the boundaries of civil discourse. There are, of course, limits to toleration (see Forst, 2004), which imply that people do not have to tolerate the intolerant, in that law, public morality, and cosmopolitan or humanitarian values regulate the differences that we have to live with and those we do not. The practices of toleration advocated by O'Neill (1993), however, ignore the intolerant in favour of an exclusive focus on people's obligations to communicate in public with civility and discursive openness that affects how we both talk and listen to others. Again there is a parallel with Habermas, for this comes close to his idea of an 'ideal speech situation' ([1981]1983), which he conceived as a situation where actors, under a 'fair play' rule, are all equally endowed with the capacities of discourse, recognize each other's basic social equality, and speech is undistorted by ideology or misrecognition. In expanding on Habermas's

---

[2] On the role of the media in assisting new forms of memory work as a peace strategy, see Brewer (2010: 153–4). With respect to sensationalist reporting, it is worth noting that the media in Sierra Leone, for example, were prevented from melodramatic and lurid reporting of the witness evidence of child soldiers at the truth and reconciliation commission, and much of their evidence was considered in private (see Brewer, 2010: 71, 160ff).

notion, Kingwell entitled his book *A Civil Tongue* (1995), which simplifies the meaning but captures its thrust.

Sociologists, however, have tended to side with the more popular view that civil society is the locus of particular values. Trust rather than tolerance has received the attention in sociology (for a selection, see: Lewis and Weigert, 1985a, 1985b; Misztal, 1996; Seligman, 1997, 1998; Sztompka, 1999; Gambetta, 2000; Mollering, 2001). It is untrustworthiness that motivates this interest, whether as the result of increasingly fragile interpersonal relations (see Giddens, 1990: 14ff), the rise of semi-detached relationships (which Bauman, 2002, refers to as 'liquid love'), the growth of terrorism (O'Neill, 2002: chapter 2), or the general deterioration in the legitimacy of governments and public institutions (survey data on which is discussed in Newton, 2001). The decline in trust is felt to be all the more serious because trust is foundational to stable societies. Two sorts of trust relationship exist—interpersonal trust as part of normal social role expectations (on which, see Shapiro, 1987), and public trust (O'Neill, 2002: 8), what others call 'generalized trust' (Seligman, 1997: 6) or 'abstract moral trust' (Mollering, 2001: 404). Public trust describes the place of trust within society's moral codes as well as the level of actual trust that is placed in social and public institutions. Interpersonal trust describes the level of trust we place in those we relate with. Interpersonal trust is seen as the necessary building block of public trust, as both a precursor to social cooperation and its outcome. Moral or public trust is portrayed as essential to people's feelings of solidarity (see particularly Lewis and Weigert, 1985b); social order can break down to the extent that distrust becomes the primary moral assumption. For this reason, Mollering (2001: 403ff) argues, public trust has to involve 'suspension' of feelings of untrustworthiness, that is, bracketing off the unknowable until, if ever, it becomes known, in order to work on the basis of trust rather than distrust. He describes this as taking 'the leap of trust'.

The connection between public trust and civil society peacemaking is clear. While Levi and Stokes (2000) argue that respecting social norms about trust is an obligation of citizenship, communal conflict can destroy these norms, increasing senses of untrustworthiness in the post-conflict setting. Civil society theorists, however, portray trust as one of the key values that arise in civil society, thus making it essential to the stability of post-conflict societies. Trust is portrayed in this literature as grounded in the level of people's civil society engagement and of their participation in voluntary associations (on trust and voluntary associations, see Fenton, Passey, and Hems, 1999; Tonkiss and Passey, 1999; Anheier and Kendall, 2002). Civil society is therefore seen as both the arena for the display of trust and the place for its cultivation (on trust and civil society, see Seligman, 2000; Tonkiss, Passey, and Fenton, 2000), the space in which people learn to trust and get used to taking 'the leap of trust' without it backfiring. In this regard trust is also linked to social capital (see Newton, 2001) and is thus one of the civic virtues that motivates and enhances democracy (on trust and democracy, see Warren, 1999; Misztal, 2001), including in newly emerging democratic societies (see Sztompka, 1997). Peacemaking thus requires a vigorous and vibrant civil society where victims and ex-combatants alike can learn—or learn again—to trust each other through participation in cross-community voluntary associations and by their joint value commitments to new forms of solidarity.

This emphasis on civil society as the foundation for democratic and moral values unites the different arguments of Putnam (2000) and Alexander (2006) on civil society. Both Putnam and Alexander agree that civil society garners and disseminates democratic values, embedding peaceful politics in a civic culture that produces trust, empathy, active citizenship, and senses of community. Although neither author discusses peace processes, the driving force of civil society peacemaking would differ for each; it is social capital in the one case, social solidarity in the other. Putnam premises social capital on social connectedness, as the civic virtues of trust, empathy, and the rest extend outwards to generalized others, on the basis of their development first amongst people closely known to each other through myriad cross-cutting social networks that bind everyone loosely. Herein lays the value of third sector, voluntary institutions in post-conflict societies as Putnam portrays it, for as overlapping social networks they constitute the medium through which civic virtues are both garnered and disseminated. The problem with Putnam's formulation is when social connectedness remains socially exclusionary, restricting people's social networks to others just like themselves, making post-conflict values partisan and one-sided.

Alexander, on the other hand, bases civil society on universal shared values, that extend to people unknown and unconnected to us, even loosely, but with whom we feel empathy based on commitment to wider humanitarian and cosmopolitan social bonds. Voluntary associations are irrelevant to this moral landscape; what matters are the values disseminated by the institutions of cultural reproduction, such as the media, public opinion, and popular culture. The measure of the civility of post-conflict society is thus the treatment accorded to, and the moral representation of, the stranger; not meant in the sense of stranger as newcomer or outsider (which is how sociology has problematized 'the stranger' in the past[3]) but as the former 'enemy' no longer able now to be morally enervated and denuded as a result of the peace process (see Jansen, 1980, for the distinction between strangers as 'outsiders' and 'enemies within'). The problem for Alexander's account is when victims and ex-combatants remain locked within separate moral codes. For both Alexander and Putnam it is not that civil society fails in these instances, it is that it

---

[3] We have in mind here the work of Georg Simmel and Alfred Schutz on the stranger, both of whom cast the stranger as an outsider. For a comparison of their treatment, see McLemore (1970).

remains partisan by succeeding all too well *within* the group boundaries of the erstwhile protagonists.

The third conceptual linkage between civil society and peace places emphasis on institutions. This is the approach of the global civil society literature that prioritizes the international network of progressive peace groups that traverse local, national, and international stages and which mobilize a further array of special interest groups across the globe—such as women's groups, peasant organizations, human rights groups, charities, and INGOs—as part of their peace campaigns (associated, for example, with Kaldor, 2003; Banchoff, 2008; Brewer, 2010; for criticism, see Keane, 2003; Anderson and Rieff, 2005). These institutions are not important for the values they inculcate and spread—global civil society theorists assume activists already have progressive values as the motivational precursor to participation—but for their global reach. These global institutional networks equip and skill local peace activists, provide resources to sustain local peacemaking, and bestow a regulatory framework of humanitarian law and practice to monitor peacemaking, for example such as through UN peacebuilding initiatives, war crimes legislation, and UNIFEM's emphasis on gender mainstreaming as a peace strategy (see Brewer, 2010: chapter 4, for a discussion on gender and peacemaking). Together with a range of philanthropic foundations and research centres, these institutions financially, materially, and intellectually underwrite civil society peacemaking.

However, as Brewer noted (2010: 206–7), it is naïve to assume that civil society is always progressive and works towards the same peaceful end. On the contrary, fissures in global civil society reproduce themselves locally in specific peace processes in two ways. Leaving aside for the moment those regressive parts of global civil society that oppose peace, first, progressive groups can be divided over means. In Sri Lanka, for example, civil society is a politically contested space and tends to be divided along ethnic lines, with separate Tamil and Sinhalese NGOs (Orjuela, 2008). In Rwanda, for example, global human rights groups criticize transitional justice in the *gacaca* courts, while global women's groups applaud them for empowering women (Cobban, 2006); and both are right if we conceive of global civil society as containing fractures that differentiate groups locally within particular peace processes. Second, progressive groups can be divided over ends. There is no discord over commitment to peace, but peace means different things. For these reasons, Holton (2005: 139) refers not to one global civil society but several, as different parts occupy distinct spaces, globally and locally.

However, by far the most widely recognized fissure in civil society, global or otherwise, is that between its progressive and regressive elements. The expansion in the quantity of civil society groups in the post-Cold War era, with its end-of-history euphoria around the universalization of Western forms of democratic association, gave, according to Paris (2004: 160), no thought to the *quality* of civil society that was being formed, noting that civil society need not necessarily promote tolerance, trust or democratization. This is encapsulated in most of the theorizations of civil society (for example, Putzel, 1997; Putnam, 2000; Chambers and Kopstein, 2001; Alexander, 2006); none can be accused of idealizing civil society or utopianism. However, for all this honesty in acknowledging the fissures and fragmentations within civil society, with the commensurate highlighting of its regressive features, the mapping of the landscape of civil society does not go far enough and we are none the clearer about the processes by which religious peacemaking can succeed in a setting where religion is itself problematic.

If we are to understand this process (and how it can be accomplished by religious groups in other conflict societies), the current maps of the landscape of civil society are required to be redrawn. One way to conceptualize the role religion plays in peace processes as a form of bridging social capital or civic repair, is to distinguish the strategic social spaces it occupies in civil society as special locations for religious peacemaking. These socially strategic spaces in civil society give religion weight well beyond that carried by the number of adherents—which in some places is declining—and they bring into higher relief the mechanisms by which religion transforms into becoming part of the solution. They are useful for deconstructing the idea of progressive civil society as itself necessarily always homogeneous by illustrating that religious groups can work differently from each other—and sometimes in opposition—despite their shared peace orientation.

THE FOUR STRATEGIC SOCIAL SPACES IN CIVIL SOCIETY

We suggest there are four strategic social spaces in progressive civil society involved with advocacy of positive peace, giving potential for civil repair and bridging social capital (see also Brewer, 2010: 55–6; Brewer, Higgins, and Teeney, 2010). After describing them, we illustrate each in turn.

- *Intellectual spaces*, in which alternative ideas are envisaged and peace envisioned, and in which the private troubles of people are reflected upon intellectually as emerging policy questions that are relevant to them as civil society groups. Civil society groups can help to rethink the terms of the conflict so that it becomes easier to intellectually contemplate its transcendence or ending, and through their championing of alternative visions come to identify the range of issues that need to be articulated.

- *Institutional spaces*, in which these alternatives are enacted and practised by the civil society groups themselves, on local and global stages, making the groups role models and drivers of the process of transformation. Civil society thus lives out the vision of peace and, in its own practice, transgresses the borders that usually keep people apart, being institutions that practise, say, non-racialism or non-sectarianism well in advance of the general citizenry.

- *Market spaces*, in which cultural, social, and material resources are devoted by the civil society groups—drawn from local and global civic networks—to mobilize and articulate these alternatives, rendering them as policy issues in the public sphere, nationally or internationally. With practices that implement, within their own terms of reference and field of interest, this alternative vision of peace, civil society groups commit resources—labour power, money, educational skills, campaigning, and debate—to underwrite their own commitment, to persuade others to share this commitment, and to draw society's attention to the policy transformations that peace requires.

- *Political spaces*, in which civil society groups engage with the political process as backchannels of communication or assisting in negotiation of the peace settlement, either directly by taking a seat at the negotiating table or indirectly by articulating the policy dilemmas that the peace negotiators have to try to settle or balance. These political spaces can be domestic and international, inasmuch as civil society groups can focus on facilitating political negotiations internally, as well as internationalizing the negotiations, either by using diaspora networks to pressure domestic governments and policymakers to come to the table, or by urging involvement of third parties and neutral mediators in the negotiations.

Intellectual space

Some world religions emphasize personal transformation through meditation, such as Yogic and Buddhist traditions. This is promoted as a strategy for peacebuilders to develop motivation for engagement and as a practice for participants in negotiations, amongst others, who are recommended to utilize space for generating peacefulness and calm to aid their discussions. The Christian traditions involved in Northern Ireland are not that different: they are liturgical, contemplative, and prayer-based, and spend a great deal of time thinking about sacred ideas and about the terminology best to express them. The preaching ministry of Christian churches and para-church organizations reinforce this emphasis on words. Experiential forms of Christian religion are bodily—speaking in tongues,[4] healing gifts, charismatic forms of participative,

---

[4] It may seem odd to describe speaking in tongues as experiential but the point is that the body is said to be inhabited by the Holy Spirit. The words spoken are unintelligible, awaiting someone else who is bodily 'channeled' by the Holy Spirit to interpret their meaning.

active worship—whereas conventional Christian religiosity appeals to the intellect through ideas and words. It is clear therefore, that Christian religious organizations within conflict zones can readily constitute themselves as intellectual spaces to challenge the terms by which the conflict is understood and to envision a new society. Some of them think about what for many others (including some other religions' traditions and Christian churches) is still unthinkable—such as non-racialism, non-sectarianism, the ending of repression, political and socio-economic reform, or the fall of communism.

The churches in Northern Ireland have readily constituted themselves as intellectual spaces to think about the conflict, and have utilized sacred spaces as physical places for this rethinking (amongst other places). The Working Party on Violence in Ireland, for example, under the direction of Cahal Daly and Eric Gallagher, was established in 1973 to enquire into the effects of violence on communities and to suggest ways by which the churches could assist in its elimination (for its terms of reference, see Power, 2007: 19). There were endless discussions within the ecumenist tradition about sectarian divisions: about the manner in which sectarianism reproduced itself, such as through mixed marriages; about theology, politics, and violence. Indeed, ecumenism was very good at thinking, writing reports, and hosting workshops, seminars, and conferences. The volume of work produced by its major organizational bodies, such as ISE, IICM, the FPG, and Corrymeela, for example, was impressive. The FPG purposely set up as a think tank catalyst in 1983, relatively late into the conflict, and published thirteen substantial pamphlets on aspects of 'the Troubles' in as many years, covering such topics as memory, forgiveness, identity, and peace (for a detailed description of the group, see Power, 2007: 175–9). Leading ecumenist intellectuals, such as the Methodist Johnston McMaster, were personally very prolific in publishing, writing pamphlets, and strategy documents intended for public rather than academic audiences, and Sister Geraldine Smyth, as another of ecumenism's intellectuals, penned many pieces for academic journals. Power (2007: 37) shows, for example, that in the ten years prior to the signing of the GFA, the IICM produced five reports (thirteen in all), culminating with a discussion document on sectarianism (discussed at length in Power, 2007: 44–8), a theme taken forward in, amongst other examples, ISE's Moving Beyond Sectarianism project, the PCI's Peace Vocation and Preparing Youth for Peace Initiative, and the COI's Hard Gospel programme and its Think Again initiative (the latter a title highly suggestive of the point).

It was not just ecumenism's main leaders who occupied intellectual space to challenge and confront communal violence, for it took on a local dimension with the involvement of neighbourhood-based ecumenical groups developing their own initiatives for thinking about issues such as identity, memory, sectarianism, and mixed marriages. Much of this space was taken up in articulating and working through the local issues that the wider sectarian division threw up. The Revd Earl Storey, referring to the Hard Gospel project he led, made the point in interview that one of its key concerns was reconciliation but that 'reconciliation means actually addressing the issues, facilitating the addressing of the issues, that actually cause separation' (21 September 2005).

Some of these local groups, however, were not as ready to hear uncomfortable truths about the churches' role in sectarianism as their own leaders would admit or their ecumenist rhetoric would imply. Naming one leading ecumenical community that had been 'meeting for years', a prominent ecumenist said, 'I am sure they did achieve good things, but when we actually started getting them to talk to one another about the issues of sectarianism, it nearly ripped the group apart' (interview 29 November 2007). At one end of the continuum, participants put up barriers, giving ecumenical groups the impression they were achieving more in these intellectual spaces than they were, while at the other extreme, some participants could easily ridicule the endless seminars and reports as just words. As one of Power's respondents put it, the IICM, 'is only a talking shop, I personally think that if it closed tomorrow it wouldn't be any great loss because they are only ever really talking round in circles' (2007: 37). Amongst our respondents, Cecelia Clegg blamed the local ecumenical groups for being 'too cosy and middle class', of not confronting strongly enough the hard gospel of reconciliation (interview 29 November 2007). Not every Christian shows the foresight and realism of the Revd David Armstrong: 'I feel that the church made a huge contribution in causing the problem to exist, so I feel therefore the church has a major contribution to play in causing the problem to cease' (interview 2 December 2005).

Ecumenism was not the only intellectual space for rethinking, however, for evangelicalism was doing its own. Two trends in Northern Irish evangelicalism eventually came together to mark a fundamental intellectual shift. The first was the emergence of liberal, 'open' evangelicalism in the form of ECONI, the other the fracture within conservative evangelicalism between those who developed a commitment to peace within the framework of a reformed GFA, and the diehards unwilling to countenance any form of power-sharing that included SF. As Ganiel (2008a: 151) documents, this division was premised on another. Shifting their emphasis towards a socially conservative moral agenda, based around opposition to abortion, divorce, homosexuality, civil partnerships, and the like,[5] allowed the pragmatists within conservative

---

[5] The Revd Lesley Carroll gave us a glimpse of this working even within the PCI. As a member of the Eames-Bradley Consultative Group on the Past she expressed disappointment that the Report caused no comment. 'I was staggered. Nobody asked a question, no comment, nothing. I mean nothing. I said there [were] a number of contentiously political issues; the only question the church rises to is around issues of sex' (interview 10 January 2008). The Caleb Foundation's website hosts the Caleb Forum (www.calebfoundation.org/userimages/forum.htm), a blog that reflects some of these shifts. The contents—some of which are admittedly posted by opponents—

evangelicalism to both move away from the single issue emphasis on the political Union with Britain and find common cause with a morally conservative Catholic Church. The diehard conservative evangelicals thus sound rather shrill and old-fashioned when now they still push the constitutional question and use rhetoric that the pragmatists—and everyone else—associates with the past. Subsuming themselves under Traditional Unionist Voice in politics and the Caleb Foundation in theology, the nomenclature seems to epitomize the Old Testament, old-fashioned, old politics of conservative evangelicals, although membership of the two bodies is not coterminous.[6]

The split in conservative evangelicalism is reminiscent of the intellectual wrangles within Afrikaner nationalism when it was first contemplating reform between what was called *verlightes* and *verkrampts* (Adam and Giliomee, 1980). Afrikaner nationalism was conservative, politically and culturally dominant, and resistant to reform, and the wings represented the less conservative Afrikaners (*verlightes*) and their opposites (*verkrampts*). One of the most significant developments within South Africa's democratic transition was the eventual link-up between the *verlightes* and the wider anti-apartheid movement in which the more liberal Afrikaners acceded to Black control of the polity in order to ensure White control of the economy in a trade-off that formed a direct part of the elite compromise that produced the negotiated deal (Brewer, 2003c: 121–3). This shift, however, was premised on a long period of re-envisioning within Afrikaner nationalism in which progressive Afrikaners redefined the nation and who had rights to its citizenship and re-evaluated their interests away from being ethnic based towards class based. This facilitated the break in the *volk* identity within Afrikanerdom (on political fissures within Afrikaners, see Adam and Giliomee, 1980; Giliomee, 1990, 1992).

It would be unwise to extend this analogy too far notwithstanding the literature that compares Afrikaners and Ulster Protestants in their covenantal thinking (for example, Akenson, 1992; Bruce, 1998), which is not the point we are making, but it is illustrative of the intellectual shifts that can take place within conflict groups. The more liberal-conservative evangelicals (a term adopted from Boal, Keane, and Livingstone, 1997)[7] and ECONI formed a

---

address moral issues such as homosexuality and the revelations concerning Iris Robinson's private life, as well as debating science, creationism and the like, but when it was consulted on 28 July 2010 not one entry concerned politics or the peace process.

[6] The Caleb Foundation was formed in 1998 to provide theological support for the campaign against the GFA (little has been written on it within social science, but see Ganiel, 2008a: 111–12). Ganiel makes the telling point that ECONI's formation in the wake of the 1985 campaign against the AIA gives both organizations political roots, although they envisage the link between evangelical identity and Northern Irish politics in opposite ways (2008a: 120–1).

[7] Ganiel (2008a: 49) correctly argues that while evangelicals in the traditional sense comprise about 25–33% of the Northern Irish population, evangelical symbolism, assumptions, and mores

sizeable constituency of evangelicals within the pro-settlement, pro-peace camp, trading a traditional Unionist political agenda for a socially conservative moral one, willing to countenance a deal that had long been championed by ecumenism but which, fortunately as it turned out, bore none of its stamp because of its lack of engagement in the public sphere. This allowed the ECONI-style evangelicals to celebrate the peace settlement as an achievement of ecumenist relationship-building (between Catholics and Protestants, evangelicals and ecumenists, and progressive Unionism and Republicanism) and the liberal-conservative evangelicals to portray it as a strategy that was entirely independent of ecumenism. The views of the Revd Mervyn Gibson, for example, a Presbyterian minister with strong connections to Loyalism and the Orange Order and the sort of liberal-conservative evangelical we have in mind here, are worth repeating on this point: 'peacebuilding hadn't to be ecumenical. I'm not an ecumenist. I believe evangelicals have a responsibility to the peace problem and actually they allowed it to become an ecumenical agenda. People will [be] ecumenical, that's fair enough. I have no difficulty with that but equally there are those who build peace without an ecumenical agenda. I think the evangelical church is only rediscovering peacebuilding and probably is still working through what it means' (interview 27 January 2006). It was thinking like this that allowed, two years later, Paisley to enter a devolved government with SF.[8]

This is not to suggest that liberal-conservative evangelicals such as Gibson identified with ECONI. In an interview on 15 July 2010, Gibson commented that while ECONI spoke from within the evangelical constituency, it was perceived as attacking Loyalism. ECONI was portrayed as full of well-intentioned but naïve people, stating that while he had good relations with them there were political disagreements. This is more open and friendly than the Caleb Foundation's view. 'My heart is still in parish ministry', Gibson said on another occasion, and 'at the end of the day I am a parish minister who became involved in peacebuilding because of my parish, because I have been working with Loyalist paramilitaries and built up those relationships' (interview 27 January 2006). The point, however, is that Gibson shared intellectual space in evangelicalism with ECONI and that liberal-conservative evangelicals like him were motivated by the same concerns. ECONI, in other words, was a bridge to several crossing points, connecting, from the one direction, the progressive evangelicalism that it represented with the non-ecumenical but

---

penetrate the mainstream Protestant churches and even non-churchgoing Protestants, making liberal-conservative evangelicalism, as Boal, Keane, and Livingstone (1997: 11) argued, the dominant attitudinal position. Ganiel's own term for this position is 'mediating evangelical' (2008a: 126–44).

[8] Kaufmann's (2007) study of the Orange Order emphasizes its hardline shift but also the number of pragmatists within it supportive of the GFA.

liberal-conservative elements within evangelicalism, and towards ecumenism in the other. It was a network of linkages that allowed the likes of Gibson to remain distant from ecumenism but which allowed Gibson's commitment to peace to solidify into an evangelical constituency that worked for a settlement. As an intellectual space, therefore, ECONI's ideas and writings were critical to mediating these splits, allowing the ecumenists opportunities to relate to progressive evangelicals and encouraging liberal-conservative evangelicals to rethink the negative features of conservative evangelicalism. This allowed evangelicals to accept they could theologically and politically buy into the discourse of reconciliation and peace on a non-ecumenical basis.

Key to this intellectual shift was ECONI's argument that traditional conservative evangelicalism misunderstood Calvinism and that the emphasis they laid on the elision of covenantal and Old Testament religion, chosen people status, nationhood, and land (discussed in Brewer and Higgins, 1998: 135–51; also see Akenson, 1992) was in their own terms idolatry and made Ulster more iconic than Christ.[9] Formed in 1985–6 as a result of dissatisfaction at the way evangelicalism was being politically mobilized against the AIA, it is thus no coincidence that ECONI's first booklet in 1988 was entitled *For God and His Glory Alone*.[10] In a series of pamphlets edited by Alwyn Thomson, then ECONI's research officer, the meaning of faith and identity within Northern Irish Protestantism was explored—*Faith in Ulster* (Thomson, 1996), *The Great White Tent* (Thomson, 1999), and *Fields of Vision* (Thomson, 2002)— all of which deconstructed, on specifically religious grounds, the shibboleths of traditional Northern Irish evangelicalism. It kept up this critique through its regular magazine, *Lion and Lamb*, a title drawn from Scripture that symbolized the healing they sought to effect. ECONI wished to modernize evangelicalism in a society needful of more tolerance and inclusivity. Anabaptism gave ECONI shared roots with the Methodists and the Baptist, mission hall tradition in Northern Ireland, firmly locating it in the pacifist strand of theology. Its commitment to peacemaking, therefore, was religiously understood and located, allowing it to speak with authority and legitimacy to the peacemakers in liberal-conservative evangelicalism who occupied spaces outside the unreconstructed and hardline corners of fundamentalism (see Vignette 8).

---

[9] Aughey (1990) makes the point that there is more to Unionism than religion and that Unionists did not necessarily need religion to anchor their sense of belonging. While evidently true, in practice certain sorts of Unionists made religion the central connection to the territory of Ulster and Protestant identity. Brewer and Higgins (1998: 129–51) refer to these as covenantal Unionists. They are to be distinguished from what has become commonly known as civic Unionists (see especially Porter, 1996).

[10] As Getty (2003: 60) shows, this was a deliberate pun on the usual Ulster Protestant refrain of 'For God and Ulster'. Within the next ten years 10,000 copies had been distributed (Ganiel, 2008a: 121).

As Getty (2003: 60) correctly writes, 'ECONI's work is effective because it is able to galvanise its target community using its own language'. The mark was not ecumenism, the already 'converted' peace activists, but other evangelicals; it was not working as a cross-community group in this sense (as Ganiel argues, 2008a: 128). Although ECONI did transcend the community divide, it was self-consciously an evangelical group seeking to transform traditional evangelicalism. This was a powerful intellectual space that facilitated dialogue of a very different kind to the ecumenist organizations. This intellectual re-envisioning was not only pursued through pamphleteering, the Anabaptist belief in social activism ensured that ECONI introduced a yearly conference, an annual ECONI Sunday, and a summer school, and organized regular workshops, conferences, and seminars on topics ranging from forgiveness, identity, Christian peacebuilding, transforming communities, and the matrix of culture–history–religion. ECONI did not just leave its peace work to intellectual spaces, for it put this re-envisioning into practice in what we call institutional spaces.

Vignette 8: Extracts of the interview with David Porter, Director of ECONI, 27 February 2006

ECONI was a reaction within evangelical Protestant circles to what was going on politically, so it was a direct catalytic pressure group, a lobby group to address the evangelical Protestant constituency about its total failure to have anything constructive, creative to say about what we understood to be the biblical requirements of discipleship around peacemaking, as part of [our] response to living in a community in conflict. That is why we began, so we were shaped by the Troubles, we came out of the Troubles, we were also shaped by a larger movement in world evangelicalism which was taken seriously. Saying 'For God and Ulster' is idolatry, bordering on the blasphemous. *For God and His Glory Alone* in 1988, it didn't say you can't be a Unionist and an Evangelical Christian. What it did say was that God is neutral on the constitutional future of Northern Ireland, that defending Ulster is not defending the Gospel, no more than Uniting Ireland is bringing about the reconciliation of the Gospel. God is not bound in to the constitutional arrangements on this Island. God is God and requires our allegiance, our commitment and our living his values in relation to our neighbour. Loving our enemy, making peace, living peace with all people as far as possible is within us. It was basically in the first instance a call to our own community to live up to that. If that is what Christian discipleship is about, then live for God and his glory alone in this community and that means forgiveness, it means love of enemy, it means commitment to being a peace maker, it means commitment to working for justice in society, it means repentance for how we have all screwed up and hated each other. This is what it means because our first citizenship call is as citizens of the Kingdom of God.

Institutional space

When the intellectual challenges and re-envisioning done in intellectual spaces is put into practice within their own institutions to change behaviours, policies, and beliefs towards peace and reconciliation, religious groups constitute an institutional space that practises peace. The importance placed on practice is reiterated in the attention we have given throughout to the idea of active peacemaking; intellectual re-envisioning that is not implemented in practical action risks remaining as passive peacemaking. In Northern Ireland's case, for example, the ecumenical churches, communities, and groups developed ideas about issues such as non-sectarianism, interfaith dialogue, and new forms of shared liturgy that challenged the basis of the division between Catholics and Protestants. For all the criticism alleged against them in Chapter 1, the clever minds that infused Northern Irish ecumenism did not remain solely within intellectual spaces, for ecumenism lived out its vision in a variety of cross-denominational activities, such as church-to-church contact, joint clergy groups, shared services, and joint prayer groups (as we saw in Chapter 1). Active peacemaking is not restricted to the social peace process, however, as we made clear in the last chapter, for institutional implementation of peace commitments reflect in the political peace process as well. Nor was ecumenism the only institutional space for religious peacemaking.

The progressive evangelical organizations also occupied institutional spaces as they put into practice their re-envisioning of evangelicalism. The Revd Gibson, for example, recalls difficult meetings within the Loyalist constituency he was trying to move, the outcome of which at the beginning of the meeting could never be taken for granted. He said of his general approach: 'it's conflict transformation, it's moving people. Every [Loyalist] Commission meeting, every contact, every relationship, is an opportunity for conflict transformation and positive change' (interview 27 January 2006). The advantage for Gibson was that the PCI to which he belonged, while split on the issue of ecumenism, was by the time of this interview constituting itself as an institutional space that put into practice the carefully crafted statements in support of reconciliation and non-violence. As an institution, it caught up with the vanguard Presbyterian ministers, such as Magee, Carroll, Newell, and Dunlop, who were practising active peacemaking ahead of the official position of the church. Indeed, John Dunlop's co-chairing of what is now called the Church and Society Committee of the General Assembly (currently chaired by Lesley Carroll) and was formerly called the Church and Government Committee—nomenclature that marked a significant shift after the signing of the GFA—oversaw many of the developments in the PCI's institutional policies; a committee that was also delegated to act on behalf of the PCI in some forms of peacemaking. As Dunlop said, it 'got itself involved in some discussions and some talks with people, sometimes quietly and sometimes on the record' (interview 23 March 2006).

Institutional spaces act as learning fields in which peace is put into practice first within the confines and remit of the organization and practised from places connected to it, allowing practitioners to remain within familiar territory and on grounds where they feel secure. It is not that peace remains as an intellectual pursuit; it is that it is first practised internally. This is often why sacred space was preferred for backchannel political communications and for dialogue with paramilitary organizations; it made the risk-taking involved in such work manageable and the space itself gave emotional reassurance. The importance of feeling oneself part of a broader institutional space, of not working alone and without wider support, was mentioned by the Revd John Morrow when he compared his period as a Presbyterian minister with leadership of the ecumenical community Corrymeela, an institutional space ahead of the PCI in practising active peacemaking: 'I was fortunate in one sense in that once I became working full time with Corrymeela I had a network of people who were 100 per cent behind me, but when I was working in an ordinary congregation I was in a much more difficult situation' (interview 7 December 2005). Occupancy of institutional spaces, in other words, not only facilitates active peacemaking, these spaces lend support to practitioners while doing it.

Similarly, the failure to back individual priests and pastors in their peacemaking activities is a barometer of the resistance of some churches to constitute themselves as institutional spaces. It can be recalled from Chapter 1 that some of the former activists in paramilitary organizations, when assessing the contribution of the churches, drew a telling distinction between the positive role of individual churchmen and women and the desultory efforts of the churches as institutions. However, as we have emphasized in Chapter 2, this criticism disguises the fact that the paramilitaries themselves were not much interested in deal-making at the beginning.

Market spaces

When religious groups focus less on themselves as institutions—as pathbreaking as this may be in some situations of communal conflict—in order to work amongst the poor, dispossessed, and victims of communal violence, they occupy market spaces in which their resources get devoted to peace; they are called market spaces because they are spaces for resource allocation. The importance of occupying strategic market spaces in this way is that it facilitates two transitions: from negative to positive peace, and from pastoral care to political engagement. This is often a two-stage process. From the initial involvement in the 'private troubles' of poor communities and victims, often comes the realization that allocating resources alone does not resolve these ills, recognizing that communal conflict makes them worse. From this can follow a wider engagement with the issue of peacemaking and the deployment of resources to help its materialization. Through global connections, religious groups are able to encourage co-religionists from outside the country to expend resources that both address the private troubles of people affected by violence and transform them into public issues on a global stage. Where religion and ethnicity elide, diaspora networks constitute a further web of co-religionists with potential to deploy resources to enhance the market spaces in which religious groups operate for the purposes of peacemaking. This marks the first transition from negative to positive peace, from conflict transformation to social transformation.

Church-based engagement in social justice, reflected in social action pro-grammes such as the Derry-based Waterside Churches Trust, now simply the Churches Trust (for fuller description, see Power, 2007: 95–100), Forth-spring's community regeneration project (see Power, 2007: 84–94), and Habi-tat for Humanity's cross-community house-building project, represent just a few of the many examples of the churches operating in market spaces, utilizing resources to impact on jobs, security, poverty, and family life as a way out of violence. As Bishop Edward Daly said of the Churches Trust, 'we felt if young people were given ownership of their city and we purchased a few properties, providing for the young people, as a contribution for young people to see that building was the way, not destroying, to be positive rather than negative' (interview 24 January 2006). Most of the cross-community work done by the churches in secular spaces, referred to in Chapter 1, and emphasized in particular by Power (2007) as their chief contribution towards the peace process, exemplifies the use of market space. 'Rather than developing proper-ty', said Bishop Edward Daly, work such as this 'was developing people'.[11]

This is more than charity and benevolent giving—a feature of all Christian practice, and something that people in Northern Ireland are noted for. As the journalist Alf McCreary put it, it involves moving out from being 'a comfort-able church' to accept a calling that involves what he called 'hassle' (interview 25 September 2007). He admitted most Christians were charitable givers but most 'don't want hassle'. 'Christians want a nice comfortable church. They want to be good neighbours, good parents, but when it comes to taking hassle it's a different matter.' Confronting the difficulties of working outside the safe confines of their own institutions, as committed to peace as they may be, requires a particular kind of Christian calling where charity becomes more

---

[11] Cardinal Daly, an inherently cautious leader, commented on his namesake's programme in Derry: 'I think that clergy haven't the skills that are needed to create jobs or enterprises that produce jobs, but they have the pastoral tact and the knowledge of their people to enable them to identify people with the relevant skills who will work with them in trying to create jobs and economically revitalize a deprived area' (interview 24 February 2006).

than giving money. It becomes giving of oneself, one's time, effort and skills, to make a difference in the lives of people adversely affected by 'the Troubles'. Market spaces take the churches out of institutional space into the 'real' world. The Revd John Dunlop worded it this way: 'I was involved in various bodies so I spent a certain amount of my life in what I called the public square; that you are not just living your life inside the bounds of the church but you are going wider than that. I am meeting a wide cross section of people which provides a certain context to your life' (26 March 2006).

The public square can be an uncomfortable, risky world, where faith commitments motivate engagement with controversial social problems such as injustice, unfairness, and inequality. This is a world all too rarely witnessed by believers in the pews. The Revd Gary Mason, for example, described the work of his East Belfast Mission and the Inner East Forum: 'we work in unemployment, we work in homelessness, we work in a youth agenda, we work in community. Yesterday it met the MLAs [Member of Legislative Assembly in the devolved government] in East Belfast, tomorrow we will meet with the Parades Commission' (interview 14 February 2006). There are many such fine examples of work like this, but all too often clerics who occupy market spaces find it difficult to take their congregations with them. Bishop Alan Harper, who subsequently succeeded Robin Eames as Anglican Primate, referred to this as the 'PLU' problem—market spaces put ordinary Christians in settings where they did not encounter 'people like us':

> If clergy, or even individual members of the congregation, attempt to step outside and engage with what may be perceived to be antisocial elements of the community, worse still if they try to bring them into the worshipping community, then they are likely to encounter a significant amount of opposition from, if you like the core, the old core of the parish, which see themselves as upholding a kind of respectability and a set of values, which they perceive as not being shared by the great unwashed, outside. So they can make life hell for somebody who tries to engage with the community within which, the church is set and its congregation meets, because they are not PLU, they are not 'people like us'. (Interview 25 January 2006)

It is fair to say that negative peace not positive peace remained the priority for most Christians, because market spaces are uncomfortable zones. The hesitancy to constitute themselves as market spaces set up an unfortunate disjuncture for the churches, which had implications for their capacity to engage with positive peace. Population relocation from working-class areas to the suburbs to escape high levels of violence meant a parallel process of church planting in 'safe' areas that has been going on as long as the conflict (Brewer, Keane, and Livingstone, 2006). Churches that remain in the troubled areas are often divorced from the communities in which they are located, with congregations in inner-city churches mostly commuting there from the suburbs, so that while the pastor may be involved locally, the flock remains aloof. Archbishop Alan Harper again: '[we] are in severe danger of having a major disjuncture between the church as a community of people and the community within which they find themselves, who may or may not be interested in being part of this church community but who are perceived by a significant body within the church community, as beyond the pale' (interview 25 January 2006). It is not just that, post-conflict, the churches have evacuated the public sphere. Many are immune to the local problems surrounding their premises and lack the social connectedness with their neighbourhood that is the building block of spiritual capital, a theme to which we will return in the Conclusion.

Political space

The second transition referred to above (the awareness that peace is necessary to solve social ills), occurs with the switch from pastoral concern in market spaces to politics and occupancy of political space. When religious organizations enter the political process and engage in the politics of reconciliation and relational change, they operate in a political space that is capable both of delivering positive peace and monitoring conformity to settlements afterwards. In Alexander's sense (2006), the churches had the potential to become social movements of civic repair, or, in Putnam's terms (2000) agents of bridging social capital.

Political space, however, is deeply paradoxical for civil society activists. The popular perception of them is one of people committed to political engagement, yet they tend to encounter politicians who dismiss them as radical, naïve, or inflexible. In Northern Ireland, as we saw in Chapter 2, the churches were wholly excluded from the formal political peace process that negotiated the GFA, in large part because of anticipated internal disagreements over the settlement, but, adding to the paradoxical qualities of political space within civil society, they were used as backchannels of communication prior to the talks, and prominent church people were afterwards co-opted by the government to lead oversight of decommissioning and to take forwards the question of how the conflict should be remembered.

It is rare in modern times for occupancy of political space to be overt, since non-fundamentalist religious groups have mostly withdrawn from direct involvement in the political process. The exclusion of Northern Ireland's churches from formal politics is not therefore unusual. But, nonetheless, churches occupy political spaces in peace processes when they mobilize against the effects of violence, criticize governments and rebels, call for peace accords, and facilitate the negotiation of second-best compromises. In cases where religious groups are open to state repression, such as apartheid South Africa, or are kept at arm's length from the peace negotiations, as in

Northern Ireland, operating in this political space can be difficult and their activities take place mostly in secret until the last stages of the conflict. This has been the churches' problem in Northern Ireland, for example, for in this political space they mostly kept well below the parapet for a very long time. But there are some examples of religious involvement in popular uprisings in open defiance and with heads well above the barricades, such as Buddhist monks in Burma and Tibet, Catholics in the Philippines, liberation theology priests in Latin America, and anti-apartheid clerics. The Northern Irish churches, however, were never part of the populist uprising; they never linked themselves to the liberation movement and always disassociated themselves from violence.

For this reason they were inside rather than external to Northern Ireland's political process. As Appleby (1998: 34–44) shows, religious peacemakers can work from positions internal to or outside the formal political process. In Northern Ireland, while they were excluded from the negotiation process that led to the GFA, their active involvement in preparing the ground for these talks placed them within political space. They had access to governments, in Britain, Ireland, the USA, and Europe; they could liaise with ministers, civil servants, and policymakers, and could enter into dialogue with political groups. Precisely because they were inside the political process they provided entrée to it for the combatant groups who were themselves outside it. This was never the case in South Africa, for example, where anti-apartheid churches could only occupy political spaces outside the sphere of government. While there are advantages to these sorts of political spaces, especially in realizing legitimacy for the churches after the political transition, which Archbishop Desmond Tutu, for example, has been able to benefit from, Northern Ireland's churches occupied political spaces that enabled them to mediate between government and opposition movements, secretly bringing in to the political process groups excluded from it. This enabled them to play a greater role in conflict transformation than did the equivalent anti-apartheid churches in South Africa, where change was driven by the internal and external liberation movements to which the anti-apartheid churches, including Tutu, were largely irrelevant. Paradoxically, therefore, despite their absence from the negotiating table, Northern Ireland's progressive churches held greater sway in the political peace process than their equivalent in South Africa. Progressive churches assisted in co-opting paramilitary groups into the political process in Northern Ireland, while in South Africa they had to wait first for the political peace process to succeed.[12] The ANC piggy-backed on the internal protest movement for their political impact, especially the UDF (see Brewer, 1986); the IRA

---

[12] We shall argue later that the South African churches played a greater role post-conflict precisely because of their anti-apartheid credibility. These credentials constrained their ability to persuade and influence the government in the lead-up to political change.

on the churches. A leading Presbyterian minister, who wishes to remain anonymous, is worth quoting at length on this:

> I think from the churches' perspective we should celebrate the fact that we as church people choose human relationships as a way to change the war and there is something transformative about relationships. Now it's not too foolish to suggest that relationships get you through everything because sometimes they break down, sometimes they reach an impasse, but there is something to be said for choosing that way of doing business. Then church people were able to provide communication links between political representatives who could not talk to each other at that time. So that was a privilege to be able to take a message from someone to someone else. That was kind of shocking. You'd get a phone call to go and [be] told something to tell somebody else, you had to meet in a car park and you had to keep walking while you were talking. Ministers lead these very sheltered lives, you know. (Interview date deleted)

These comments confirm our argument in Chapter 2, where we observed the ambivalence about occupying political space, especially that ambiguous cross-over space between government and gunmen, and there was considerable trepidation amongst religious peacebuilders in the light of the opposition from elsewhere in the churches. This opposition only served to increase their insecurity and uncertainty at occupying political space and raised their level of anxiety. It added also to the frustration of the politicians engaged through it, who wanted greater official institutional support and affirmation from the church to legitimate it. Mark Durkan drew attention to the divisions within the churches on the Hume–Adams talks: 'I always had an issue with the Protestant church people [who] were more than happy to see their role as trying to bring Loyalists forward and bring Loyalists round yet often, very pompously, were critical of what John Hume was doing at the time' (interview 17 February 2006).

Therefore we see similar sorts of divisions inside the progressive churches when acting in political space as was evident in their occupancy of market spaces. These two spaces in particular posed difficult choices for religious peacemakers—which is why it was easier for religious peacemakers to remain within the comfort of intellectual and institutional spaces. Some tore their hair at others' inaction; some at despair at what others had the temerity to do in the name of peace. The choice of getting involved in market and political spaces was sometimes made reluctantly, and the efforts of even the bravest and least risk-averse religious peacemakers were racked with ambivalence, fear, and uncertainty. The local settings that religious peacemakers found themselves in could be a powerful break on their choices. As the Revd Ken Newell estimated, a fifth of clergy in his experience were passionate about peace but were in situations where they needed to proceed 'with extreme caution and they have to move [a] half centimetre a year' (interview 20 September 2005). It was thus straightforward for church leaders such as Cardinal Cahal Daly to argue that the church should be apolitical: it avoided all complex decisions.

Other leaders knew that political spaces could not be avoided—the option for them was what to do politically and how to do it. These difficult decisions led to a variety of different choices, which we have tried to capture using the idea of strategic social spaces in civil society. There is nothing sequential about these spaces, as if religious organizations progress linearly from one to the other in an automatic manner. Religious peacemakers often decided to concentrate in certain spaces, yet they are not hermetic, for religious groups were able to merge them and work in several spaces simultaneously. The boundaries between the spaces are therefore very fluid, making them difficult to distinguish at the edges as specific activities flow around them. Nor do they imply a judgement of the quality or effectiveness of the peacemaking done on each plane, for it is hard to say that one is any more critical to the outcome of peace than another.

However, it is necessary to draw out something that by now seems obvious. The capacity of churches to constitute themselves as one or other space and to work as peacemakers within them is affected by wider structural factors. We suggest that church–civil society relations need to be set in the broader framework of church–state relations. This gives us the matrix of church–civil society–state as the conceptual apparatus with which to best understand the churches' role in Northern Ireland's peace process. We will return to this three-way relationship in the conclusion to this chapter. First we wish to outline the importance of the state to locating church–civil society relations.

Church–state relations

Sociologists routinely see civil society as occupying a space between the market and the state, modulating the selfish interests of the market and moderating the centralizing tendencies of the state. This mediation occurs not because the spheres are discrete, as is simplistically implied, but as the result of their interpenetration, the capacity of civil society to move in and out of local, national, and international political arenas. After all, this is what global civil society means; it depends for its effectiveness on working with state and interstate structures while not being absorbed by them. Churches, as part of civil society, have this same relationship with the state. There are a few sociologists of religion who locate their discussions of religion in the context of civil society–state relations. Casanova (1994), for example, argues that the re-entry of religion into civil society is constrained when the church is closely allied to the state; he feared the capacity of religion to 'seep' outside civil society into political spaces. Turam (2004) discussed the connection between Islam, civil society, and the state in Turkey, showing civil society to engage with the state in positive ways that mediated the impact of Islam in modern Turkish politics. We continue this reflection by stressing the importance of the state in linking religion and peacemaking.

The influence of church–state relations shows itself in two ways: whether the intervention by religious groups is official or unofficial, and whether undertaken from a position of majority or minority status. We take these as measures of church–state relations because majority and minority churches are in different relation with the state by dint of legal establishment, cultural legitimacy, and popular support and membership. Church–state relations can impact on the degree of criticism that majority churches are prepared to make of the state and the power relations between dominant and subordinate groups. Also, the level of state repression that minority churches might expect or fear affects the nature and level of their motivation to undertake peace work. Church–state relations impact on the choice of whether to intervene in the peace process officially, unofficially, or with ambiguous levels of institutional authority, offering opportunities to both majority and minority churches to negotiate the constraints of church–state relations. We will consider the majority–minority continuum first, giving some very broad examples from across the world to illustrate each pole before drawing on our Northern Irish data to highlight the complexities in the middle.

Church–state relations: the majority–minority church dimension

Majority–minority status has a powerful effect on the ability of religious organizations to occupy particular strategic social spaces in civil society, and constitutes an important structural factor that mediates the bridging capital of religious peacemaking in civil society and its capacity for civic repair. Minority status, in particular, is a serious constraint in accessing some of these strategic social spaces, but it is simultaneously an opportunity. The USIP Special Report on faith-based NGOs and peacebuilding wisely noted that 'conflict fomented by a religious community can best be contested by a creative minority from that same faith community' (Smock, 2001: 2). However, while true, this is only one meaning of minority status. It can be defined by one of three conditions. The first is being one of the smaller denominations or world faiths within the faith of the majority community, with the majority understood either in the common-sense way as the faith of the largest number of the population or of the dominant group (such as Methodists within Protestantism in Northern Ireland, and Christians in Sri Lanka or Israel-Palestine). Minority status is also conferred on those who comprise a small wing of an otherwise majority denomination, in the manner of the USIP argument above, such as liberal rabbis in Israel-Palestine or anti-apartheid members of the Dutch Reformed Church (DRC) in South Africa. Finally, non-established and non-national churches have minority status compared to those that are state churches.

Minority religious groups are amongst the leading examples in peacemaking, for they have less to lose and most to gain from involvement. Established religions, tied to the state and linked to the majority population's sense of nationalism, find it difficult to mount challenges to the regime or to exclusive forms of ethno-nationalism. They are 'integrated with their state and lack institutional autonomy' from it (Philpott, 2007b: 104). This is why the Sinhalese Buddhist community in Sri Lanka, for example, lags behind the country's small Christian community in peacemaking (see Wijesinghe, 2003). As Philpott (2007b: 104) shows, the Catholic Church in Argentina, for example, was closely tied to the military regime and except for a few dissidents did not help shape the national trials of the former junta or the work of civil society groups dealing with the disappeared. The DRC preached racial separation from the pulpit and it was left to a few courageous individuals within the denomination to speak out, such as Beyers Naudé, or to minority wings, such as the separate Black DRCs, notably people such as Allan Boesak, or the non-established churches, such as the South African Council of Churches and the South African Catholic bishops. Majority religions may also be restricted in their peacemaking by their previous support for state violence against minorities. Only where a national religion identifies itself with opposition to the state, as in Poland, can it distance itself from the state regime sufficiently to engage with the peace process; otherwise it is left for established or national religions to about-turn when the failed regime is on the cusp of collapse (see Herbert, 2003: 197–228).

Minority status, on the other hand, can facilitate an intellectual challenge to the way the conflict is understood and to the intellectual envisioning of peace, as well as enhance the religious critique of existing social relations and thus their commitment to the social transformation required by positive peace. Minority status can place them outside the mainstream, leading to feelings of strangeness from the majority and to empathy with other minorities, or of being in a similar position to the victims of communal violence; and it can lead to feelings of marginality and thus to extra efforts to make a difference in the peace process in compensation for what is otherwise a low profile or even relative neglect. And liberals in a denomination or world faith often find it easier to talk to liberals in another faith rather than extremists in their own. Minority status, however, can also be associated with limited material and cultural resources, restricted social capital and legitimacy for civic repair, a low profile in or exclusion from the political sphere, and hostility and oppression from members of the majority religion—as is the case, for example, amongst both Christians and the Rabbis for Human Rights group in Israel–Palestine—all of which tends to restrict occupancy to intellectual and institutional spaces. Minority status restricts access to cultural, material, and financial resources fundamental to peacemaking, limiting their occupancy of market spaces. Membership of Rabbis for Human Rights tends to be from Jews with a background in the West, educated in Western universities, and imbued with Western sensitivities towards humanitarian values, which places them in a more extreme minority position within contemporary Israel–Palestine and near total exclusion from political spaces (on this group see Brewer, 2010: 63–6).

Minorities' exclusion from market spaces is less likely for those groupings linked to dominant faith communities and wealthy co-religionists outside, financial links to which can facilitate them becoming key agents in the allocation of resources. This enables their occupancy of local political space by dint of their market power. Some world faiths are global and although placed in a minority position within particular nation states they can none-theless call on international networks and rich resources for local effect. Religious groups with majority status, conversely, gain easier entrée to the political process because of their majority status or established church position and have greater resources to dispense in key market spaces. They become powerful agents in peace processes whenever this privileged status is exploited in political spaces to help realize a settlement.

Applying these arguments to Northern Ireland, in these terms, majority churches in Northern Ireland are illustrated by the PCI and the COI, while minority churches are exemplified by the Catholic Church, Methodism, the 'new' charismatic and 'house' churches (on which in Northern Ireland see Thompson, 2000), ecumenists inside majority churches, as well as specialist ecumenical communities and para-church organizations outside the remit of a single denomination, such as ECONI. We use the term minority as it is understood in sociology to describe subordinate power relations not popula-tion numbers. The Catholic Church is the majority church on the island of Ireland and the single largest denomination in the North, but its minority status in Northern Ireland is defined by its subordinate power relationship to the British state and to the dominant ethno-religious group. Because the Catholic Church is a global organization and is able to draw on cultural, financial, political, and symbolic resources from co-religionists elsewhere, its minority position was not one of powerlessness and impotency, not least because the neighbouring state gave it majority status on the island, although Northern Catholics felt their Southern co-religionists were uninterested in them. Bishop Edward Daly remarked in interview on 26 January 2006: 'the church here was very sensitive to the idea of Catholicism being equated with Nationalism or with Republicanism. They were very conscious of the fact that we were a minority. As well as that you had a double minority situation, you had a Southern situation as well and the Southern Church basically didn't want to know about the North, they got concerned certainly, but basically, it wasn't an issue, they wanted to get on with their lives, they were that long out, they were glad to get as far [out] as possible.'

Therefore it was the Irish diaspora outside the island that provided North-ern Catholics with cultural connections and relational closeness. This global interchange helped Catholics in Northern Ireland. For example, Fr Sean McManus established the Irish National Caucus in the USA as a pro-Nationalist lobby that had powerful resonances amongst Catholics in Northern Ireland and was a major fundraiser, although Unionist critics disparaged the Caucus as gunrunners for the IRA. The Irish diaspora was able to lobby for pressure from consecutive US administrations to move the peace process along and the Catholic Church in Northern Ireland exploited these links for local gain, including politically, such as persuading Clinton to give Adams a visa.[13] It was also influential in the development of the McBride Principles, which required local firms in receipt of US investment to adopt fair employment policies well ahead of subsequent legislative changes in this direction.

But ecumenists, new church groups, and ECONI were also able to mobilize global ties for the purposes of peace, bringing in internationally known peacemakers and thinkers, such as John Paul Lederach, Stanley Hauerwas, and Mark Amstutz, and buying into the resources and skills of wider ecumenical, charismatic, and Pentecostal networks. Minority status, in other words, is relative. The Methodists were perhaps the only minority church in these terms that lacked the same extensive global network, although world Methodism should not be belittled. Indeed, it could be argued that it was their relative marginality and powerlessness that helped sensitize them to the problem in particular ways and motivated them to make a difference. Methodists in Northern Ireland, representing 3 per cent of respondents in the 1998 Life and Times survey (see Brewer, 2003b), have been disproportionately involved in the peace process for these sorts of reasons; Methodists from Ireland have won the World Methodist Peace Award on three occasions in its thirty-year history.

This conceptual distinction has more value than denomination for understanding the diverse strategic social spaces religious peacemakers occupied within Northern Irish civil society and in explaining the impact on their work of wider church–state relations. At the two extremes of the continuum it is easy to see how majority status can lead to identification with the state and the dominant group and minority status the reverse, impacting on the stances taken by the churches on war and peace and shaping moral positions on justice, equality, fairness, the elimination of oppression, and democratization generally. However, the distinction is much more complicated than these crude polar extremes imply, especially in communal conflicts where there is no moral high ground and the categories of victim and perpetrator are ambiguous and overlap, such as in Northern Ireland.

The identification of the majority faith with the British state, support for union with Britain, and loyalty to the Crown meant that, at a minimum,

---

[13] We do not here intend to discuss the role of the international community in the peace process, on which there is an extensive literature (see Cox, Guelke, and Stephens, 2006).

members wanted negative peace, either through the military annihilation of the state's opponents or a compromise deal that stopped the violence. The former meant peace through the defeat of terrorism; the latter through a negotiated deal. The former is not peace at all. The latter could be articulated passively or worked for actively. Active peacemaking, however, could include involvement in the social peace process, emphasizing societal healing and restoration of broken relationships, and in the political peace process, dealing with the preparation of the ground for negotiations, participation in deal making, and monitoring the terms of the agreement afterwards. It could also include support for positive peace, for social transformation of Catholic–Protestant relations in a context of greater fairness, justice, and equality. This view of peace might not be expected from members of majority churches, but for some it was; and it might have been expected from members of minority churches, but for some it was not. This is the paradox that the conceptual distinction throws into high relief.

Northern Ireland's majority churches were paralysed by their initial failure to develop official policies with respect to the peace process and by bureaucratic red tape when making or changing policy. Beyond the ritualized condemnations of violence (the articulation, in other words of negative peace), a policy towards more positive peace emerged slowly when conflict transformation was initiated by the 1994 ceasefires. As a consequence, lone runs by small groups and individuals were the norm prior to 1994, not institutional policy engagement. It took some time, for example, for Protestant majority churches to stop thinking, as the Anglican Revd Charles Kenny put it, 'that any talk of civil rights was code for a United Ireland' (interview 15 September 2005). The Revd Lesley Carroll observed that in the majority Presbyterian Church, the initial focus of its 'peacemaking committee was all [on] conflicts in other places not on the conflict here; I think it was all we could get through the General Assembly, so it was a pragmatic choice. And then it began to shift into the more liberal scene which many of us were glad about' (interview 10 January 2008). John Dunlop, at the heart of Presbyterian shifts towards the development of official church policies on peace, noted that it was difficult enough to establish these—even with the ceasefires—given the legacy of the intense conflict: 'Now that [institutional policy reform] would have been very difficult whenever you were in the intensity of the heart of the conflict to do it, but there came a time whenever that was possible, but it was not without some controversy and not without some risk even at that stage. Nevertheless it was done' (interview 23 March 2006).

It is reasonable to ask, therefore, where the majority churches were in policy terms at the height of the violence; hence the criticism of their late entry as institutions into the policy debate. Even evangelicals within the PCI—themselves late into this sphere—criticized the absence of church policy. The Revd Mervyn Gibson remarked, 'the biggest question that paramilitaries ask church leaders when they meet them is, "where were the churches for thirty-five years?" I think there are notable exceptions in the churches, but that's what they ask the church leaders. Church leaders [now] throw their hands up and say, "you're right'" (interview 27 January 2006). In response to the conflict, he went on to say that, as institutions, 'I think the churches battened down the hatches.' This was a source of frustration to the peace activists in the majority churches, who wanted the church to develop policies towards positive peace. As Archdeacon Gregor McCamley said with respect to the COI: 'there was never a church policy. The Church of Ireland is a church that embraces North and South, it is a church that has within its membership Nationalists and Unionists and wide political opinions. In individuals cases there was a lot of work going on behind the scenes and so on [but] it was never church policy' (interview 14 September 2005). 'Take Drumcree,' he said. 'Drumcree is a hobby horse of mine and I disagree with Robin Eames and his approach. Robin Eames at a General Synod stood up and said in the presidential address that he had done everything possible in relation to Drumcree. I stood up during that Synod and stated that factually he was right but what he and nobody else had done was to change the law of the church, to give the bishops greater power to cancel a service—he did not have that authority, strange as it may seem to you. But there was nothing to stop General Synod bringing in a bill that if there was fear of disruption and civil disorder after a service then the diocesan bishop had the authority to cancel that service. The bishops did not want that authority. And they did not want it because if they had it, they would either have to use it or not use it and have fingers pointed at them.'

One of those bishops, Harold Miller, told us of the problems that arose as a majority church when he proposed policies that conservative members of the church disagreed with: 'I remember being at a Synod and asking that a long march planned from Derry to Drumcree [by the Orange Order] be called off. When I got home I had fifteen phone calls on the answering machine. The first one was, "If I'd been there I'd have thrown you in the river." Now, OK, what I'm saying is, a bishop, a church leader has to some degree, either choose a prophetic model, a pastoral model, a chieftain model, a leader model, whatever, you have [to] choose some kind of model. Now I would have to say, that in choosing that model, and in declaring cross-community bridge-building and reconciliation as the central plank of the diocese, right, I was probably seen at that time as being kind of slightly friendly towards Rome' (interview 25 January 2006). Institutional inaction, in other words, is a way of managing the internal difficulties that arise for majority churches when they attempt to formulate policies that undermine the majority status of members of their congregations. Members of the dominant faith community can thus be amongst those least in favour of policies of positive peace.

Mavericks and critics within the majority churches can, therefore, misinterpret the nature of the obstacles facing them in the religious peacemaking.

These constraints can be attributed to the personality and leadership style of individual leaders, and Eames in particular has provoked widespread criticism of his leadership style, or the lack of theological or political vision within the institution (see Vignette 9). They are rarely seen as residing in the majority status of the church itself, making majority churches institutionally unwilling to countenance splits within their membership that might arise from taking stances on the peace process that end up critical of the state. It is within this framework that lack of vision or effort in the majority churches has to be located and which gives meaning to the wriggling that progressive leaders and mavericks engaged in to move their church forward.

Minority Protestant churches, such as the Methodists, faced fewer institutional hurdles than the minorities in the progressive wings of the majority churches, such as Miller, Newell, Dunlop, McCamley, and Kenny. Methodists had no institutional leviathan to move only slowly and haltingly, no establishment links with the state to negotiate, and had members with an ambivalent history towards establishment Unionism that facilitated criticism of it. Harold Good, a former President of the Methodist Church in Ireland, recognized the advantages and summarized our argument very well: 'We start off at an

---

**Vignette 9: *Extracts of the interview with the Revd Ken Newell,
Presbyterian minister, 29 September 2005***

Let me talk about the role of the church in the Protestant community. Largely speaking, it is a very disappointing story because any observer would recognize that only about 10 per cent of local congregations in any of the denominations are actively involved in serious [peace] work. Therefore it is a rather depressing story. The reasons for this is first of all the church [here] has never had a theology of peace. So it doesn't have a conviction bank of motivating beliefs. And because it doesn't have a conviction bank like this—no petrol tank you know—it works a wee bit on solar heat—because where there is heat in the community you get a wee bit of energy coming out for a while and then clouds come over and it settles back to normal. But the biggest problem in the church is that it does not have a conviction bank, it reads the Bible every Sunday in church and a lot of people would read the Bible every day, but they are missing the challenge of God to his people to be involved in the peacemaking ministry of Christ. The church has never connected into a Christ who has a passion for peacemaking and reconciliation. And because of that there is very little energy coming out. The second thing is that the church has been very slow to respond to the Troubles because it lacks what I would call a theological reservoir of passion in this area. It does not know how to interpret the Troubles and as a result of that it doesn't read the Troubles as 'What is God saying to us through the Troubles in this country?' Is there something being revealed, a very serious default in the mindset and in the conviction base and in the life and ministry of the church?

advantage. Two things are to our advantage. One is we're small, we're a minority and I think minorities can perhaps understand other people who feel themselves to be minorities and you haven't got much to lose in one sense. The other thing is we don't carry the baggage of history. We are essentially neither the sector people nor the establishment people so we don't have those burdens of history' (interview 25 September 2005). Norman Taggart, a Methodist minister active in ecumenism, expressed this similarly: 'I think for a small church we have taken initiatives because we're small. We are a small church, not capable of doing very much by ourselves except in this role as facilitator, mediator, prompter, initiator' (interview 30 January 2006).

Smallness—for all intents and purposes here meaning minority status—was something that had to be surmounted by disproportionate activity. This disproportionate involvement is only in part to stake a claim in the struggle for credit, credibility through credit-taking—minorities within the dominant faith community face fewer problems in risk-taking because of their smallness. ECONI, a minority in precisely these terms, responded to the space opened up by the ceasefires without the hesitation or ambivalence that John Dunlop earlier described. As David Porter put it, 'as soon as the ceasefires were declared it was our job then to say, let's make this public. So we organized a series of events called Christian Citizenship Forum and we invited Sinn Féin to address it in the YMCA in Belfast. It was the first public occasion. It became a public forum for debate and discussion of the issues around the peace process, from policing to decommissioning and so on' (interview 27 February 2006). The self-confidence that attaches itself to membership of the majority community can extend even to those who occupy minority spaces within it.

In sharp contrast, the minority position of the Catholic Church made it feel vulnerable at entering political spaces that placed it in opposition to the British state. The policy of the Catholic Church towards peace engagement allowed some individualism but two things stand out: church policy was heavily influenced by the personality and style of the leader of the day, and when going too far, the church silenced and ostracized maverick religious peacemakers. Under Cardinal Cahal Daly, activists felt restrained and went underground in unofficial peacemaking; under his predecessor Tomas O'Fiaich they could get away with more. O'Fiaich was resoundly condemned as pro-Republican and treated with suspicion by Unionists and the British state; Fr Joe McVeigh described O'Fiaich as being 'targeted by the British government' (interview 14 August 2008). O'Fiaich's predecessor was Cardinal Conway, who was very conservative indeed. Conway was cardinal when it became known to the British government and the Catholic Church that Fr Chesney was an active IRA volunteer with blood on his hands, knowledge of which was kept secret by both of them for fear of enraging opinion against the church, justice being thought less important on this occasion than political stability. Except for the period of O'Fiaich's leadership, therefore, the Catholic Church's leadership in the North has not wished to antagonize the British state and loyalists to it.

Minority churches are doubly vulnerable when they represent relatively powerless groups, some of whose supporters utilize violence, for their ministry cannot avoid engagement with social transformation but they need to avoid being seen as promoting the use of force. This fine balancing act was not carefully managed under O'Fiaich's leadership; under Daly's, the Catholic Church's policy was more circumspect. It was enthusiastic about participation in the social peace process, therefore, especially, after initial reservations, in ecumenism, and in those spaces within civil society where it did not directly confront the British state—notably institutional and market spaces. In political space the risk was high that it would be placed in a situation where it would have to overtly criticize the British state.

In a sense, it was O'Fiaich who was out of kilter not Daly, for historically the Catholic Church in Ireland always sought an accommodation with the British state. It was also always vehemently anti-Republican. It is often forgotten that it excommunicated participants in the 1916 Easter Rising, including the later 'father of the nation' Eamon de Valera, and it was keen to avoid any suggestion of support for SF or violence. Cahal Daly's reaction was therefore to formally eschew politics, to declare the Catholic Church as apolitical, and when it acted politically, it did so with heads well beneath the barricades, mostly in private in backchannel dialogue, with public declarations that urged peace carefully crafted to avoid implying any support for the state's opponents. Mavericks such as Fr Denis Faul, who felt unable to refrain from criticism of legal and political injustices, were firmly disciplined by Cardinal Conway, O'Fiaich's predecessor. 'That aroused my anger a lot,' Fr Faul said, 'I felt the judicial system was unjust, I made a protest against it, a public protest, said the judges were not fit to do their job. Cardinal Conway wasn't pleased and he silenced me for a while, a couple of months' (interview 23 January 2006). Cahal Daly was equally intolerant towards politicization of the church. For instance, when being interviewed by a reporter on the shoot-to-kill policy by out-of-control sections of the security forces, he rebuked the reporter for trying to make him use the words 'shoot to kill'. As Cahal Daly said in interview on 24 February 2006:

> I did everything in my conscience I thought possible and appropriate, and everything that carried hope of peace and reconciliation in Northern Ireland I tried to do, but I did it in the open because I have always believed that any dialogue that there is between political leaders, government and so on must be in the open. There must be transparency; there must be no backstairs shuttling and no secret deals because it is wide open to grave misunderstanding. I was quite certain that if I engaged in talks with people associated with paramilitaries, that this would very quickly become public knowledge, that it would be exploited as an indication as the church's secret sympathy with people of violence.

Fr Tom Toner, someone who pushed Daly's boundaries as far as was possible, remembers this hardline position dictating church policy even towards the burying of the hunger strikers, who had come to benefit from a wave of popular sympathy in Ireland—one of the few occasions when Southern and Northern Catholics appeared agreed on 'the Northern question'. 'I can remember when Bobby Sands was reaching the end of his time', he said, 'and we'd had our normal conference at Easter time, beginning of May and someone asked the bishop, "what do we do if Bobby Sands dies", and the bishop said, "you bury him like any other parishioner". That is exactly what happened. Outside it was entirely different, of course' (interview 15 March 2006).

Entry of the Catholic Church into the political peace process was therefore late. Even the utilization of backchannels for political dialogue—a form of private political space—revolved around Alec Reid and the Clonard Redemptorists, a religious order that constitutes a minority space within the Catholic Church, out of the control of Cahal Daly. Daly himself saw the contrast, although he challenged our use of the term 'control' despite seeming to confirm it:

> I had no direct involvement with the Clonard peace process whatever and that is just a statement of fact, it doesn't imply that I disapproved of it, it was quite independent of my activity and if I may take exception to the use of the word 'control', Clonard was not under my control in that sense of the term, nor did I regret that or feel that I should have control. No, there is a degree of independence on the part of Religious Orders, they have a different relationship with a bishop than the diocesan clergy. I wouldn't use a control term even with the diocesan clergy but I would be responsible for nominating them. I would have discussed pastoral and other problems with them, they could be broadly said to have been in agreement with my general approach and so on, but at the same time they had their own independence. Nor did I expect people in Clonard to inform me of what they were doing and planning and so on. (Interview 24 February 2006)

The irony was thus that majority faith Protestant clergy—although admittedly mostly from its minority denominations and wings—found it easier to talk to SF and the paramilitary organizations than Catholic diocesan priests. Fr Tom Toner again: 'we were under the shadow of Cardinal Daly. He was virulent in his attacks on SF and IRA and caused a great deal of alienation. That eventually changed but there is a certain degree of truth in that the Protestant clergy were talking for quite some time with Sinn Féin' (interview 15 March 2006).

While the minority status of the institutional Catholic Church restrained the leadership, it was an opportunity rather than a constraint for minorities within this minority. Maverick diocesan priests and the religious orders were more eager occupants of political space. Maverick diocesan priests recognized therefore that this meant they had to confront the British state. In what is a classic statement of the minority church position, one such priest, Fr Joe McVeigh, said in interview on 14 August 2008: 'The official Catholic Church role has been very negligible. Over the forty years of the war they played a very pro-government role; instead of taking the side of the people as far as I'm concerned they took the side of the government. We should all learn lessons from this; the church's role should never be to support the establishment or political powers; it should support the people and confront the powers and principalities that exist in our world; to challenge injustice wherever it is.'

Fr Alec Reid, another representative of the 'minority within a minority' came close in one radio interview to explaining his motivation that violence necessitates a political response: 'I was at the wake of a man who had been assassinated by Loyalists and there was a young woman, I'd say she was about thirty. I've a feeling she was his daughter and she was kneeling at the coffin and suddenly she got into a state of agony where she started to kind of wail and cry out in a most heart-rendering way. I remember saying to myself people shouldn't have to go through this kind of agony, this kind of suffering, something should be done. The whole feeling [in the Catholic Church] was that we couldn't do anything because it was a political matter and only the government could solve the problem.'[14] He went on to explain that from that point, sometime in 1974, he tried initiative after initiative, some lasting a few months, others as long as six, over a ten-year period to try to get the IRA to stop the violence: 'I said to him, Gerry [Adams] look there's another man dead can we not do anything about this? He said the church is the only organization that can do anything because it only has the creditability, the moral standing, and especially the lines of communication.' In another radio interview for Radio Ulster's Sunday Sequence on 31 January 2005, Fr Reid said: 'It's a political mistake to think that through war you can solve political conflicts of any kind. One of the great lessons of the Irish peace process is that dialogue is the powerful dynamic, dialogue will solve every conflict.' Minorities within minority churches were thus as influential as minorities within the majority churches in occupying what for churches are the most sensitive and dangerous strategic social spaces in civil society.

Church–state relations: the official–unofficial intervention dimension

Majority versus minority status does not neatly overlap with the contrast between official and unofficial intervention. Sometimes engagement with injustice and oppression is official church policy in opposition to the state—as

---

[14] 'The Clonard Priest', 29 November 2006, BBC Radio 4.

with the Catholic Church's involvement with Solidarity and the collapse of communism in Poland—and on other occasions it is unofficial, representing unsanctioned reactions by religious organizations in fear of state repression or avoiding the constraints imposed by conservative and cautionary church hierarchies. This tends to be the case for monks in Buddhist countries that have political dictatorships. Religious hierarchies sometimes withhold official backing of local peace initiatives but nonetheless stomach it, while on other occasions the official church can try to prevent local priests challenging the status quo. For example, liberation theology in Latin America was attacked by the same pope as sought the liberation of his Polish homeland, although local priests in Latin America often disregarded him and were active agents for social change. In Nicaragua, for example, commentators stress that it was 'popular religion' not the official Catholic Church that assisted social change (Lancaster, 1988; Linkogle, 1998). In Latin America, the official church position often changed only with the government, being wary of exposing itself to threat. The official church often restricted itself to negative peacemaking—the provision of pastoral care to the affected communities, criticisms of the violence, calls for restraint, formulaic statements after each tragedy, and the promotion of national dialogue between the protagonists. However, in some instances, restrictions on local priests are not imposed in order to defend corrupt regimes or to protect the church against repression, but as a control mechanism intended to make peace work the preserve of the religious hierarchy or, at least, to afford leaders the opportunity of doing the high-profile peacemaking.

At the extreme ends of this continuum, the distinction between official and unofficial interventions is thus clear but the relationship between them is flexible and there are grey areas in the middle. The Northern Irish case illustrates that the relationship is affected by three factors: church governance structures, leadership styles, and the fluid dynamics of peacebuilding itself. We will deal with these factors in reverse order.

We have alluded throughout this book to the way in which peacebuilding sometimes requires secrecy and confidentiality. Secrecy can be a problem to some people when the dogs in the street seem to know, or suspect they know, that backchannel discussions are occurring. Secret work does not have to be unofficial. The sensitivity of the dialogue, however, and the potential controversy surrounding it, encourages unofficial interventions as a way of limiting the damage when disclosures risk injuring the image of the churches and the reputations of individuals. Dialogue can be painstakingly slow, premised as it is on relationship-building, but once it has a head of steam, the dynamics are very fast flowing. This often requires autonomy and independence on the part of the churchmen and women doing it. This again persuades the use of unofficial interventions. But such is the ambiguity of this distinction in the grey centre-ground that there may be official authorization given to religious peacemakers to act autonomously. The Revd Harold Good explained his position in the Methodist Church: 'We had this little group which was totally free, we didn't have to run back to the church to say can we go and meet somebody or can we do this and that. It was a very clear understanding, "look you're free to talk with whomsoever you wish whenever you wish. If there's anything that you want to feed back to us in our understanding or when we are going to make a statement, that's alright, but you don't have to." That was very important because it gave us freedom. There was trust' (interview 24 January 2006). Another Methodist, the Revd Norman Taggart also told us that this group was 'authorized, actually authorized by the Council [Council of Social Responsibility]'. Part of the reason for this ambiguous official stamp was disclosed by Taggart when he went on to say, 'there was a lot of controversy about that within Methodism' (interview 30 January 2006). Secrecy keeps critics inside and outside the churches in the dark while peacebuilding proceeds apace and an unofficial or semi-official cloak helps keep it hidden. As the Revd Ruth Patterson said of her work, 'it wasn't publicized, otherwise the process would not have been possible' (interview 29 November 2005).

The cloak of semi-official interventions covers the peacemakers as well, and can act as protection from accusers. Deliberate ambiguity thus becomes a strategy to manage the anxiety and strains involved in peacebuilding. Unofficial status is highly problematic, however. The tendency for Protestant critics to abuse Fr Alec Reid with the appellate of 'Provo priest' can be explained because his work never came with the official authority of the Catholic Church. He could be more easily dismissed that way. Yet, the very strains of peacemaking require some sort of official sanction and support as a form of psychological protection. It is worth recalling the discussion in Chapter 2 on the Hume–Adams talks, where Reid wanted freedom on the one hand but a loose form of institutional support as well. This is what Harold Good and Norman Taggart were referring to. In the Methodists' case it came in the form of authorization to act independently within a bond of trust. Sometimes, however, it comes only in the form of nods and winks. There is a level of uncertainty with tacit understandings about what official authority religious peacemakers bring to the task. Again it is worth recalling that the politicians involved in the Hume–Adams talks all assumed that Alec Reid's venture was authorized. Only with public disclosure was it revealed that, by a nod and a wink, a small self-selected group, which included Bishop Edward Daly, was acting as an emotional support group and a sounding board but lacked any official status to authorize Reid's work. It was unofficial, but nods and winks disguised this fact. This helps explain the additional strain on Reid, who has had two emotional breakdowns and has moved to Dublin.

Tacit authorization comes with the knowledge of the official leadership but not their formal consent. Sometimes the consent is implied as a form of quiet toleration. As the Revd David Armstrong explained, 'I had a boss who was saying "David, I'll turn a blind eye to it", and really, that's all I needed. I didn't have his 100 per cent blessing [but] he wasn't blocking me' (interview 2 December 2005).

But where even tacit authorization is unlikely, and there are no nods and winks, knowledge is kept from the official leadership so that the intervention is unambiguously unofficial and unsanctioned. Fr Des Wilson, for example, explained that under the leadership of Cardinal Cahal Daly, 'the attitude of the Catholic hierarchy was, "don't tell me about it, I don't want to know, but if you want to go on doing it you do it on your own responsibility"' (interview 9 November 2005). This can be experienced as abandonment by religious peacemakers. As Fr Wilson went on to say, 'therefore, they [religious peacemakers] get into a position which Alec Reid got into, where he was reviled and hated, "sorry Alec, you're on your own"'. This did not just happen within the Catholic Church. A third party, who wishes to remain anonymous, told the following story about a colleague in the Presbyterian Church who was dialoguing with paramilitary groups: 'he was extremely critical of the fact that the church authorities were giving him no support, he said "nobody rings up to ask"' (interview 26 January 2006).

The larger point here is that churches are institutions operating within the legal framework of the state and, where repression or criticism can be expected from the state arising from religious peace work, unofficial interventions are a reasonable strategy. They readily lend themselves to deniability by the institutional church and allow the leadership to separate themselves from conduct that can then be portrayed as unsanctioned, protecting the church as an institution but exposing the peacemakers to considerable personal risk.

Fear of repression and criticism, of course, can be real or imagined. Indeed, they can be exaggerated as an excuse for restricting the church to passive forms of peacemaking. It is worth asking, therefore, why so much intervention in a formally democratic society such as Northern Ireland was unofficial or came with only tacit authorization. It was, we contend, the result of church–state relations that made churches into being part of the problem so that they found it difficult to determine how best to be part of the solution. Some of the sensitive backchannel communication obviously required secrecy, but that was no reason for the churches to keep it unofficial and hence deniable. Religious peacemaking was controversial and was so for different reasons to the various parties involved. The state wanted deniability, should exposure of their involvement in backchannel communications in sacred spaces be damaging. The church leaders wanted deniability, because their membership was divided over the peace process and they did not want to risk losing more numbers in a context where secularization threatened haemorrhage. Preserving church unity was a priority—a similar preoccupation, of course, for the political parties. The churches were also afraid of public criticism because peacemaking was so controversial. The fear of state repression was not a consideration (as in South Africa) but the fear of ostracism was. With their majority status, the mainstream Protestant churches in particular felt this as a constraint; and the minority Catholic Church sought an accommodation with the British state. As Cecelia Clegg said, 'when the fear got too much', the church leaders just 'backed off' (interview 29 November 2007).

This emphasizes how important leadership and leadership styles are to the relationship between official and unofficial interventions. It is feasible for leaders to use unofficial and tacit activities to test water, fly kites or whatever euphemism is used to describe exploratory peace moves. The journalist and broadcaster Malachi O'Doherty suggested that Cardinal O'Fiaich, Cardinal Daly's predecessor, used Fr Denis Faul 'to play footsie with the Provos, out there doing a job' (interview 4 September 2007). Some church leaders preferred to make the overtures themselves. Much of the Anglicans' peace efforts were centred on Archbishop Eames as primate. This reflected his personal leadership style. As Archdeacon Gregor McCamley explained 'it was part of his personality, he likes to keep things strict and to have control'. 'Collegiality was the important thing', to Eames, 'and it was controlled by him'. Reflecting on the situation now, McCamley went on to say, 'I understand individual bishops will, as it were, stand up on their own much more than they would have done say ten years ago' (interview 14 September 2005).

The contrast in leadership styles between Cardinals O'Fiaich and Daly is also indicative of our argument. O'Fiaich wished to push the boundaries of his relationship with the British state. He used Fr Faul indirectly to criticize the British over allegations of torture. Fr Faul recalled an incident at the time of the 1980–1 hunger strikes when he was told not to bring Faul to a meeting between him and Jim Prior, Secretary of State at the Northern Ireland Office, but O'Fiaich ignored them anyway and Faul 'did all the talking' (interview 23 January 2006). O'Fiaich very early on involved the Irish state in the peace process to put pressure on the British state, having talks when Charles Haughey was Taoiseach, which included Alec Reid. Looking back on his leadership, Dr Des Wilson said: 'O'Fiaich would talk to anyone, he talked to Loyalists, he talked to Republicans, he talked to anybody who wanted to talk to him, but the others, their policy was, no, you don't talk to them, stop doing whatever you're doing, let them stop their opposition to the government, sure, what was the point of talking to them then?' (interview 9 November 2005). Cardinal Cahal Daly, however, avoided criticism of the British state (see Vignette 10). He said of the comparison in styles between him and O'Fiaich, 'I'm not Cardinal O'Fiaich. Cardinal O'Fiaich acted according to his own conscience and the opportunities and situations in which he found himself, mine were different.'

Daly was apolitical, conservative, and cautious, fearful of British and Unionist criticism of the church as being meddlers or full of the likes of Fr Chesney, the real 'Provo priest'. The risk takers, even amongst the bishops,

---

Vignette 10: *Extracts of Cardinal Daly's interview, 24 February 2006*

Well, given the situation here and the suspicions which many people on the Unionist Protestant side of the community divide, their suspicion of the Roman Catholic Church and their sometimes openly stated belief, postured by some of their leaders, that secretly, behind everyone's back, the church was in conspiracy with the IRA, that the IRA was in some kind of way the arm of the church. Now, given that attitude on the part of some in the Protestant community, I was deeply convinced that any kind of direct contact between myself as bishop and the leadership of the IRA would become known and would do great, very great harm to the Catholic Church and do very great harm to the hope of Protestant Catholic mutual understanding and mutual respect. Therefore I declined several attempts to pressurize me into meeting with the leadership. I couldn't speak with Gerry Adams or Martin McGuinness, they never talked to me about their faith. They wanted to talk to me to change my opinion about their armed struggle. My conviction is that this would have done terrible harm to the church because it would have been exploited as a coup for the IRA, as proof at last in the open that the church was in collusion with the IRA. The church is not involved in politics and it's very dangerous for the church to be seen as it were in political party or a pressure group or whatever. The church encourages its members to work for peace but the work of peace is a complicated issue, it requires a great deal of skills which are not necessarily the skills of a pastor of souls. If asked for advice he will give it but he will publicly proclaim the teaching of the church, publicly and openly condemn evil wherever he finds it, particularly the evil that is emanating from within his own faith community. If I may modestly say so, I did everything that I could to push the British government along, but I did so openly and I don't doubt, but that what I was saying had some degree of influence. I think there is a grave danger in trying to decide who did most for peace; I don't think that was what it was about at all. The church was involved at every level each person doing what was thought to be most advantageous for the cause of peace, but I don't like any sort of attempt to award brownie points to the various people working for peace.

---

such as Edward Daly, were refused when they requested church leaders to intercede with SF (interview with Edward Daly 24 January 2006). The maverick priests were on an even tighter leash. If O'Fiaich exploited maverick peacemakers who were willing to operate under weak forms of tacit authorization, or unofficially under none, Daly reined them in. This is what we meant when we used the term leash leadership in Chapter 2, a style that controlled peacemakers for fears of stirring up political problems for the churches. 'On big political things', Fr Denis Faul said, as a maverick himself and nicknamed 'Denis the Menace' for his outspokenness, 'priests would accept direction' (interview 23 January 2006), suggesting that there were limits placed even on unofficial interventions under Daly's leadership.

Governance structures within the respective churches are also important to the relationship between official and unofficial peace interventions. Church authority structures determined the levels of autonomy for individual peace-makers and the nature and severity of the punishment if breached. Bureau-cratic structures needed to be negotiated as part of church–state relations, determining the space within which religious peacemakers could operate. Anglicans and Catholics are Episcopalian and have hierarchical authority structures centred on the bishops, upward eventually to the Archbishop of Canterbury and the Pope. Anglicans tie the authority of this bureaucratic office to the democratic notion of Synod as the ultimate decision-making body, but Archbishop Eames was skilful in manipulating Synod to avoid maverick clergy from placing issues on the agenda. Irish cardinals have no democratic pretence and can openly act autocratically, if they wish. The more democratic churches, such as the PCI and Methodism, have rotating heads, precisely in order to avoid personal power being attached to the bureaucratic office, and local structures of accountability; they rotate on an annual basis in the PCI, so quickly that moderators can be out of office before they get the hang of the system, as Alf McCreary put it (interview 25 September 2007). Para-church organizations, ecumenical communities, new church move-ments, and the like were accountable only to themselves and to whatever loose management structure they had established. David Porter, Director of ECONI, recognized this: 'The churches get hung up on that because they have got institutional integrities to protect. We are a focus group, we are a lobby group; we are a small organization, we don't have a membership that we have to hold ourselves accountable to, we have just got a board like any charitable voluntary organization. We have never said that we spoke for anybody other than the thirty to forty members of ECONI at any one time who were on the steering group' (interview 27 February 2006).

The peacebuilding process often requires quick decision-making, and bureaucratic governance structures are incompatible with the speed at which peace negotiations move. Official intervention within both democratic and Episcopalian structures can be slow given the pace at which presbyteries, assemblies, and synods work, especially on matters that are controversial and raise internal opposition. The Catholic Church, with the least democratic governance structure, thus missed an opportunity for speedy official interven-tion and enforcing anti-sectarian decrees, which puts its conservatism in an even more negative light. Ironically, the Catholic Church was in a similar position to the IRA as a hierarchical organization with a centralized gover-nance structure that enabled it to better enforce its peace strategy on volunteer units, a position quite different to the fissiparous Loyalist paramilitaries. The COI could act speedily only by Eames working outside his authority by manipulating Synod and thus acting unofficially, which puts criticisms of his personality and leadership style in a different light. Speedy action en-courages unofficial interventions for simple bureaucratic reasons. This is why the Methodists and ECONI could move quickest of all; the former gave its peace workers tacit authorization to work autonomously within a bond of trust, while the latter had only a minimal bureaucracy to bind its director, David Porter.

Bureaucracies encourage unofficial interventions for another reason. In bureaucratic systems where hierarchical leaders imposed limits on religious peacemaking for whatever reason—and the motivations of Eames and Cahal Daly were different given the respective relations of their churches to the British state—unofficial interventions became a reasonable strategy to what was perceived, rightly or wrongly, as official church reticence. Unofficial interventions in these situations, however, need skilful manipulation of bureaucratic space to avoid limits and controls from above. This is partly the reason why activist Catholic priests and Anglican clergy linked themselves with, and worked through, ecumenical communities and groups not under Episcopalian control, and with broader initiatives such as the Faith in a Brighter Future group and ISE, which had diffuse lines of authority and did not come under the authority of any particular church. Civil society groups such as this provided wriggle room for unofficial intervention amongst those otherwise working under tight church governance structures. This is also why bureaucratic spaces less under the control of bishops were exploited for peacemaking, notably religious orders, why Redemptorists and Jesuits dominate on the Catholic side in occupying unofficial spaces, and why monasteries in particular were popular sacred spaces for backchannel work. As Sean Farren, SDLP MP, said when reflecting upon what he saw as the relative inactivity of the institutional churches in the peace process, diocesan priests had less room for manoeuvre 'but Reid, because he was outside the authority of the bishops, was able to take the initiative' (interview 27 May 2007).[15]

Democratic decentralized forms of governance, however, worked in two ways. They helped evade leadership control but expanded the opportunity for localized control. Bishops could move troublesome priests within a diocese, but, as Fr Des Wilson said, reflecting on personal experience, 'that's not a penalty at all' (interview 9 November 2005). They could be rebuked but never sacked and left penniless without house and home. Anglican clergy can be moved only after a very long process and this is not determined by the congregation. Decentralized churches, however, can punish more quickly and heavily, rescinding a minister's right to preach. Congregations have the power to oust ministers. Thus it was that after wishing the neighbouring parish priest a happy Christmas, the Revd David Armstrong was hounded

---

[15] It is necessary also to remember the question of time. Parish ministers of every denomination have so many calls on their time that peace work has to fit alongside very many other duties. Non-parish priests, members of religious orders, and full-time workers in the ecumenical groups were amongst those with the time to utilize their bureaucratic position for the purpose of peace. We address this in Chapter 4.

out of his church in Limavady, then out of the country, and eventually from Presbyterianism, ending up in a COI parish in the Republic of Ireland. Consider the following. The Methodist Church had policies that allowed some of its peace workers to hold secret talks with official authority to act autonomously. They invited other churchmen and women into these talks. Some were Presbyterians acting with tacit authorization at best, others Catholic or Anglican acting entirely independently of their church leadership; others from the ecumenist communities or para-church organizations were accountable to no one. They faced different levels of risk from exposure and different degrees of censure, entirely because of church governance. It meant that religious peacemakers not only acted in different ways, they did so with varying levels of official authority.

CONCLUSION: THE CHURCH–CIVIL SOCIETY–STATE MATRIX

Fr Des Wilson, in interview on 9 November 2005, told of how he and Alec Reid had tried for years to persuade the leadership of the Catholic Church to talk to SF because 'we believed that this was one way of stopping the war'. Why them though? In part, the answer lies in their role as churchmen. Fr Wilson again: 'The only people who would have had the credibility and who could take the risk of talking to all parties, including the military group, the only people were the church. The church had nothing to lose. In fact they had everything to gain.' The answer also lies in their particular location within the Catholic Church as double minorities,[16] a status that persuaded them towards unofficial interventions and backchannel communication, a type of activity most suited to their category of religious peacemaker and to the use of sacred spaces, which had special qualities appropriate to the purpose.

Minority status such as this is simultaneously both an opportunity and a constraint. Limited as minorities in the strategic social spaces that can be occupied within civil society arising from church–state relations, and subject to structures of church governance and leadership that potentially limited their capacity for religious peacemaking, these weaknesses were turned into strengths, pushing them, and people like them, into particular kinds of peace work, in specific physical locations and with particular forms of organizational autonomy. It shaped the contribution made to the political peace process by restricting it to backchannel dialogue, which reaped so much reward by preparing the ground for negotiations and formal politics. Unofficial

---

[16] Fr Faul was a maverick diocesan priest; Fr Reid was a member of a religious order.

interventions in this form of political space were recognized by politicians such as John Major and Albert Reynolds as unusually helpful. And it determined the concentration on the social peace process, notably ecumenism, conflict resolution, and anti-sectarianism, where intellectual, institutional, and market spaces could be occupied without overtly criticizing the British state and confronting the essentially political nature of the conflict. These spaces dictated the heavy emphasis placed on negative peace (conflict transformation) rather than positive peace (social transformation). With the exception of market spaces, where churches dealt with the social problems of a hostile world through the social gospel, churches preferred safe spaces to effect the social peace process and many eschewed public political space for the relative security of deniable backchannel political dialogue, although this was dangerous enough for the people doing it. Reid and Eames in their different backchannel work were prisoners of church–state relations. Cahal Daly's fears of antagonizing the British forced Reid down the same route as Eames, who feared antagonizing his majority community members.

It makes sense in our view to locate the minutia of religious peacemaking over the years in Northern Ireland in this kind of conceptual field. Church-civil society-state relations are critical to understanding religious peacemaking, for some of the strategic social spaces in civil society were especially suited to civic repair and bridging capital by the churches, notably intellectual spaces and private backchannel political spaces, although like any other institution beginning to rethink and re-envision the conflict, the churches could put this into practice within their own domain, as some did. Some spaces were more suited to engagement with the social peace process, others the political peace process, allowing religious peacemakers to narrow their efforts and to avoid others. These spaces help define the variety of different sorts of activities that religious peacemaking comprises. Some religious peacemakers restricted themselves to one or more of these spaces, or were constrained by church–state relations to one or more of these spaces. Activities in these spaces sometimes contradicted each other and some religious peacemakers were at odds with others working in different spaces and across time.

Ecumenism, for example, facilitated backchannel communication with protagonists as a practical form of ecumenism, but provided no intellectual space for justifying the work of evangelical peacemakers. Ecumenism's religiously motivated cross-community activities encouraged occupancy of market spaces but cut off collaboration with secularists and evangelicals working in the poorest neighbourhoods, where social conditions spurred on Loyalism. Ecumenism's links with Catholics and to Republican paramilitaries were stronger than with evangelicals and Loyalist paramilitaries. Ecumenism, for example, was a hindrance to liberal-conservative evangelical peacemakers. The Catholic Church, for example, was constrained in its utilization of political space by the controversy associated with it as a result of church–state relations, pressuring diocesan and non-diocesan priests into particularly stressful forms of secret work, where 'the can', as it were, was carried on a few shoulders rather than stronger institutional ones. Eames's brave shoulders bore a great deal within Anglicanism, but more than was necessary if ordinary clergy had only been empowered to act in these social spaces. What he was doing—almost alone—in secret dialogue, actually restrained the COI's activities elsewhere as the primate sought to avoid his work being impugned by possible controversy surrounding the potential work by others—controversy rooted in the COI's placing within wider church–civil society–state relations.

The church–civil society–state matrix is represented diagrammatically in Figure 5. This diagram is not meant to give the impression of hierarchy, in which the superstructure dominates over the base, but more to define a set of sedimentary layers that, while distinct, are all equally important to determining the substance of the whole, the absence of one layer of which substantially changes its form. Church–state relations shaped the kinds of peacemaking done by majority and minority churches, restricting the majority churches in the extent to which they challenged majority community dominance and power relations, and making certain forms of minority church activity particularly vulnerable, whether these threats were real or imagined.

The constraints imposed on majority and minority churches by church–state relations were managed by different forms of official and unofficial intervention, allowing majority church peacemakers some autonomy when acting secretly and facilitating minority religious peacemakers, some of whom were in a double minority position and whose capacity for engagement

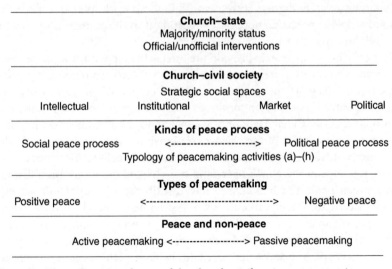

Figure 5. The sedimentary layers of the church–civil society–state matrix

required creativity in sidestepping official constraints. Officially the churches mostly moved quite late to develop policies for engagement, which is why unofficial forms of religious peacemaking dominate as path-breaking activities during the worst of 'the Troubles'.

It is possible to delineate specifically religious factors when explaining the course of religious peacemaking in Northern Ireland, as with the impact of church governance structures and forms of church leadership, theological relations and disputes that opened or closed opportunities for collaboration and networking, and the effect of different institutional forms, such as the organizational and bureaucratic differences between established and non-established churches, religious orders, para-church organizations, religious lobby groups and the rest that mediated the capacity for religious peacemaking. We contend, however, that these narrowly religious factors need to be located in a broader relationship between church, civil society, and the state. After all, governance structures, organizational forms, and styles of religious leadership, for example, can be managed and manipulated if the commitment to peace engagement is present, especially persuading some minorities to imaginative types of mediation to circumvent the constraints. Religious peacemakers in the North of Ireland found ways around the restrictions imposed by insecure or frightened leaders, or the restraints in established churches in moving synods or presbyteries towards a critical position against the British state. It remains the case, however, that as institutions, the churches contributed less than the individual members they compromise. This is why some of the most effective religious peace work was done in non-denominational organizations, such as the ecumenical communities and ECONI, or in organizational settings outside the control of conservative church hierarchies, such as in monasteries, or done in secret, as with Eames's work. We can explain this kind of religious peacemaking best by locating it in the church–civil society–state relationship.

Not only does this matrix provide the intellectual apparatus to understand the nature and forms of religious peacemaking in Northern Ireland, it proffers a conceptual leap. It moves us beyond the emphasis on personality and religious leadership styles, important as these are when considering the role of people such as Cahal Daly and Robin Eames, by locating the churches' activities in the context of their wider relationship to the British state. It also successfully advances our understanding of civil society, for church–civil society relations in the North of Ireland transcended the rather tired distinction between 'good' and 'bad' civil society. By utilizing the idea of four strategic spaces in civil society, it can be shown that while all 'good' in these terms, religious peacemakers were pulled in different directions; sometimes in contradiction to each other. Progressive civil society can oppose itself by its internal divisions; and some majority faith believers can be more progressive in their utilization of strategic social spaces than some minority faith believers, contrary to what might be expected from the normal structures of power governing majority–minority relations.

We contend that this matrix also absorbs the equally tired contrast between bonding and bridging social capital, not only in the sense that some religious networks were both bridging and bonding at the same time, such as ecumenism and liberal-conservative evangelicalism, but also in the sense that the priority placed on social capital as the mechanism by which peace is realized in democratic transitions is overdone. In the next chapter we elaborate on this last conceptual advance when discussing the limitations of religious peacemaking.

4

Weaknesses in the Churches' Peacemaking

INTRODUCTION

It was not until 1994—the year of the paramilitary ceasefires—that the Presbyterian Church endorsed its 'Peace Vocation' statement, calling on its members to distinguish their faith from their nationalism; the COI's Hard Gospel anti-sectarianism project did not begin until well after the signing of the GFA, and the Catholic Church at the time of writing still has no central peacemaking statement or initiative involving grass-roots members.[1]

Being 'behind the times', however, is a vacuous criticism to make with the benefit of hindsight. Rather, in what follows we intend to discuss a range of grievances against the churches' peacemaking that emerged from our interview data and which respondents felt negatively affected their contribution. We then address a series of weaknesses that we attribute to the churches, culminating in what we consider to be the major weakness, the failure to link up other sections of civil society in an integrated and unified peace movement. This enables us to continue our reflection on the opportunities and constraints of civil society peacemaking in settings where civil society is itself part of the problem.

---

[1] In November 2001 the Catholic Church produced a statement on the value of Catholic education entitled *Building Peace, Shaping the Future* (Catholic Bishops of Ireland, 2001), which came close to providing a public statement in support of peace. That they integrated their statement on peace within a document defending Catholic education indicates their sensitivity to the claim that segregated education contributed to division. In a remarkable development in October 2010, SF's Deputy First Minister Martin McGuinness came out in support of segregated education when criticizing the DUP First Minister Peter Robinson for commenting that segregated education created social apartheid. SF have hardly converted to segregated education; it is a further and sad reflection that the traditional principle still holds—'my enemy's enemy is my friend'.

RESPONDENTS' COMPLAINTS

One of the indisputable facts about Northern Ireland is that a population of 1.7 million people has at least the same number of opinions about the roots of the conflict and its potential solutions. At the same time that there have been people who understated their involvement in peacebuilding, others offer opinions more than actions. However, since our interviewees are amongst the central figures in the progressive churches and para-church organizations in Northern Ireland or are members of the main political parties, paramilitary bodies, and civil society groups, their perceptions of the weaknesses of the churches are instructive, offering 'insider accounts' richer than our own. We encountered many complaints. There are almost as many as people interviewed. Some represent real weaknesses that we expand on below; others have been mentioned in earlier chapters or are not worth dwelling on in detail, but we list the major ones for the sake of completeness.

- The churches have often reflected and not challenged a highly sectarian community, making them indistinguishable from society at large.
- Church leaders have often been predictable and verbose, and unable to respond in a timely fashion to both urgent and ongoing need.
- At their worst, churches amplified the fears of the community and did not present a theology of reconciliation and peacebuilding as a normal part of what it means to be a Christian.
- Lack of analysis/risk-taking amongst church leaders.
- There were rarely, if ever, sizeable clusters engaged in active peace work, or of the kind that people could be recruited to as a movement for change in everyday life.
- A vision of the purpose of religion that could transcend political division was made secondary to pastoral care to one's tribe.
- Denial, passivity, by-standing, sometimes as a result of fear of engagement.
- Amongst some Protestants, there was early acquiescence in Loyalist violence, then disengagement.
- Lack of financial, theological, or political commitment to work for peace.
- Focus on individual piety and internal church politics at the expense of underemphasizing sectarianism, neglecting local social issues and forging senses of identity that were inclusive.
- Church structures were not adapted to the requirements of the socio-political crisis.
- Churches did not equip clergy and church members to respond to the situation.

- Churches were often disengaged from the working class.
- Engaging in high-level or political elite—and elitist—activities not grass-roots activism.
- The mainstream church did not challenge Paisley, thereby allowing militant fundamentalism to have an influence vastly disproportionate to its numbers.
- Not challenging congregations to act beyond their self-interest or working with their congregations to encourage personal commitments to peacemaking.
- No development of a radical movement for peace.
- Equating the conflict with broken relationships alone led to misdiagnosing the problem, so inter-church worship was used far too often as a bandage on conflicts that were far deeper than can be resolved through ecumenism.
- A sense of abandonment felt by (some) victims against churches that did not attend to their needs.

While this list appears rather long, when unpicked it reveals considerable concord. It is plain that chief amongst the grievances is the view that Northern Ireland's churches reflected the society in which they functioned. The Revd Norman Hamilton, later to become Moderator of the Presbyterian Church, put this succinctly: 'Historically the thing that has disappointed me most is that the Protestant church leaders have not articulated the needs, the hopes, and the fears of the Catholic, Republican, and Nationalist constituency. If I can say so, the same applies to the senior Catholic clergy: you have not articulated to your people the fears, the hopes, and the needs of the Unionist community. So, all we have done is to mirror the politics of our own community. I think that has been a serious and damaging weakness' (interview 26 January 2006).[2] In one sense this is inevitable because churches are part of the institutional structure of society, operate within the framework of laws that mark the state, and comprise members and believers who are embedded in local cultural beliefs and values. This grievance, however, articulates more the idea that we could have expected something different from churches. Where the churches' social and political location is dramatically at odds with their principles and ethos, they should offer a critique of society rather than mirror it. Rather than positioning themselves on a moral high ground, however, leading society forward with a vision from the privileged heights, Northern Ireland's churches sunk in its morasses, leaving relatively few individual churchmen and women,

---

[2] As an illustration of the constraints operating on the holders of the office of moderator, despite these views, and a courageous history in standing up against Loyalists to defend Catholic schoolchildren in the Holy Cross incident, Hamilton declined to shake the hand of the Pope when he visited London in 2010, although he did agree to meet him.

mostly mavericks and independents outside the control of conservative and cautious hierarchies, to struggle to pull themselves up above the mire. This complaint has a number of constituent elements.

At their worst, churches simply reinforced the terms of the conflict. By endorsing and nurturing the equation of religion with ethno-national identity—from matters as ostensibly trivial as Irish dancing in Catholic churches to barn dances in Protestant ones—they reinforced cultural exclusivity. By the trappings of flags and emblems inside the respective denominations, such as paramilitary funerals or regimental standards and Boys/Girls Brigade emblems, churches displayed the colours of their loyalties, no matter how ambivalent some individual clergy were about them (see Vignette 11). The larger churches never engaged in a systematic or credible challenge to religious

---

Vignette 11: *Extracts from the interview with Bishop Edward Daly, 24 January 2006*

The whole funeral culture was very difficult, the whole paramilitary funerals, it was a point of enormous sensitivity both for church and for people and caused quite a lot of confrontation here in Derry. It caused huge confrontation between myself and the Provos [Provisional IRA]. You talk about the church being used. I mean at that time everyone used the funerals to gain publicity. You had a situation where you had a young priest somewhere out in [name deleted] and he was confronted with this funeral of some young person from this parish who turned out to be in the Provos and was shot by the SAS or something, and you had this massive funeral with Gerry Adams and Martin McGuinness and all the luminaries of Sinn Féin arriving with flags and coffins and bands and shots being fired; with about four or five television crews banging on his door night and day for the forty-eight hours beforehand; with families who were grieving and the whole circus there; with the police guarding or surrounding the place, army surrounding the place to make sure that shots weren't fired. And he was caught in the maelstrom and then half an hour after the funeral everybody was gone, he was left with the grieving family and the people in the parish round him and that was extraordinarily difficult. I found myself a lot of times, working with priests who found themselves in that situation, spending maybe two or three days before a funeral with them, they'd dread it and it's something that nobody could have prepared anybody for, you know, that sort of situation. So, and he was left subsequently to pick up the pieces afterwards. And in some cases, too, you had a family who were split, some brothers in the family supported the Provos, others didn't want to, some wanted a flag on the coffin, some didn't, some wanted a military funeral, some didn't. And you went on and you had to be very careful what you said because what you said was simply taken and analysed and maybe sometimes taken completely out of context. Conflict in one's own community is extraordinarily difficult to deal with. You can comment away on things in other parts of the border when you're nice and in an armchair, but when you are sitting in the eye of the conflict it's extraordinarily difficult to think on your feet.

extremists, who always punched politically above the weight of their congregational numbers. Paisleyism was more than a person, it was a way of thinking and Christian politeness towards the man often inhibited attacking the system he once embodied.

The flip side of the denominational diversity in Northern Ireland (with more than fifty indigenous denominations) is a disunited church. Protestantism is internally schismatic (Bruce, 1990) and the Catholic Church had its internal strife over policy and practice, including towards involvement in active peace. But there was disunity on another level. No one could agree on the reasons for the conflict, nor its solutions.

The voices calling for a peace vision were drowned; and not only by the extremists. The progressive churches shouted across each other. What was missing therefore was leadership of a peace movement inside the churches that could be projected outwards into society generally. Clergy have often appeared to see themselves as 'managers' rather than leaders. They felt inhibited from challenging their congregations. And among those in leadership positions, there was a culture, both in politics and church authority, that bishops, moderators, and presidents saw themselves as committee chairs rather than prophetic leaders, seeking consensus rather than setting the pace for change. They criticized violence, and its perpetrators, but gave little prophetic leadership by moving society beyond condemnation, agreeing around negative peace but divided by positive peace. As Fr Des Wilson said, so wonderfully astutely, 'it always seemed to me that what the churches were looking for was peace without change' (interview 9 November 2005).

Lying behind this grievance, in its many formulations, is the idea also that church leaders misdiagnosed both the problem and the solution. Emphasizing only the relational dimensions of the conflict, ecumenical worship services were overstated as potential peacemaking solutions by bringing (some) people together. While 'proper relationships' *are* important to positive peace, the conflict was also about social injustice, economic disparity, and unequal life chances (for working-class Protestants as much as Catholics). Social transformation is part of the solution as much as relational togetherness. Positive peace, as far as the churches were concerned, would have involved them messing about in local communities with hands dirty from practising social witness. Their neglect of this dimension goes hand in hand with church leaders avoiding grass-roots activism in preference for high-level and elite engagements. It is consistent with clergy extolling personal piety on their congregations rather than commitments to social transformation.

All this is summed up perhaps as a lack of critical self-reflection within the churches as institutions. The ecumenist movement was smug in not exposing to criticism its grounding assumption that relationship-building would eventually break down all barriers; and the mainstream churches were sluggishly comfortable in restricting themselves to engaging with people just like themselves. In class terms this meant the suburban, 'polite' middle classes, in theological terms the liberals, leaving working-class communities and fundamentalists adrift, both thought of as sunk in sectarianism, 'people not like us'. This lack of reflexivity meant, above all, that most religious peacemakers could not see the mote in others' eyes for the beam in their own. They did not critique sectarian society, they reproduced it; mostly unintentionally, it has to be said, and without realizing this was the case given the uncritical view of themselves as leading the charge against it (a point which Garrigan, 2010, makes forcibly).[3] Mavericks and independents, on the other hand, used to mediating their way through hierarchical controls and restrictions and with imagination and initiative to find ways to engage with the social and political peace processes regardless of institutional constraints, were forced by this circumstance to be reflexive; it was the only way they could protect themselves within church bureaucracies. Their insecurity tended to militate against sloth and smugness.

WEAKNESSES AND CHALLENGES

In this section, we want to build on respondents' complaints to develop an argument that the churches' religious peacemaking was constrained by a series of weaknesses and challenges that as institutions they could not surmount, leaving key individuals to mediate their own personal way around them. This had the effect of individualizing the churches' contribution to peace. Some of these weaknesses are familiar from the above analysis and, where this is so, we are able to elaborate and provide extracts from the data in support.

1: A disunited church

Northern Ireland's churches are just that: churches, with a myriad of distinct approaches and differences. There has never been a fully unified approach amongst the churches to addressing conflict. The Revd David Armstrong voiced the opinion that in fact the churches were 'very pleased with the division in society because it made them able to rein in [their] own people'; they feared that a coming together would 'cause a certain amount of power to be lost' as institutions (interview 2 December 2005). Indeed, when the Roll of Northern Irish Christian peacemakers is read, most of the names are likely to be less known to the general public, as these tended to be low-profile, even

---

[3] The Catholic Church's persistent support for segregated education, however, does not qualify to be excused under this generosity caveat.

maverick figures, whose peace engagements meant that they were unlikely to rise to senior leadership positions in churches that preferred more cautious approaches. These people are well known locally, of course, for in getting close to the paramilitaries and their communities, strong reputations became rooted in their own neighbourhoods, although a few rose to such prominence that they transcended this localism. In a setting where peace work marginalized them from their leaders, especially in the beginning, women religious peace-makers were doubly suspect. As the Revd Ruth Patterson remarked, 'to be seen as an ordained woman and as someone involved in reconciliation was anath-ema to a lot of my male brothers within the Presbyterian tradition' (interview 29 November 2005).

There are various levels of disunity, however. The most obvious is between the pro- and anti-peace churches. The very ideology promoted by some churches (such as the FPC) actually reinforced the perception of the civil conflict as being religious in nature. David Porter, ECONI Director, put it as follows in interview on 24 September 2007: 'You are told the Catholic Church is the antichrist, that no Catholic can really be a Christian. You are being taught on a regular basis of the political threat of Romanism, of the antichrist as the big system that is going to control the world before Jesus comes again. How can you be taught that week in and week out and then sit down and make peace with your Catholic neighbour on a Monday?' The history of bigotry was on all sides, however. Cardinal O'Fiaich was fond of remarking that 'the Protestant people are 90 per cent religious bigots and the Catholic population are 90 per cent political bigots'. In telling us this tale, Fr Denis Faul went on to comment, 'that's something to quell you know, this clash between the two types of bigot' (interview 23 January 2006). The residual anti-Catholicism in mainstream Protestantism (on which see Brewer and Higgins, 1998) was matched by Catholic self-righteousness, 'smugness' as the SDLP Sean Farren termed it (interview 27 May 2007), as privileged possessors of religious truth.

One of our respondents who asked for the following comment to be unattributed, which is itself a reflection of the divisiveness in the church, was very perceptive in drawing comparison with the prophetic leadership of the civil rights movement in the USA shown by some churches:

> I think [there are] church politicians who [are] faultless in [their] capacities for diplomacy and at times the focus on keeping [their] own church together limited [their] ability to take the risks that are necessary to be celebrated as a peacemaker. Martin Luther King wasn't worried about holding his congregation together when he walked down a street or when he led a thousand people. The difference here is Martin Luther King didn't have a denomination which had some people who were in favour of segregation and he didn't have to try and hold the segregationists together with the integrationists. I went to a theological college that didn't even have a module looking at the theology of conflict, and there was no reconciliation training. This was after the peace process, this was

1998, and there still wasn't something like that in place. They were arguing about seventeenth-century theological disputes. (Interview date deleted)

But even those leaders in the progressive churches who might otherwise have incarnated a truly risk-taking vocation for peace, were frequently opposed from within their own denominations. Very broad political divisions could be represented even within congregations and there were a myriad of subtler distinctions over strategy and objective that separated people who shared a commitment to change. Silence or apathy became a management strategy to contain congregational conflicts as a priority over confronting societal conflict. As Cecelia Clegg said in interview on 29 November 2007: 'A sin of omission, which relates mostly to the Catholic Church, is that there were very few occasions on which the clergy got together and had a chance to talk about what was actually going on. In the Derry diocese, I was never able to verify it, but several people told me that there had not been a single meeting of the clergy in which the situation had been discussed in the first twenty-five years of "the Troubles"'. It is worth noting in support of the argument that there were significant differences between the Belfast and Derry Catholic dioceses caused largely by personnel. Bishop Edward Daly in Derry was a very active grass-roots peace practitioner; Cahal Daly in Belfast was not. This affected the respective engagements of the church leaders with SF, but had the opposite effect on ordinary priests. Cahal Daly's disengagement gave impetus in Belfast to ordinary clergy striking out on their own, Edward Daly's contacts made it unnecessary in Derry.

Disagreement over strategy and practice amongst progressive churches, however, is not what we mean here, for there was genuine disunity. The paradox of ecumenism is that while it reflected an important unity amongst practitioners, it restricted itself to other ecumenists and was itself a source of disunity. It provoked considerable opposition within the mainstream Protestant churches (many of whom continued to look over their shoulder at the menaces from Paisley and the Loyal Orders, as well as fundamentalist mission halls and organizations), and was an obstacle to developing meaningful relationships with peace activists in the liberal-evangelical tradition. ECONI was the only route for ecumenists to link with evangelicals. But the disunity went further. Peace initiatives, ironically, tended to be carried out on a denominationally exclusive basis, with one notable but indicative example being the Presbyterian Youth for Peace project established in 2000, which omitted any obligation for contact with Catholic youth, as this was considered too controversial to be approved by the General Assembly. Outside ecumenism, the Faith in a Brighter Future group was perhaps the only initiative that was genuinely interdenominational.

As another example, the boundaries of trust required for highly sensitive backchannel communication were often narrowly construed in denominational terms and participants were restricted to small groups within the one denomination. As secret activities, the duplication between denominationally competing backchannel initiatives only came to light afterwards. Fr Denis Faul recalled the overlap in efforts to bring about a ceasefire at the time of the 1974 Feakle talks between Protestant clergy and the IRA: 'There [were] two efforts made by me and a few priests to bring about a ceasefire, but they wouldn't listen to you. It was around about the time of the Feakle thing'. The Revd William Arlow was the unofficial leader of the Protestant clergy involved in the Feakle talks and when asked whether Faul was aware of what Arlow was doing and vice versa, Fr Faul replied, 'No, No'. When the interviewer put to him that the initiatives were run separately, Faul went on, 'oh, completely. All the time you have the split and you have two different groups' (interview 23 January 2006).

There was an element of covetousness and competition involved on top of the confidentiality. There is direct evidence that the Faith in a Brighter Future initiative was briefed against by the leader of a para-church organization that was well known for running initiatives of its own. This briefing included potentially dangerous bad-mouthing of the facilitators to SF—'mischievous' was how Monsignor Tom Toner referred to them in conversation with Francis Teeney at the big SF funeral for Jimmy Drumm. Toner revealed that the matter had been discussed as high in SF as Gerry Kelly. The Revd John Dunlop referred to the counterproductive effects of this denominationalism when interviewed on 23 March 2006: 'You find individual people will do very significant things whereas the total corporate body may not themselves be able to go as far as some individuals would be able to go. The danger is that you get a very strong attitude of "ourselves alone", ourselves alone as Republicans, ourselves alone as Unionists, ourselves alone as Presbyterians, ourselves alone as Methodists, ourselves alone as Catholics. But ourselves alone won't work because God never meant us to work in a way that is essentially divisive, inward looking, selfish.'

2: Clergy as 'managers'

The role of clergy as representatives of their own denomination is noteworthy as an instance of disunity across these religious boundaries. It reflects another major weakness, however, with respect to prophetic leadership. Many clergy felt constrained by their congregations and did not speak out about sensitive topics. The shift towards a morally conservative agenda noticeable amongst evangelicals (for example Ganiel, 2008a) was not just premised on post-GFA realities, where political preaching became problematic, nor was it restricted to evangelicals. A dose of hell fire and damnation about moral looseness was the stock in trade of many a Sunday, irrespective of denomination, well before the political peace process delivered agreement. Indeed, criticizing moral looseness was safe in a way that praying for political agreement was not. Suppressing political and other fissures within their congregations marked the managerial aim of many clergy, whether with respect to the tensions wrought by the hunger strikes and paramilitary-style funerals, or Remembrance Sunday and Orange Order services. This view of the clergy's role as manager could be used to disguise political preferences that otherwise could not be publicly revealed, both for and against the peace process. Those 'clergy managers' who otherwise withdrew reluctantly from peacemaking tended to lionize the mavericks and treated them as the 'conscience' of their denominations.

This kind of clergy manager provided a considerable degree of moral support to others' peacemaking, often turned up at meetings, swelled the audiences measurably and voiced enthusiasm (especially when their own congregations could be kept in the dark), and were the mavericks' strongest supporters, pushing them forward from behind. Sometimes done from fear of putting themselves in the position of advance guard, or caution at working without the imprimatur of the senior leadership, preference for this role also reflected their realization that parish clergy had daily responsibilities in the church bureaucracy and for the pastoral needs of parishioners. Brother David Jardine explained the problem facing clergy managers: 'Clergy are so busy in their parishes that it's very hard to spend a lot of time working outside, and sometimes if you neglect visitation of people within the parish to spend time working outside, you're going to have to face a lot of criticism' (interview 6 December 2007). And it is the case that the mavericks and independents were on the whole free of parish chores and had opportunities for peace work that clergy managers lacked. The religious peacemakers themselves often failed to recognize the advantages of their institutional location. Dr Cecelia Clegg, for example, noted that churches have always been 'preoccupied with church life and issues', seeing it as easy enough for other clergy 'to clear their diaries so there was some space for inter-community meetings and things' (interview 29 November 2007).

It is ironic that parish management should be a constraint with Catholicism, since Vatican II was supposed to bring in the laity to do these things, but Irish bishops, and indeed some parish priests, resisted this for fear of diluting their authority. Preference for the role of manager not only measured people's (varying) inability to transcend the tyranny of the diary, it sometimes reflected also the advice of their church leaders to avoid peace work, whose displeasure they feared. Displeasure could grow into real threat when presbyteries, bishops, or other leaders could remove someone's capacity to preach and with it perhaps house and home. The real weakness with the role of clergy manager, therefore, at least for those for whom it was a genuine constraint on their peacemaking rather than a disguise for inactivity, was the slow recognition on the part of the institutional churches to establish a large cadre of skilled activists with the bureaucratic space and time to become specialists in peace. The journalist Malachi O'Doherty said when asked what he would do now if we could return to the start of 'the Troubles': 'what I would have done in the churches, I would have singled out your most eloquent people and said your job is going to be to make the case against violence and hypocrisy by whomever and you're going to be really good at it you're going to study this and you're going to be dedicated to this and this is what you're going to do' (interview 4 September 2007).

3: Fear, real and perceived, including the fear of 'losing your people'

Clergy and grass-roots Christians alike were sometimes legitimately afraid of involvement in peacemaking. It may be entirely reasonable to be anxious about what might happen if you 'put your head above the parapet'; sometimes not. Suburban sensibilities sometimes caused fear. The Revd Gary Mason often complained with respect to participation in the social peace process that some clergy were fearful of social witness since it involved mixing with working-class people in ghetto-like estates where the paramilitaries held strong command and which were subject to high levels of antisocial behaviour, crime, and drugs. 'We are taught well, in inverted commas, to pastor congregations, to preach sermons but there is a major weakness as regard the whole thesis of engaging with civic society and social holiness' (interview 14 February 2006). This caused a distance between most Protestant clergy and Loyalists in working-class areas that was never matched by priests in working-class Catholic estates. As Loyalist community worker Billy Hutchinson said of the Protestant churches, 'I suppose they didn't understand what was going on in working-class communities, they didn't understand the fear issues and they didn't understand why people were in paramilitary organizations. I think that was because what they were interested in was people's spiritual side rather than the whole notion of how we deal with conflict and all the rest of it' (interview 26 September 2007).

   Involvement in the political peace process, however, brought more dangerous fears. Some clergy and church workers suffered genuine intimidation—bullets in the post, threatening phone calls, abusive letters, and threats to burn churches (sometimes carried out). As the Revd Lesley Carroll remarked, 'those were scary days' (interview 10 January 2008). It was not just the range of threats that provoked fear but, as Robin Eames said, it was knowing that paramilitaries had a mindset that gave them permission to carry them out (interview 29 January 2008). Protestant clergy were always the more vulnerable; the IRA considered attacks on clergy beyond the pale in a way that Loyalist paramilitaries never did, and Protestant parochial houses mostly had husbands, wives, and children living there, to add to the level of fear. The Revd David Armstrong remembered an occasion: 'The police called saying, will you lie low tonight, we believe that your life is in danger, and I can remember people putting away their guitars and coming over and shaking my hand and saying, "David and June we'll be praying for you", or even people coming a big a distance to present us with copies of Bonhoeffer [Dietrich, theologian executed by the Nazis], leather-bound copies. But when Police Inspector [name deleted] arrived and said "I'm afraid your life today may be in danger would you please, please be careful", my wife brought the tray of tea in and sandwiches, she said, "where are the men with the Bonhoeffer books?" I said, "love if you look out the window you can see them running across the field as fast as their legs will carry them"' (interview 2 December 2005).

SF realized the peculiar problems facing the Protestant clergy with whom they were having secret meetings: 'You know, it's a difference in attitude. For them to go back into their community and say listen, we were meeting with Shinners [Sinn Féin], it would be ah, traitor, you know, Lundys, all that' (Denis Donaldson, interview 14 November 2005). The Revd Harold Good described this in interview on 24 January 2006: 'I was getting people phoning up, I've still got some of the nasty letters somewhere, [saying] I had betrayed the Protestant people, let down the Protestant people. Then I came home the next afternoon and there was a petrol bomb sitting in the middle of our back yard in [name deleted] where we lived, somebody had put this petrol bomb. So I packed my wife and kids off down to Granny's, down the country, you know and said, you go away and have a bit of a holiday and leave me to get on with my work and I won't have to worry about your health and safety.' He said that his anxiety was not whether his activities put him in danger but whether or not they put his ultimate goal of peace at risk.

Sometimes there was fear of being too far ahead of their congregations and in saying and doing unpopular things that risked splitting the congregation. Some things Catholic priests did not speak up about, Fr Denis Faul said, 'because, basically, I suppose they were afraid of splitting their parish' (interview 23 January 2006). The Presbyterian minister Ken Newell lived a ministry of great courage in his work at Fitzroy Church in South Belfast but explained, 'it is also a very risky thing because you move into the whole prophetic area, and have to say things to challenge your own people in the community' (interview 20 September 2005). Low levels of personal courage interacted with a manager mentality to persuade some clergy that the mavericks, such as Newell, should do all the pushing, pulling, and heavy lifting.

At the same time, it is important to recognize that use of 'fear-language' by some clergy was an excuse for not being involved. Sometimes the 'fears' were not real or were exaggerated as part of the ongoing cliché in Northern Ireland that 'whatever you say, say nothing'.[4] But personal courage *is* a necessity for religious peace work when religion is part of the problem. Bishop Samuel Poyntz said on one occasion about receiving a bullet through the post: 'On it was printed, "the next one's for you", that's all, but I mean, I never worried about it, I never worried about it in the least, I didn't even tell my family' (interview 23 September 2005). It might be thought simplistic, but it can be argued that while Catholic priests feared their cardinal rather than the IRA, at least in Belfast, and in effect had nothing serious to worry about from their own community,[5] Protestant peacemakers faced more benign church hierarchies but a murderous threat from Loyalists.

4. Misdiagnosing the problem

There are two particular dimensions to this challenge: the failure of the churches to acknowledge the *religious* dimension to the conflict in Northern Ireland, thus failing to address robustly the problem of sectarianism and their own contribution to it; and their narrow emphasis on the relational dimensions of division between Catholics and Protestants rather than on the structural and systemic features of conflict.

The debate about whether or not Northern Ireland's conflict was religious (summarized well in Barnes, 2005; Mitchell, 2006) misrepresents it for it was both religious and not religious; there was much more to 'the Troubles' than theology, but it was in part experienced as a religious conflict because of the boundaries of the groups involved and the deployment *inter alia* of religious discourses to understand it in lay terms. Paradoxically, the progressive churches sought to underplay the religious elements of the conflict, in part because they wished to distance themselves from religious extremists who emphasized it and also to avoid the self-realization that they helped contribute to it. This neglect revealed itself in the avoidance of any discussions in the churches about sectarianism until the period of the ceasefires, when the political peace process was coming to fulfilment, and unwillingness even then to analyse and confront the religious contributions to it, such as through patterns of worship, the scriptural texts used in sermons, hymnody, and religious rituals generally (see Garrigan, 2010, for elaboration of this point). And while discussions of sectarianism were initiated in the churches in the 1990s, they were primarily led by ISE and suffered from ecumenism's

---

[4] This is taken from a famous poem by Seamus Heaney 'Whatever you Say, Say Nothing', published in 1975 as part of the anthology *North*, and immortalized in song as a caricature by Colum Sands in his 1981 album *Unapproved Road*. It finds its parallel in another popular euphemism in Northern Ireland 'see no evil, hear no evil', which Knox (2002) made the title of a paper on public reactions to paramilitary violence in Northern Ireland.

[5] Several Catholic priests were attacked by Loyalists and had churches burned.

marginalization both from the mainstream churches and the grass roots, and proved very difficult to embed in either. It is worth noting here that the COI's anti-sectarian project was disguised under the label 'Hard Gospel' and based in Derry, a Catholic majority city, although it had an office in Belfast.

The 'problem' was perceived by most religious peacemakers to be political violence itself rather than religion, such that the solution became negative peace—the cessation of violence. Bishop Alan Harper, later to become Anglican primate, admitted, 'the church was attempting to distance itself from the conflict in Northern Ireland, and still does to a degree, by siding with those who argue that this is, first and foremost, a political issue and not a religious issue' (interview 25 January 2006). When the conflict was more broadly understood, the violence itself was located in a very limited backcloth, namely the constitutional question and the separate identities that were thought to lay behind this, rather than social structural factors that cause it, such as unemployment, poverty, bad housing, poor education, and local subcultures of violence. Galtung (1969; also see Ho, 2007) calls this 'structural violence' and sees its solution as positive peace—the (re)introduction of fairness, justice, equality of opportunity, and social redistribution. The emphasis on the separate 'conflicting' identities of Catholics and Protestants rather than systemic or structural violence led to an inevitable focus on 'proper relationships' between what appeared as the warring groups. The disadvantaged structural position of working-class Loyalists thus went by neglect. Ecumenism was as much at fault here as mainstream Protestant churches, preferring instead to focus on building bridges between middle-class people like themselves. This is precisely why evangelicals got interested in the peace process in the first place, by trying to respond to the needs of working-class Loyalist neighbourhoods affected by the violence and its structural causes.

The emphasis on 'proper relationships' meant that 'reconciliation' was the mantra not social justice, social redistribution, fairness, and equality, wherever they were found wanting, including in Loyalist ghettos. We are not suggesting that an emphasis on social justice would have found any greater grounds for unity amongst working-class Loyalist and Republican groups. No matter how socially deprived, Loyalists did not like Catholics getting a larger slice than they of social justice. But as a basic Christian principle, preaching social justice rather than relational togetherness might have fostered greater unity *amongst the churches*. ECONI's seminar programme on social justice, that included talks on policing, human rights, and the like, only served to further isolate this para-church body from the mainstream. The focus on reconciliation, however, was divisive, for as Garrigan (2010: 48) outlines, it meant different things across the denominations based on how they understood sin and salvation.

The term 'reconciliation' was controversial in Presbyterian circles until relatively recent times and evangelicals within the mainstream churches and outside sought to monopolize the word as a purely theological term referring to the role Christ plays in reconciling people to God. They assumed that political and social reconciliation could be the consequence only of widespread evangelical conversion, as only the 'saved' could be reconciled with each other. They therefore focused exclusively on what they called 'preaching the gospel'— which in practice meant a pietistic personal Protestant morality that actually reinforced the religious-ethnic boundaries of Northern Irish society.

By conflating evangelical spirituality with the trappings of Ulster Protestantism, sincere Christian people ended up fuelling the conflict through their own evangelism by reinforcing the identification of Protestantism with land, nation, and Union, 'for God and Ulster'. Understating his point significantly, former SF Mayor of Belfast Tom Hartley said: 'I would have thought churches are open to criticism when they associate with one particular view of history and one particular view of the conflict' (interview 2 February 2006). Insiders in the churches admitted the same. Cecelia Clegg said, 'I suppose that was the biggest problem, people let their political or national identities affect their religious identity and the demands of the gospel' (interview 29 November 2007). The Revd Charles Kenny put it this way: the churches 'tended to act as chaplains to a particular tribe and that is the great tragedy of it all' (interview 14 September 2005).

Therefore, while Bishop Harold Miller is absolutely correct to observe that many Protestants saw churches as havens during the violence, as places of quiet calm no matter how fleetingly (interview 25 January 2006), this made churches places of retreat and escape, where difficult and challenging confrontations with religious-ethnic boundaries was avoided by default. A critic of the churches, Dawn Purvis, who was at the time of her interview leader of the PUP, commented: 'I found the churches very closed, not ignorant of the conflict but really a sense of "we provide a spiritual haven for our members". It was nearly a separation [from] all the bad things that were going on. That's the [problem with] exclusive Christianity' (interview 11 September 2007). The journalist and broadcaster Malachi O'Doherty agreed: 'I think they were full of pious humbug a lot of the time. I think they were afraid, they didn't want to involve themselves much in "the Troubles", except for a few who did so constructively' (interview 4 September 2007).

Northern Irish religious peacemaking therefore offers an excellent illustration of Turner's (2009: 254–61) argument that piety (what he calls 'pietization') is strangely problematic for churches. When churches are faced with social division and have the subsequent responsibility to assist in civic repair, piety increases the cohesion of the religious group and meets their requirement for righteousness, but carries social exclusion that inhibits empathy with less or non pious 'others', including even when they have been subject to mass atrocity. This is not necessarily by deliberate design but by dint of concentration on personal piety as the religious goal. The Revd Harold Good, for example, was aware of the danger: 'What I'm saying is [that] we've been so concentrating on getting ourselves saved and spreading the faith and sharing our witness that we've never really actually sat down to think what does all this mean [for society]. We've got to be painting the [peace] vision' (interview 24 January 2006).[6]

The paradox was that even for those religious peacemakers who challenged the churches about sectarianism, such as Harold Miller, or called for a peace vision, such as Harold Good, rendered the solution to be cross-community relationship-building at the personal level. Ecumenism's major strength was simultaneously its greatest weakness, for while it laid bare the dynamics that nurtured religious sectarianism, it was constrained by the emphasis on improving relations between individual Catholics and Protestants. Thus, one of the chief champions of anti-sectarianism inside the churches, Cecelia Clegg, said in interview: 'I believe in the power of prayer. But it wasn't prayer we needed. It was real communication and real relationship and a real willingness to take chances together' (29 November 2007). Indeed—and much more besides. The journalist and commentator, William Crawley, ordained a Presbyterian minister but now post-Christian and strongly critical of the churches, said that this misdiagnosis is no more than we should have expected: 'If you have a theology overwhelmingly that is about personal righteousness rather than social reconciliation don't be surprised then that the ministers produced by that church and that theological context are people who inhabit that world and embody that kind of limited perspective' (interview 23 September 2007). Advocates of social witness who were themselves addressing the problem of sectarianism but from outside ecumenism, such as the Revd Earl Storey, were equally trenchant: 'How can a church express Christian faith and not address sectarianism? The churches' contribution, the gospel's contribution, has got to be much more incisive, much more proactive than just condemnation' (interview 21 September 2005). Alf McCreary, a religious journalist, saw the blame for this lying in the sorts of people who were attracted to join the clergy and their inadequate training in preaching social witness: 'A lot of young priests that I know come from fairly sheltered backgrounds; and the theological training they get would not challenge them to think anyway radically about social justice as it affects the North of Ireland' (interview 25 September 2007).

---

[6] The irony is that many of the great social reformers in the eighteenth and nineteenth centuries were evangelicals, but evangelicalism in the early twentieth century took against the social gospel since its emergence coincided with the growth of theological liberalism and the loss of confidence in the scriptures as an authoritative source of faith and practice, the downgrading of understanding of the cross, and the need for redemption, repentance, and forgiveness. So evangelicals resisted the social gospel not because of its social content but its association with what they saw as the abandonment of certain theological truth claims. We owe this insight to David Porter in interview on 27 February 2006.

Robin Eames, in a remarkable admission after he had retired as primate of the COI, when asked to name one thing that he would have done differently, replied that it would be 'to get more Protestants, Unionists, [and] Church of Ireland to accept that long before "the Troubles" there was great injustice in the Catholic community' (interview 29 January 2008).[7] SF's Jim Gibney agreed with this view: 'The mainstream churches failed to deal with the issues which were part of the conflict. They had people who would have known the extent of the injustices that led to the conflict' (interview 25 September 2007). When the follow-up question was put to Eames on what he would recommend to clergy and churchgoers today, he was forceful: 'Come out of your pulpits, come out of your sanctuaries, come out of your comfortable pews and recognize that the way you live, the people you talk to, and the way you talk to them [should be] made relevant and stop wasting so much time on irrelevancies.'

Not only Protestant clergy suffered from narrowness of perspective. Fr Denis Faul admitted in interview on 9 November 2005 that, 'yeah, well, very early on we were under the mistaken impression that the major problem was one of relationships between people and therefore if you maximize the coming together of people, of all kinds of shapes and sizes talking to each other, you would help to solve the problems'. He later came to the recognition, he said, that this 'wouldn't actually solve problems unless at the same time you had some mechanism whereby you dissolved the power of the various organizations that split people apart'. Many would include the churches as one of those institutions.

5: The role of mistrust

If truth is the first casualty of conflict, trust is close behind. Mistrust was unbounded in 'the Troubles' and the churches are hardly to blame for that, even though they might have spoken more volubly against it. Eric Smyth, a Protestant pastor who resigned from the DUP over Paisley's support for power-sharing, was reputed to be fond of saying that while he did not know what his opponents were talking about, he was against it anyway. However, for every ten like Smyth inside the churches, for whom mistrust was their watchword, there was perhaps one or two who, through back-channel communications, for example, did all they could to build trust. Trust not mistrust was their moral assumption. We therefore mean

---

[7] It is worth noting that the defining feature of most Unionist politicians was to deny allegations of injustice towards Catholics, any intimation of which was sufficient to lead to the accusation of being Republican and in favour of terrorism, as happened on one occasion to Teeney. Some Unionist politicians hold fast to this view today.

something quite specific by our criticism here: namely, the failure of the churches to trust *each other* in the very backchannel peacemaking by which trust was garnered. The suspicious, suspect 'other', whom faith commitments should have made churches open towards, was as much the marginalized 'insider' from within the churches. Suspicion amongst excluded churchmen and women about secret dialogue encouraged denominationalism, as sense of trusting ourselves alone, and reproduced the political divisions of the wider society inside the churches.

The failure to trust each other meant the churches offered no lead in the public sphere to encourage ordinary people to abandon mistrust. The late Revd John Morrow, one of the original founders of Corrymeela, illustrated this point well. Referring to clergy involved in secret talks, he said: 'some members found it difficult to carry on in the light of events which they felt somehow or other the people they were talking to bore some responsibility for. They [the talks] were fairly private because some sections of the church didn't agree with them and therefore we didn't go around [emphasizing them] publicly. There was always a danger, we were always risking to some extent actually causing further divisions within our own churches by what we were doing because it was disapproved of that we should be talking to people who were regarded simply as murderers. We didn't feel that that was a justifiable reason for not having contact' (interview 7 December 2005).

Part of this mistrust was politically motivated, describing people's fears over the possible outcome. Marginalized insiders were sometimes accused of being duped, of believing the 'mistruths' they were being fed by devious interlocutors, of going 'native'. Interestingly, it was Catholic priests who tended to be accused of going Republican, never Protestant clergy of going Loyalist, a reflection of where these sorts of criticisms emanated from rather than observed fact.[8] Looking at the situation from outside the churches, the journalist Brian Rowan, who specialized in security issues, felt that 'the secrecy of all of this stuff suggests to people, well it is wrong. When it's out in the open people begin to think it's more right, and I think that was part of the problem, it was not a properly managed process' (interview 4 April 2006). This fails to recognize that no one else was doing this sort of peace work and the churches could do it best because of the special qualities of sacred space that associate it with confidentiality. Another element to the mistrust of each other, therefore, was the sense that secrecy corrupts, an irony given the large number of

---

[8] To SF, it appeared that many Protestant clergy were immersed in these loyalties anyway. In interview with Jim Gibney, one of SF's leadership team responsible for developing contacts with Protestant clergy, he said 'without naming any individuals, we talked at length to them [Protestant clergy] about the scale of collusion, for example, between the state forces and Loyalist paramilitaries in the killing of Catholics, not only did they not want to believe it they did not believe it. And it was not about not wanting to believe it: they just refused to accept it' (interview 25 September 2007).

Protestant ministers suspected of membership of the Masonic Order.[9] There is a deep irony here. Some religious peacebuilders helped garner trust but were mistrusted by their colleagues for doing so. It is in this sense that the churches contributed to the problem of mistrust.

6: Self-aggrandizement and the battle for credit

There is a paradox with secrecy that has gone unrecognized in the usual complaints against it. The backchannel facilitators within the churches were mostly quiet people who preferred being out of the public limelight—many still are reluctant to talk about their activities and tend to be self-deprecating when doing so, avoiding aggrandizement. However, their critics were mostly much more at ease in the public gaze and were better suited to making public statements of condemnation—of violence, the paramilitaries, and, occasionally, of secrecy itself. We do not wish to suggest that public statements were intentional means to self-aggrandizement but they had the effect of raising the person's profile and their importance in the media, increasing their visibility, and, if the dash of rhetorical condemnation was flamboyant enough, they became regular commentators, readily and routinely asked for public statements. Dawn Purvis, who resigned as leader of the PUP as a result of the UVF's breach of its ceasefire by murdering Bobby Moffett in 2010, and someone critical of the progressive churches' failure to stand up to Paisleyism, was dismissive of such grandstanding: 'I think there are [some clergy] who regard themselves as fitting nicely and snugly into that role and talking about their constituency and their involvement at every opportunity. I think in all of this, people need to guard their own personal integrity because it's the only thing they come into life with and it's the only thing they can leave with' (interview 11 September 2007).

Thus starts a vicious rather than virtuous circle. Senses of self-importance rose, and with it the belief that public statements made a difference; and the more statements that were made, the greater the belief that statements—and the person making them—mattered. This makes it easy for those who are antagonistic to religion to criticize religious peacebuilders for hypocrisy—for condemning violence but not living in areas where violence was prevalent, for reverting to public statements rather than long-term action on the ground, and for criticizing church people for backchannel secretive activities that in the longer term spoke more than their own thousands of words. Indeed, some of those church figures, very well known for making public statements, came

---

[9] As a secret organization it is impossible to provide figures to support this claim but anecdotal evidence supports it given the strong association in membership between the Orange Order and the Masons.

only very lately to active participation in dialogue—bishops of the COI, for instance, did not meet Gerry Adams officially until 2005, although they had been meeting him unofficially since at least 2000.

Some Catholic priests articulated their frustration at a having a church leadership eager and willing to make ritualized statements of condemnation but which failed to support their activities on the ground. Fr Egan said he had a sense 'of being with Catholic people who were not being supported and [felt] very let down by the institutional church. The leaders at the time did not understand their plight. They were issuing condemnations but were doing it from a distance, and that upset and alienated a lot of people. They felt they were not being ministered to by those who should have been serving them. I think if they [Catholic leaders] had been more willing to stand at the coalface and be with people on the front line . . .' (interview 22 November 2007). As one example, the Catholic bishops of Ireland had a letter read out at Mass denouncing violence after the IRA Enniskillen Remembrance Day bombing in 1987, and it provoked large-scale walkouts in Catholic areas. Cahal Daly said at the time that those who had walked out had seldom walked in—serving only to show how detached the hierarchy was from churchgoers in Republican strongholds. Indeed, one Catholic cleric only half-jokingly said that if you wanted to know what was going on within the Republican movement you had to ask a Protestant minister—some Protestant clergy had more meetings with Republicans than did Catholic priests.

Ironically, the measured nature of some of the public statements against violence, designed as calls for peace but without offending the factions within their denomination, sometimes ended up devoid of rhetorical flourish. William Crawley remembers 'some of the statements coming out from the Presbyterian Church in Ireland which were nervously formulated to avoid giving offence to some section of the church. [There] was a very significant section of the church that was nervous about the Good Friday Agreement, but the church wanted to be encouraging of a peace process but didn't know how to' (interview 23 September 2007).

The more sensitive church leaders admitted to what we might call 'the calculation problem': of saying what people will accept rather than what they need to hear. Robin Eames said: 'You got the blasting of criticisms when you said something the public did not like or did not agree with. And you searched, if you were like me, you searched and searched and searched when you wrote something to say, because you really [thought to yourself] what effect this was going to have on the people on the ground' (interview 29 January 2008). Harold Good, a senior leader of Irish Methodism and located within one of the most pro-peace traditions, also faced the same problem: 'I can tell you I've been there as a church leader to try and prepare a statement, by the time it comes out it is so bland that no journalist is interested in it' (interview 24 January 2006).

Vanity is the least dangerous aspect of aggrandizement, however. Churches are made up of human beings; no more or less subject to the typical competitions between people over status and ambition. Just as the peace process generally was hamstrung in its early days partially by the fight over who would get the credit for starting it—the British or Irish governments, John Hume or Gerry Adams—the churches have sometimes competed with each other to be seen 'taking a lead' in peacebuilding. A leading Christian peace activist once told Gareth Higgins that a member of an English prayer group had let him know that they believed their prayers to be the reason for the restoration of the IRA ceasefire in 1996; his response was to say that while he was grateful for their prayers, he assumed that secret meetings between clergy, the IRA Army Council, and the Irish and British governments might also have had something to do with it. Competition for credit prevented cooperation among the churches as the other side to denominationalism and this contributed to gaps in Christian responses to the conflict. There was competition within denominations and across them. Some displayed what we might call 'the cuckoo complex': wishing to suppress and supplant any other activity than their own. Methodists in particular have celebrated their own contribution to the peace process through international peace awards, books that highlight the specific contribution of particular Methodists (on Eric Gallagher, see Cooke, 2005), in pamphlets (for example, Taggart, 2005), and lectures (for example, McMaster, 1996). Their minority status, as outlined in Chapter 3, is compensated for by this attention.

BUILDING FENCES NOT BRIDGES
WITHIN CIVIL SOCIETY

Mistrust and misdirection, disunity and denominationalism, managerialism and megalomania—these are some of the alliterations that measure the weaknesses of the churches. Given the weaknesses described above, it should come as no surprise that the churches failed to form an alliance with secular civil society to develop an umbrella movement committed to peace and social change. There are four dimensions to this criticism, not all of which are faults to be laid against the churches: the churches' peace work continued alongside their reproduction of sectarian civil society; pro-peace, progressive parts of the churches did not cultivate links with secular equivalents; secular civil society ostracized the church; and there was no forum to argue for or develop an umbrella organization to coordinate a fragmented civil society. We expand on these below.

With respect to the first point, we want to make a distinction that avoids us being misunderstood. We are not referring in this criticism to the inability of

churches to constrain sectarian demagogues. Structures of power and authority within churches as bureaucracies protected and constrained the fanatics as
much as they did progressive mavericks. Even such a pro-peace denomination
as the Methodist Church, for example, had its hotheads that confused the
clarity of its peace message. The Revd Robert Bradford MP, for example, was a
supporter of British Israelism (on which, see Brewer, 2003d) and was reputed
to be a member of the clandestine Loyalist network Tara, although Roy
Garland, an expert on these matters, thinks this is probably untrue (interview
1 November 2010). Bradford is remembered as the clergyman who asked
for public prayer for a long hot summer during the 1980–1 hunger strikes
so that the dirty protest could be brought to a quicker conclusion because
of the stench (the act that reputedly led the IRA to murder him). At the 1979–80
Methodist Annual Conference held in Cork, Harold Good (interview 1
November 2010) remembers the presidential speech by the Revd Harold
Sloan being ahead of its time in urging Methodists towards working actively
for peace. This was met by a motion of no confidence from the floor by
Bradford, which fellow Methodists complained bitterly against and prevented
being put to the vote. The Methodist Church later passed a rule preventing
parish ministers from working full-time in politics, because it displaced
ministry as the full-time preoccupation, which caused Bradford to resign his
parish rather than his parliamentary seat, although he remained within the
Methodist Church.[10] Every denomination had their equivalent, and accounts
such as this can be repeated often.

Our point is that the churches did not cut their links with sectarian civil
society, so irrespective of the very courageous peacebuilding undertaken by
some people in the churches and the constraints on fanatics, as institutions
they retained links with other civil society groups, such as the Loyal Orders
and the GAA, which continued to mark them as part of the problem rather
than the solution.[11] In such a situation it was never clear which priestly hand
was dealing what cards and thus what the game actually was; the patient work
of religious peacebuilders could be undercut in an instance by their own
institution's link to sectarian bodies. For example, the COI Primate at the
time, Robin Eames, on the one hand felt he could not rein in the Anglican
minister at Drumcree, where the stand-off between the Orange Order, local

[10] The Catholic Church had internal regulations that precluded priests from public office, but
Protestant clergy sometimes doubled up as politicians, particularly hardline ones, whose public
pronouncements against political compromise often forced fellow clergy into secret backchannel
work, where, ironically, they proved very effective.

[11] This forms the complaint of those who challenge the role of civil society in Northern
Ireland's peace process by arguing civil society is dominated by sectarian groups such as the GAA
and the Orange Order, notably McGarry (2001b: 117). While McGarry overlooks the splits
within the Orange Order noted by Kaufmann (2007), in practice the dominant ethos in both civil
society groups was ethno-national exclusiveness not inclusiveness.

Catholic residents, and the security forces led annually to considerable disruption and violence for much of the 1990s, including the murder of a policeman by Loyalists and the burning to death of the children of the Catholic Quinn family in their home on a Loyalist estate in Ballymoney in July 1998.[12] Conversely, Eames was persistent in utilizing backchannel dialogue to the point where Loyalist paramilitary organizations were persuaded into agreeing to the DSD, as well as into making a public apology and a statement of contrition for their role in the violence, and accept a ceasefire (on which they later reneged, although so did the IRA).

To have cut their ties as institutions to ethno-national bodies that epitomized the level and extent of sectarian division in Northern Ireland, would have forced the churches to confront their own affinities with these identities and thus their constitutional preferences. They refused to do this: they wanted peace but without disturbing the traditional political landscape. Remaining in the 'tribe' proved more important to them as institutions in the end than dismantling tribalism. This aptly described the extent of the problem that mavericks and independent religious peacebuilders faced when trying to change churches from within—hence their frustration—and explains the preference of many for working in para-church organizations and ambivalent institutional spaces. Politicians who were working to dismantle tribalism after having moved from similarly very traditional ethno-national identities, held the churches in contempt for this. David Ervine, for example, former Loyalist combatant and ex-prisoner, and leader until his untimely death of the PUP, described religious sectarianism as like piss down people's legs, giving a warm feeling that soon went cold (interview for Brewer and Higgins, 1998: 211).

We should recognize, however, that progressive churches were trenchantly criticized by politicians whenever they floated ideas that threatened ethnonational loyalties. They were subject to constraint—rather than control—by the cultural and political processes that reproduced 'politics as usual'. Of course, in attaching themselves so closely with ethno-national identities and the political preferences embedded in them, the progressive church people opened themselves up to this pressure, but it was politicians who applied it and critics amongst their congregations in the pews who reiterated it. Politicians used allegations aplenty to try to pull them back from any radicalism—accusations of being traitors, of letting down 'their' community, and the like, made with a level of vociferousness that persuaded paramilitary organizations to reinforce the criticism with threats of physical violence, as we saw in earlier interviews.

---

[12] The Revd William Bingham was vociferously shouted down by Orangemen when he linked the deaths to the Orange protests in Drumcree. This offers another example of the constraints placed on religious figures when they step outside and threaten 'politics as usual', a point we develop further below.

We can give an example from outside the progressive movement. The Revd Martin Smyth, a Presbyterian clergyman, South Belfast MP for the Unionist Party, and Grand Master of the Orange Order between 1972 and 1998, but also a strong supporter of the ecumenical initiative of prayer breakfasts, in 1993 surprisingly issued the call for Unionists to open up talks with Republicans. Within hours, his party leader at the time, James Molyneaux, dissociated himself from the idea and Smyth withdrew it, saying he had been misunderstood. The DUP also criticized him heavily. He later voted against the GFA. An instance from the early peace efforts of the churches is the Feakle talks, so named because they were held in the village of Feakle in County Clare, with the full knowledge of the British ambassador in Dublin who did not discourage the initiative (Cooke, 2005: 212).

These talks have become iconic in the memory of religious peacebuilders in Northern Ireland, referenced by many of our interviewees when reflecting on the history of church engagement with the peace process (an excellent account from the perspective of the churchmen can be found in Cooke, 2005: 212–24). They assume so large an impression because the talks were both highly successful in their direct practical effects and very damaging for subsequent engagement by Protestant clergy. For example, Walter Lewis, a COI canon in South Belfast, recalls them: 'you had the Feakle talks with Bishop Butler and Jack Weir and so on. They were the sort of pioneers, they were the sort of visionaries, they risked an awful lot within their own churches and within the Protestant community to be identified with any talks with the "other side", at great cost to themselves. But those people I think were seen as prophetic leaders' (interview 3 September 2008).

There are good grounds to lionize the clergymen for what was at the time an exceedingly daring and courageous initiative. Cooke (2005: 212) reports that the Revd Eric Gallagher thought the talks to be so sensitive he did not even tell his wife beforehand. Taking place in 1974, when violence was very intense, they occurred on the back of a series of initiatives from the Conservative government in Britain that established a line of communication with the IRA. Senior Protestant clergymen from all the main denominations held secret talks with the IRA as a channel to the British government; the Revd William Arlow, Assistant Secretary to the Irish Council of Churches, who unofficially led the delegation, subsequently reported the results to Merlyn Rees, Secretary of State at the time. According to Ruairi O'Bradaigh, who later left SF over its peace strategy to become President of Republican Sinn Féin linked to the dissident Continuity IRA, the talks led to a six-month ceasefire by the IRA and debate in the British government about the long-term presence of Britain in Ireland. Almost farcically, the talks were raided by armed Special Branch officers of the Garda, according to O'Bradaigh on the instruction of the Irish government who opposed the British having contact with a movement which at the time was being criticized heavily by a new Irish government elected on law and order issues (see McCann, 2005). Cooke (2005: 217) reports that SF had been alerted 'by their man in Dublin Castle' that they were to be raided and the three 'activists' in the IRA left early, with SF members remaining. Arlow reports that doors were smashed, voices were raised, and chaos ruled for a few hours (cited in Cooke, 2005: 218). The talks reconvened when Special Branch left and the excitement was over. That was merely the beginning of the problem faced by the churchmen.

Most Unionist politicians in Northern Ireland were furious when details of the talks became known, demanding the RUC interview the clergymen for details that might lead to the identification and imprisonment of the IRA personnel concerned. The word 'Judas' was banded around, designed for its special wounding connotations to Christians. Paisley and the Unionist Vanguard Movement, led by another firebrand William Craig, were menacing. Unionist Vanguard (on which, see Teeney, 2004) held Nuremberg-style rallies, with meetings marshalled by men wearing armbands, and rows of flags, with Craig accompanied by motorcyclists in black dress as outriders. Their emphasis was on 'direct action', and rhetoric included phrases such as 'liquidation of the enemy'. The clergymen received death threats and abusive phone calls and were vilified for allegedly wanting peace at any price. The Revd Eric Gallagher's wife took a call informing her that he would be dead by midnight. Even the Methodist Church was provoked into criticizing those of its members at the talks: the president and secretary disassociated themselves and the Methodist Church from the initiative, even though on the same day as news broke of the Feakle talks the Methodist Church was launching its own peace initiative. The talks never resumed.

Sean Farren, the SDLP politician, wished to correct the impression that everything else stopped along with the talks: 'the notion that somehow there was no dialogue except at Feakle, and then Feakle stopped and then Gerry Reynolds met a few people in the early 90s and nothing happened between times. That's a lie that needs to be nailed' (interview 27 May 2007). He could not have had Protestant clergy in mind, for the criticism heaped on their heads proved far dirtier than coals and it was many years before Protestant clergy met the IRA again in systematic dialogue, although casual contacts were kept: the Revd William Arlow maintained regular contact with Jimmy Drumm, a well-known Republican whose wife, Marie, was involved in the talks (and later murdered by Loyalists). So sensitive had the talks become that Jimmy Drumm and Arlow ended up having to contact each other via a neighbour's phone, the home of a young Francis Teeney. When we interviewed Arlow twice for this research in 2005 he would not let us record on tape or write notes; the experience still remained highly controversial in his mind. The lessons of stepping outside 'politics as usual' had been forcibly learned.

Not only did the churches *not* distance themselves from sectarian civil society, they reproduced it in another way. They did not prevent the duplication of separate civil society groups across the denominational divide within their own organizations. The Catholic Church had their scouting organization (the Catholic Boy Scouts of Ireland), for example, and the Protestant churches their Boys and Girls Brigades (which are separate from the British scouting movement, which is also present in Northern Ireland). This sort of duplication is repeated for church-based aid agencies and charities, let alone schools, religious sporting associations, and church-based leisure activities (for a classic study of sectarianism in sport, see Sugden and Bairner, 1993; after the GFA, see Bairner, 2004). Women's groups in the Protestant churches, for example, particularly prevalent in evangelical Protestantism (on which, see Porter, 2002), did not link with the putative feminization of Catholic women independently of participation in gender-blind ecumenism. In interview on 10 December 2007, Fran Porter complained bitterly of the failure of groups in the respective churches to unite on tackling common issues that affected women, such as domestic violence. The main Christian traditions 'gave God a father heart. Heaven forbid that God should have a mother heart.'

Ours is not a complaint about the failure of churches to collapse denominational boundaries; it is about their failure to work together in key sectors of civil society irrespective of formal denominational distinctions as models of cooperation for secular groups in the same field, thus leaving sectarian distinctions between these sectors intact *within* the churches. Failure to work with each other therefore gave the institutional churches no inspiration or motivation to link up with secular groups working in the same civil society sector or to the same peaceful end. There was no sharing of resources or personnel across the sacred-profane boundary and no evidence of any desire for such on the part of the churches. Boundaries were even tighter than these broad categories suggest, for finer distinctions were drawn within the sacred domain, often ruling out cooperation across denominations, let alone with secular groups. The Revd Lesley Carroll mentioned this:

> The church should be an equal player in civil society. That we are not is not just
> the churches' fault. Other players in civil society don't necessarily see the church
> as having any significant role to play. But the churches themselves don't necessarily see themselves as having a significant role to play. I think the question for
> the churches is how do we insert ourselves into civil society in a way which is
> meaningful and effective, in a way that we get heard? That means we have to be
> running real hard and we're not running real hard, we're mostly just complaining. (Interview 10 January 2008)

This comment makes it clear that as the churches saw it, secular civil society shied away from working with them. Civil society activists blame the churches for this. The businessman Chris Gibson put it this way: 'If the businessmen said we need to get the churches involved, well, which church?'—although he admitted that 'business has tried to stay outside that [conflict] so they could assist the debate' (interview 19 September 2007). This is a remarkable admission, but those sectors of civil society that were interested in peace still on the whole avoided the churches. Paula Curran, who works in civil society for a victim support group called Families Achieving Change Together, said: 'I have been here since 2003 and we haven't worked with the clergy or the churches. We have more or less gone down the road of working very hard to secure funding to provide services for our members that hasn't included working with clergy' (interview 5 April 2006). SF developed a strategy for developing links with the Protestant churches, but there was nothing similar in other political parties or churches. Community peace and reconciliation groups funded by the Community Relations Council and various tranches of EU peacebuilding money, sometimes linked up with ecumenist bodies (prompting the argument that the churches only had influence when they transformed from ecumenism into community relations, see Power, 2007), but this was within a narrow range of organizations and ambitions. PCROs—peace and conflict resolution organizations—as they are called (see Ganiel, 2008a: 30) have been applauded for their contribution to a culture of dialogue and for informing elites (Wilson and Tyrell, 1995: 246) but they operated within a narrow horizon that overlapped with ecumenism to the exclusion of other religious expressions and civil society interests.

Bridges were not built within civil society to harness its skills, resources, and expertise for the purposes of empowering individual groups; fences were constructed instead. This ensured that in many of the civil society spaces in which they worked, sacred and secular groups did not coordinate their activities, even, in many cases, inform others of their initiatives, resulting in overlap and omission, both too much in some areas (especially relational reconciliation) and too little in others (such as social justice). Civil society activists draw particular attention to the overlap between the churches and secular groups on prison issues (Fitzduff and Williams, 2007: 32). Appleby (2000), Smock (2006: 36), Ganiel (2008a: 28) and Brewer, Higgins and Teeney (2010) are amongst commentators that stress the importance of religious peacemakers cooperating with secular allies. It extends the strategic social spaces in civil society in which the churches work and expands the size of the peace movement. Civil society activists interviewed by Fitzduff and Williams (2007: 25) bemoaned that there was no shared analysis of Northern Ireland's situation and no agreed strategy about how to change it. Fitzduff and Williams argue this was to be expected given societal divisions.

We argue that it could have been otherwise, for above all, there was no umbrella organization in civil society with sufficient breadth of vision or with enough widespread legitimacy to command, mobilize, and coordinate its separate parts into a single movement for peace and social change. There was coordination enough in Northern Ireland *behind* fences. ECONI, ISE, and

Corrymeela worked together, for example, to mobilize ecumenism; civil society umbrella bodies such as Democratic Dialogue accomplished unity amongst some local deliberative forums, as did Community Dialogue with many local community development groups; the Women and Peacebuilding Programme did a great deal in working with local women's groups, as did the Northern Ireland Council for Voluntary Action with third sector voluntary groups. There were networks with the potential for breaking down the fences, such as the Peace People, which imploded from internal factionalism; the Woman's Coalition, sadly also becoming defunct; and the Faith in a Brighter Future group, which could not shed its religious character. Every portent was short-lived. Civil society groups thus spoke and acted independently. The trade unions organized actions against sectarianism but did not incorporate the nascent critique of sectarianism within the progressive churches. Some in the churches criticized them for this, feeling that as a group the trade unions had little influence, paling against that of the churches (Fr Egan, interview 22 November 2007). Peter Bunting, one of the more prominent trade unionists in Northern Ireland said, on the other hand, 'I would blame the churches for that [lack of cooperation]' (interview 30 January 2008).

The blame lies with neither but with the fissures in civil society itself. Fragmentation precluded the development in Northern Ireland of the equivalent of the UDF in South Africa (on whose coordinating role, see Houston, 1999; Knox and Quirk, 2000: 164; Brewer, 2003c: 137–8) or the civil rights movement in the USA (on whose role in 'civic repair', see Alexander, 2006: Part III), groups able to link the churches with secular bodies within an umbrella organization that motivated and managed the overarching alliance in civil society. This meant that civil society engagements with politics—political parties, paramilitary organizations, governments, and international actors—were dissolved to the level of the individual group or person; the fragmentation of civil society individualized its influence, and while this impact was great for certain key players and groups in civil society, it could have been much greater had there been an alliance led by an umbrella body. Civil society in South Africa mediated between the grass roots and the state, filling the democratic deficit left by a failing state (see Brewer, 2003c: 129–39). Brewer (2003c: 137–9) has argued that this meant that civil society was able to slow the slide into violence that seemed to threaten the townships, was able to mediate between the grass roots, ANC, and government in the negotiating process to ensure representativeness, and during the interregnum while the new constitution was being deliberated, it monitored the National Peace Accord by which political parties and groups agreed to conduct their competition for power peacefully (on which they were only partly successful). In the interregnum there were local peace committees—more than 200 in all—and the churches were well represented, working alongside community and voluntary groups, NGOs, women's groups, trade unions, tribal authorities, residents' groups, and the like in a powerful display of the advantages of coordinated planning in civil society. There was no possibility that the churches could have provided this leadership in Northern Ireland, perceived, as they were, as part of the problem, and torn asunder by weaknesses that prevented them showing any lead whatsoever. It also has to be admitted that progressive churches in South Africa earned considerable legitimacy from their anti-apartheid activities that carried over into acceptance of their mediating role (as well as into their post-conflict activities), which the churches as institutions lacked in Northern Ireland—this legitimacy was extended only to certain individuals known to have been key players in the peace process.

In all probability, the churches as institutions would not have been a significant contributor to this umbrella body had fractures within civil society not made the alliance inconceivable. Clem McCartney (1999), a prominent civil society organizer, made the telling point that the polarization—perhaps a better term might be fragmentation—of Northern Irish civil society prevented interaction with the political process. This helps explain the exclusion of civil society, including the churches, from the political peace process that negotiated the GFA (as well as from the AIA), resulting in the top-down negotiation processes that civil society activists complain about (see Fitzduff and Williams, 2007: 23).

CONCLUSION

Civil society in Northern Ireland was not only divided between its regressive and progressive elements, as we should have expected given the centrality of the distinction between 'good' and 'bad' civil society in the literature (Chambers and Kopstein, 2001), but the progressive elements were further fractured. One way to understand these fissures is through the spheres or strategic social spaces in which civil society operated within the peace process, as we illustrated in Chapter 3. Another analytical device is to separate sacred and secular civil society groups and, within that, to divide the progressive churches in terms of how they responded to the need for peace. This is what we have attempted in this chapter. Some of these divisions were caused by the sensitivity surrounding 'the sacred' in a conflict where religion was perceived to be part of the problem, making other sectors of civil society unwilling to work with the churches. The weaknesses did not just lie with others, however. Turning themselves into part of the solution was difficult for the progressive churches partly because, irrespective of the wider society's need for peace, they had imbibed its sectarianism, misdiagnosed the problem, and misdirected their efforts. Violence itself was the problem as they perceived it, to be counteracted by relational reconciliation, resulting in negative peace becoming the priority over positive peace. This allowed the progressive churches to urge for peace without disturbing traditional politics in Northern Ireland or disrupting its patterns of class, wealth, and power, of which, of course, as individuals and groups they were major beneficiaries. Most religious peacemakers had a poverty of vision, and whereas the odd maverick or two railed against this constraint, the institutional churches mostly pulled them back, absorbed them, marginalized them or, occasionally, ostracized them. And where 'politics as usual' was being threatened by religious peacemaking, the politicians did all they could to rein them in as well. The churches' fear of splitting congregations did likewise.

Religious peacemakers were mostly highly critical of their institutions because of this but occasionally they defended their churches with the argument that prophetic leadership can only be shown by individuals; corporations have no soul. The Revd John Dunlop put it this way: 'Do you remember Jack Weir, who was the Clerk of the Assembly [of the PCI], he was involved in this stuff away early on at Feakle. Somebody asked Jack one time if the church could have a prophetic role and he said, and I think it was a wise statement, that it was doubtful if the church collectively could have very much of a prophetic role. But what the church ought to be able to do, out of the body of the church ought to come some prophetic people who would be supported by the rest of the church or not be undermined by them or be criticized by some people in the church. You find individual people will do very significant things, whereas the total corporate body may not themselves be able to go as far as some individuals would be able to go' (interview 23 March 2006).

This is an apt description of Dunlop's life as an individual prophetic leader but not his church. The PCI was slow, cumbersome, hesitant, and unsure, giving little support to individuals but plenty of criticism. For example, the Revd Ken Newell, Presbyterian minister in Fitzroy until 2009, was accused of representing the antichrist by some colleagues inside the PCI. Religious peacebuilding was an individualized and individualizing process, which not only reflected the paucity of the institutional churches' peace vocation, it measured their lack of progress as institutions in moving from being what Jakelic (2010) calls 'collective religions'.

Before we expand on the notion of 'collective religion' it is necessary to show that our terminology here is not contradictory. Because the churches remained as collectivizing institutions as part of the wider process of ethnonational identity formation in Northern Ireland, churches got wrapped up with the reproduction of group identity. Religious peacemakers therefore either worked within the framework of traditional ethnic 'politics as usual' or separated themselves from and stepped outside their institutions on an individual basis, working with no or ambivalent authority from the institutional churches. We call this the process of individualization. Collectivization and individualization are therefore concomitants rather than contradictions. It is in their failure to resist these collectivizing tendencies that the institutional churches in Northern Ireland assisted in the reproduction of social conflict and failed to provide the sort of prophetic leadership that as an institution the DRC displayed in South Africa during the collapse of apartheid, when it admitted its past mistakes, distorted theologies and racist practices, and made public apology for them. It might well be that Archbishop Tutu was a prophetic leader in the way that the Anglican Church in South Africa was not, as Dunlop claimed in interview (23 March 2006) as proof that corporations are soulless, but prophetic leadership was evidenced at an institutional level in South Africa by the DRC when eliminating its collectivizing practices. Let us therefore now explore the idea of collective religion as the Northern Irish churches' chief weakness.

Within contemporary sociology of religion the emphasis is upon two processes—the decline in religious observance in the West and the importance of choice for those remaining believers when determining their preferred form of religiosity. Choice is seen as the necessary concomitant of late modernity, in which the decline of tradition and the dissolution of rigid social structures gives people limitless horizons to construct for themselves, as Beck (2010) says, 'a god of their own'. However, in the West (and especially elsewhere) some societies still remain where religious identification is almost ascribed, giving people little or no choice about membership or practice. This is because religion stands in for ethnicity, national origin, cultural, and linguistic differences to such a degree that religious identification and membership is coterminous with group identity. In these societies, individuals are not immune to the global processes that promote individualization and personal choice, but individual identity is absorbed to a greater extent in the group. Social conflict undermines this process and pulls people's identity formation in collective directions. Jakelic has the Balkans in mind (2010: chapters 2–3) but recognizes the persistence of collective religion in Northern Ireland (2010: chapter 4(b)). Collective religions may well represent an anomaly against global trends towards 'post-traditional society', as Giddens (1996: 8–64) puts it, but in places where group loyalties persist as part of social conflict, collective religions survive effortlessly as part of the cultural reproduction of 'groupness', as Brubaker (2002) describes it.

This is the error made by Beck (2010) in failing to recognize the persistence of tradition under limited social structural circumstances, where choice in religion is secondary to the duty to belong (if not necessarily to faithfully practice). Thus, while there was a pronounced fall in observance amongst Christians in Northern Ireland at the turn of the millennium, there was no increase in religious independents (roughly still about one in ten people; see

Hayes, Fahey, and Sinnott, 2005) or decrease in religious identification, espoused roughly by nine out of every ten people (see Brewer, 2003b).[13]

It is tragically ironic that in pursuit of activities designed to eliminate conflict, Northern Ireland's progressive churches reproduced themselves as collective religions that perpetuated it. But we have emphasized in this chapter that one of the central weaknesses of the progressive churches was their continued association with sectarian identities as part of the elision between religion and ethno-nationalism. Even progressive churches worked within the tramlines of tribalism and 'groupness' by not challenging systemic injustice, inequality, and unfair social distribution and instead translating religious peacebuilding into interpersonal reconciliation and relational togetherness. The collectivizing character of Catholicism and Protestantism continued; what mattered was that members of the religions could relate to one another 'properly'. This may have involved a critique by many religious peacemakers of the sense of superiority 'as the one true church' within Irish Catholicism and the equation of land, nation, and religion within conservative evangelicalism that made 'Ulster' seemingly their own, disabusing both of their inherent self-righteousness, but few religious peacemakers queried that violence itself was the main problem and thus did not move beyond seeing the solution as improving personal relations between individual Catholics and Protestants. The churches' chief weakness was thus to focus on conflict transformation at the expense of social transformation, because to do otherwise was to break up collective religion itself by changing the political and class landscapes of Northern Ireland. Fr Des Wilson summed this up well, and we can conclude this chapter no better than by repeating his earlier comment. 'It always seemed to me that what the churches were looking for was peace without change' (interview 9 November 2005).

---

[13] Hence the colloquialism in Northern Ireland that there is no such thing as a lapsed Catholic or Protestant, for while observance might decline, even stop, identity formation processes retain the association with them as groups.

Conclusion

Religion and the Northern Ireland Peace Process

INTRODUCTION

The seventeenth-century historian William Nicolson, after attempting to write an account of Edward IV's reign, felt compelled to warn readers that it had proved difficult to 'form a regular history out of such a vast heap of rubbish and confusion'. This is a commentary on sources. In the *Decline and Fall of the Roman Empire*, Edward Gibbon referred to Titus Antoninus Pius as leading a reign 'marked by the rare advantage of furnishing very few materials for history'. This is a commentary on substance. To adopt the first observation would be far too harsh a judgement of the quality of what has been written so far about the churches' contribution to the Northern Ireland's peace process, and the second seriously undervalues the importance of our topic and its cross-national and comparative significance. While the role of the churches is sometimes dismissed (for example, Knox and Quirk, 2000: 201), we have tried to show that such a view is whimsical in the least. But filling gaps in history does not give this volume its rationale.

While we have attempted to correct various misapprehensions in the literature about the nature of religious peacebuilding and move the focus away from the main participants whose work is commonly known, we have approached the topic conceptually rather than descriptively. If history is represented best by chronology, as historians themselves feel, we as sociologists fall prey to Nicolson's criticism, for our attention has been on developing a conceptual apparatus that assists in making sense of history rather than describing its fine detail sequentially. Contrary to Gibbon, however, we suggest that our material is important.

In this conclusion we summarize the set of ideas and concepts through which we have approached religious peacebuilding in Northern Ireland, highlight what the framework illuminates about the case that enables us to celebrate the important contribution of the churches as well as their main challenges, and identify three weaknesses that our conceptual apparatus elucidates, and which point to significant problems within the literature so far. It will be clear that we do not subscribe to the view that religion is a force for ill in society but, for the churches, turning themselves into a force for good in Northern Ireland's ethno-religious conflict was difficult and not accomplished to the degree it might have been.

ACCOUNTING FOR RELIGIOUS PEACEBUILDING

Much is lost when analysts transcend time and depart from chronology. The use of phrases such as the 'Irish peace process' sometimes place the stress on the first word in order to emphasize that it was the culmination of a protracted process of decolonization from Britain (for example see Dawson, 2007). Mostly, however, the phrase suggests inadvertently a unitary development occurring in a more or less coordinated fashion that is captured by the last word—'process' has connotations of progression, method, and procedure. A chronology of religious peacebuilding in Northern Ireland, however, would forcibly show it to be the opposite. It was non-linear and pauses rather than progression was its dominant feature, as developments were put on hold, even stopped temporarily; occasionally for a very long time. If Northern Ireland's politicians were unadventurous—with the GFA of 1998 famously described by Seamus Mallon as the 1973 Sunningdale Agreement for slow learners—most people in the churches lacked the motivation and commitment to peace that facilitated them quickly to depress the pause button and start again. The habit of critics of the power-sharing Sunningdale Agreement to portray it as a popish trick—'Rome is but Sunningdale away'—added further controversy to church involvement in the peace process.

Public outrage at an atrocity closed the space for dialogue—the 'latest atrocity syndrome' meant that pauses were sometimes the natural outcome of public disquiet. On occasions, pausing reflected the moral qualms of the religious peacemakers themselves. The Revd Ken Newell once told the IRA, for example, that he could not hear what they were saying about peace above the sound of their guns (interview 29 January 2005). Pauses were so frequent as to be commonplace. For example, the habit of annually electing a new moderator inevitably introduced delays in the PCI's peace work. Some pauses were thus routine, others dramatic. Public exposure of sensitive backchannel communications were sometimes done deliberately to pause developments.

The peace process also exemplifies paradoxical dynamics, in which developments in one area worked against those in another. Counterproductive activities made the pace and direction of change uneven over time. Paramilitary-style funerals in Catholic churches, for example, while reflecting the integration of local priests in the communities from which the deceased came—critical to their backchannel dialogue with the IRA—alienated most Protestant clergy and closed the space for Protestant engagement with Republicans. The British government's desire for an early agreement with the IRA in the 1970s, which had churchmen hosting secret meetings between MI5 and the IRA in diocesan houses, by 1974 produced the Feakle talks that delivered both a ceasefire as a form of negative peace and a commitment to positive peace by a commitment to reassess Britain's long-term interests in Ireland. But they were scuppered by the new Irish government's law-and-order platform that was designed to evince to Unionists no tacit support in the Irish Republic for terrorism. Paradoxical dynamics often resulted in long pauses, as people did not know what to do next without provoking ire or outrage. John Major, for example, was livid when Gerry Adams, with whom there were secret meetings, carried the coffin of Thomas Begley, one of the Shankill Road bombers killed in October 1993 when the device exploded early but which nonetheless led to ten civilians being killed. The talks were interrupted. He contacted Albert Reynolds asking how he could now be expected to endorse the Hume–Adams document, to which Reynolds replied, perceptively, that Adams could not deliver the IRA unless he had carried the coffin (discussed in Duignan, 1995: 106). Those with strong senses of personal motivation to peace learned to live with disappointment, frustration, and anguish caused by the unevenness of the process, driven along as it was by kangaroo petrol, as Dawn Purvis once remarked (interview 11 September 2007).

Much of this non-linear movement is lost in a conceptual rather than chronological account. But much also is gained. We have argued that our conceptual framework assists in understanding the different kinds of religious peace work undertaken in Northern Ireland, captured analytically by three sets of distinctions: the contrast between active and passive peace, negative and positive peace, and between the social and political peace processes. The different kinds of active peace work in the churches were represented in our typology of active peacemaking that encompassed a range of activities in both the social and political peace processes. Further differences in religious peacebuilding were captured in our conceptualization of the four strategic social spaces in civil society in which the churches and para-church organizations worked. This considerably extends the familiar distinction between 'good' and 'bad' civil society and showed the different locations progressive civil society occupies. These spaces offered particular opportunities and constraints and are one way to analyse the strengths and weaknesses of the churches' activities, some imposed by the churches themselves as institutional, biblical, and bureaucratic barriers, others as a consequence of the relationship between church and state. Church–civil society–state relations focused our attention on styles of leadership, governance structures, the minority or majority status of the churches, and para-church organizations, as well as the official versus unofficial engagements made by the churches. This conceptual apparatus is, we contend, a particularly enlightening way of explaining the paradoxical dynamics of religious peacebuilding in Northern Ireland. Let us show how.

Our intellectual apparatus helps explain the individualization of religious peacemaking in Northern Ireland as the institutional church withdrew from prophetic leadership. Individualization is both cause and effect of the churches' weaknesses and describes the *process* by which religious peacebuilding was conducted (done mostly by independents and mavericks rather than the institutional church) and its *outcome* (a focus on improving individual relations between Catholics and Protestants within a framework of 'politics as usual' rather than dismantling collectivized religion). Individualization is the necessary consequence of a weak institutional church containing within it several highly committed mavericks and independents, who sought to circumvent conservative and cautious church hierarchies.

Individualization, however, constitutes a problem. 'The Troubles' were not located by these otherwise well-meaning and highly committed mavericks in the continued capacity of the churches to reproduce themselves as collective religions and thus in the social structural conditions that sustained two mutually exclusive ethno-religious blocs. Symptom and cause were confused. The problem was perceived to be violence itself rather than a sectarian social structure of which the churches were themselves an integral part, so negative peace became the solution rather than positive peace, conflict transformation the emphasis rather than social transformation. This predicated even the efforts of mavericks and independents; it was about normalizing relations between people rather than attacking the system that distorted them in the first place. This sort of work was recognized by the mavericks (and others) as inherently political, pushing the institutional churches and the mavericks into political spaces where they felt uncomfortable (in varying degrees), but the aim was to demilitarize politics rather than change the society that created the conditions for abnormal politics. Thus, while there were differences between those churchmen and women who wanted to stop killings by promoting reconciliation and those who wanted to do so by promoting political dialogue—the difference, say, between the Revd John Morrow and Fr Alec Reid— political blueprints were still conceived as working within ethno-religious political structures.[1] 'Politics as usual' was a standard utilized by politicians, regressive civil society groups, and hardliners in congregations to constrain

---

[1] We mean by this that the Hume–Adams document, the DSD, and the GFA are not political blueprints that introduce political integration but enshrine ethno-religious power blocs in typical consociational style. This is the substance of the complaint made by the civil society group Platform for Change, chaired by Robin Wilson, formerly of Democratic Dialogue. It is worth noting that few church figures have signed the 2010 petition of Platform for Change calling for full political integration.

any religious peacebuilding or political blueprint that appeared to disrupt them.

In this sense, quite incongruously, religious peacemakers continued to contribute to the problem rather than solve it. Ironically, peacemaking helped to sustain and lengthen the conflict by dint of neglect of its causes and by narrowing on only one of its symptoms. For all the valorization of this remarkable generation of courageous religious peacemakers, in the academic literature, in popular culture, and common hearsay, their efforts contributed to the reproduction of the conditions of sectarianism. This is not what they thought they were doing and they will likely recoil from the suggestion that this was even an unintended consequence of their peace work. We agree that this was not intended or designed. Individualization of religious peacebuilding, however, permitted the collectivization of religion by default, leaving unanalysed the churches' own contribution to sectarianism and unchallenged the social structure that created it. This is despite the efforts of the handful of champions of anti-sectarianism in the churches, such as Joe Liechty, Cecelia Clegg, and Earl Storey. Their complaints at the difficulties of embedding anti-sectarianism in the churches, articulated in earlier chapters, describe the extent to which collectivization was reproduced unthinkingly by the individualization of religious peacebuilding.

This occurred at the same time as which religious peacemakers, of course, displayed very high levels of personal motivation to peacemaking (and often great bravery). The value of our conceptual approach, however, is precisely that it moves debate beyond personal motivation and moral commitments to peace work (which is the problem with the case studies of individual religious peacemakers in Little, 2007) in order to focus on wider opportunities and constraints. Understandably enough in interviews, mavericks themselves placed great emphasis on people's levels of commitment and interest as the mediating factor in religious peacebuilding. The Revd Ken Newell is often cited in the literature, for example, for his estimate that only one in ten of his colleagues in the PCI had motivations to work for peace (Getty, 2003: 61; Fitzduff, 2010: 21). It is unquestionable that some people in the churches lacked motivation while others had it aplenty, but personal motivation interacts with opportunity and constraint in such a way as to disclose that, despite the high levels of motivation in some religious peacemakers from the very beginning, the churches' peacemaking activities did not prove effective until the conditions were ready for it in the mid-1990s. And they *were* effective— but only when the time came.

For a quarter of a century, faith-based peace activism in Northern Ireland was dominated by secret engagement between church figures and political and paramilitary leaders on the one hand and by the question of improving relations between Catholics and Protestants on the other. The intellectual reflection exemplified by ISE's Moving Beyond Sectarianism project, the encouragement to Protestants to rethink their identity, the development of meaningful positive political relationships through individuals such as the Revd Ken Newell, Fr Gerry Reynolds, the Revds John Dunlop and Harold Good, the activities of ECONI, and the continued witness of inter-church communities, in the form of Corrymeela and others, stand as icons of what Christians have tried to do to challenge the terms, and ameliorate the consequences, of the vicious conflict. To those atheists such as Richard Dawkins, who claim that religion inevitably kills, we agree that without religion there would have been no conflict in Ireland, but it is also certainly the case that without religion there would have been no ceasefires and thus no negative peace. The motivations of the religious peacebuilders never diminished over this period. It is not that they were motivated in the mid-1990s and not earlier. What varied were the conditions that shaped their opportunities and constraints.

We can distinguish between internal and external opportunities and constraints. Amongst the external conditions, premier must be the spaces that were opened up for the churches as a result of developments in the political peace process that provided peacemaking opportunities, such as transitions towards a political strategy within the paramilitary organizations, the formation of a single military command in Loyalism with which to negotiate, the active interest of the Irish government in working with the British government in delivering their respective client groups, the good personal relations between Major and Reynolds, as well as the involvement of other international third parties. The deterioration in the level of violence that occurred in the lead-up to the Hume–Adams talks and the DSD seemed so bad as to counteract the delaying effects of the 'latest atrocity syndrome' and to reflect the truism that violence in the North had to get worse before it got better (a point made by O'Malley, 2001). The backchannel dialogue that various religious peacemakers had established over the years with Loyalist and Republican paramilitaries, which were so suited to sacred spaces as places of secrecy, confidentiality, and anonymity, were able to be mobilized later to deliver support for the political peace process and ceasefires, and key religious figures such as Reid, Magee, and Eames orchestrated the manoeuvres in combination with the respective governments.

The churches' long-standing contributions to the social peace process were not irrelevant to this: the extensive development of ecumenist contacts between clergy, congregations, and denominations; the involvement of neighbourhood clergy in instances of local conflict mediation and dialogue; and the churches' participation in public peace initiatives and secular cross-community activities, which comprised the main activities by which societal healing and relationship-building was attempted in the social peace process. These contributions continued throughout 'the Troubles', although there is no real evidence that they were effective on their own terms. However, our earlier argument that the relationship between the social and political peace processes is recursive enables us to contend that while spaces were opened up for the *social* peace process only by advances in the *political* peace process, progress in political negotiations was facilitated by the social peace process, such as when church dialogue with protagonists as a form of conflict mediation developed later into backchannel political communications that assisted the political peace process. Religious peacemakers, however, could not proactively initiate these backchannel communications—perhaps with the exception of the Hume–Adams talks instigated by Fr Alec Reid. They had to wait until the external conditions made the paramilitaries and the governments *want* to utilize sacred spaces for the purpose. This requirement was outside the churches' control.

There is a need for further research that places Northern Irish churches in these wider national and international political developments to explore how political actors manipulated the churches for their own ends.[2] Our interest, however, has been with the opportunities and constraints internal to the churches: the institutional and leadership barriers to engagement with peace; the church systems of authority that constrained mavericks and squeezed the institutional spaces for prophetic leadership; the resort to unofficial interventions that made practitioners vulnerable, insecure and open to marginalization by their own church leaders; the tendency towards both denominationalism within the churches and separatism from other civil society groups that prevented an umbrella civil society alliance; their ambivalent attitude towards anti-sectarianism as a result of the realization that 'politics as usual' formed part of the ethno-religious boundaries that sustained them as churches; and the dominance of 'clergy manager' role expectations that limited the ambitions as well as the time of individual clergy.

It was easier for some religious peacemakers to evade these internal constraints and to exploit opportunities, notably non-parish clergy, those in religious orders, the independent para-church organizations, ecumenical communities, and the mavericks impervious to any censorship and control from church leaders. Clergy outside these categories desirous of involvement in the peace process chose highly ambivalent institutional locations outside the purview of church leaders. Only those with the tacit knowledge of the hierarchy, such as Methodists, could claim any authority for their peace work, further individualizing the process of religious peacebuilding in Northern Ireland (see Vignette 12). For the rest, it put them on the margins of devel-

---

[2] The interesting point here is that Christian churches are global institutions and Northern Irish churches were locked in a network of connections that facilitated their manipulation on an international scale, as well as giving them political influence globally. Northern Irish churchmen and women often exploited these connections for their effect locally, such as pressure from Fr Reid to get Adams a visa to enter the USA.

Vignette 12: Extracts of an email sent to Gareth Higgins by the Revd Harold Good after being interviewed, dated 26 September 2007

Reflecting on what I was saying about the role of the 'institutional church'—and institutions in general—our history will remind us all too clearly of those times when the institutional church was silent when it should have spoken, reactive when it should have been pro-active, timid when it should have been bold, ambiguous when it should have been un-ambiguous, impotent when it should have been a potent force in our society, self-protective when it should have taken risks, confused in its loyalties to the kingdoms of this earth and the Kingdom of God etc.— with all of this—and more—I totally agree! However, as always, there is another side to the story! At the risk of being accused of being over-protective of the institutional church and making excuses for it, I should add to the above: 1) I do not dismiss an institution which has fed me, housed me and clothed me from birth. More importantly it has nurtured me in my faith, trained me for my chosen vocation and entrusted to me the enormous privilege of ministry, and allowed me the freedom to be myself, even when I may have made demands which were not in the interests of the institution. I would suggest that my experience of my institution is not unique; 2) frustrated though I have been at times with the institution, I also believe that there are times and situations when with the best will in the world institutions are not best positioned to produce what they would want to see achieved. This, of course, can be used as a 'cop out' but there are times when an institution cannot achieve consensus—and will therefore only confuse. Also, by its very structure there are times when the institution, like an army, would only get in the way of initiatives which are best left to individuals. In such circumstances, it is the role of the institution to 'send forth', 'delegate', 'allow', 'permit', 'support', bless' and—above all—trust its representatives to act on its behalf. This for me has been my personal experience of my institution, for which I am extremely grateful. Doesn't mean that everyone within it agreed with me—or even knew what I and others were 'up to'—but I always felt that I was trusted and allowed an enormous amount of freedom by my congregations as well as the 'body politic'. Good wishes for the road ahead.

---

opments, limited their availability for meetings, and encouraged them to voyeuristic involvement in the peace process, keen and enthusiastic but from a distance, urging on the mavericks well from behind. These sorts of church people were not against peace, their institutional position made them vulnerable and afraid. The ambivalence of these institutional spaces therefore either pushed them towards a 'fellow traveller' role or, as a way of supplying a source of social and moral support, garnered an attitude amongst them of 'ourselves alone', fostering religious denominationalism within the churches and separatism from the rest of civil society.

It may appear ironic therefore, that Methodists, acting under a secure bond of trust and with tacit authority, should be the most denominational of religious peacebuilders, but we explain this as deriving from their minority position within the church–civil society–state matrix, which led to overcompensation to want to make a difference. Minority status, as we argued, was a powerful internal constraint on the strategic social spaces religious peacebuilders could occupy, precluding heavy participation in market and political spaces, but also an opportunity, particularly with respect to intellectual and institutional spaces. It fits this argument that majority churches such as the COI, the PCI, and the Catholic Church (a majority at least on the island of Ireland) were the most heavily engaged in political spaces, both backchannel dialogue and in the political negotiation process over the DSD, and minority churches and para-church groups such as the Methodists, ISE, the ecumenical communities, and ECONI most active in intellectual and institutional spaces. There were exceptions to this, of course, based on key individuals' reputations; the Revd Harold Good and ECONI's David Porter, for example, although from minority positions were peripatetic in the spaces they occupied.

One further virtue of our conceptual approach is that it illuminates other cases, placing Northern Irish religious peacebuilding in a broader framework. There is a need to transcend space as much as time and proffer an intellectual apparatus that provides the scaffolding to build cross-national comparisons. This allows cases to be set in conjunction with one another and comparisons drawn along a common set of parameters. The case-study approach that dominates the field sorely calls for the kind of theoretical and conceptual study we have attempted here. In moving from the micro to the macro, or the minor to the major and back again, as Liz Stanley (2009) put it, through this conceptualization, we subscribe to a view of sociology that recognizes that narratives, stories, and interview accounts are not small-scale or limited in compass but, as Charles Tilly (1984) once described it, are capable of dealing with 'big structures, large processes, huge comparisons'. It is an approach Burawoy (1998) calls the extended case-study method, whose hallmark is 'extending out' from the ethnographic field not only to broader issues and concerns but also over time and space in a way that 'extends theory'. We achieve this through conceptualizing religious peacebuilding in Northern Ireland in terms of the church–civil society–state matrix. We believe this to be a model that permits wider comparisons.

However, we do not intend here to engage in this comparative analysis (but see Brewer, Higgins, and Teeney, 2010), but rather to discuss the limitations in the current characterization of religious peacebuilding that derive from our analysis of Northern Ireland as an 'extended case'. This literature is mostly hugely overoptimistic, very naïve, and idealistic. Smock (2006: 2), for example, endorses the earlier arguments of Johnston (2003) on faith-based interventions in conflict, suggesting that religion can be a particularly significant factor in peace when one of more parties to the conflict has strong religious identities and when religious leaders come from all sides of the dispute. Churches are portrayed as having credibility as trusted institutions, respected for their set of values, having moral warrants in opposing injustice, unique leverage in promoting reconciliation, and possessing the capability to mobilize and follow through locally in the wake of political agreement. In earlier work, Smock (2002) listed several key roles for faith-based NGOs in peace processes, amongst them are: training, mediation, conflict prevention, dialogue, and reconciliation.

It has to be said in Smock's defence that the case-study approach in the literature on religious peacebuilding (for example, Coward and Smith, 2004; Little, 2007; Shore, 2009), precludes programmatic and generalized claims, but this caveat notwithstanding, there are very narrow assumptions behind these general claims. It might be feasible to consider churches and faith-based NGOs as neutral outsiders when the conflict is not about religion and is not experienced as religious. They may have an important role to play in civil society when states are weak or fail, as alternative political voices and sources of welfare, or when the state represses civil society, since churches and faith-based NGOs are often the last set of institutions to be suppressed. But Smock's claims simply do not apply where religion is involved in the contestation or elides with ethnicity, 'race', and structural cleavage, when churches take sides and associate with specific parties to the conflict and form part of regressive civil society, or where churches and para-church organizations uphold failed or failing states. We would suggest, therefore, that existing programmatic statements do not apply to cases where religion is itself part of the problem. It is one thing to develop a vision of the role of religious peacebuilding where religion is irrelevant, quite another where religion is integral to the conflict. Northern Ireland sets the advocates of religious peacebuilding a stern test (which may be why Smock neglects it in his case studies, see Smock 2006).

Its challenging character, however, is the very importance of the Northern Irish case. In a society where religion is part of the problem, elements in the churches were nonetheless able to become part of the solution. Theirs was not the sort of activity others might have wanted from them or they themselves should have aimed for. Nor was the transition easy. The institutional church found it hard to establish itself firmly as part of progressive religious peacebuilding precisely because collective religions constituted a critical element of the structural conditions for the reproduction of sectarianism, and individual peacemakers were as much hampered by the institutional church as wider circumstances. Internal constraints operated alongside external ones. However, religious peacebuilders were able to rise above the morass of which religion itself was a factor, but in individualized ways and by making individualization the intended outcome of the peace process (improving relations between individual Catholics and Protestants in a context of 'politics as usual'). The way they did this is conceptualized here in terms of the sedimentary layers within the church–civil society–state matrix, as in Figure 5 in Chapter 3 (see page 169), which we proffer as a general model for conceptualizing the role of religion in peace processes where religion is itself wrapped up in the conflict.

Our theorization involves no light-headed notions of churches somehow being above the fray, or repositories of moral values, impartial in practice and wise and independent in judgement. It is full of sociological realism at the scale of the difficulties in Northern Ireland faced by brave and courageous religious peacebuilders who had to take on the institutional church almost as much as the gunmen and bombers. That they provided only a partial solution is a measure of the immense difficulty in moving themselves and their colleagues on from being part of the problem.

SO WHAT?

There are three bodies of literature to which our study is relevant and to which it offers contentious, even provocative conclusions. The first concerns the lionization of the ecumenist movement as the main religious carrier of peace; the second the tendency to romanticize the contribution of civil society in democratic transitions; the third the championing of the idea of 'spiritual capital' as a special kind of social capital in societies where religious belief and identification are high. We devote more attention to the latter because of its novelty.

Ecumenism and the peace process

It appeared to outsiders that during Northern Ireland's atrocious civil conflict, when perpetrators regularly sunk to new lows on a downward spiral of barbarity, that glimmers of enlightenment inevitably emanated from the ecumenists. This in part reflected the external view that the conflict was religious in nature, but also measured the quiet decency with which ecumenists conducted themselves against the hell-fire and brimstone political preachers who otherwise represented the public face of religion in Northern Ireland. Theirs was the 'other side' of religion in the North, reflecting its humanitarianism rather than ambivalence, its compromising not conflictual tendencies. Ecumenists were the 'natural' carriers of religious change, with 'proper relations' in sacred settings being the model to counteract distorted ones more generally; its handmaidens groups such as Corrymeela, ISE, FPG, Cornerstone Community, and the Rostrevor Christian Renewal Centre. Many local commentators (McCreary, 2007; Power, 2007) joined international ob-servers (Appleby, 2000; Grant, 2004) in celebrating ecumenists as the main, in some cases the only peacemakers; praise that seemed justifiably all the louder given that there were no other sectors of civil society offering the same lead. Ecumenism *was* the peace process.

This observation cannot be sustained. It reflects the unfortunate tendency to prioritize efforts in the social peace process (societal healing and relationship-building) above the political peace process (effecting political dialogue prior to and during the negotiation process and monitoring conformity to the settlement afterwards). Ecumenists were very active in the former but the recursive nature of the relationship between the two types of peace process means that developments in the social peace process were primarily facilitated by political progress. Ecumenists mostly eschewed direct involvement in politics, in part because they withdrew from engagement in the public sphere but also their emphasis on relationship-building in ordinary Protestant–Catholic interactions was perceived as the better way to destroy problematic politics. As Brewer (2010: 201–2) has argued elsewhere, it is a moot point how far ecumenism improved 'proper relationships' before the political peace process gave it considerable push by the opening up of critical spaces that allowed it to penetrate secular society and become part of the community relations industry; if ecumenism was peace, Power (2007) argues, it was so through its transformation into 'community relations'.

The lionization of ecumenism has benefited from a broader misjudgement, however; the tendency to prioritize religion above politics as the main carrier of peaceful change. The distinction between religion and politics is difficult to perceive in Northern Ireland, and not just because of the way religion is part of the effortless reproduction of 'politics as usual' as a result of churches functioning as collective religions. The political dialogue engaged in effectively by some religious peacebuilders was done using backchannel communication that was so secret and confidential that some participants will not talk about it years after the events, still feeling obligated to honour confidences. This secrecy meant that in one sense the religious peacebuilders seemed, to outsiders at least, to avoid politics, being unable without breaching confidentiality to show their active political engagement. In this regard, it could be argued that the main religious carriers of change were not ecumenists but those from strong denominational positions (mostly Catholics, Methodists, and Anglicans) who pioneered backchannel political dialogue to facilitate broader negotiations, people who on the whole do not receive the international attention of ecumenism precisely because their work was secret.

While all this is true, religious peacebuilders were effective only when the political conditions were right. Religious change, measured through growing support for ecumenism or backchannel dialogue, was secondary to wider political developments that gave religious peacebuilders opportunities that proved fruitless before. The emphasis on ecumenism as the carrier of religious change, therefore, allows the distinction between religion and politics to be maintained and for religious change wrought by them to become the progenitor of the whole peace process. It sustains the fiction that politics was the dirty game that religious peacebuilders did not—could not—understand, nor have truck with, when this very illusion meant the opposite was the case.

However, irrespective of the guiding assumption that religion not politics matters, the observation that ecumenism drove the peace process is plainly wrong-headed. We mean this in two senses. First, ecumenism was conservative not radical and failed to mobilize outside its small constituency of committed ecumenists already converted to peace. But more than this, it was exclusionary. The Revd Professor James Haire, a well-known theologian from Charles Sturt University, Canberra, but native born in Northern Ireland, in a personal communication with John Brewer (dated 21 December 2009) referred to the conservative nature of Northern Irish ecumenism and its exclusivist mindset. He had in mind the 'in-club language of ecumenism' whose code words of 'ecumenism', 'inter-church relations', and 'ecumenical dialogue and co-operation' not only put off others outside this tradition but precluded practical relationship and alliance with them. A more inclusive language—Haire suggested use of terms such as 'united Christian voice', 'Christian inter-denominational activity', and 'united evangelical concern'— was disregarded in order to badge themselves as separate and different. This ended up as self-righteousness in believing theirs was the true way to do religion amidst 'the Troubles'. It was unity but within a very narrowly conceived band of Christian brothers and sisters rather than with the churches as a whole.

In this way, the development of admittedly difficult relations with evangelicals and other religious hardliners was eschewed in favour of relating to people just like themselves within the ecumenical constituency. Their avowal of 'proper relations' between Catholics and Protestants missed the point that ecumenists should have been mindful of improving relations within the churches more generally, thereby helping to deliver a united church not one divided by ecumenism itself. The difficulties of this task reduced them to developing a laager of a very different kind to that within conservative Afrikaner religion but separatism nonetheless.

Second, there are two other sources of religious motivation for peace that can also rightly be claimed as the principal carriers of religious change that presaged the political peace process. The first we have alluded to in the form of those strong denominationalists who from a position of embedment within their 'own tradition', developed backchannel political dialogue with the paramilitary organizations as an eventual link to political parties, governments, and international political actors. These religious peacebuilders had to be denominational rather than ecumenist to enable them to develop trustworthy contacts with paramilitary bodies on the relevant 'side'. While these later crossed over to contacts with paramilitaries on the 'other side', trust was first built up denominationally. The Redemptorists in Clonard, such as Reid, the maverick priests in parishes in Catholic West Belfast, such as Toner, Wilson, and Faul, the peace activists in the PCI, such as Magee, Newell, Carroll, Dunlop, and Weir, in Methodism Good and Arlow, or Kenny and Eames in the COI, are treated unfairly in the international literature as being secondary to ecumenists, when in fact backchannel communications pioneered by them had by far the greater effect on political negotiations. The weakness of ecumenism in this respect is that it did not connect these backchannel activities with its own efforts in the social peace process, nor did it help manage the balance between the need for denominationalism in some circumstances and church unity in others. Ecumenism was absorbed into the prevalent mindset of 'ourselves alone', not a provocateur against it.

The other process of religious change that presaged the political peace process is evangelicalism. Normally seen as the antithesis of ecumenism— and ecumenism's main religious opposition, both by ecumenists and evangelicals themselves—the conversion of evangelicalism to the rhetoric and idea of peace was a late and surprising instance of religious change in Northern Ireland. The literature on this feature of religious change is represented mostly by Gladys Ganiel (2008a; also see Ganiel and Dixon, 2008; Rankin and Ganiel, 2008) and pales in number compared to that on ecumenism. Appleby (2000: 184), for example, mentions evangelicalism in his account of religious peacebuilding in Northern Ireland but accords it significance only as religiously motivated opposition to ecumenism. But it is arguably more significant for the peace process than its much valorized counterpart.

Evangelicalism's contribution is rooted in the immersion of evangelical ministers and pastors in the local Loyalist communities that were as adversely affected by sectarianism, violence, and civil conflict as were working-class Republican areas. Loyalist paramilitarism came to be seen as much the symptom of these social problems as cause, and evangelical ministers drew on their good contacts with Loyalists in local neighbourhoods to begin dialogue with them in the context of advancing both social witness and political engagement. This was as near to replicating the tightly integrated Catholic parish system as is possible within Protestantism; while ecumenist communities spoke for no one but their like-minded selves, and often from leafy backwaters in suburbs or coastal towns, evangelical pastors in the thick of sectarian decay and deindustrialization felt the pressure of different sorts of problems from their congregations. Loyalists were incorporated into backchannel communications with politicians, governments, and Catholic peacebuilders such as Fr Reid, primarily through the evangelical wing of the PCI, such as the Revds Mervyn Gibson and Roy Magee, the Anglican Archbishop Robin Eames, and ECONI.

ECONI had several advantages compared to ecumenism. It made the same repudiation of covenantal Calvinism as ecumenism, and its Anabaptist pacifist commitments equally focused it on active peacemaking, but its roots in evangelicalism gave it by definition the solid commitment to social witness characteristic of the tradition, a desire to act in the public square rather than retire to quiet contemplation and prayer behind the scenes, and none of the queasiness that suburban and middle-class Protestants felt at engaging overtly in politics and, in particular, with working-class Loyalists and paramilitaries. ECONI was also inclusive in its willingness to work with every faith community, even those unlike themselves, including non-evangelical Protestants, harder line fundamentalists (what Ganiel, 2008a: 4 *passim*, calls 'traditional evangelicals') and Catholics (although harder line fundamentalists remained its most ardent critic). Whereas ecumenism felt threatened by conservative evangelicalism and protected itself against this religious opposition by reproducing the 'ourselves alone' mentality that should have been anathema to ecumenist principles, ECONI always felt secure in its evangelical identity and was never threatened by the prospect of religious pluralism (Ganiel, 2008a: 50). Its willingness to break from the cross-community emphasis within ecumenism by means of 'own identity' work amongst working-class Protestant communities, and with citizenship education workshops addressing Protestant history, culture, and identity, gave it prophetic presence in Loyalist areas that ecumenism lacked. This was reinforced by two things: the local integration of evangelical pastors in these areas that middle-class ecumenists never matched; and the social witness strategy within ECONI (what it called its Transforming Communities programme). Reconciliation, the main direction of ecumenism's route to 'proper relationships', was never that prominent in ECONI (contrary to the claim by Ganiel, 2008a: 51), not because of absence but, simply, there was so much more to its Christian peacebuilding programme than within ecumenism.

Writing at a time when hindsight might have proven to him otherwise, Patrick Mitchell (2003: 297–8) wondered whether ECONI's 'open' character within evangelicalism would militate against its peace ambitions. ECONI's inclusivity, however, was a virtue as much as a weakness. For example, it gave ECONI strong links to the ecumenist movement and in this respect ECONI was the mediating network that linked liberal evangelicals, ecumenists, paramilitary bodies, and politicians. Prominent ecumenists to which some of the above criticisms do not apply, such as Johnston McMaster and Geraldine Smyth, are exempt precisely because they worked as much through ECONI as ISE. And someone like the Revd Ken Newell, co-founder of the Fitzroy-Clonard group with Fr Gerry Reynolds, can sit easily with the name as both ecumenist and evangelical. Many of ECONI's affiliates had close links with Fitzroy.

However, herein lay ECONI's weakness, for it was perhaps too narrowly religious in its ethos. ECONI had potential to be the umbrella organization that linked sacred and secular civil society, for the web of its connections spread beyond religious groups and churches to Zero28, a peace organization oriented to young people, the One Small Step Campaign, the Healing Through Remembering project, and others (Ganiel, 2008a: 126). Its former Director, David Porter, was enmeshed in backchannel dialogue that placed ECONI at the fulcrum of other networks that linked it with political parties, governments, and paramilitary organizations. Some of its funders included banks, philanthropic foundations, the Parades Commission, the EU, and the Irish government (Ganiel, 2008a: 182 n 11). Yet ECONI's ambitions were restricted. It wanted to change evangelical ideas about politics away from 'chosen people' notions of land, nation, and religion, for 'God and Ulster', but not to disturb 'politics as usual' by leading a thoroughgoing peace movement to overthrow sectarian social relations completely. It saw itself as a specifically *religious* response to distorted Protestant politics in Northern Ireland, not the head of a peace movement that might forge alliances with other secular civil society groups to change Northern Ireland's social structure. There were advantages in the way ECONI saw itself, for it marshalled the process of religious change within evangelicalism and assisted in redirecting it towards the political peace process, but it was everyone's loss that ECONI failed to take more innovative leaps forward to disturb the whole system of 'politics as usual'. It wanted to normalize politics by ridding Unionism of the worst distortions of religious nationalism rather than dismantle collective religions in their entirety.

Romanticizing civil society

'Is civil society the "big idea" for the twenty-first century?' asks Michael Edwards (2004: vi). As Director of the Ford Foundation's Governance and Civil Society programme he could respond in only one way: civil society addresses moral questions about the nature of the good society, speaks to people's needs for associational life, and to society's necessity for a vibrant public sphere. Its force, however, derives in large part because it is linked to another 'big idea', the notion of 'good governance'. Democratization, civil society, and active citizenship hang together within the remit of good governance, renewing the democratic culture of established nations at risk of shrivelling from within through apathy, and underwriting the democratic transitions of former authoritarian societies. As Edwards wrote, 'the preconditions for a true civil society' are 'a deeper commitment to equal citizenship and democratic self-government' (2004: 96), which need to be made the object of public policy and practice in democratic and democratizing states alike. Research institutes and centres, like his own, analysed the nature of the idea; philanthropic foundations funded civil society programmes in newly democratic regimes in order to bolster political reform; peace accords sometimes made the promotion of civil society an integral part of the negotiated agreement; and analysts of peace processes placed civil society as a key factor in consolidating the ending of wars. It was an idea whose time had come precisely because it seemed an antidote to the growth of new forms of organized violence in late modernity—forgetting in fact that it was a very old idea that could be traced back to the Stoics and that modern reflections began with Adam Ferguson in the eighteenth century (Ferguson, [1767] 1967). But modern conflict undoubtedly rekindled interest in civil society (and along with it in Ferguson).

The churches comprise a key sector of Northern Irish civil society and their uneven role in the peace process serves as a precaution against romanticizing civil society. Appleby (2000: 236) thought Northern Ireland was saturated with religious peacemakers able and willing to cooperate with secular counterparts to the point that they made themselves part of the 'institutional and social landscape'. This view from Notre Dame is not the local perspective (it is also criticized by Ganiel, 2008a: 51–2). On the contrary, we suggest that the churches reproduced the divisions within wider society. They were split between regressive and progressive sectors, popularly presented as the distinction between 'good' and 'bad' civil society (Chambers and Kopstein, 2001), and the progressive sectors within the churches suffered from denominationalism, the cuckoo complex and the battle for credit. They could not form a united movement for peace within sacred space, let alone in combination with secular groups. Unity of a sort was found around minimalism: the agreement to condemn acts of violence, but even then only violence from the paramilitaries. They left unchallenged the sectarian social structure that caused the violence in the first place; to do otherwise was self-destructive since they benefited from the reproduction of themselves as collective religions.

The churches' contribution to social capital was no better. Social capital dominates discussion of civil society in Northern Ireland (and elsewhere) for three reasons. The popularity of the concept in academic discourse offers analysts a familiar lens through which to characterize civil society; the language of social capital has penetrated lay discourse and is part of the rhetoric of civil society itself; and the bonding versus bridging debate offers practitioners in civil society some self understanding of the limitations of their role. Churches in Northern Ireland are not immune to the popularization of social capital in lay discourse and interviewees were free with the notion that religion excels at garnering and disseminating bonding social capital, poor at developing bridging social capital.

However, an interesting way to conceptualize their contribution to bridging social capital was recently provided by Geys and Murdoch (2010), who expanded the distinction by contrasting internal and external bridging. External bridging is normally understood as Putnam's original idea of bridging social capital, where links are made between different groups across a divide. However, internal bridging occurs when connections are built between groups *within* this divide. It is said to be different from bonding social capital because groups within this divide need not be like one another. Internal bridging evinces the heterogeneity characteristic of bridging social capital but only within a range. If bridging social capital is inclusive and bonding exclusive, internal bridging capital has elements of both.

This has great potential for understanding the role of Northern Ireland's churches. It is too extreme to castigate progressive elements as contributing merely to bonding capital, and too optimistic that they transcended sectarian structures by developing networks that bridged them. Ecumenism is often portrayed as having the most bridging potential since its rationale and purpose was to develop 'proper relations' across the communal divide. Yet as we argued, ecumenism restricted its activities to like-minded ecumenists in the Catholic and Protestant traditions and evinced no effort to bridge broader divisions, such as those with non-ecumenical Protestants, especially conservative evangelicals. We take this to be an excellent illustration of what Geys and Murdoch (2010: 524) call internal bridging. As we have argued, ECONI also had bridging dimensions, given that it linked evangelicals, ecumenists, Protestants, and Catholics. However, it, too, was restricted in its bridge-building by excluding non-religious groups and, above all, bridging only within the framework of support for 'politics as usual' not with those seeking to eradicate all vestiges of collective religion. There was indeed heterogeneity within both ECONI and ecumenism as religious networks, but only within a range, giving them both inclusive and exclusive qualities, although in different degrees. What inclusivity they had, however, did not extend to a level that they were successful at external bridging.

Our analysis suggests, however, that there is need to move beyond the hegemony of social capital when it comes to understanding the role of the churches in civil society. Notions of 'bonding' and 'bridging' need to be supplemented with Putnam's (2007) elaboration of constrict capital, which fits well with our arguments. Constrict capital does not bridge and thus has no positive effect in raising levels of trust, empathy, and altruism between people and groups across a social cleavage and divide. It has none of the virtuous consequences of social capital because, in the face of intractable division, people and groups are said to withdraw—to constrict—by hunkering down within themselves, overcome with pessimism that attempts to bridge these cleavages are as pointless as they are fruitless; with no cross-cutting social networks, people turn inwards.

This might be one way of characterizing dimensions of religious peace-building in Northern Ireland. There are elements of hunkering down in the 'ourselves alone' mentality that marked the denominationalism of most people's efforts. Even more so, it is one way to understand the exclusivity of ecumenism, hounded as it was on all sides from opponents inside their own churches as well as from traditional quarters in conservative evangelicalism, and burdened by the scale of the reconciliation task as ongoing violence polarized ordinary people even more. A life of principled commitment to peace could be lived a lot easier for ecumenists by withdrawing into themselves, hunkering down, and restricting—constricting—their engagements to like-minded others already committed to ecumenism and peace. Our findings are portents of the usefulness of constrict capital as an additional element of the conceptual apparatus to understand civil society. Can the same be said for spiritual capital?

The failure of spiritual capital

The idea of spiritual capital is being pushed by the Metanexus Institute, which has developed a research programme in order to show the positive contribution of religion to society (see www.spiritualcapitalresearchprogram.com/), with the suggestion that it is as powerful as social capital in the moral economy that disseminates social virtues. Religion is not just good for individual believers, it is good for society. What motivates this view is partly Putnam's observation that religion is an important contributor to social capital (2000: 67),[3] but it is also part of the peculiarly US debate about the separation of church and state (see Audi and Wolterstorff, 1996), for it legitimates the view that religion ought to feature in the public square not because of its spiritual significance but its social, political, and economic benefits.

Spiritual capital is consistent with the growing emphasis in the USA on, amongst other things, religious diplomacy (Johnston, 2003), the contribution of religion to transitional justice (Philpott, 2006, 2007b), and the importance of religious perspectives on international and public affairs (Appleby, 1998; Gill, 2001), which a new journal *Review of Faith and International Affairs* embodies. The developing field of religious peacebuilding is part of the same zeitgeist. The USIP, for example, established its research programme in this area in 1999 and several publications have appeared from its research leaders (Smock, 2001, 2002, 2006, 2008; Little, 2007). There is a religion and peacebuilding programme as part of the peacebuilding initiative of the International Association for Humanitarian Policy and Conflict Research (www.peacebuildinginitiative.org/index), developed in conjunction with the United Nations' Peacebuilding Support Office. There is no evidence that the Metanexus Institute is linked to these bodies but a member of the US Foreign Policy Research Institute sits on its main board (see www.metanexus.net/board.asp).[4]

We wish to apply the concept of spiritual capital to Northern Ireland because it is new ground, but in so doing move the debate on to the

---

[3] Putnam is on the Advisory Board of the Spiritual Capital research programme. See www.spiritualcapitalresearchprogram.com/about_advisory.asp consulted 25 November 2010.
[4] Consulted 25 November 2010.

post-agreement phase in order to examine evidence of spiritual capital in dealing with social reconstruction in the aftermath of 'the Troubles'. A consultation paper by the DUP in late 2010 entitled 'Empowering Faith Groups to Benefit Local Communities', makes several recommendations that, without referring to it directly, endorse the principle of spiritual capital (see www.dup.org.uk/default.htm). The suggestion that faith groups can make positive contributions to local communities through the provision of services, support structures, and generally being the heart of the neighbourhood, is ahead of its time in one sense. But in another, this is precisely what churches used to do before secularization. Sensing this return to 'the golden age', the conservative evangelical Caleb Foundation and the Evangelical Protestant Society responded enthusiastically to the consultation (www.calebfoundation.org/page4.htm). The resistance of mainstream churches, however, may by default turn this idea into an opportunity for fundamentalism to try to reassert itself following the DUP-SF power-sharing deal.

The COI Archbishop and Primate Alan Harper, for example, recognized the need for churches to change focus now that (negative) peace has been achieved: 'Obviously over thirty odd years of conflict most of the attention at local level has been paid to survival, to pastoring the survivors and dealing with that multiplicity of pastoral issues that surround both injury and death on the one hand and criminality on the other. That continues to be for clergy on the ground probably their primary focus, but things have changed since overt violence was switched off, and that enables us to take a second look perhaps at what the church ought to be doing, in other words out of survival mode into something which might be more appropriate and pro-active' (interview 25 January 2006). The diffidence with which these sentiments are expressed is a measure of the scale of the problem in convincing progressive churches they have a role to play now violence has stopped. The weaknesses they displayed in the pre-agreement phase seriously constrain their ambitions and activities in the post-violence period. Therefore, we argue as a generalization, the potential for spiritual capital in societies where religion was part of the problem is mediated by the churches' activities in the pre-agreement phase and can be severely limited by it.

Spiritual capital in the post-agreement stage is reflected in the churches' activities in the public sphere in dealing with the legacy of violence, both for individual victims and society more generally. It is measured by the translation of members' private troubles into public issues, not by rendering this activity into pastoral care dealt with only in individual congregations. Pastoring to the individual needs of churchgoers has an accumulative effect in society but it is random, restricted to church members, and does not meet the obligations of the churches to respond to the wider needs of societies emerging out of conflict (contribution to society, after all, is the defining characteristic of spiritual capital). High levels of spiritual capital would signal a strong commitment to work in the public square on issues that violence has left as ongoing problems: such as mobilizing public discussion about post-conflict emotions and emotion management—for instance, in the appropriate balance between righteous anger and forgiveness, or the cultivation of public senti-ments around hope, reconciliation, compromise, compassion, and empathy; within their domains of influence assisting in the management of the risks of renewed outbreaks of violence, and supporting ex-combatants with the de-construction of violent masculinities and with their wider social reintegration; work amongst victims and in bringing victim issues into the public sphere; assisting in the correction of distorted notions of the conflict and of history generally, as well as empowering local communities to engage in informal 'truth' recovery procedures; encouraging new notions of identity and new processes of identity formation; and, encouraging the deconstruction of sec-tarian shibboleths from the past, particularly confronting ethno-religious group structures that perpetuate segregation rather than facilitate integration. This is not an exhaustive listing but it gives an indication of the scale of the task if spiritual capital is to be meaningful in post-'Troubles' Northern Ireland.

However, the churches' approach to peace in the pre-agreement phase, which we characterized as individualization, reproduces the failure of the institutional church in all these matters and the continued dependence on individual religious peacebuilders, independents, and mavericks. This should come as no surprise. If the problem was misdiagnosed to be violence itself, the introduction of negative peace marks the end of the institutional churches' role. The peace process, as far as the institutional church is concerned, has come to an end. Taking no responsibility for the past, or their contribution to sectarianism, the institutional church does not accept it has any responsibility to the future, save ministering to the pastoral needs of their congregations on a piecemeal basis. Hesitant and uncomfortable in displaying prophetic leader-ship in the public sphere during the violence, they are at a loss to know what to do publicly after it. It is thus left to individual religious peacebuilders to address the legacy of violence, equally piecemeal.

Representatives of victim groups, for example, feel the churches abandoned them once (negative) peace was negotiated. Victim issues tend to be enfolded into the pastoral duties of congregations, leaving unchurched victims ignored and victim issues individualized. Willie Frazer, for example, one of the most public campaigners for victims of Republican violence and who runs Families Acting for Innocent Relatives (FAIR) said, 'the churches as a whole [have] done nothing whatsoever to help victims. My father was murdered and he was sexton of the Church of Ireland for twenty-eight years. His reward from the churches was to be forgotten, the churches have nothing to offer' (interview 15 April 2006). Frazer is an ardent critic of the GFA and this affects his view of religion. He went on to say that 'our clergymen'—by which he meant good Protestants—'were prepared to throw justice out of the window for the sake of a so-called peace agreement. Justice didn't come into it with them.' Feelings of abandonment as a victim are thus wrapped up with feelings of abandonment as a Protestant, but this notwithstanding, Frazer's complaint about the absence of public campaigning on behalf of victims by the churches is fair; although it would be fairer if Frazer saw public campaigning as necessary for all victims.

While campaigners such as Frazer say victims feel under pressure from the churches because of their public stance—'the only thing we hear from our churches is, we must forgive, we must move on, we must forget the past' (interview 15 April 2006)—in fact there is no public religious discourse on forgiveness, hope, and compassion; still less on resentment and anger (on the importance of victims being able to express 'righteous anger' after conflict, see Brudholm, 2008, 2009; Muldoon, 2008). Forgiveness as a process is often feared by liberal human rights activists and victims alike because it is assumed to mean amnesty, although it need not. But debates about what forgiveness is politically, and whether or not it first requires repentance, on which churches should be expected to take the lead after conflict (Smock, 2006: 38; Garrigan, 2010: 39), are not entering the public arena.[5] And hope is not a word in the lexicon of the churches—at least not this-worldly hope. As part of the same phenomenon, the churches are silent on transitional justice issues. There is no religious discourse in Northern Ireland on human rights issues (on faith-based human rights NGOs elsewhere, see Livezey, 1989; Bush, 2007), on truth-recovery (on religion and truth recovery in Latin America, see Hayes and Tombs, 2001), or on other transitional justice themes such as reparation, memory, or restorative reintegration of ex-combatant prisoners. As we saw in Chapter 1, in the lead up to the GFA, religious peacebuilders placed a very high priority on working with prisoners while they were in jail, and their families, but not when released, nor once they gave their imprimatur to the deal.

In order to show the potential of what is missing with respect to spiritual capital, it is worth mentioning some examples of work done by individuals, independents, and mavericks in this area. That these are sketchy and uncoordinated reflects the individualized nature of religious peacebuilding before and after the agreement. Activists in the social gospel, for example, have been very prominent in managing the risk of renewed outbreaks of violence as one instance of this kind of work. Locally integrated in hard-hit neighbourhoods and serving a local population, some clergy have been active in the North and West Belfast Parades Forum, for example, which includes members of

---

[5] A series of Lenten lectures was held on forgiveness in St Anne's Cathedral in 1996 (COI, 1996), ECONI had a fifteen-volume pamphlet series on forgiveness running between 2001–3 and in 1996 the FPG published a pamphlet on remembrance and forgiveness (FPG, 1996). This is discussed more fully in Chapter 1, pp. 81–2. Note that it was mostly done in the pre-agreement phase as part of the groundwork for agreement, not as part of societal accommodation afterwards.

paramilitary bodies, political representatives, community groups, and local churches, trying to defuse the conflict around contentious marches. The Revd Norman Hamilton's participation was recognized by him as the consequence of his earlier conflict resolution work in the Holy Cross dispute (interview 26 January 2006). Without realizing it, he described the benefits of spiritual capital in Northern Ireland: 'the churches are part of the fabric of this society, for good or ill, and in the normal course of social dialogue, we will be engaging with each other'. Another advocate of the social gospel, the Revd Gary Mason, heads a similar venture, the Inner East Forum, which is a mixed group that includes Loyalists, and mediates with the Parades Commission as well as concerning itself with the structural causes of conflict in the area around poverty, poor housing, and unemployment.

The principled commitment to social witness in evangelicalism not surprisingly encouraged ECONI to be active in social justice issues, concerning itself with international fair trade, climate change and the environment, multiculturalism, policing and racism, amongst others. Ganiel (2008a: 134) notes that its decision in 2005 to become the Centre for Contemporary Christianity in Ireland was in order to expand its interests into community and citizenship—a lead it takes from the London-based Centre for Contemporary Christianity to which it is now linked.[6] Ganiel quotes an activist from the more conservative Evangelical Alliance as saying that social justice is just as important to the gospel as getting people 'saved' (2008a: 134). While at one level this seems to widen the gulf with traditional evangelicalism, the common interest in family values as part of their shared moral conservatism pulls in the other direction. It is precisely this link between social justice and 'family values' that grounds ECONI and others in grass-roots evangelicalism. Ganiel's criticism (2008a: 143) that the support base of ECONI is unclear applies more to ecumenism, which was essentially elitist. This elitism lay behind the difficulties of ISE, for example, to entrench its anti-sectarian work in the grass roots and the failure of the booklets by the FPG on history, remembrance, sectarianism, and the like, to embed in ordinary people's practice.

ECONI took interest in the public sphere; ecumenism did not. In 2003 ECONI obtained funding from the EU Peace II Programme to undertake a pilot study on the future of the church in the public square, the report on which (see Kiess and Thompson, 2004) formed the basis of a seminar in April 2004. Interviews were conducted with a sample of representatives from the churches and civil society on religious contributions in three areas—human rights, politics, and community relations. Data from civil society representatives disclose ignorance about the churches' contribution in these fields, a

---

[6] Perhaps we can infer from it becoming defunct by 2010 that it found this transition problematic and the agenda unpopular. It also had difficulty in surviving the loss of its popular and dynamic leader, David Porter, who has moved to Coventry Cathedral.

strong perception that the churches still 'did not know how to engage in a positive, non-divisive way' (Kiess and Thompson, 2004: 5) and a feeling they were wholly ineffective. More worryingly, representatives from the churches (admittedly only four were interviewed) felt that because they are still associated with sectarianism, sustained partnerships were not possible, nor was it feasible for the churches to contribute to public debate. ECONI made some suggestions for how churches might be empowered to enter the public square, such as through modelling the practice of forgiveness, doing 'single identity work' so that congregations address relevant post-conflict issues, engagement more with wider culture and with NGOs in relevant fields, creating public statements, and so on (Kiess and Thompson, 2004: 11–13). To date none have been implemented in anything like a strategic or comprehensive fashion.

There is no authoritative religious voice in public debate on post-violence issues. This is partly a skills issue. Liam Clarke, a well-known journalist on Irish affairs, Kathryn Clarke, and Revd Earl Storey, from the Hard Gospel project, responded by establishing a suite of courses for clergy in 2010 on the theme of 'Speaking Publicly for Peace' (Storey, 2010). Primarily, however, public silence is a motivational issue. ECONI spoke essentially to (and about) itself when the Report's authors wrote: 'the church is not absolved from engaging directly. Engagement flows directly from the public life of the church, whether in poverty alleviation, peacebuilding or education' (Kiess and Thompson, 2004: 10). While there have been a few instances of religion entering the public square dealing with post-violence issues—for example, the Healing Through Remembering project; the Eames-Bradley Consultative Group on the Past; the Journey Towards Healing project on trauma, grief, and faith; and the Northern Ireland Association of Mental Health/University of Aberdeen project on religion and ex-combatant prisoners—these are independent of the institutional church, done freelance by individual religious peacemakers (in some cases done after they retired from active ministry) and undertaken in conjunction with other civil society representatives in a way that they carry no strong religious stamp. Thus it was that some of our interviewees eager for a higher profile by the church in the public sphere complained at the churches' evacuation of public space. David Porter, for example, referred to their siege mentality, a survival mode, more concerned about declining numbers than owning up to their contribution to the conflict (interview 24 September 2007). Cecelia Clegg said, 'at a very high level our churches are living in cloud cuckoo land' by not being able to deal with ongoing differences between people and communities (interview 29 November 2007). These sentiments hint at the main problem for the churches in visualizing a role for themselves in the public square.

The essential problem derives from the critical weakness churches displayed in the pre-agreement phase. Namely, their motivation to continue to reproduce themselves as collective religions by individualizing their efforts to independents and mavericks, which in turn reflects their enduring loyalty to ethno-religious 'groupness' (Brubaker, 2002). Negative peace triumphed not positive peace, leaving churches uninterested in post-violence reconstruction. As Brother David Jardine put it, 'we didn't do enough to come together as churches. We should have been creating more relationships across the divide' (interview 6 December 2007). Again it is the odd maverick or two that sees the churches having the responsibility to speak out publicly about the dangers for Northern Ireland if groupness goes unchallenged. The Revd John Dunlop articulated these fears well: 'One of the most worrying things about Northern Ireland is that we are moving into homogeneous communities. The demographic shifts of the population are very serious and very worrying. The only way we can start to overcome that is when local church communities decide they are going to move across these divisions and try to sustain integrated communities or mixed communities or good neighbourliness. That is part of the Christian vocation where [you] have to have a concern not just for your own congregation but for the community' (interview 23 March 2006).

Homogenization creates walls not bridges between ethno-religious communities and some perceptive interviewees see that reconciliation, the motif of the churches during the conflict, is becoming more difficult now. The Revd Ruth Patterson, for example, judged in 2005 that reconciliation work is more difficult than ten years ago. Polarization has been left intact and in this quiescent phase without overt violence she thinks there is 'no kudos, no glory' for the churches to get involved anymore (interview 29 November 2005). The Revd Lesley Carroll, herself active in the public domain as part of the Eames-Bradley Consultative Group on the Past, was strident in criticism of the churches for not exploiting the space opened up by negative peace to push for more positive change: 'The greater sin of the churches wasn't in the days of "the Troubles" but when space came we didn't then face down all the things that we needed to' (interview 10 January 2008). It is perhaps fitting that we give the last word on this to the late Revd John Morrow, pioneer of ecumenism, co-founder of Corrymeela, and the champion of reconciliation approaches to Ireland's conflict, who was speaking in 2005:

> It's a difficult phase we are at now because a great effort was made to bring about the ceasefires. People are having a hard time coming to terms with what we really agreed here and therefore there has been a certain drawing back from the difficulty of the task because we now realize that in order to carry this through we have all got to be changed, all of us. And we are not really that willing to be changed. To carry through in policing, with dealing with the wounds of people who are victims, dealing with the remaining injustices, it was easier when the simple opposition was violence—that was the simple target we could all put our aim into. Now we are in a much more messy situation. People have seen how deeply sectarian we actually are. When we are not all just simply against violence,

which is nice to agree about, we recognize the deep-seated sectarianism which still has to be overcome. (Interview 7 December 2005)

This is a measure of what spiritual capital needs to accomplish in Northern Ireland in order to make religion a positive contribution to post-violent society and a vivid testimony of its absence.

CONCLUSION

How to finish on the right note? In *Aspects of Aristocracy*, the historian David Cannadine (1994: 210), writing about the lives of British aristocrats, begins his account of the couple Harold Nicolson and Vita Sackville-West by saying they were a remarkable pair but not as remarkable as they are thought to be. This only in part serves as an analogy to our ending. Most commentators attribute no significance to the churches in Northern Ireland's peace process, while a few exaggerate it. We have tried to avoid overcompensating for this neglect by claiming religious peacebuilders to be more remarkable than they actually were—but they are more remarkable than most people take them to be. A famous Irish phrase has been appropriated by Republican ex-combatants to honour their role—'it is not those who inflict the most but those who endure the most who will conquer in the end'. Ironically, this applies better to clergy.

We are sure that for some we have merely proved a negative: with one or two notable exceptions, the churches in Northern Ireland were not thumping their Bibles and exhorting their flocks to holy war. What of proof positive? While they acted as a restraining force on avowedly secular violence, the churches could have done more to assist the peace process. The institutional church was not proactive and the group of individuals, independents, and mavericks who were engaged were noble amateurs. Untrained and unskilled, they were not professional peace negotiators; they succeeded nonetheless in several important ways. While some of their fellow travellers played ignobly at peacemaking, the serious and committed religious peacebuilders made an honourable difference, in both the political and social peace processes. They had a prophetic presence at the same time as which the institutional churches deserted prophetic leadership. But individualization shaped their pre-agreement efforts and blinded them to the necessity for implementing positive peace in the post-agreement phase. This suggests that the rhetoric of spiritual capital could usefully be popularized in the churches to the same level as social capital as a way of motivating them for the new challenges ahead.

One last question needs to be asked, though. Are Northern Irish churches capable any longer of doing anything? Paradoxically, their condition post-agreement is worse than before. Secularization and anti-clericalism diminishes their influence and respect. They lack moral legitimacy for having missed opportunities for prophetic leadership during 'the Troubles'. Individual peace-makers are ageing, retiring from active ministry, or burning out, becoming ill and moving out of Northern Ireland. Religious peacebuilding is in crisis as individualization disappears with the peacemakers who bore its brunt and as the institutional church still evades its responsibilities in the public square. If our arguments suggest there was too much reliance on individuals and mavericks when undertaking faith-based peacebuilding, the flip side is that too much religion continues to be done through the institutional church. Northern Ireland needs more faith-based NGOs free of bureaucratic con-straints and institutional limitations if religion is to play any part in spiritual capital and assist Northern Ireland to make the transition from negative to positive peace. We fear, however, that the capacity of the institutional church to inherit the future is diminished by the irresponsibilities in its past.

Bibliography

Abbott, D. (1973) 'Ian Paisley: Evangelicals and Conflict in Northern Ireland', *Communication Quarterly* 21: 49–55.

Adam, H. and Giliomee, H. (1980) *The Rise and Crisis of Afrikaner Power*. Cape Town: David Philip.

Adams, G. (2007) *An Irish Eye*. Dingle: Brandon Books.

Alexander, J. (2006) *The Civil Sphere*. New York: Oxford University Press.

Akenson, D. H. (1992) *God's People*. London: Cornell University Press.

Amstutz, M. (2004) *The Healing of Natious*. London: Rowman and Littlefield.

Anderson, K. and Rieff, D. (2005) 'Global Civil Society: A Sceptical View', in Anheier, Glasius, and Kaldor (2005).

Anheier, H. and Daly, S. (2005) 'Philanthropic Foundations: A New Global Force?', in Anheier, Glasius, and Kaldor (2005).

—— and Kendall, J. (2002) 'Interpersonal Trust and Voluntary Associations', *British Journal of Sociology* 53: 343–62.

—— and Simmons, A. (2004) *The Role of Philanthropy in Globalisation*. International Network on Strategy Philanthropy. Gutersloh: Bertlesmann Foundation.

——, Glasius, M. and Kaldor, M. (2005) *Global Civil Society 2004/5*. London: Sage.

Appleby, S. (1998) 'Religion and Global Affairs: Religious Militants for Peace', *SAIS International Review* 18: 38–44.

—— (2000) *The Ambivalence of the Sacred*. Lanham MD: Rowman and Littlefield.

Ashe, F. (2006) 'Gendering the Holy Cross School Dispute', *Political Studies* 54: 147–64.

—— (2007) 'Gendering Ethno-National Conflict in Northern Ireland', *Ethnic and Racial Studies* 30: 766–86.

Audi, R. and Wolterstorff, N. (1996) *Religion in the Public Square*. Lanham, MD: Rowman and Littlefield.

Aughey, A. (1990) 'Recent Interpretations of Unionism', *The Political Quarterly* 60: 188–99.

Bairner, A. (2004) 'Inclusive Soccer, Exclusive Politics? Sports Policy in Northern Ireland and the Good Friday Agreement', *Sociology of Sport Journal* 24: 23–41.

Banchoff, T. (2008) (ed.) *Religious Pluralism*. Oxford: Oxford University Press.

Barnes, L. P. (2005) 'Was the Northern Irish Conflict Religious?', *Journal of Contemporary Religion* 20: 55–69.

Bauman, Z. (2002) *Liquid Love*. Cambridge: Polity Press.

Beck, U. (2010) *A God of One's Own*. Cambridge: Polity Press.

Bell, C. and O'Rourke, C. (2007) 'The People's Peace?', *International Political Science Review* 28: 293–324.

Beresford, D. (1987) *Ten Dead Men*. London: Harper Collins.

Berger, P. (2005) 'Religion and Global Civil Society', in M. Juergensmeyer (ed.) *Religion and Global Civil Society*. Oxford: Oxford University Press.

Bew, J., Frampton, M. and Gurruchaga, I. (2009) *Talking to Terrorists*. London: Hurst.

Boal, F., Keane, M. and Livingstone, D. (1997) *Them and Us? Attitudinal Variation Among Churchgoers in Belfast*. Belfast: Institute of Irish Studies.

Braithwaite, J., Braithwaite, V., Cookson, M., and Dunn, L. (2010) *Anomie and Violence: Non-Truth and Reconciliation in Indonesian Peacebuilding*. Canberra: Australian National University Press.

Brewer, J. D. (1986) *After Soweto*. Oxford: Clarendon Press.

—— (1991) *Northern Ireland's Experiences of the Parallels Between Sectarianism and Racism in terms of the Models of Work, Classroom Issues and Preparation for Practice*. London: Report for the National Steering Group on the Teaching of Race and Anti-Racism in the Personal Social Services, Central Council for Education and Training in Social Work.

—— (1992) 'Sectarianism and Racism, and their Parallels and Differences', *Ethnic and Racial Studies* 15: 352–64.

—— (2001) *Taking to One's Opponents*. Armagh: Centre for Social Study of Religion, Queen's University Armagh.

—— (2003a) 'Northern Ireland', in Cejka and Bamat (2003).

—— (2003b) 'Are There Any Christians in Northern Ireland?', in A. M. Gray, K. Lloyd, P. Devine, G. Robinson, and D. Heenan (eds), *Social Attitudes in Northern Ireland: The Eighth Report*. London: Pluto Press.

—— (2003c) *C. Wright Mills and the Ending of Violence*. Basingstoke: Palgrave.

—— (2003d) 'Contesting Ulster', in R. Robin and B. Strath (eds), *Homelands*. Brussels: Peter Lang.

—— (2004) 'Continuity and Change in Ulster Protestantism', *The Sociological Review* 52: 265–83.

—— (2010) *Peace Processes: A Sociological Approach*. Cambridge: Polity Press.

—— and Higgins, G. (1998) *Anti-Catholicism in Ireland*. Basingstoke: Macmillan.

——, Bishop, K., and Higgins, G. (2001) *Peacemaking Among Protestants and Catholics in Northern Ireland*. Belfast: Centre for the Social Study of Religion, Queen's University of Belfast.

——, Higgins, G., and Teeney, F. (2010) 'Religious Peacemaking: A Conceptualisation', *Sociology* 44: 1019–37.

——, Keane, M., and Livingstone, D. (2006) 'Landscape of Spires', in F. Boal and S. Royal (eds), *Enduring City*. Belfast: Blackstaff Press.

——, Lockhart, W., and Rodgers, P. (1997) *Crime in Ireland 1945–95*. Oxford: Clarendon Press.

Brubaker, R. (2002) 'Ethnicity Without Groups', *Archives Européennes de Sociologie* 43: 163–89.

Bruce, S. (1990) *A House Divided*. London: Routledge.

—— (1998) *Conservative Protestant Politics*. Oxford: Oxford University Press.

—— (2003) *Religion and Politics*. Cambridge: Polity Press.

—— (2007) *Paisley*. Oxford: Oxford University Press.

Brudholm, T. (2008) *Resentment's Virtue*. Philadelphia: Temple University Press.

—— (2009) 'On the Advocacy of Forgiveness after Mass Atrocity', in T. Brudholm and T. Cushman (eds), *The Religious in Response to Mass Atrocity*. Cambridge: Cambridge University Press.

Burawoy, M. (1998) 'The Extended Case Method', *Sociological Theory* 16: 1–30.

Bush, E. (2007) 'Measuring Religion in Global Civil Society', *Social Forces* 85: 1645–65.

Call, C. (2008a) (ed.) *Building States to Build Peace*. London: Lynne Reiner Publishers.

—— (2008b) 'Building States to Build Peace?' in Call (2008a).

Campbell, A. (2007) *The Blair Years: Extracts from the Alastair Campbell Diaries*. London: Hutchinson.

Cannadine, D. (1994) *Aspects of Aristocracy*. New Haven: Yale University Press.

Carothers, T. and Ottaway, M. (2000) *Funding Virtue: Civil Society Aid and Democracy Promotion*. Washington, DC: Carnegie Endowment for International Peace.

Casanova, J. (1994) *Public Religions in the Modern World*. Chicago: University of Chicago Press.

Catholic Bishops of Ireland (2001) *Building Peace, Shaping the Future*. Armagh: Catholic Bishops of Ireland.

Cejka, M. and Bamat, T. (2003) (eds) *Artisans for Peace*. Maryknoll, NY: Orbis Books.

Chambers, S. and Kopstein, J. (2001) 'Bad Civil Society', *Political Theory* 29: 837–65.

Chesterman, S. (2004) *You The People*. Oxford: Oxford University Press.

——, Ignatieff, M., and Thakur, M. (2005) (eds) *Making States Work*. Tokyo: United Nations University Press.

Church of Ireland (1996) *Lectures at St Anne's 1996: Brokenness, Forgiveness, Healing and Peace in Ireland. What Should the Churches Do?* Belfast. St Anne's Church of Ireland Cathedral.

Clark, J. (2009) 'From Negative to Positive Peace: The Case of Bosnia and Herzegovina', *Journal of Human Rights* 8: 360–84.

Cobban, H. (2006) *Amnesty after Atrocity?* Boulder, CO: Paradigm.

Cochrane, F. (1997) *Unionist Politics and the Politics of Unionism Since the Anglo Irish Agreement*. Cork: Cork University Press.

—— (2001) 'Unsung Heroes? The Role of Civil Society in the Northern Ireland Conflict', in McGarry (2001a).

—— (2005) 'Bowling Together within a Divided Community: Global and Local Understandings of Civil Society—The Case of Northern Ireland', in S. Robteutscher (ed.), *Democracy and the Role of Associations*. London: Routledge.

—— (2006) 'Two Cheers for the NGOs: Building Peace from Below in Northern Ireland', in Cox, Guelke, and Stephen (2006).

—— and Dunn, S. (1997) *People Power? The Role of the Voluntary and Community Sector in the Northern Ireland Conflict*. Cork: Cork University Press.

Cooke, D. (1996) *Persecuting Zeal: A Portrait of Ian Paisley*. Dingle: Brandon.

—— (2005) *Peacemaker: The Life and Work of Eric Gallagher*. Peterborough: Methodist Publishing House.

Coward, H. and Smith, G. (eds) (2004) *Religion and Peacebuilding*. New York: SUNY Press.

Cox, M., Guelke, A., and Stephen, F. (2006) (eds) *Farewell to Arms?* Manchester: Manchester University Press.

Cox, W. H. (1987) 'Managing Northern Ireland Inter-Governmentality: An Appraisal of the Anglo Irish Agreement', *Parliamentary Affairs* 40: 80–97.

Darby, J. (2001) *The Effects of Violence on Peace Processes*. Washington: United States Institute of Peace Press.

Dawson, G. (2007) *Making Peace with the Past?* Manchester: Manchester University Press.

De Breadun, D. (2008) *The Far Side of Revenge*. London: Collins.

Delanty, G. (2009) *The Cosmopolitan Imagination*. Cambridge: Cambridge University Press.

Desroche, H. (1979) *The Sociology of Hope*. London: Routledge.

Donnan, H. and O'Brien, M. (1998) ' "Because You Stick Out, You Stand Out": Perceptions of Prejudice among Northern Ireland Pakistanis', in Hainsworth (1998).

Dryzek, J. (2005) 'Deliberative Democracy in Divided Societies', *Political Theory* 33: 218–42.

Duignan, S. (1995) *One Spin on the Merry-Go-Round*. Dublin: Blackwater Press.

Durward, R. and Marsden, L. (2009) *Religion, Conflict and Military Intervention*. Farnham: Ashgate.

Du Toit, A. (2001) *South Africa's Brittle Peace*. Basingstoke: Palgrave.

Edwards, M. (2004) *Civil Society*. Cambridge: Polity Press.

Faith and Politics Group (1989) *Living the Kingdom*. Belfast: Inter-Church Group on Faith and Politics.

—— (1991) *Remembering Our Past: 1690 and 1916*. Belfast: Inter-Church Group on Faith and Politics.

—— (1993) *Sectarianism: A Discussion Document*. Belfast: Inter-Church Group on Faith and Politics.

—— (1996) *Forgive us Our Trespasses?* Belfast: Inter-Church Group on Faith and Politics.

—— (1998) *Remembrance and Forgetting*. Belfast: Inter-Church Group on Faith and Politics.

—— (2001) *Transitions*. Belfast: Inter-Church Group on Faith and Politics.

Farrington, C. (2006) *Ulster Unionism and the Peace Process in Northern Ireland*. Basingstoke: Palgrave.

—— (2008a) (ed.) *Global Change, Civil Society and the Northern Irish Peace Process*. Basingstoke: Palgrave.

—— (2008b) 'Models of Civil Society and their Implications for the Northern Ireland Peace Process', in Farrington (2008a).

Fearon, K. (2006) 'Whatever Happened to the Women? Gender and Peace in Northern Ireland', in Cox, Guelke, and Stephen (2006).

Fenton, N., Passey, A., and Hems, L. (1999) 'Trust, the Voluntary Sector and Civil Society', *International Journal of Sociology and Social Policy* 19: 21–42.

Ferguson, A. ([1767] 1967) *An Essay on the History of Civil Society*. Edinburgh: Edinburgh University Press.

Fey, M. T, Morrissey, M., and Smyth, M. (1999) *Northern Ireland's Troubles: The Human Costs*. London: Pluto Press.

Finke, R. (2003) 'Spiritual Capital: Definitions, Applications, and New Frontiers', paper for the Spiritual Capital Planning meeting, Metanexus Institute, October. Accessible at www.spiritualcapitalresearchprogram.com/pdf/finke.pdf

Fitzduff, M. (2010) 'Just Enough to Hate–Not Enough to Love: Religious Leaders and Conflict Management in Northern Ireland', unpublished manuscript, accessed March 2010.

Fitzduff, N. and Williams, S. (2007) *How Did Northern Ireland Move Towards Peace?* Cambridge, MA: Collaborative Development Action, Reflecting on Peace Practice Project.

Forst, R. (2004) 'The Limits of Toleration', *Constellations* 11: 312–25.

Frazer, H. and Fitzduff, M. (1986) *Improving Community Relations*. Belfast: Standing Commission on Human Rights.

Frazer, J. G. (1922) *The Golden Bough*. Abridged edition. London: Macmillan.

Fukuyama, F. (1992) *The End of History and the Last Man*. New York: Free Press.

Galtung, J. (1969) 'Violence, Peace and Peace Research', *Journal of Peace Research* 6: 167–96.

—— (1976) 'Three Approaches to Peacebuilding', *Peace, War and Defense*, Vol. 2. Copenhagen: Ejlers.

—— (1996) *Peace By Peaceful Means*. London: Sage.

Gambetta, D. (2000) *Trust*. Oxford: Oxford University Press.

Ganiel, G. (2008a) *Evangelicalism and Conflict in Northern Ireland*. Basingstoke: Palgrave.

—— (2008b) 'A Framework for Understanding Religion in Northern Ireland', in Farrington (2008a).

—— and Dixon, P. (2008) 'Religion, Pragmatic Fundamentalism and the Transformation of the Northern Ireland Conflict', *Journal of Peace Research* 45: 419–36.

Garland, R. (2002) *Gusty Spence*. Belfast: Blackstaff Press.

Garrigan, S. (2010) *The Real Peace Process*. London: Equinox.

Gesthuizen, M., van der Meer, T., and Scheepers, P. (2008) 'Ethnic Diversity and Social Capital in Europe: Tests of Putnam's Thesis in European Countries', *Scandinavian Political Studies*, 32: 121–42.

Getty, E. (2003) 'Building Peace in Northern Ireland: Christian Reconcilers in an Economy of Hate', *Journal of Hate Studies* 2: 47–62.

Geys, B. and Murdoch, Z. (2010) 'Measuring the "Bridging" Versus "Bonding" Nature of Social Networks', *Sociology* 44: 523–40.

Giddens, A. (1990) *The Consequences of Modernity*. Cambridge: Polity Press.

—— (1996) *In Defence of Sociology*. Cambridge: Polity Press.

Giliomee, H. (1990) 'The Elusive Search for Power', in H. Giliomee and J. Gagiano (eds), *The Elusive Search for Power*. Cape Town: Oxford University Press.

—— (1992) '*Broedertwis*: Inter-Afrikaner Conflicts in the Transition from Apartheid 1969–91', in N. Etherington (ed.), *Peace, Politics and Violence in the New South Africa*. London: Hans Zell.

Gill, A. (2001) 'Religion and Comparative Politics', *Annual Review of Political Science* 4: 117–38.

Godson, D. (2004). *Himself Alone: David Trimble and the Ordeal of Unionism*. London: Harper Collins.

Gormley-Heenan, C. and Robinson, G. (2003) 'Political Leadership: Protagonists and Pragmatists in Northern Ireland', in O. Hargie and D. Dickson (eds), *Researching the Troubles*. Edinburgh: Mainstream.

Grant, P. (2004) 'Northern Ireland: Religion and the Peace Process', in Coward and Smith (2004).

Griffin, V. (2002) *Enough Religion To Make Us Hate*. Dublin: Columba Press.

Guelke, A. (2003) 'Civil Society and the Northern Irish Peace Process', *Voluntas* 14: 61–78.

Habermas, J. ([1981] 1983) *Theory of Communicative Action*, Vol. 1. Boston: Beacon Press.

Hadley, M. (2001) (ed.) *The Spiritual Roots of Restorative Justice*. Albany, NY: State University of New York Press.

Hainsworth, P. (1998) *Divided Society: Ethnic Minorities and Racism in Northern Ireland*. London: Pluto Press.

Hamber, B. (2009) *Transforming Societies after Political Violence: Truth, Reconciliation and Mental Health*. New York: Springer.

Harpviken, K. B. and Roislien, H. E. (2008) 'Faithful Brokers? Potentials and Pitfalls of Religion in Peacemaking', *Conflict Resolution Quarterly* 25: 354–65.

Hayes, M. A. and Tombs, D. (eds) (2001) *Truth and Memory*. Leominster: Gracewing.

Hayes, B., Fahey, T., and Sinnott, R. (2005) *Conflict and Consensus: A Study of Attitudes and Values in the Republic of Ireland and Northern Ireland*. Leiden: Brill Academic Publishers.

Herbert, D. (2003) *Religion and Civil Society*. Aldershot: Ashgate.

Higgins, G. (2000) 'Great Expectations: The Myth of Antichrist in Northern Ireland', unpublished Ph.D. thesis, Queen's University of Belfast.

Hirsh, D. (2003) *Law Against Genocide: Cosmopolitan Trials*. London: Glasshouse Press.

Ho, K. (2007) 'Structural Violence as a Human Rights Violation', *Essex Human Rights Review* 4: 1–17.

Holton, R. (2005) *Making Globalization*. Basingstoke: Palgrave.

Hooghe, M., Reeskens, T., Stolle, D., and Trappers, A. (2009) 'Ethnic Diversity and Generalized Trust in Europe. A Cross-National Multilevel Study', *Comparative Political Studies* 42: 198–223.

Houston, G. (1999) *The National Liberation Struggle in South Africa*. Aldershot: Ashgate.

Huddock, A. (1999) *NGOs and Civil Society*. Cambridge: Polity Press.

Iannaccone, L. (1990) 'Religious Participation: A Human Capital Approach', *Journal for the Scientific Study of Religion* 29: 297–314.

Jakelic, S. (2010) *Collective Religions*. Farnham: Ashgate.

Jansen, S. (1980) 'The Stranger as Seer or Voyeur', *Qualitative Sociology* 2: 22–55.

Johnston, D. (2003) *Faith-Based Diplomacy*. Oxford: Oxford University Press.

Jones, P. (2006) 'Toleration, Recognition and Citizenship', *Journal of Political Philosophy* 14: 123–43.

Jordan, G. (2001) *Not of This World*. Belfast: Blackstaff Press.

Juergensmeyer, M. (2000) *Terror in the Mind of God*. Berkeley: University of California Press.

Kaldor, M. (1999) *New and Old Wars*. Cambridge: Polity Press.

—— (2003) *Global Civil Society*. Cambridge: Polity Press.

—— , Anheier, H., and Glasius, M. (2003) *Global Civil Society 2003*. Oxford: Oxford University Press.

Karl, B. and Katz, S. (1987) 'Foundations and the Ruling Class', *Daedalus* 116: 1–40.

Kaufmann, E. (2007) *The Orange Order*. Oxford: Oxford University Press.

Keane, J. (2003) *Global Civil Society?* Cambridge: Cambridge University Press.

Keen, D. (1998) *The Economic Functions of Violence in Civil Wars*. Oxford: Oxford University Press.

Kemp, A. (1985) 'Images of the Field', *Journal of Peace Research* 22: 129–40.

Kennedy, D. (2004) *Nothing But Trouble?* Dublin: Irish Association.

Kenny, A. (1986) *The Road to Hillsborough*. Oxford: Pergamon Press.

Kerr, M. (2006) *Transforming Unionism*. Dublin: Irish Academic Press.

Kiess, J. and Thompson, A. (2004) *The Future of the Church in the Public Square Final Report*. Belfast: Evangelical Contribution on Northern Ireland.

Kingwell, M. (1995) *A Civil Tongue*. Philadelphia: Penn State University Press.

Knox, C. (2002) ' "See No Evil, Hear No Evil": Insidious Paramilitary Violence in Northern Ireland', *British Journal of Criminology* 42: 164–85.

—— and Quirk, P. (2000) *Peace Building in Northern Ireland, Israel and South Africa*. Basingstoke: Macmillan.

Lancaster, R. (1988) *Thanks to God and the Revolution*. New York: Columbia University Press.

Landau, Y. (2003) *Healing the Holy Land: Inter-Religious Peacebuilding in Israel/ Palestine*. Washington: United States Institute of Peace Press.

Larsson, J. (2004) *Understanding Religious Violence*. Aldershot: Ashgate.

Lederach, J. P. (1997) *Building Peace*. Washington: United States Institute of Peace Press.

Leonard, M. (2004) 'Bonding and Bridging Social Capital: Reflections from Belfast', *Sociology* 38: 927–44.

Letki, N. (2008) 'Does Diversity Erode Social Cohesion? Social Capital and Race in British Neighbourhoods', *Political Studies* 56: 99–126.

Levi, M. and Stokes, L. (2000) 'Political Trust and Trustworthiness' *Annual Review of Political Science* 3: 475–502.

Lewis, J. and Weigert, A. (1985a) 'Trust as a Social Reality', *Social Forces* 63: 967–85.

—— (1985b) 'Social Atomism, Holism and Trust', *Sociological Quarterly* 26: 955–71.

Liechty, J. (1993) *Roots of Sectarianism in Ireland*. Belfast: Irish Inter-Church Meeting.

—— and Clegg, C. (2001) *Moving Beyond Sectarianism*. Blackrock: Columba Press.

Linkogle, S. (1998) 'The Revolution of the Virgin Mary: Popular Religion and Social Change in Nicaragua', *Sociological Research Online* 3. Accessible at: http://www.socresonline.org.uk/socresonline/3/2/8.html

Little, D. (2007) *Peacemakers in Action*. Cambridge: Cambridge University Press.

Livezey, L. (1989) 'US Religious Organizations and the International Human Rights Movement', *Human Rights Quarterly* 11: 14–81.

Lundy, P. and McGovern, M. (2005) *A Critical Evaluation of the Role of Community-Based Truth-Telling Processes for Post-Conflict Transition: A Case Study of the Ardoyne Commemoration Project*. Belfast: Community Relations Council. Accessible at http://cain.ulst.ac.uk/issues/victims/ardoyne/lundymcgovern05.htm

—— (2006) 'Participation, Truth and Partiality', *Sociology* 40: 71–88.

—— (2008) 'Whose Justice? Rethinking Transitional Justice From the Bottom Up', *Journal of Law and Society* 35: 265–92.

Lynch, J. and McGoldrick, A. (2005) *Peace Journalism*. Stroud: Hawthorne Press.

McAdam, D. (1982) *Political Process and The Development of Black Insurgency*. Chicago: University of Chicago Press.

McCann, D. (2005) '1974 Talks for Peace "Scuppered', *Saoirse 32*, 4 January.

McCartney, C. (1999) *The Role of Civil Society.* Accord Series 8. London: Conciliation Resources.

McCreary, A. (2004) *Nobody's Fool.* London: Hodder and Stoughton.

—— (2007) *In War and Peace.* Belfast: Brehan Press.

McGarry, J. (2001a) (ed.) *Northern Ireland and the Divided World.* Oxford: Oxford University Press.

—— (2001b) 'Northern Ireland, Civic Nationalism and the Good Friday Agreement', in McGarry (2001a).

McLemore, S. (1970) 'Simmel's "Stranger": A Critique of a Concept', *The Pacific Sociological Review* 13: 86–94.

McMaster, J. (1996) Lecture 4. *Lectures at St Anne's 1996: Brokenness, Forgiveness, Healing and Peace in Ireland: What Should the Churches Do?* Belfast: St Anne's Church of Ireland Cathedral.

Major, J. (1999) *John Major: The Autobiography.* London: HarperCollins.

Mallie, E. and McKittrick, D. (2001) *Endgame in Ireland.* London: Hodder and Stoughton.

Maney, G., Higgins, I., and Herzog, H. (2006) 'The Past's Promise: Lessons from Peace Processes in Northern Ireland and the Middle East', *Journal of Peace Research* 43: 181–200.

Mansergh, M. (2003) *The Legacy Of History For Making Peace In Ireland.* Dublin: Mercier.

Metanexus Institute (2006) *Spiritual Capital Research Program.* Metanexus Institute at http://www.spiritualcapitalresearchprogram.com/index.asp

Miller, F. (2008) *David Trimble: The Price of Peace.* Dublin: Liffey Press.

Misztal, B. (1996) *Trust in Modern Societies.* Cambridge: Polity Press.

—— (2001) 'Trust and Co-operation: The Democratic Public Sphere', *Journal of Sociology* 37: 371–86.

Mitchell, C. (2005a) *Religion, Identity and Politics in Northern Ireland.* Aldershot: Ashgate.

—— (2005b) 'Behind the Ethnic Marker: Religion and Social Identification in Northern Ireland', *Sociology of Religion* 66: 1–22.

—— (2005c) 'Catholicism and the Construction of Communal Identity in Northern Ireland', *Irish Journal of Sociology* 14: 110–30.

—— (2006) 'The Religious Content of Ethnic Identities', *Sociology* 40: 1135–52.

Mitchell, G. (2000) *Making Peace.* Berkeley: University of California Press.

Mitchell, P. (2003) *Evangelicalism and National Identity in Ulster 1921–1998.* Oxford: Oxford University Press.

Mollering, G. (2001) 'The Nature of Trust', *Sociology* 35: 403–20.

Morgan, V. (2003) 'The Role of Women in Community Development in Northern Ireland', in O. Hargie and D. Dickson (eds), *Researching the Troubles.* Edinburgh: Mainstream.

Morrow, D., Birrell, D., Greer, J. and O'Keefe, T. (1991) *The Churches and Inter-Community Relationships.* Coleraine: Centre for Study of Conflict. Accessible at http://cain.ulst.ac.uk/csc/reports/churches/htm

Morrow, J. (2003) *On the Road to Reconciliation.* Dublin: Columba Press.

Mowlam, M. (2002) *Momentum: The Struggle for Peace, Politics and the People.* London: Hodder and Stoughton.

Muldoon, P. (2008) 'The Moral Legitimacy of Anger', *European Journal of Social Theory* 11: 299–314.

Newton, K. (2001) 'Trust, Social Capital, Civil Society and Democracy', *International Political Science Review* 22: 210–14.

Nordlinger, E. (1972) *Conflict Regulation in Divided Societies*. Cambridge, MA: Harvard University Press.

Norris, P. and Inglehart, R. (2004) *Sacred and Secular: Religion and Politics Worldwide*. Cambridge: Cambridge University Press.

O'Leary, B. (1987) 'The Anglo Irish Agreement: Folly or Statecraft?', *West European Politics* 10: 5–32.

Oliver, J. E., and Ha, S. (2008) 'The Segregation Paradox: Neighbourhoods and Interracial Contact in Multiethnic America', in B. A. Sullivan, M. Snyder, and J. L. Sullivan (eds), *Cooperation: The Political Psychology of Effective Human Interaction*. Malden, MA: Blackwell.

O'Malley, P. (2001) 'Northern Ireland and South Africa', in J. McGarry (ed.), *Northern Ireland and the Divided World*. Oxford: Oxford University Press.

O'Neill, O. (1993) 'Practices of Toleration', in J. Lichtenberg (ed.), *Democracy and the Mass Media*. Cambridge: Cambridge University Press.

—— (2002) *A Question of Trust*. Cambridge: Cambridge University Press.

Onyx, J. and Bullen, P. (2000) 'Measuring Social Capital in Five Communities', *Journal of Applied Behavioural Sciences* 36: 23–42.

Orjuela, C. (2008) *Building Peace in Sri Lanka*. London: Sage.

Paris, R. (2004) *At War's End*. Cambridge: Cambridge University Press.

Patterson, R. (2003) *Journeying Towards Reconciliation*. Dublin: Veritas.

Philpott, D. (ed.) (2006) *The Politics of the Past*. Notre Dame: University of Notre Dame Press.

—— (2007a) 'Explaining the Political Ambivalence of Religion', *American Political Science Review* 103: 516–28.

—— (2007b) 'What Religion Brings to the Politics of Transitional Justice', *Journal of International Affairs* 61: 93–110.

Playboard (1990) *Play Without Frontiers*. Belfast: Playboard Northern Ireland.

Porter, F. (2002) *Changing Women, Changing Worlds*. Belfast: Blackstaff Press.

Porter, N. (1996) *Rethinking Unionism*. Belfast: Blackstaff.

Portes, A. (1998) 'Social Capital: Its Origins and Applications in Modern Sociology', *Annual Review of Sociology* 24: 1–24.

—— and Landolt, P. (1996) 'The Downside of Social Capital', *The American Prospect* 26: 18–21.

Potter, M. (2008) 'Women, Civil Society and Peace Building in Northern Ireland' in Farrington (2008a).

Powell, J. (2008) *Great Hatred, Little Room: Making Peace in Northern Ireland*. London: Bodley Head.

Power, M. (2007) *From Ecumenism to Community Relations*. Dublin: Irish Academic Press.

Protzesky, M. (ed.) (1990) *Christianity Amidst Apartheid*. London: Macmillan.

Putnam, R. (1993) *Making Democracy Work*. Princeton: Princeton University Press.

—— (2000) *Bowling Alone*. New York: Simon and Schuster.

Putnam, R. (2007) '*E Pluribus Unum*: Diversity and Community in the Twenty-First Century. The 2006 Johan Skytte Prize Lecture', *Scandinavian Political Studies* 30: 137–74.

Putzel, J. (1997) 'Accounting for the "Dark Side" of Social Capital', *Journal of International Development* 9: 939–49.

Rankin, A. and Ganiel, G. (2008) 'DUP Discourses about Violence and their Impact on the Northern Ireland Peace Process', *Peace and Conflict Studies* 15: 115–35.

Rappaport, R. (1999) *Ritual and Religion in the Making of Humanity*. Cambridge: Cambridge University Press.

Raven, J. (1999) 'Protestant Jews or Catholic Jews'. Unpublished M.Phil thesis, Queen's University of Belfast.

Richardson, N. (1998) (ed.) *A Tapestry of Beliefs: Christian Traditions in Northern Ireland*. Belfast: Blackstaff Press.

Rothstein, R. (1999) (ed.) *After the Peace*. Boulder, CO: Lynne Rienner.

Rowan, B. (1995) *Behind the Lines: The Story of the IRA and Loyalist Ceasefires*. Belfast: Blackstaff Press.

Ruane, J. and Todd, J. (1999) (eds) *After the Good Friday Agreement*. Dublin: University College Dublin Press.

Scheff, T. (1997) 'Deconstructing Rage', online paper accessible at http://www.soc.ucsb.edu/faculty/scheff/7.html

Schlack, A. (2009) *The Role of Religion in Peacebuilding and Conflict Transformation*. Saarbrucken: VDM Verlag.

Scott, F. E. (1976) 'The Political Preaching Tradition in Ulster: Prelude to Paisley', *Western Journal of Communication* 40: 249–59.

Segal, R. (1998) (ed.) *The Myth and Ritual Theory*. Oxford: Wiley-Blackwell.

—— (2005) 'Myth and Ritual', in J. Hinnells (ed.), *Routledge Companion to the Study of Religion*. London: Taylor and Francis.

Seligman, A. (1997) *The Problem of Trust*. Princeton: Princeton University Press.

—— (1998) 'Trust and Sociability', *American Journal of Economics and Sociology* 57: 391–404.

—— (2000) 'Trust and Civil Society', in Tonkiss, Passey and Fenton (2000).

Servaes, J. (2008) (ed.) *Communication for Development and Social Change*. London: Sage.

—— (2010) 'Advocacy for Peace', *Media Development* 57: 60–4.

Shapiro, S. (1987) 'The Social Control of Interpersonal Trust', *American Journal of Sociology* 93: 623–58.

Shirlow, P. and Murtagh, B. (2006) *Belfast: Segregation, Violence and the City*. London: Pluto Press.

Shore, M. (2009) *Religion and Conflict Resolution*. Farnham: Ashgate.

Shriver, D. (1995) *An Ethic for Enemies*. Oxford: Oxford University Press.

Simpson, K. (2009) *Truth Recovery in Northern Ireland*. Manchester: Manchester University Press.

Smock, D. R. (2001) *Faith Based NGOs and International Peacebuilding: Special Report*. Washington, DC: United States Institute of Peace Press.

—— (2002) (ed.) *Interfaith Dialogue and Peacebuilding*. Washington, DC: United States Institute of Peace Press.

—— (2006) (ed.) *Religious Contributions to Peacemaking*. Washington, DC: United States Institute of Peace Press.

—— (2008) *Religion in World Affairs: Its Role in Conflict and Peace*. Washington, DC: United States Institute of Peace Press.

Stanley, L. (2009) 'Narratives From Major to Minor', *Sociological Research Online* 14 (5). Accessible at http://www.socresonline.org.uk/14/5/25.html

Stark, R. and Finke, R. (2000) *Acts of Faith: Explaining the Human Side of Religion*. Berkeley: University of California Press.

Stedman, S. (1997) 'Spoiler Problems in Peace Processes', *International Security* 22: 5–53.

Stephen, F. (2006) 'Integrated Schools: Myths, Hopes and Prospect', in Cox, Guelke, and Stephen (2006).

Stevens, D. (2005) 'The Churches and Ten Years of the Peace Process', in Community Relations Council (ed.) *Beyond Sectarianism? The Churches and Ten Years of the Peace Process*. Belfast: Community Relations Council.

Stolle, D., Soroka, S., and Johnston, R. (2008) 'When Does Diversity Erode Trust? Neighborhood Diversity, Interpersonal Trust and the Mediating Effect of Social Interactions', *Political Studies* 56: 57–75.

Storey, E. (2002) *Traditional Roots*. Blackrock: Columba Press.

—— (2010) 'What Clergy Say Publicly Can Contribute to Reconciliation', *The Irish News* 28 October.

Sugden, J. and Bairner, A. (1993) *Sport, Sectarianism and Society in a Divided Ireland*. London: University of Leicester Press.

Sztompka, P. (1997) 'Trust and Emerging Democracies: The Lessons from Poland', *International Sociology* 11: 37–62.

—— (1999) *Trust: A Sociological Theory*. Cambridge: Cambridge University Press.

Taggart, N. (2004) *Conflict, Controversy and Co-operation* Dublin: Columba Press.

—— (2005) *Methodism and 'The Troubles'*. Belfast: Catalyst. Pamphlet 12.

Taylor, C. (2004) *Modern Social Imaginaries*. Durham, NC: Duke University Press.

Taylor, P. (1998) *Provos: The IRA and Sinn Féin*. London: Bloomsbury.

Taylor, R. (2001) 'Northern Ireland: Consociationalism or Social Transformation?', in McGarry (2001a).

—— (2009a) (ed.) *Consociational Theory: McGarry and O'Leary and the Northern Ireland Conflict*. London: Routledge.

—— (2009b) 'The Injustice of a Consociational Solution to the Northern Ireland Problem', in Taylor (2009a).

Teeney, F. (2004) 'The Transition of Sinn Féin and The Progressive Unionist Party into Constitutional Politics: A Social Movement Analysis'. Unpublished Ph.D. thesis, Queen's University of Belfast.

Thompson, L. (2000) 'The House Church Movement'. Unpublished Ph.D. thesis, Queen's University of Belfast.

Thomson, A. (1996) *Faith in Ulster*. Belfast: Evangelical Contribution on Northern Ireland.

—— (1999) *The Great White Tent*. Belfast: Evangelical Contribution on Northern Ireland.

—— (2002) *Fields of Vision*. Belfast: Centre for Contemporary Christianity in Ireland.

Tilly, C. (1984) *Big Structures, Large Processes, Huge Comparisons*. New York: Russell Sage Foundation.

Tonkiss, F. and Passey, A. (1999) 'Trust, Confidence and Voluntary Organizations', *Sociology* 33: 257–74.

Tonkiss, F., Passey, A., and Fenton, N. (2000) (eds) *Trust and Civil Society*. Basingstoke: Macmillan.

Tuomela, R. (2002) *The Philosophy of Social Practices*. Cambridge: Cambridge University Press.

Turam, B. (2004) 'The Politics of Engagement Between Islam and the Secular State: The Ambivalences of "Civil Society"', *British Journal of Sociology* 55: 259–81.

Turner, B. (2009) 'Violence, Human Rights and Piety', in T. Brudholm and T. Cushman (eds), *The Religious in Responses to Mass Atrocities*. Cambridge: Cambridge University Press.

Ure, M. (2008) 'Introduction', *European Journal of Social Theory* 11: 283–98.

Van Leeuwen, M. (2009) *Partners in Peace: Discourses and Practices of Civil-Society Peacebuilding*. Farnham: Ashgate.

Vogel, A. (2006) 'Who's Making Global Civil Society: Philanthropy and US Empire in World Society', *British Journal of Sociology* 57: 635–55.

Wallis, R., Bruce, S., and Taylor, D. (1987) 'Ethnicity and Evangelism: Ian Paisley and protestant Politics in Ulster', *Comparative Studies in Society and History* 29: 293–313.

Warm, D. (1998) 'The Jews in Northern Ireland', in Hainsworth (1998).

Warren, M. (1999) *Democracy and Trust*. Cambridge: Cambridge University Press.

Wells, R. (2005) *Friendship Towards Peace*. Dublin: Columba Press.

Wijesinghe, S. (2003) 'Sri Lanka', in Cejka and Bamat (2003).

Williams, T. and Falconer, A. (1995) *Sectarianism*. Dublin: Dominican Publications.

Wilson, D. and Tyrell, J. (1995) 'Institutions for Conciliation and Mediation' in S. Dunn (ed.) *Facets of the Conflict in Northern Ireland*. Basingstoke: Macmillan.

Woodbury, R. (2003) 'Researching Spiritual Capital: Promises and Pitfalls', paper for the Spiritual Capital Planning meeting, Metanexus Institute, October. Accessible at www.spiritualcapitalresearchprogram.com/pdf/woodbury.pdf

Index

Adams, Gerry xv, 7, 64, 104, 105, 108, 110, 111, 113, 115, 117, 123, 147, 152, 159, 161, 164, 175, 191, 192, 206, 207, 209, 210

African National Congress 35, 146, 199
　　See also Mandela, Nelson

Ahern, Bertie 6, 8

Alexander, Jeffrey 19, 20, 21, 24, 55, 126, 131, 145

Anabaptists 140, 217

Anglican Church of South Africa 202
　　See also South Africa

Anglicanism 1, 3, 8, 29, 47, 52, 58, 74, 75, 93, 97, 102, 108, 118, 124, 144, 154, 163, 165, 166, 167, 169, 185, 193, 215, 217
　　See also Church of Ireland

Anglo Irish Agreement 98, 110, 137, 139, 200

'An Sagairt Maith'/The Good Priest 6

anti-Catholicism xi, 178

anti-clericalism 21, 229

apartheid 9, 17, 35, 86, 93, 113, 137, 145, 146, 149, 200, 202
　　See also South Africa

Appleby, Scott 3, 9, 48, 94, 98, 146, 198, 214, 217, 220

Arlow, Revd William 180, 195, 196, 217

Armstrong, Revd David 52, 67, 70, 80, 136, 161, 166, 177, 183

Ashe, Fidelma 61

Aughey, Arthur 139

backchannel dialogue xiv, 6, 7, 25, 34, 40, 55, 56, 63–6, 94, 100, 101–18, 119, 121, 122, 127, 128, 134, 145, 158

Baptist Church 43, 139
　　See also Anabaptists

Beck, Ulrich 10, 202

Belfast 5, 11, 15, 43, 46, 49, 50, 52, 53, 55, 61, 63, 70, 72, 75, 80, 91, 100, 109, 113, 115, 144, 156, 179, 183, 184, 185, 186, 195, 217, 225

Bell, Christine 12, 128

Bible, the 39, 43, 51, 54, 55, 61, 64, 120, 137, 139, 155, 229

Bingham, Revd William 194

Bishop, Ken xiv, 10, 31, 51, 82, 87

Blair, Tony 6, 7, 8, 115

Bloody Sunday incident v, 62, 98, 113

Bonhoeffer, Dietrich 183

Bradford, Revd Robert 193

Bradley, Denis 85, 107, 113, 121, 136, 227, 228

Brady, Cardinal Sean 44

Braithwaite, John 35, 36, 105, 120

Brethren Church 43, 109

Brewer, John xiii, xiv, xvii, 7, 21, 35, 37, 110, 119, 129, 132, 139, 198, 199, 215, 216

Brighton bombing 110

British Broadcasting Corporation 5, 47, 50, 59, 65, 159

British Israelism 193

British government v, xvii, 7, 15, 33, 40, 47, 60, 66, 67, 68, 83, 85, 86, 93, 99, 107, 110, 111, 113, 114, 120, 151, 156, 157, 159, 163, 164, 166, 168, 170, 192, 195, 206, 209

British security forces
　　army/M15 7, 101, 104, 107, 110, 113, 121, 206
　　Royal Irish Constabulary xiii, xiv
　　Royal Ulster Constabulary xiii, xiv, 101, 110

Britishness, Protestants and 83, 106

Bruce, Steve 47, 78, 124, 137, 176

Bunting, Peter 199

Burawoy, Michael 212

Call, Charles 34, 35

Carroll, Revd Lesley 65, 73, 74, 97, 101, 136, 141, 153, 182, 197, 217, 228

Caleb Foundation 3, 119, 136, 137, 138, 223

Calvinism 139, 217

Campbell, Alastair 6, 7, 8, 54

Carlin, Fr Neal 56

Casanova, José 11, 148

Catholic Church
　　in Ireland 3, 4, 8, 42, 43, 44, 51, 52, 60, 61, 62, 73, 90, 93, 97, 98, 99, 102, 103, 112, 137, 151, 156, 157, 158, 159, 161, 162, 163, 164, 165, 167, 168, 172, 176, 178, 179, 193, 197, 212
　　in Latin America 76, 146, 150, 160, 225
　　in Poland 9, 93, 150, 160
　　in South Africa 150

Catholicism 2, 11, 29, 42, 47, 48, 54, 61, 76, 78, 90, 100, 116, 150, 151, 165, 175, 178, 181, 203, 217
　　See also anti-Catholicism

ceasefires xvi, 6, 7, 8, 16, 44, 51, 58, 59, 66, 67, 76, 93, 103, 108, 110, 114–18, 122, 123, 153, 156, 172, 180, 184, 190, 194, 195, 206, 209, 228
Chambers, Simone 18, 126, 133, 200, 220
Chesney, Fr James 3, 156, 163
Christian Fellowship Church 109
Christian Renewal Centre 48, 49, 69, 214
church/churches, the
  and prisoners 35, 39, 50, 59, 60, 61, 65, 66–7, 84, 85, 86–7, 89, 93, 99, 106, 108, 125, 127, 128, 225, 227
    See also Prison chaplains
  and voluntary sector 2, 11–12, 15–16, 24, 68, 131, 165, 199
  authority structures in 72, 100, 116, 123, 124, 149, 154, 161, 165, 167, 176, 193, 202, 210, 211
  contribution to sectarianism 3, 26, 177, 184, 187, 199, 200, 208, 210, 213, 224, 227
    and anti-sectarianism 40, 53, 79, 80–3, 88, 127, 128, 134, 135, 141, 168, 172, 187, 208, 210
  institutional church xvi, 73, 112, 162, 166, 181, 191, 197, 201, 202, 207, 211, 213, 214, 224, 227, 229, 230
  leadership in v, 4, 44, 89, 92, 94, 101, 112, 117, 118, 119, 121, 122, 123, 142, 155, 157, 158, 160, 162, 163, 164, 165, 166, 167, 170, 176, 178, 180, 181, 189, 191, 200, 201, 202, 206, 207, 210, 224, 229, 230
  moral agenda of 84, 86, 136–7, 138, 180, 226
  size of 2, 11
  young people, and 2, 49, 70, 71, 72, 73, 75, 92, 144, 179
church–civil society–state nexus 10, 126, 148–71, 206, 211–12, 213
Church of Ireland 3, 40, 44, 46, 47, 48, 49, 67, 74, 75, 76, 82, 85, 95, 99, 108, 117, 135, 151, 154, 165, 167, 169, 172, 185, 188, 191, 193, 195, 212, 217, 223, 224, 225
  and 'Think Again' project 74–5, 135
  See also Hard Gospel project
civil society 1, 8, 10, 11, 12–25, 26, 27, 28, 31, 37, 38, 70, 79, 82, 83, 85, 86, 92, 94, 109, 110, 118, 126, 127, 128–48, 172, 173, 192, 193, 196, 197, 198, 199, 200, 206, 208, 210, 211, 212, 213, 214, 215, 218, 219–22, 226, 227
  See also global civil society
  regressive versus progressive civil society 18, 19, 21, 24, 26, 27, 28, 126, 127, 132–3, 170, 200, 206, 207, 213, 220

civil sphere 19, 20, 24, 55, 85, 126, 128
Clarke, Liam 227
class, social v, 46, 52, 58, 64, 94, 109, 125, 137, 144, 174, 176, 177, 182, 186, 201, 203, 217, 218
Clegg, Cecelia 31, 47, 73, 81, 82, 136, 163, 179, 181, 186, 187, 208, 227
Clonard Monastery xv, 8, 27, 43, 44, 50, 51, 58, 66, 96, 103, 105, 106, 111, 113, 126, 159, 216, 218
  See also Redemptorist Order
Cochrane, Feargal 24, 25, 110
collective religion 210, 202, 203, 221
Columba Community 48, 50, 56, 69
Combined Loyalist Military Command 59, 114, 116, 122
Community Dialogue 71, 79, 199
community relations 26, 51, 52, 57, 67–74, 88, 187, 198, 215, 226
Community Relations Council 68, 69, 198
consociationalism 23, 207
Consultative Group on the Past 86, 120, 136, 227, 228
Conway, Cardinal William 95, 99, 156, 157
Cooke, Denis 10, 91, 192, 195, 196
Cornerstone Community 39, 46, 48, 50, 56, 69, 214
Corrymeela Community 27, 39, 42, 46, 48, 56, 64, 69, 81, 135, 142, 189, 199, 209, 214, 228
cosmopolitanism 17, 19, 21, 129, 131
Craig, William 196
Crawley, William 42, 44, 66, 73, 74, 119, 187, 191
Curran, Paula 198

Daly, Cardinal Cahal xvii, 42, 61, 67, 90, 91, 100, 103, 104, 113, 116, 117, 123, 135, 143, 148, 156, 157, 158, 162, 163, 166, 168, 170, 178, 191
Daly, Bishop Edward vi, 6, 7, 49, 59, 60, 61, 62, 67, 87, 102, 104, 107, 111, 112, 113, 116, 143, 151, 161, 164, 179
decommissioning v, 5, 7, 40, 59, 78, 79, 85, 120, 145, 156
Democratic Unionist Party xv, 4, 61, 78, 91, 105, 107, 172, 188, 195, 223
democratization 13, 17, 18, 20, 23, 35, 128, 133, 152, 219
denominationalism 180, 189, 190, 192, 210, 211, 212, 220, 221
Derry/Londonderry vi, 7, 8, 49, 50, 51, 53, 56, 69, 104, 111, 112, 114, 143, 154, 175, 179, 185
Devlin, Bernadette 114
Donaldson, Denis xvi, xvii, 33, 66, 104, 183

Donaldson, Jeffrey 119
Down and Connor Diocese (Catholic) 90, 100
Down and Dromore Diocese (Anglican) 74, 75, 76
Downing Street Declaration xv, xvi, 8, 59, 103, 110, 114–18, 194, 207, 209, 212
Drumcree 3, 78, 100, 154, 193, 194
Drumm, Jimmy 180, 196
Dublin 15, 53, 80, 82, 90, 110, 116, 161, 195, 196
Dunlop, Revd John 41, 43, 58, 62, 64, 73, 98, 101, 104, 109, 117, 118, 122, 141, 144, 153, 155, 156, 180, 201, 202, 209, 217, 228
Durkan, Mark xv, 104, 110, 111, 112, 114, 115, 147
Dutch Reformed Church 93, 149, 150, 202

Eames, Archbishop Robin 3, 6, 8, 58, 59, 67, 85, 93, 94, 102, 103, 105, 108, 115, 116, 117, 118, 122, 124, 136, 144, 154, 155, 163, 165, 166, 168, 169, 170, 182, 188, 191, 193, 194, 209, 217, 228
Economic and Social Research Council xiv, xvii
ecumenism 3, 10, 26, 27, 38–9, 40–55, 67, 68, 73, 77, 81, 87, 88, 89, 94, 104, 128, 135, 136, 138, 139, 140, 141, 156, 157, 168, 171, 174, 179, 184, 185, 187, 197, 198, 199, 214–19, 221, 222, 226, 228
    compared to ecumenicalism 26, 42, 67
Edwards, Michael 14, 16, 219
Egan, Fr Adrian 43, 44, 59, 96, 106, 191, 199
Enniskillen bombing 78, 102, 191
Ervine, David xvi, 67, 116, 119, 194
European Union 11, 15, 20, 21, 68, 69, 75, 120, 146, 198, 219, 226
Evangelical Catholic Initiative 54
Evangelical Contribution on Northern Ireland 1, 2, 3, 27, 40, 47, 55, 64, 76, 77–8, 85, 91, 95, 100, 101, 112, 136, 137, 138, 139, 140, 152, 156, 165, 170, 178, 179, 185, 198, 209, 212, 217, 218, 219, 221, 225, 226, 227
evangelicalism 2, 3, 10, 25, 27, 43, 47, 54, 77, 87, 136, 137, 138, 139, 140, 141, 171, 187, 203, 217–18, 219, 221, 226

Faith and Politics Group 2, 27, 42, 52, 81–2, 135, 214, 225, 226
Faith in a Brighter Future group 7, 119, 166, 179, 180, 199
Families Acting for Innocent Relatives 224
Families Against Intimidation and Terror 78
Farren, Sean 46, 166, 178, 196

Farrington, Christopher 6, 18, 23, 24
Faul, Fr Denis xv, 60, 61, 98, 99, 157, 163, 164, 167, 178, 180, 183, 188, 217
Feakle talks 6, 66, 180, 195–6, 206
Fitzduff, Marie 11, 12, 68, 98
Fitzduff, Niall 6, 24, 198
Fitzroy Presbyterian Church 43, 51, 55, 66, 104, 114, 183, 218
forgiveness 36, 40, 49, 52, 54, 77, 82, 85, 86, 106, 120, 135, 140, 187, 224, 225, 227
Forthspring Inter-Community Group 71, 143
Frazer, Willie 68, 224, 225
Free Presbyterian Church 3, 42, 43, 44, 53, 78, 91, 107, 119, 178
    See also Paisley

Gaelic Athletics Association xv, 18, 193
Garrigan, Siobhán 2, 122, 184, 185, 225
Getty, Eric 139, 140
gacaca courts 22, 132
Gallagher, Eric 10, 42, 95, 135, 192, 195, 196
Galtung, Johan 4, 32, 34, 185
Ganiel, Gladys 2, 9, 10, 76, 136, 137, 198, 217–18, 226
Garland, Roy xiv, xvi, 46, 58, 64, 66, 67, 94, 111, 188, 189
gender xv, 11, 15, 22, 23, 36, 39, 50, 70, 71, 72, 79, 132, 178, 197, 199, 224
Gibney, Jim xv, xvi, 63, 66, 83, 106, 114, 188, 189
Gibson, Chris 197
Gibson, Revd Mervyn 44, 68, 77, 78, 103, 138, 139, 141, 153, 197, 217
Giddens, Anthony 130, 202
global civil society 13–15, 20–2, 27, 132, 133, 134, 143, 148, 152
globalization 9, 202
Godson, Dean 7
Good Friday Agreement xiv, xv, 5, 6, 7, 8, 24, 25, 33, 40, 44, 45, 59, 62, 68, 79, 82, 85, 88, 94, 106, 118, 119, 124, 135, 136, 137, 138, 141, 145, 146, 172, 180, 191, 195, 197, 200, 205, 207, 224, 225
Good, Revd Harold v, 6, 7, 11, 45, 50, 64, 83, 85, 94, 95, 96, 99, 120, 155, 161, 183, 187, 191, 193, 209, 211, 212, 217
Grant, Patrick 7, 10, 47, 214
Guelke, Adrian 6, 23, 152
Guild of Uriel xii, 1

Habitat for Humanity 40, 143
Habermas, Jurgen 128, 129
Haire, Revd James 216
Hamber, Brandon 36–7
Hamilton, Revd Norman 62, 63, 94, 174, 226
Hard Gospel project 40, 74, 82, 135, 136, 172, 185, 227

Harper, Archbishop Alan 144, 145, 185, 223
Hartley, Tom xvi, 64, 83, 186
hate speech 129–30
Hayes, Bernie 11, 203
Heath, Edward 99
Herbert, David 93, 150
Higgins, Gareth xiii, xi, xiii, xiv, xvii, 73, 77,
    141, 192, 198, 211
Holy Cross incident 39, 55, 61–3, 88,
    174, 226
hope 28, 40, 79, 80, 84, 85, 86, 88, 120,
    224, 225
Hume-Adams talks xv, 104, 110–14, 147, 161,
    209, 210
Hume, John xv, 64, 90, 104, 110, 111, 112,
    113, 114, 115, 123, 147, 161, 192, 206,
    207, 209, 210
hunger strikes, the 60, 61, 88, 110, 163–4,
    181, 193
Hurley, Fr Michael SJ 53
Hutchinson, Billy xvi, 182

individualization 202, 207, 208, 213, 224,
    229, 230
Indonesia 120
integrated education 3, 23, 39, 42, 70, 82, 83,
    122, 177
Irish Council of Churches 4, 39, 95, 195
Irish Inter Church Meeting 27, 40, 42, 52, 76,
    81, 96, 135, 136
Irish National Liberation Army 67, 123
Irish Republic 1, 8, 15, 16, 80, 90, 116, 146,
    151, 206
Irish Republican Army *see* Provisional Irish
    Republican Army
Irish School of Ecumenics 2, 3, 27, 40, 46, 48,
    52, 53, 56, 76, 81, 82, 85, 135, 166, 184,
    198, 208, 212, 214, 218, 226
    and 'Moving Beyond Sectarianism'
    project 53, 81, 82, 135, 208

Jakelic, Slavica 201, 202
Jardine, Revd Brother David 181, 228
Jesuits/Society of Jesus 100, 111, 166

Kaldor, Mary 12, 13, 16, 17, 20, 21, 88,
    128, 132
Kaufmann, Eric 52, 138, 193
Kelly, Gerry 107, 180
Kelly, Grainne 36, 37
Kenny, Revd Charles xv, 44, 45, 99, 109, 153,
    155, 186, 217
Kerr, Revd Cecil 49
King, Revd Martin Luther 33, 178
Knox, Colin x, 184, 199, 204
Kopstein, Jeffrey 18, 126, 133, 200, 220

Lederach, John Paul 57, 87, 152
Leonard, Madeleine 18
Lennon, Fr Brian SJ 96, 100
Leverhulme Trust, The xi, xii
Lewis, Revd Walter 65, 195
Liechty, Joe 82, 208
Londonderry See Derry
Loyalism/Loyalist 58, 59, 61, 62, 64, 65, 66,
    67, 87, 89, 102, 103, 104, 111, 114, 116,
    117, 122, 138, 147, 157, 159, 163, 168,
    174, 182, 184, 185, 194, 196, 209, 217,
    218, 226
Lundy, Patricia 36

Magee, Revd Roy 6, 58, 59, 67, 114, 116, 117,
    118, 122, 141, 200, 217
Major, John xv, 8, 103, 107, 114, 115, 116,
    117, 168, 206, 209
Mallon, Seamus xv, 205
Mandela, Nelson xvi, 7
Mandelson, Peter 6
Mansergh, Martin 8, 103, 111
Maruna, Shadd 105
Mason, Revd Gary 81, 92, 100, 144, 182, 226
Masonic Order 190
Mayhew, Patrick 59, 107
McAllister, Brendan 57
McCamley Archdeacon Gregor 52, 99, 104,
    154, 155, 163
McCarthy, Kevin xii–xiv
McCartney, Clem 23, 200
McCrea, Revd William 107
McCreary, Alf 143, 165, 187
McGarry, John 2, 18, 193
McGuinness, Martin 4, 107, 113–14, 121, 164,
    172, 175
McKinley, Jim 87
McManus, Fr Sean 152
McMaster, Revd Johnston 47, 135, 192, 218
McVeigh Fr Joe 156, 159
Meath Peace Group xii, 1
Mediation Northern Ireland 39, 56–7
memory/remembrance 36, 40, 82, 84, 85, 117,
    120, 129, 135, 225, 226
Metanexus Institute 22, 222
Methodism 27, 44, 45, 64, 65, 73, 83, 92, 99,
    139, 150, 151, 152, 155, 161, 180,
    191, 192, 193, 210, 211, 212, 217
    See also Methodist Church in Ireland
Methodist Church in Ireland v, 44, 91, 95,
    155, 161, 167, 193, 196
Miller, Frank 7–8
Miller, Bishop Harold 44, 45, 47, 74, 75, 76,
    78, 154, 155, 186, 187
Mills, C. Wright xiii, 17
Mitchell, Claire 2, 11, 43, 184, 206

Mitchell, George 6, 7
Mitchell, Patrick 2, 9, 218
Moffett, Bobby 190
Molyneaux, James 116–17, 123, 195
Monaghan, Paddy 54
Morrow, Duncan 11
Morrow, Revd John xv, 41, 42, 64, 119,
    142, 189, 207, 228
'Mountain Climber' 7, 107
Mowlam, Mo 6, 7

Nationalism, Irish 2, 59, 65, 90, 96, 102,
    111, 123, 152, 154, 173
    See also Social Democratic and
    Labour Party
new church movement/new churches 43, 75,
    109, 151, 152, 165
New Ireland Forum 90
Newell, Revd Ken 6, 10, 43, 44, 64, 66, 119,
    141, 147, 155, 183, 201, 205, 208, 209,
    217, 218
North and West Belfast Parades Forum 63, 225

O'Bradaigh, Ruairi 195
O'Doherty, Malachi 163, 182, 186
O'Fiaich, Cardinal Tomas 60, 61, 67, 111, 113,
    116, 156, 157, 163, 164, 178, 187
O'Neill, Onora 129, 130
O'Reilly, Fr Myles SJ xvii
Orange Order xv, 3, 5, 18, 43, 52, 63, 99, 138,
    154, 179, 181, 190, 193, 195

Paisley, Revd Ian v, 4, 8, 44, 47, 78, 91, 97,
    105, 110, 119, 138, 174, 179, 188, 196
Paisleyism v, 99, 176, 190
Palestine 9, 149, 150, 151
paramilitary organizations, dialogue with xv,
    xvi, 4, 6, 39, 40, 51, 58, 59, 63, 65, 89,
    105, 108, 122, 125, 126, 142, 158, 162,
    182, 194, 199, 208, 216, 219
Paris, Roland 17, 129, 132
Patterson, Revd Ruth xvii, 10, 69, 73, 161, 178, 228
peace
    passive versus active 4, 5, 29, 31, 32, 37,
        38–41, 72, 94, 121, 141, 142, 153, 169,
        176, 206, 218
    positive versus negative 4, 29, 32–3, 34, 35,
        37, 38, 41, 84, 92, 122, 125, 133, 142,
        143, 144, 145, 150, 153, 154, 168, 169,
        176, 185, 201, 206, 207, 228, 229, 230
    social versus political 4–5, 25, 26, 28, 29,
        30, 35, 36, 37, 38, 41, 68, 84, 86, 87, 88,
        90, 100, 118, 122, 125, 126, 141, 153,
        157, 168, 169, 182, 209, 215, 217, 224
Peebles, Clifford 2
'People Moving On' project 79

philanthropy 13–16, 18
Philpott, Daniel 3, 86, 150
Playboard Northern Ireland 82–3
Poland 9, 150, 160
Porter, David 2, 47, 64, 78, 95, 96–7, 99, 101,
    102, 111, 140, 156, 165, 166, 178, 187,
    212, 219, 226, 227
Porter, Fran 197
Powell, Jonathan 6, 7
Power, Maria 25, 42, 48, 67, 135, 136, 143, 215
Poyntz, Bishop Samuel 67, 184
preaching styles, Ulster 47, 134, 180, 185,
    186, 187
Presbyterian Church in Ireland 1, 3, 40, 44,
    48, 68, 73, 76, 77, 91, 97, 98, 114,
    117, 119, 135, 136, 141, 142, 151,
    153, 162, 165, 172, 201, 205, 208,
    212, 217
    and 'Peace Vocation' statement 3, 40, 135, 172
Presbyterianism 1, 27, 43, 44, 50, 55, 65,
    66, 73, 97, 99, 101, 153, 162, 167, 178,
    180, 185
Prior, Jim 163
Prison chaplains 66, 67
Progressive Unionist Party 109, 119, 186,
    190, 194
Protestant And Catholic Encounter xviii, 70, 79
Protestantism v, 11, 44, 46, 47, 62, 90, 100,
    139, 150, 178, 186, 197, 203, 217
Provisional Irish Republican Army v, 3, 7, 33,
    43, 58, 60, 65, 66, 67, 72, 78, 87, 95, 99,
    102, 103, 104, 107, 110, 113, 114, 115,
    116, 117, 121, 146, 152, 156, 158, 159,
    163, 165, 175, 180, 182, 184, 191, 192,
    193, 194, 195, 196, 205, 206
Purvis, Dawn xvi, 91, 119, 186, 190, 206
Putnam, Robert 16, 17, 18, 20, 22, 23, 55, 73,
    131, 145, 220, 221, 222
Putzel, James 18

Rabbis for Human Rights 150–1
Rea, Desmond 45
reconciliation 5, 23, 27, 28, 30, 34, 35, 36, 37,
    40, 44, 48, 49, 51, 53, 55, 56, 62, 64, 69,
    70, 75, 76, 77, 78, 79, 80, 81, 86, 96,
    101, 106, 120, 127, 129, 136, 140, 141,
    145, 154, 155, 157, 173, 178, 185, 186,
    187, 198, 201, 203, 207, 213, 218, 221,
    224, 228
Redemptorist Order 27, 58, 67, 100, 113, 158,
    166, 216
Rees, Merlyn 195
Reid, Fr Alec xvii, 6, 7, 43, 50, 58, 63, 64, 65,
    66, 67, 85, 102, 105, 108, 110–18, 120,
    158, 159, 161, 162, 166, 167, 168, 202,
    209, 210, 216, 217

Reid, Paul 109
religious peacebuilding xii, xv, 9, 100, 101,
    125, 126, 128, 201, 203, 204, 205–14,
    217, 221, 222, 225, 230
  as inter-faith dialogue 9–10
Republican/Republicanism v, xv, 2, 27, 45, 60,
    61, 64, 65, 66, 73, 82, 83, 87, 89, 96,
    97, 99, 102, 106, 109, 110, 111, 113,
    114, 117, 125, 138, 151, 156, 157, 158,
    163, 168, 174, 180, 185, 188, 189,
    191, 195, 206, 209, 217, 224, 229
  See also Sinn Féin
Republican Sinn Féin 195
Restoration Ministries 69, 81
Restorative Justice Ministries 87
Reynolds, Albert xv, 8, 59, 99, 103, 105,
    114–18, 121, 168, 205, 209
Reynolds, Fr Gerry 6, 10, 43, 58, 63, 196,
    209, 218
Robinson, Iris 137
Robinson, Peter 4, 172
Rowan, Brian 59, 67, 105, 117, 189

Sands, Bobby 60, 158
Sandy Row 51, 52
Segal, Robert 54
sectarianism 3, 24, 26, 40, 52, 53, 71, 74, 75,
    77, 85, 92, 99, 100, 135, 136, 174, 177,
    184, 187, 199, 200, 208, 213, 217, 224,
    226, 227, 229
secularization 11, 23, 162, 223, 229
Shankill 43, 68, 77, 116, 206
Sinn Féin xv, xvi, xvii, 4, 7, 8, 60, 63, 64,
    65, 66, 73, 78, 83, 102, 103, 104, 105,
    106, 107, 109, 110, 111, 112, 113, 115,
    136, 138, 156, 157, 158, 164, 167, 172,
    174, 179, 180, 183, 186, 188, 189, 196,
    198, 223
Sloan, Revd Harold 193
Smallwood, Ray 114–15
Smock, David 9, 10, 198, 212, 213
Smyth, Eric 188
Smyth, Sister Geraldine 47, 73, 135, 218
Smyth, Revd Martin 53, 195
social capital 16, 17, 18, 19, 22, 28, 68, 130,
    131, 133, 144, 150, 214, 220–22, 229
  bonding versus bridging 10, 18, 19, 24, 28,
    126, 171, 220–22
  constrict 20, 221–22
  regressive 18, 126
Social Democratic and Labour Party 7, 46, 90,
    111, 114, 166, 178, 196
social gospel 31, 92, 109, 122, 125, 128, 168,
    187, 225, 226
sociology 16, 17, 19, 22, 31, 32, 87, 106, 130,
    131, 151, 202, 212

South Africa 6, 9, 14, 35, 36, 62, 84, 86, 93,
    113, 128, 145, 146, 149, 150, 163, 199,
    200, 202
space, social 5, 11, 21, 24, 94, 102, 124, 126–7,
    198, 209, 213
  bureaucratic space 166, 182
  sacred space 23, 26, 27, 40, 55, 67, 73, 88,
    102–7, 109, 111, 113, 119, 121, 123,
    124, 163, 166, 190, 210, 220
  strategic spaces 10, 26, 126–8, 133–4, 149,
    150, 152, 167, 168, 169, 170, 198, 200,
    206, 212
Spence, Gusty xvi, 58, 65, 66, 67, 114, 116
spiritual capital 22, 23, 25, 28, 72, 85, 87, 145,
    214, 222–9
  compared to religious capital 22
Sri Lanka 9, 13, 18, 24, 132, 149, 150
St Andrew's Agreement xv
St Anne's Cathedral 85, 225
Stanley, Liz 212
Stevens, David xvii, 46, 68
Storey, Revd Earl xvii, 52, 74, 82,
    135, 136, 187, 208, 227
  See also Hard Gospel project
Sunningdale Agreement 205
Swift, Jonathan 6

Taggart, Revd Norman xvii, 4, 92, 104, 156,
    161, 192
Tara 193
Taylor, Rupert 11, 23
Teeney, Francis xiii, xvii, 7, 110, 119, 180, 188,
    196, 199
terrorism 6, 29, 91, 102, 130, 153, 188, 206
Thatcher, Margaret 60, 61, 62, 110
Thomson, Alwyn 47, 139
Tilly, Charles 212
tolerance 16, 17, 18, 40, 52, 85, 129, 130, 133, 139
Toner, Monsignor Tom 51, 158, 180, 217
Tosh, Bert 47
trade unions, and the peace process xv, 40, 79,
    82, 199
transitional justice 12, 36, 39, 85, 86, 87, 89,
    92, 125, 127, 128, 132, 185, 222, 224,
    225, 226
Trimble, David xv, xvi, 7, 8, 119, 120, 123
'Troubles, the' 2, 4, 7, 12, 17, 27, 28, 30, 42, 43,
    47, 50, 56, 67, 73, 80, 81, 85, 92, 94, 99,
    109, 114, 117, 125, 135, 140, 144, 155,
    170, 179, 182, 184, 186, 188, 207, 209,
    216, 223, 224, 228, 230
Troy, Fr Aidan 62
trust v, 16, 17, 18, 20, 22–3, 28, 43, 45, 51, 63,
    69, 84, 85, 86, 94, 101, 102, 125, 130–1,
    133, 161, 166, 179, 188–90, 192, 211,
    216, 221

Turner, Bryan 186
Tutu, Archbishop Desmond 62, 113, 146, 202

Ulster Covenant 76
  compared to Presbyterian Peace
    Vocation 76
Ulster Defence Association 61, 62, 64, 114, 122
Ulster Unionist Party xv, 47, 65, 116, 119, 195
Ulster Volunteer Force 63, 67, 87, 109, 122, 190
Unionism/Unionists xv, xvi, 62, 64, 65, 73, 96,
    107, 111, 117, 120, 138, 139, 154, 155,
    157, 180, 188, 195, 206, 219
United Nations 15, 21, 222
United Prayer Breakfasts 53, 195
United States of America 9, 11, 14–15, 16, 17,
    18, 20, 23, 27, 30, 33, 53, 68, 69, 105,
    120, 152, 178, 200, 210, 222, 223
United States Institute of Peace 9, 42, 149, 222

Van Leeuwen, Mathijs 12, 17, 24
Vatican II 52, 54, 181

victims/victim issues 36, 40, 57, 72, 84,
    85, 131, 142, 150, 174, 223, 224,
    225, 228

Waterside Church Trust 49, 50, 143
Weber, Max xiv
Weir, Revd Jack 64, 83, 95, 106, 195,
    201, 217
Wells, Ronald 10, 43
Wijesinghe, Shirley Lal 150
Wilson, Cedric 120
Wilson, Fr Des 6, 108, 162, 163, 166, 167, 176,
    203, 212
Wilson, Gordon 102
Wilson, Robin 207
Wilson, Sammy 61
Women's Coalition 199
Women Together for Peace 71,
    72, 79

Zero28, 72, 73, 218

Lightning Source UK Ltd.
Milton Keynes UK
UKOW03f2231221113

221669UK00001B/2/P